Kirkus Reviews

CHICO'S CHAPMANS

THE CALIFORNIA YEARS 1861–1899

By Michele Shover

A California history scholar explores the life and legacy of a relatively obscure West Coast settler.

In the late 1970s, after buying an old farmhouse in the Chapmantown neighborhood in Chico, California, Shover became interested in the area's eponymous Augustus "Gus" Harley Chapman, an entrepreneur and politically active Republican who died in 1899. After decades of research, she presents readers this history of Chapman and his family, Chico, and late-19th-century Northern California. Originally drafted in the 1980s, the book includes Shover's more recent research, which made use of internet search tools and genealogical services. The author notes that most other histories of Chico emphasize the role of John Bidwell as its founder, but this book places Chapman an important town leader. Admirably, Shover's recentering eschews a fawning tone, and although she highlights Chapman's personal charisma and entrepreneurial spirit, she doesn't shy away from noting, for instance, his "questionable ethics by modern measures." Chapman is also engagingly portrayed as a man plagued by "an inability to find satisfaction in any one accomplishment"; at various times, he was a lawyer, politician, and entrepreneur who dabbled in mining, real estate, and his prominent lumber company. The book's first section focuses on Chapman's early life and decision to move to California;

the second and third concentrate on his political and economic ventures in the 1870s and '80s. The final part surveys his tumultuous final years, concluding with a chapter on his descendants ("The Twentieth Century Chapmans") and a 1909 fire that ravaged his former "big house."

Shover, a former political science professor at California State University, Chico, and the author of multiple works on the history of the Golden State, effectively demonstrates that Chapman and Chico were "so intertwined that the history of one illuminates the other." She does so through the use of numerous vignettes and deep dives into the daily dramas of post–Civil War California. As such, this is also a rich local history of Chico's economic, political, and social life. Moreover, Shover connects Chico—a town of 100,000 people now, which was home to only 4,000 residents at the time of Chapman's death—to the wider history of the West, exploring anti-Chinese violence, Republican and Democratic politics, gender dynamics, and shadowy Gilded Age business practices. The book's impressively thorough endnotes and bibliography, however, demonstrate a firm grasp on the relevant historical literature and commendably centers on primary sources. Archival collections across the state—including diaries, letters, scrapbooks, and public records, as well as Chapman's own personal writings and ephemera—provided the author with ample material to analyze her subject's contributions to Northern California. They also provide an intimate perspective on a complex man who was always looking for a new project. In addition, the author's extensive use of local newspaper stories provides a colorful portrait of the daily lives of Chicoans.

A well-researched, biography of a forgotten Californian and his times.

Chico's Chapmans

The California Years 1861–1899

MICHELE SHOVER

STANSBURY
PUBLISHING
Chico, Ca.

Chico's Chapmans
The California Years 1861–1899

ISBN 978-1-935807-70-4
Library of Congress Control Number: 2022937352

Stansbury Publishing
An imprint of Heidelberg Graphics
Chico, CA 95928-9410

Cover art by Connie Ballou

Library of Congress Subject Headings. Hillsdale College |
Rural Northern California, 1860–1899 | Michigan Central
State Prison at Jackson | San Quentin and Folsom Prisons |
Civil War in a farm town | Gov. George Perkins | Oroville,
CA | Constitution Convention, 1879 | Workingmen's Party
| Nonpartisan Party | farm town business culture | partisan
political rivalry

In Memoriam

Professor Murray Markland
Department of English
California State University, Chico

His advice and commitment to this account of the 1880s
sustained the author's intent to publish this fuller, deeper
version forty years later.

"What's remembered, lives."

Nomadland
The film, 2021

Augustus "Gus" Harley Chapman and Sarah Sickley Chapman

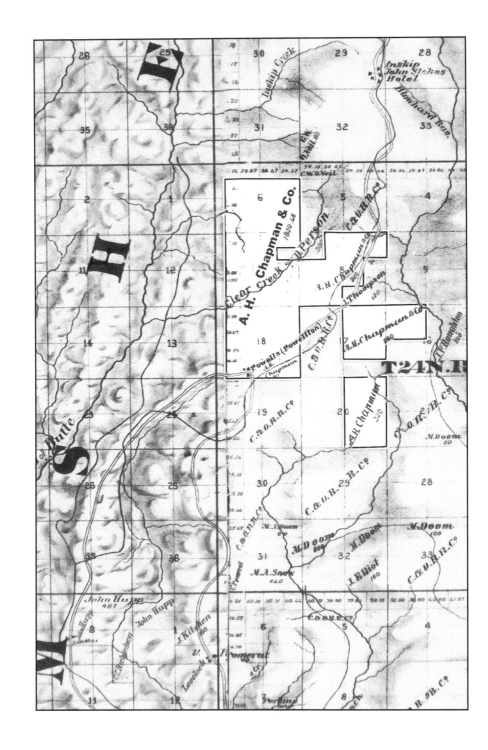

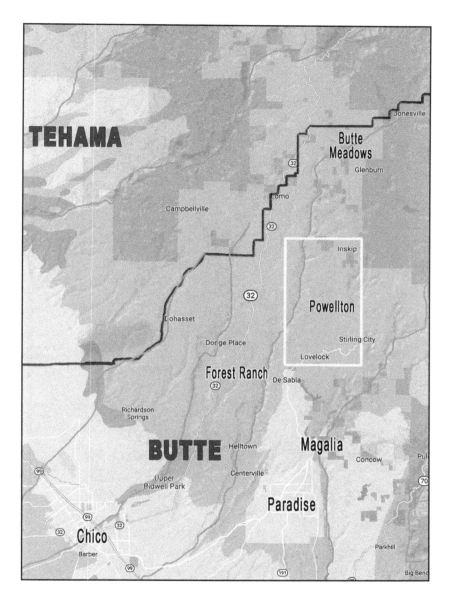

(Left) Agustus Chapman's main lumber mill was located in Powellton in the Sierra Nevada foothills. Note the lumber sites owned by Chapman.

(Above) Powellton, Magalia (formerly Dogtown), and Paradise in the Sierra Nevada foothills.

Chico Village in 1871. Rancho Chico headquarters is on the lower right-hand corner.

Contents

1890s and After

Preface

Augustus Harley Chapman's name hovers like the wisp of a phantom in Chico, California, a township of 1,500 or less residents when he arrived from Michigan in 1861 and under 4,000 when he died in 1899. Today few of its more than 100,000 residents could identify much more than the name Chapmantown—a section of town they've heard about (and perhaps lived in) visible from Highway 99, just northwest of the Twentieth Street overpass.

Research to explain this anomaly took a serious turn in 1979, when local historian John Nopel gave me a copy of Chapman's 1899 newspaper obituary. He had learned I was curious about the provenance of the old farm house my husband Barney Flynn and I bought in the original Chapmantown—the neighborhood he created out of open land in 1870, which has been part of the city since 1918. No one could tell me more than it once belonged to the Chapmans. Its neighborhood, later neglected by owners and the city, is only now experiencing revival by a new generation appreciative of its old-fashioned large lots and shaded houses in styles from every period.

After Gus Chapman died in 1899, the need to house low-wage workers for the new Diamond Match factory created a flurry of construction on grazing land that adjoined the original Chapmantown on its east side. That name unofficially expanded to also cover the haphazard housing development to the east. Unlike sightly Chico developments by proud investors who named their creations after themselves, as Chapman had done, the new area sprouted from no single entrepreneur's vision. In contrast, from its start this area was a jumble of hardscrabble cottages scattered around a county "pocket" where building regulations, already weak, were ignored. As the twentieth century unfolded, public understanding conflated the middle- and upper-middle class Chapmantown A. H. Chapman founded and the working-class addition on land he never owned.

The obituary remembered A. H. Chapman as a prominent, politically courageous entrepreneur in Chico and a significant Republican in state government. With time, Chico memories of him shrunk to only his Chapmantown development. The city did not annex the newer Chapmantown until 2020.

Forty years of my research followed from this initial curiosity about why or how the memory of A. H. Chapman, once considered remarkable, was reduced to the name of a neighborhood. The family had so far disappeared from Chico's memory that only the grave of an early infant marks the site where he and his children are buried. And, why was his wife not buried with them?

In order to illuminate the Chapman family's experiences, I had to reconstruct extensive parts of Chico's early years. I found Chapman and Chico so intertwined that the history of one illuminates the other. He became an entrepreneur whose businesses were vital to the valley farm town and Butte County's lumber regions. From private business he would move on to become a key appointee of Republican Governor George Perkins. In his work for Perkins he achieved remarkable accomplishments but was caught in such a deadly political game that a new Democratic governor's effort to destroy Perkins's accomplishments caught Chapman in his sights.

I soon recognized that Chapman was not the only town father forgotten over time. Local history progressively narrowed its remembered shapers to just one remarkable man. By the late twentieth century the enduring impression, although incorrect, was that the single figure whose wisdom and leadership shaped Chico was John Bidwell who, in 1849-1851, acquired a vast former Mexican land grant on which he established Rancho Chico, his headquarters and the beginnings of a village, on the north side of Big Chico Creek. In 1860 he moved the small village of Chico to its present site on the south side of the creek. However, the understandable obsession with the large role of the founder had the unintended side effect of erasing the contributions of other Chico leaders.

The focus on Chapman and his family yielded evocative and nuanced glimpses of small town life. It is to our benefit that, as a merchant and community volunteer, he observed the town from multiple vantage points. California State University, Chico (CSUC) librarian Bill Jones made an important contribution when he acquired Charles Lewis Stilson's diaries for the library's Special Collections. Stilson—Charlie in his early years and Lewis later—started out as a young clerk at John Bidwell & Co. under the supervision of Gus Chapman, the store's chief clerk and sales manager. When Chapman left with Bidwell's store partner to open their own competing store, Stilson moved with them. In addition to Stilson's accounts, other sources, including local newspapers, followed the development of the lumber industry which Chapman and his partner joined with their purchase of a pioneer lumber mill. The newspapers were also valuable in following his life in Chico because they followed political issues and other activities important to him.

Economist Henry George, a close student of California who visited Chico during the depression of the 1870s, cautioned his eastern readers: "It is yet a mistake to regard California as a community widely differing from more Eastern states. I am in fact inclined rather to look on California as a typical American state and San Francisco [read "Chico"] as a typical American city."[1] True to George's surmise, the political and economic conditions that Gus Chapman encountered in Chico resembled those he had encountered in Michigan.

Gus's compulsion to rise up the economic ladder was evident in Michigan and Chico. His acquisition of one business after another speaks to his chronic restlessness—an inability to find satisfaction in any one accomplishment and a seeming lack of center. Easy goals never tempted him. He courted risk, was never cowed by complexity, stood up to controversy, ignored physical exhaustion and considered all of his travails a benefit to his advancement and his family's well-being. This chronicle about Chapman's challenges reveals the fluid ethical environment in the nation at large was no less a factor in a remote nineteenth-century farm town. Even small villages and hamlets were not simple places. Time and again Chapman's and his friends' or rivals' competitive attempts at success revealed how class strains and personal disputes affected public and private conduct.

As an ambitious striver with no independent resources upon his arrival in California, Gus Chapman fell back on the strategy he had benefited from in his years in Michigan. At key points throughout much of his life, he became the indispensable manager for senior partners who then provided financial or political backing. As the right hand of each partner and later on his own, Chapman adapted to every stage of Chico's changing identity. Before becoming a lumber entrepreneur, he was a lawyer, justice of the peace and trader to miners, farmers and ranchers. He adjusted to two depressions, the settlers and Indians' war and confronted anti-Chinese violence. Evidence of his rise will demonstrate how, despite questionable ethics by modern measures, he built an overall reputation for responsibility, honesty and savvy that eventually led him to qualify for and accept an important position in state government.

Archival sources that bring Gus Chapman to life also summoned insights about the lives of Chapman neighbors and rivals. Like people today, residents then cooperated and shared — and competed and quarreled. They forged deep friendships and life-long rivalries over great national and petty personal issues. Over the years the Chapmans and others were confronted with juvenile crime, education issues, racial clashes, infrastructure neglect and utility crises. At various stages, Gus Chapman addressed one or another of those problems as a businessman, parent or high-level political appointee. While his challenges in the nineteenth-century's second half were characteristic of that time but may seem foreign to ours, their essential nature and their impact on his and his family's lives make his experiences and those of his family recognizable today.

For example, Gus Chapman and John Bidwell, who regularly "re-earned" his position as Chico's most prominent citizen, became well-acquainted businessmen who worked together and with others to advance Chico's development for thirty years. However, on a deeper level, Chapman's choices in the mid-1860s permanently estranged him from Bidwell, who waited until the 1870s and 1880s to render retribution. Bidwell left no obvious evidence that this was his intent, but the allegation here rests on strong circumstantial evidence from their characteristics, personal diaries, timing, parallel ambitions, rival interests and each man's behavior relative to the other on issues important to both.

The author drew on the John Bidwell collections at the California State Library in Sacramento, the UC Berkeley Bancroft Library and CSUC Meriam Library. They reveal a man whose values and perspectives are unmistakable. He meant to do well and do good. As rich as his archives are, they do not furnish all that is necessary to take his measure. The fullest picture of John Bidwell looks beyond his person to his place in the business, religious and civic communities where he interacted with other complex people. Readers interested in John Bidwell will value *John Bidwell and California* by Michael Gillis and Michael Magliari and publications by this author. Additional nuance has been reserved for the present account.

§

Finally, the present account so heavily relied on the *Enterprise* and the *Record* newspapers for information about events or persons, "local color" and incidental data—weather, clothing, foods, general conditions—that mentions would have required one or two thousand citations. Therefore, only the sources of direct quotes are identified. However, dedicated researchers will find the primary items tucked away in the *Enterprise* or the *Record* during the year(s) the text addresses. This will require effort, but keen researchers will find what they need and other interesting information about all parts of Chico life along the way. Unlike this researcher who had to grind her way through these sources on microfilm, her modern counterparts can quickly tap computers, laptops or even smartphones for digital versions.

The author built the narrative from items in the archival collections in CSUC Meriam Library's Special Collections, the California Collection at the State Library in Sacramento and the California State Archives. The documents speak—often indirectly—to the multiple issues that shaped the lives of Chapman, his wife Sarah and their four children. Also useful were diaries, interviews, public documents, scrapbooks and letters. Private individuals who provided information include the late Mary

Hanson of the Wesley Lee family, the late Sybil Gage of the C. J. Sommer family, John R. and the late Joan Robinson of the George and Sydnia Jones's family, the late Ted Meriam, the late Larry V. Richardson, Betty Boyd Owen of the Mary (Wood) Hallet family, Marja Miller of the George Sisk family, the late Vera Hintz Ekwall of the Charles Hintz family, the late John Nopel and Adriana Farley. Of all the student assistants over thirty years, Robert Gastineau set the high mark for industriousness, thoroughness and integrity. Bill Jones's CSUC Special Collections staff, especially the late Mary Ellen Bailey, was indispensable.

David Nopel has shared files of local history data from the John Nopel Collection. Interviews in the 1980s with the late Ted Meriam and other Chico descendants added important refinements to this account.

Anne Russell, editor of *Chico Standoff,* made her services available for *Chico's Chapmans.* She took this on even though she and her husband lost their Paradise home in the Camp Fire in 2018 and she had to restructure her life before she could begin this round of work for me. When I had to step back from this work, she agreed to edit all the writing, sort out hundreds of notes and construct the index. I have been fortunate in her steadiness and patience, not to mention her technical help, analytical insights and chronological sensibility. She benefited from a much earlier edit by Linda Walker, a Jane Austen scholar in Ann Arbor, Michigan.

I am also grateful to Larry Jackson of Heidelberg Graphics for publishing this book, as well as his experience, patience and unfailing good advice. Connie Ballou prepared illustrations that introduce the existence and meaning of a historic street, Old Chico Way, that David Nopel and I discovered. Ms. Ballou also rendered an image of the earliest part of the still existing Chapman home that architect Henry Cleaveland later remodeled and expanded. She also created a map that clarifies the location of the Chapman's mansion in the original Chapmantown that Gus Chapman created. David York, a specialist in photo restoration and image composition, fine-tuned the archival photographs which add an important dimension to the narrative here. Photos that illuminate the Chapmans' lives are from the John Nopel Collection, Randy Taylor Collection and others in CSUC Meriam Library's Special Collections.

Interwoven, the data they provided made it possible to reconstruct the Chapmans' lives, sometimes at a fairly intimate level. It was out of necessity, but with considerable forethought and confidence, that the author has interpreted reasons and motivations from the facts, patterns and inferences that appear in those documents. Readers, of course, may find other motives and assumptions more compelling. All that materially remains of the Chapmans' existence in Chico is their original remodeled farm house in Chapman's Addition and a thin scattering of personal ephemera that has surfaced over the years: Gus's 1855 pocket ledger, his father's 1812 dictionary, four other books, four photographs, two essays he probably wrote, and his wife Sarah's 1899 diary.

The Chapmans arrived in Chico as accomplished adults, ready to invest their talents and experience in a new town. This account of him and his family illuminates how, even though they were residents of a remote rural town, the Chapmans' lives were steeped in the major social, economic and political issues important to the broader American experience. Along the way, it does not neglect their personal lives nor both the benefits and the costs to their children of Gus Chapman's ambition or judgment.

In reflecting at my advanced age I realized I have been remiss in never adequately appreciating my Shover and Dickey families: the backing they gave their scholarly girl has seen me through the decades of my full and fortunate life. Their help extends to today, when, in my home, I rely on people of diverse talents. The core of my team, Melissa Hughes Land, has kept many aspects of my life in order so I could make this book a priority. My stepdaughter, Cathy Lillibridge, R.N., has provided useful advice with her regular ministrations. Weekly visits by Dawn McNulty and Marie Peterson have kept me physically strong for decades. The always capable and caring Delores Davey has joined that crew. Jim Thorup of One Stop Mobility equips me for independence. Ramona Flynn of Chico and Linda Walker remain all that "best" stands for in "best friends." I am no less fortunate in my late husbands Bernard Flynn Jr. and Don Lillibridge and their children, Elena Flynn, Bernard Flynn III and Cathy Lillibridge.

To sum up my life, loosely translated,
Quod capio mecum est —What I want is what I have.

—Michele Shover
Chico, 2022

1860s and Before

1

A Way Out—West

In September 1861 Augustus and Sarah Chapman reached their California destination: Chico Village. Its founder John Bidwell used that name to differentiate it from the cluster of houses and stores north across Big Chico Creek spreading around his sprawling Rancho Chico headquarters. By the late 1850s his employees, their families and visitors had begun thinking of the ranch headquarters as a small hamlet they were calling "Chico." The Chapmans' mid-September arrival fell in the early stage of Bidwell shifting the ranch village south across the creek to create Chico Village. This meant that, after the Chapmans' grueling travel across the country and through the Sacramento Valley's desiccated grasses, the village they reached was so new it was more a promise than a reward.

Chico, as they saw it, required imagination. Compacted dirt staked out as streets evoked fine lines on surveyor's maps. Bounded by two creeks to the north and south, there was not a lot to see. Duncan Neil's saloon had already been in business a year, and two houses were going up in the scattering of scrub oaks and alders along the east side of the new Main Street, still better known as the Oroville-Shasta Trail, originally established by Native peoples. "Starter" businesses in scattered frame shacks were underway and there were two "bricks" handsome enough to encourage Gus and Sarah's aspirations.[1]

Until 1860 Main Street's predecessor, the north-south Indian trail, had cut through former owner John Potter's grazing grounds in what was to become Bidwell's Chico Village. Where the trail ran through his ranch he had installed a gate at each end to protect its operations from settler traffic. Therefore, traffic heading south had to turn east at Potter's northern gate. This detour, remembered as Old Chico Way (now Olive and East

Twelfth streets), turned south through open land to the ford across Little Chico Creek on Chico Village's eastern border.[2] (The ford was most likely near the location of Bidwell's abandoned trading post, about which a transcribed Indian elder spoke.) Old Chico Way then emerged into forest on Dr. J. B. Smith's "Sunflower Farm," where it turned west onto now East Twelfth Street, to reenter the Oroville-Shasta Trail. When newer rancher John Bidwell acquired Potter's land in 1860, he pulled down both gates and fences and designated the Indian trail as Chico Village's Main Street, once again part of the Oroville-Shasta Trail.

The Chapmans drove straight into Chico on the reopened Oroville-Shasta Trail, which was funneling a constant train of north- and southbound traffic along the town's length. An observer who climbed Bidwell's water tower thought the wagons resembled a moving train of ants, rendering Main Street dangerous to cross. New blocks just east along Wall Street, parallel to Main, would soon fill with a jumble of boarding houses and family cottages amid a scattering of brothels.

Despite the raw edges, signs of construction promised commerce and domesticity: Chico was slated to grow into a farm town like those Gus and Sarah knew back home. They strolled through the designated downtown, where family pigs lay in the shade or grazed on fresh garbage dumped into the streets. Gus and Sarah recognized, but didn't "hear," the curses of wagon drivers who swerved to miss a cow languidly munching on green sprouts in the middle of Main Street. Although the friendliness of fellow speculators and "old hands" buoyed their hopes, could any of those people ever mean as much to the Chapmans as the family and friends they had left in Michigan's Lenawee County?

Most of Bidwell's employees, still in their ranch-based cottages and shops that had turned his front yard into the original Chico, would soon be moving across the creek. To protect his Valley Maidu workers from Mountain Maidu raiders and White harassment he moved their bark huts behind his long, two-story federal farmhouse with its busy office. He gave or sold village lots to new settler arrivals who could provide labor and services to the ranch and others who might make desirable townspeople.

Chico's most impressive attribute was John Bidwell, a

substantial figure in his twentieth year as a resident of California. He and Pearson Reading, both of whom had worked for John Sutter, were the most prominent men north of Sacramento. Along with the Mechoopda village, far-reaching *Rancho Arroyo del Chico* or Rancho Chico, John Bidwell's more than 22,000-acre land grant, was home to vast herds of cattle and horses, storehouses, stables, maintenance shops and the bunkhouses of male Indian workers. Bidwell's mill, which processed his winter wheat, sold flour throughout the area. With little cash left to make their start, the Chapmans probably stayed across from the mill at Bidwell's adobe hotel, although the new brick Chico Hotel (on now West Second Street between Salem and Broadway) must have been an inviting option.

Between Bidwell's ranch headquarters and his new village site, a buffer of thick cottonwood trees and willows were curtained by wild grape vines and anchored in blackberry bushes along both banks of Big Chico Creek. Across the creek from his office and in sight across his large, fenced cattle pen was John Bidwell & Co.'s general merchandise store on the southwest corner of Front (now First) Street and Broadway, which paralleled Main to the west. This two-story "brick" declared the high standard Bidwell intended for his town.[3] The Chapmans had just missed its grand opening ball at the only other impressive structure, the Chico Hotel. Its presence would free Bidwell to demolish his adobe hotel with its attached saloon, a favorite of ranch workers, travelers, soldiers and farmers. Because saloon owners had been valuable wholesale buyers in his Michigan store, he felt comfortable in that milieu and occasionally headed there for his evening glass of porter and to compare his impressions of Chico and its prospects with old hands or other newcomers.[4]

Although Gus and Sarah's son Freddie was only about a year old, they were already planning his education and wanted to know about schools. Classes were about to begin in rooms on the upper floor of a Greek Revival house its teacher was building in the projected residential district west of the downtown.[5] They were skeptical about a public school near Mud Creek because it was several miles north. Another option to consider was the schoolroom in teacher Lavinia L. Sproul's country farmhouse south of town where the Oroville-Shasta Trail crossed Little Chico Creek, the town's southern boundary. Although Chico proper had no public school, Gus knew how to start one.

He was impressed that Chico's new streets could handle wide turns by freight wagons, signaling Bidwell's commitment to development. At such an early stage, though, Chico's fragility was also obvious: it was remote, twenty miles from the heaviest trafficked road to Oregon (now Interstate 5). It had no established churches and railroad service was non-existent. Chapman had to figure out where he could fit in in Chico. At 34, his Michigan legal practice and then his store had taught him about businesses' need for a school, good roads, productive markets and railroads. He had seen Spring Arbor, Michigan, his college town, evaporate when the railroad ran its tracks a few miles away.[6]

As Gus and Sarah absorbed the scattered buildings on open land and admired Bidwell's vision, answers to their questions about the climate were cause for unease. They learned the upper Sacramento Valley has little to no rain between June and November and the summer months present intense heat. This contrasted to the heavy rains at home where a dozen or more lakes produced stifling heat, humidity and the mosquitos that likely infected Chapman with malaria. Compensating for its inclement weather, California's wild grasses were suited to cattle ranching and its winter rains produced heavy wheat crops.

The Chapmans were familiar with life in a remote location. This one had a population of about fifty families—fewer than 400 people. In addition, its economy drew on 1,100 outlying township residents, bolstered by travelers and the prospect of more newcomers.[7] As he peered up and down Chico's raw streets, although confident due to his education and experience, Gus was "dead-broke" and had to find work.[8]

It was second nature for Chapman to observe, consider, calculate. True to the historical English origins of his family name (a bartering or dealing man), he was inclined toward marketing, sales and merchant life. Always on the move, he had constantly engaged in the present challenge, all the while staying alert to the next opportunity. Because he was reticent by nature and hardships in his youth made him socially tentative, those

characteristics sometimes led new acquaintances to underesti-
mate him. However, colleagues and friends recognized intensity
in the gleam of his dark eyes beneath a heavy brow. They also
could not miss his restlessness. He found his true self in work,
where he eagerly ran toward, not away from, problems. No new
business, family or civic challenge intimidated him. As his present already suggested and his future would underline, Gus's
wife, partners, employees and children would have to learn to
live in his churning wake.

The Chapmans Who Chose Chico

Before the Civil War the Chapmans were committed to life in
Michigan despite political changes. Through the 1850s, because
Confederate-sympathizing northern Democrats had allied with
southern Democrats to make up the majority in Congress, their
western expansion policies became increasingly unpopular in
the North. Nevertheless, Chapman remained a Democrat and
his run for public office in November 1860 demonstrates he did
not intend to leave Michigan. However, with Southern states
seceding and war unfolding, and desiring to avoid being drawn
into war, he sold his business and left for California with Sarah
and their child Frederick Willis. Even though, by any measure
then, Chapman already had a successful life underway, he put
it all behind him and made ready, as he later recalled, to "begin
at the bottom of the ladder again."[9]

In addition to avoiding the war, several conditions suggest
an additional reason for leaving. Americans in the early 1860s,
indeed, until at least the early-to-mid-1900s, considered it normal to repeatedly pick up and start over elsewhere to chase a
better life. Abraham Lincoln's father moved his family from Kentucky to Indiana to Illinois. The writer Hamlin Garland's family
moved from Maine to Wisconsin to Minnesota to Iowa to South
Dakota.[10]

Gus Chapman's father David Chapman and his brother
Charles had moved from pre-Revolutionary Connecticut to
western New York in 1818. David Chapman launched the later
famed Cataract Hotel, which still overlooks Niagara Falls and
became a stop on the future Underground Railroad. Augustus
Harley Chapman was born there in 1827, but remembered little

because his family left for Michigan Territory when he was a young child.[11]

David Chapman and his wife Ann Rogers Chapman, a Connecticut native, were among the many who gave up on the hope that New York's great manorial estates would break up and provide land for small farms.[12] Later, in Gus's Chico years, it became a common refrain that residents hoped the Sacramento Valley's vast land grant ranches would break up, making space for small farmers whose patronage could support many villages. New York-born and Michigan-raised, Gus grew up in the culture of transplanted Easterners who honored "the man whose eye was the quickest and whose grasp was the strongest"—and "every man for himself." This belief would make him—and break him. In his lifetime nothing taught him otherwise.

In Michigan, several Chapman families settled in Jackson County, named for the president its new residents revered. Hopes for their future on the frontier collapsed, however, with the early deaths of David Chapman and his brother. Gus's mother Ann next married Lenawee County farmer William Babcock with whom she had a second son, George, in 1837. When Babcock died sometime in the late 1840s, Ann and her boys shared their farm with her widowed sister-in-law Hannah Chapman and Hannah's child Betsy.[13]

New farms like theirs in the Michigan wilderness required constant tree felling, stump pulling, marsh draining, fence setting and more. With Gus and George's help, their mothers and their cousin Betsy managed to keep the Babcock farm going. In addition to Gus's chores, he also found work with neighboring farmers. The "many hardships" and struggles he recalled from those years explain why Gus Chapman, who later could afford to invest, never bought farmland and apparently resolved never to be poor or live on a farm again.

School Days

Gus Chapman's first glimpse of a bigger and more generous world took place in a one-room schoolhouse. Across Michigan, transplanted Yankee teachers instilled traditional New England's ethic of civic responsibility and respect for learning. Students like Chapman were "farmer boys [who] walked behind the plow with their books in hand and sometimes forgot to turn at the end of the furrow."[14] Alonzo Smith, a community leader and businessman in Woodstock, was Chapman's teacher and mentor at the village's public school. For much of his life, Chapman's talent, integrity and motivation would convince such men they could rely on him; in return, they became his backers and supporters.

When Quakers opened a high school, the Raisin Valley Seminary, Chapman enrolled there because it permitted poor students to work off their tuition. Although the faculty immersed him in their school's religious beliefs, which included firm anti-slavery principles, he remained a Baptist. By 1849, at the age of 22, he had saved enough money to enter Michigan Central College, a Free-Will Baptist institution in nearby Spring Arbor.[15]

At Michigan Central, his talent and motivation came to the attention of its president Edmund Burke Fairfield. Thirty years later, Gus recalled that Fairfield became his mentor and role model. Although an "advanced student," he typified Michigan Central alumni by quitting after two years. Of the 700 young men and women who enrolled between 1844 and 1853, only 13 graduated.[16] Gus left with a liberal education that included mathematics, science, Latin and Greek. His later polished reports suggest he mastered composition along the way. Weekly Testament recitations in Greek at Michigan Central enhanced Gus's talking rights on the subject of religion. However, as a worldly man who kept his own counsel, he would rarely, if ever, opine on religious matters. By leaving college early, however, he missed advanced work in history and philosophy—subjects applicable to the political and ethical dilemmas he would encounter throughout his life.[17]

Soon after Gus left college, he won election as Lenawee County's justice of the peace. This was a significant job for a 24-year-old novice because waves of land speculators then descending on Michigan inundated its county courts with land disputes. During his tenure he became aware of the higher incomes of lawyers who handled such cases. In short order, while still tending to his duties in the minor court, he apprenticed himself to a local lawyer.

In 1854, ready to launch his legal career in the Jackson County farming village of Brooklyn, he rented a room in a boarding house. Eager to make a proper appearance, he bought new calf boots and picked out fabrics for a tailor to make his dress pants and silk shirts. Gus's ambition "jumps off the page" of his pocket-sized leather ledger where, among other items, he reserved a page to record "Lost time." Here he jotted down every full and half day that did not advance his future. This short list noted infrequent sick days and rare trips to see his mother. His most extended break took place when he returned to the Babcock farm to help her with harvests. He also allowed himself one-and-a half days each month for "flings."[18]

Following a common practice before banks were established, Chapman made small loans at interest, methodically keeping track of each transaction. His earnings bought gloves for his mother and garters for George Babcock, now 12. He also allowed himself an occasional brandy or sarsaparilla. However, while Gus had advanced his circumstances, he realized legal practice would still not provide the income he envisioned. While land disputes produced abundant cases, the clients were a difficult, transient lot, who had little compunction about stiffing their lawyers, often taking off for other parts overnight. In 1855 he recorded his and his mother's personal property: "our buggy," two cows, a "fancy mill," some loose tools and a wagon. His only significant asset at the age of 28 was himself. He had a good name in the community and had achieved professional standing, but his fortune still eluded him. So he turned to farm town commerce, which Jacksonian values blessed as a favored path to advancement.[19] This time Chapman apprenticed himself to work for three years at a large general merchandise store in Brooklyn, Michigan.

Smith & Chapman

Chapman's skills made a good fit with trade. For one thing, although quiet, he was good with customers. The discovery that he could anticipate their needs and tastes eventually led him to become the firm's buyer on trips to Chicago, where he discovered the appeal of urban interludes. Now confident that business was the right path for him, he joined with an investor and opened Smith & Chapman, a general merchandise store in the farm community of Addison, Michigan. By 1857 he was established well enough to extend his reach into the community. To New England-rooted Michiganders like himself, "the habit of community life" was a proper extension of personal life. He became a Master Mason and was active in the county's Democratic Party. In the Midwest, called the "Valley of Democracy," Chapman became a staunch Jacksonian Democrat who always had respect for people who struggled, even during his most successful years as a local Republican leader in Chico.[20]

Gus Marries

Sarah Ann Sickley married Augustus Harley Chapman on March 27, 1858, the same day she turned 24 and he 31. Her father William Sickley was, like Chapman, a Democrat who admired Andrew Jackson. The Sickleys descended from a Dutch immigrant who no sooner started his young family in New Jersey than he died in the Revolutionary War. The son of that patriot, William Sickley, and his wife Sarah made their first move in 1833, when they acquired a 120-acre farm in western New York in time for young Sarah's birth in 1834. When she was a teenager, the large Sickley family set off by wagon for Buffalo where they boarded the steamship *Mayflower* for Michigan. Family members never forgot their terror on Lake Erie's turbulent seas during the five days' passage. Once on land, Sarah and William and their eight children settled on farmland near that of Gus Chapman's mother in the vicinity of Woodstock.[21]

Nothing documents Sarah's education. However, both her older brother and next older sister Mary attended normal schools and became teachers. The high demand for teachers in Michigan's full-to-bursting country schools opened up opportunities for women. Sarah's later commitment to provide her children the most advanced education infers she had been a teacher, the only paid work allowed "respectable" women. Whatever her employment, if any, it ended with her marriage. Gus's wedding gift was an elementary primer for homemakers, *The Ladies' New Book of Cookery*, in which he inscribed, "To Mrs. A. H. Chapman."[22] His choice hints at concerns about her mastery of the "domestic arts." The book's worn condition, well over 150 years later, suggests frequent use. Whatever her education, Sarah was a reader and became the writer of a surviving straightforward diary. When she followed her husband to California, Sarah Sickley Chapman left behind not only libraries, colleges and "culture," but all the family and friends who had shaped her life.

Immigration from the East to southern Michigan in the late 1850s brought Whigs and Republicans whose numbers began to overtake those of the Democratic settlers who had established the state. Nevertheless, Chapman remained a loyal Democrat. His contributions earned him the Buchanan administration's appointment as Addison's postmaster—a plum for his ego and his wallet. In the years before general delivery, any merchant whose store handled the mail drew virtually every area resident to his store at least once a week.

He remained a loyal county Democrat at the same time anti-Andrew Jackson Republicans, disaffected Democrats and other party members were crossing over to the Whigs. Addison had become known as Coon Town because so many residents had nailed raccoon pelts, a Whig symbol, over their doors.[23] They blamed the South's control of the Democratic Party for subverting federal financing of Michigan improvements. With heightening partisanship and intense rivalry on all sides, the Chapman business must have suffered customer losses.

Although there is no evidence Chapman approved of slavery, he evidently concluded war against the South could undermine the security of all private "property," including slaves. He campaigned as a Doughface Democratic candidate for Lenawee county clerk in 1860. Doughfaces were northern Democrats who questioned war on the South to expunge slavery. Twenty years later, he recalled to a biographer that the campaign was "one of the most spirited elections ever known in that largely Republican county."[24] The new Whig majority trounced him.

That winter Gus mulled over his defeat as he followed the news of successive secessions in the South. Breadwinners like Chapman calculated the likely effects of war. If he joined the Union, he would have to leave Sarah and their son to fight against the South. However, for Chapman, who did not even hunt, to fight in battles was unthinkable. Should he refuse to serve but remain in Michigan, he would face challenges to his loyalty. So he followed the current American pattern and left his problems behind by moving to California and out of the government's reach.

His lifelong financial hardships and recent political engagements made Chapman a realist. Avoidance of the war dilemmas he faced in Michigan drew him to California—not the romance of the West. In leaving, he carried a largely private stigma attached to those who headed west while their neighbors headed east and south to fight. The crossing to California had its dangers too. Plains Indians had intensified their attacks on wagon trains because protective state militias had not fully replaced federal troops who had pulled out of the Dakotas to enter Union and Confederate service.[25]

Immigrants like the Chapmans often chose their destinations on the advice or example of friends. Forty percent of the immigrants in California during the mid-1860s settled in its agricultural valleys rather than along its coast. As the Civil War continued, those in search of peace who settled in Butte County and elsewhere included war avoiders like Chapman, Missouri families in flight from violence and a steady trickle of both armies' veterans.

It appears that for Gus Chapman, who did not know California, Chico represented the best place he could pick on short notice from 2,000 miles distance. He probably relied on the reports of Alfred D. Nelson, a New York native who, in 1859, had left his home in Addison, Michigan, where Chapman's store was located, for an area south of Chico where he farmed wheat.

For whatever reason, Augustus and Sarah Chapman settled in Chico. But they arrived as fully formed Midwesterners who carried the stamp of their families' New England roots. That heritage shaped the goals he meant to achieve and the standards they both strove to meet in California.

2

The Chief Clerk and Manager: John Bidwell & Co.

For Augustus Chapman, California represented a refuge from political disappointment in Michigan, perhaps an escape from the draft and certainly a financial opportunity. He was better educated than most, possessed a business aptitude and was ambitious and resilient. In addition, like other new arrivals such as miners, lawyers and businessmen, he was ready to work hard and sacrifice for financial success. He was imbued with the American hallmark of personal virtue and national progress.

But first, Chapman needed a job. He found one at John Bidwell & Co., the general merchandise store in Chico where George Wood hired him to be chief clerk/sales manager, Wood's own position before becoming Bidwell's managing partner.[1] Customers headed there for retail and wholesale trade, to use the new telegraph service and the post office. Readers gravitated to the shelved books intermixed with donated newspapers that made up the town's library. The stagecoach stop was out front and Bidwell Hall upstairs, a community center in the store's new location, the southwest corner of Front (now First) and Broadway streets, across Big Chico Creek from Bidwell's Rancho Chico.

Chapman's boss Wood knew John Bidwell better than most. In California since the early 1850s, Wood had been a partner in the Morrill lumber mill, but moved to Rancho Chico to manage Bidwell's original general store on his ranch. With Bidwell's financial backing, Wood developed "the largest and best arranged [store] in the Co[unty] filled with a general assortment of merchandise."[2] The Alabama transplant from his New England birthplace called on his son Jo Wood to do odd jobs at the store or to ride out, find and repair the telegraph line regularly cut by Indians.

Otherwise, Jo usually avoided daylight, only rousing himself for horse races. A regular at the night-long faro games, he drank his way through pitchers of spruce beer. Because George Wood had no control over his son, he became all the more dependent on Chapman's work ethic and retail savvy. An active entrepreneur, Wood was often away from the store for days, entrusting the store's entire operation to Chapman. Although Gus's closeness to Wood would benefit the new arrival, before long it would antagonize John Bidwell.

While Wood became Chapman's mentor, an even better one might have been John Bidwell, the area's most remarkable leader by any measure. However, single and childless, he never made a lasting personal commitment to cultivate younger men as potential partners or heirs. In that light, Chapman was lucky to connect with Wood, who was such an "honored and respected" man that, as a resident told him, "There are men in this community ready to sneeze the moment you point your nose at the snuff box."[3]

Wood and Chapman's mutual understanding extended to political views controversial in Chico. Both were skeptical about the war's merit. Chapman had arrived with the concerns he dealt with in Michigan. Personal experiences also shaped Wood's political beliefs: his wife Caroline was an Alabama native and, until he moved to California, George Wood, born in Massachusetts, lived in the South. Wood, as California correspondent to the *Mobile* [Alabama] *Advertiser,* maintained financial interests that kept him deeply connected to that Confederate state. Beyond that, John Bidwell's Union Party leadership also explains the men's discretion about war issues.

In store matters, Bidwell left the operation to Wood; but, as co-owner of the store, he took a keen interest in its profitability. Store staff had a glimpse of how that worked in 1864 when the 1863 store profits were tallied. According to customary practice, it was common for customers to sign a running tab for purchases over the year and then, in the new year, pay the balance after crops were harvested and sold. On a designated payment day in early January, Wood, Chapman and Stilson followed the retail bill collection tradition and set out food and liquor to soften the blow when customers received and paid their bills. Later that week store clerk Charles L. Stilson overheard Wood infer to Bidwell that employees were responsible for store losses that reduced the partners' profits. However, in Stilson's diary, he blamed Wood for underpriced store goods.[4]

In short order Chapman realized the weight of Bidwell's presence in Chico. Townspeople admired, envied and resented him by turns. Stories of his dramatic rise encouraged aspiring new arrivals. A tall man who weighed over 200 pounds, his direct gaze, full black hair and dignified bearing conveyed assurance that declared power. His financial stake in Chico's expansion was apparent at every turn and fed residents' expectation that immigrants from "the states" would descend and snatch up all his empty lots. John Bidwell's success as an entrepreneur who built his ranch from raw "prairie," still the residents' word for the Sacramento Valley, vindicated Chapman's decision to leave home and stake his family's future on Chico.

Born in New York, then living in Pennsylvania and Ohio, John Bidwell was a man of modest origins and a decent education. He emigrated to California in 1841, when it was still Mexican territory. After several years as an administrative employee of John Sutter, an early California pioneer, he made his initial fortune in 1847 when he was one of those who discovered gold in the Sierra Nevada, helping give rise to the Gold Rush the following year. During the late 1840s he switched to agriculture, settling in the Sacramento Valley where he established Rancho Chico on his former Mexican land grant that included local Maidu Mechoopda territory.[5]

Such vast property astonished Chapman and others from the farmlands of the East and Midwest where forty-acre farms were the rule. Rancho Chico was so expansive that its farm was able to feed most of the county, including the gold country, from great herds of cattle, orchards and row crops. Bidwell's ranch even had enough left over to ship its products for wider sale.[6] Until the twenty-first century, no Northern Sacramento Valley resident equaled Bidwell's achievements, which spanned economics, politics, town development and agronomy.

Moving about the store assisting customers, Chapman was able to size up his new neighbors. In fall 1861 these were Chico's "first families," querulous and grizzled veterans of the 1850s'

gold camps who wintered in the Valley, living in boarding houses and working in village trades or as ranch hands. On their
stops at John Bidwell & Co. these men cast skeptical glances at
the energetic and optimistic newcomers.

The old hands knew these young men would find farming
near Chico little resembled what they had known near Gale-
na, Illinois, Monticello, Iowa, or Charleston, South Carolina.[7]
Like Chapman, new Butte County farmers were puzzled by California's water pattern. He recalled Michigan farmers had so
much rainwater they had to tile their fields to run it off. Here,
in a normal year, there was little or no rain between late May
and November; some years the rains they counted on for grazing cattle and nourishing their winter wheat amounted to mere
sprinkles. At other times, heavy storms would flood the valley
floor. In addition, the new arrivals who, back home, were used
to large numbers of poor men eager for work at any wage, found
the Valley's labor shortage an expensive problem. As a manager intent on becoming an owner, Chapman sympathized with
employers' complaints about high wages. At the same time, as
an employee, his wage of $100 a month fed his family, but not
his aspirations.

Store talk informed Chapman about lingering tensions
between foothill farmers and gold miners east of Chico. Meanwhile, miners who traded at the store told about clashes with
Mountain Maidu still trying to drive the outsiders off their historic territory.[8] To East Coast arrivals, such talk seemed merely
colorful, resembling their elders' hazy ramblings about "history"
back home. The Chapmans and other newcomers became familiar with ongoing debt issues, market nuances, concerns about
the impacts of Chinese immigrants and water issues.

John Bidwell stood at an intersection between the old hands
and the newcomers. He knew his town's future hinged on the
recent arrivals' self-discipline and traditional standards to turn
the new town in a more polite and "conventional" direction.[9]
Even so, he never condemned the "rough" miners he knew from
his own days in the gold camps—and upon whom the early
town's fortunes had relied. Bidwell tried to look beyond their
heavy drinking, chronic gambling and violent disputes. To the
dismay of many, rough conduct remained a subtext to Chico's

postwar development. Cultural tensions would linger, making unity and stability hard to establish over the next decades.

Let the Challenges Begin

The Chapmans' first year tested their commitment to this new town. As the 1861 California winter approached, repercussions persisted from the previous winter's drought when, they learned, tens of thousands of cattle were reduced to heaps of bleached bones. Dread set in that 1862 would again not deliver enough water for crops and cattle. The county newspaper counseled that "all classes [must buckle down to] industry and rigid economy."[10]

However, in January 1862 a once in a thousand years-size storm descended on California. Rain in sheets forced creek and slough waters through Chico's dirt streets. At Bidwell & Co. all hands hastily moved barrels and boxes above the water's reach. Cattle that survived the previous drought drowned in creek and Sacramento River floodwaters. Just southeast of Chico, the Boucher brothers lost 5,000 head of cattle. Water swept away outbuildings and fences, leaving grain in moldy shreds, forcing farmers to import grain to feed the cattle.

When the floods finally subsided, frost whitened the ground and a three-day storm produced an inch of snow. Did the snow evoke Gus and Sarah's wistful memories of Michigan firesides? Or, did they congratulate one another on their escape from their old home's blizzards?

While most businesses suffered that winter, some prospered. Chico's boot repairmen were so busy they fell three to six months behind and the Bidwell store realized record sales. Accounts due climbed higher in 1862 than in any year afterward.[11] However, farmers' ability to pay off their debt to the store became doubtful when wet ground delayed the wheat planting.

With summer's approach in 1863, aggressive north winds pushed fine, powdered grit into every crevice. The store extended credit to ranchers and businessmen, both of whom signed petitions to the State Legislature to allow debtors more time to pay off their creditors before the sheriff could post auction signs at their gates.[12]

Keenly interested in politics and always looking for

advancement, Chapman drew on his Michigan experience. A year after his arrival, he was elected one of two justices of the peace.[13] Deputy sheriffs brought in "miscreants and debtors" to appear before him and the other justice, Andrews Hallet.[14] Roughhousing was entertainment and poverty the norm in the swarm of young miners who wintered in town. Both justices worked part-time out of their office in the What Cheer Hotel at the southwest corner of Third and Main streets. Bad debts often poisoned personal relationships, leading to frequent grievances, so Chapman ran newspaper advertisements to solicit private lawsuits. It was the mark of a slow day when he wasn't presented with at least one new case.

His legal work required Gus to master California's legal code and immersed him in the townspeople's personal and financial affairs, both of which prepared him for potential new business deals. With circuit-riding preachers only periodically on hand, Chapman also performed weddings. His various incomes allowed him and Sarah to buy a cottage at Sixth and Chestnut.[15] Nonetheless, handling acrimonious debt cases did not advance his political ambitions and diverted his attention from business opportunities.

By the mid-1860s normal rain levels enabled winter wheat crops to prosper in northwestern Butte County. However, Chapman believed Chico needed a broader, more steady economic base to make up for the sporadically shaky condition of wheat crops and cattle ranching.

When bootmaker Bob Bill Baker reached Chico in 1864, he was struck by the village's modesty: he remembered one of the two brick buildings and "fifteen little shacks."[16] While the village actually was somewhat more advanced than that by 1864, John Bidwell must have realized that, with thousands of immigrants fleeing to California from the war, his grand ranch and a few other businesses could not meet all the new arrivals' retail needs.

While mining in the Sierra Nevada had dried up by the mid-1860s, Idaho gold mines were still at peak production. Its isolated mining camps, some with exotic names like Boise, Orofino and Owyhee, required an endless stream of supplies. A solution for Chico's need to grow could be increased trade with miners there. However, Chico goods meant for Idaho had to be shipped south to Oroville, the county center, where the closest existing route to Idaho began. Oroville merchants became anxious, therefore, when John Bidwell began to talk about building a road from Chico directly east to Idaho mines, which would make Chico a rival of Oroville in cross-mountain trade.[17] Bidwell found fellow investors who shared his desire to build such a road.

The *Record* newspaper at the county seat in Oroville printed vigorous denunciations of the valley town's pretensions. Although in 1862 Chico's population was still under a thousand, over the next few years it more than doubled. With this sign of the town's potential, its aspiring business owners increasingly resented Oroville's monopoly of the Idaho trade. Farmers around Chico needed a wider market for their produce and cattle. Other businessmen in town, just as eager to grow their markets, believed that a direct route from Chico through the mountains to the Idaho mines would draw immigrants from the usual Plains routes that entered California south and north of there. George Wood, who had an interest in the pioneer Morrill lumber mill, envisioned such a road transporting lumber directly to the Chico Landing, northwest of Chico on the Sacramento River, for shipments to the coast. At present, Oregon lumber companies used ocean transport to monopolize coastal lumber demands.

In 1863 the State Legislature, after lobbying by Bidwell and his partners, approved a $2,000 grant secured by Bidwell property. With that, their Humboldt Road Co. set to work.[18] Led by Bidwell's man Henry Landt and heavily relying on Mountain Maidu labor, the company built a toll-funded highway—Humboldt Road—from the Chico Landing to Honey Lake (now Lake Almanor) in the Sierra Nevadas. This initiated the passage to Soldier Valley in Nevada and thence to Silver City, Idaho.

New access to timber lands and trade led promoters to proclaim Chico "The Gateway to Idaho." Despite competition from Oroville, Red Bluff, Marysville, Portland, Oregon, and Council Bluffs, Iowa, once the Humboldt Road was in place, Chico's economy received a financial boost from burly, longhaul teamsters whose freight wagons carried produce and other goods. Additionally, although many were tough and boisterous men, few townspeople complained about their conduct because they patronized boarding houses, stores, saloons, hotels, blacksmiths, bootmakers and carriage builders. Their early morning stops to load up at Bidwell & Co. before heading out on Humboldt Road led George Wood to revive his waning interest in lumber milling as an investment.

Gus Chapman was away from home most of every day. In addition to his six-and-a-half days at the store, the disputes he handled in his years as a justice of the peace were ongoing. An example of those arose in July 1863, after an Indian revenge raid killed white children from a foothill ranch. The aftereffects threw the countryside into chaos and the Chico business community experienced losses.

On August 17 businessmen elected Chapman to chair a meeting about this crisis. In the unfinished public schoolhouse the men engaged in a heated exchange as they struggled to understand why raids in the foothills had led farmers to turn against Chico, to the point of threats to withdraw trade from its stores. They argued over whether, as charged by the farmers, Indians living on Bidwell's ranch were among the raiders. In addition to his Mechoopda ranch hands, a large camp of Mountain Maidu were temporarily housed in a separate, solely federal camp under government custody. Men close to Bidwell denied any Mechoopda, whose camp was near ranch headquarters, were responsible for the killings. In the end, the participants agreed somehow to come up with a response to mollify the farmers. Their statement endorsed removing the Indians in federal custody and, at the same time, keeping Bidwell's Mechoopda labor force in place.

After three days Chapman presented the draft he wrote with advice from druggist Wesley Lee and Dr. Samuel Sproul. His lawyerly wording was fine-tuned to keep Bidwell Indians working on Rancho Chico and assure the farmers that the Mountain Maidu in the federal camp would be removed. The farmers who read the document closely caught the Mechoopda exemption from removal and resumed their boycott threats. The document satisfied no one and Chico trade continued to suffer. By the end of August three companies of soldiers were camped at Rancho Chico to impose order and organize removal of the Mountain Maidu on Bidwell's ranch and others who walked down to the valley and surrendered to save their own lives. Bidwell's Indian workers stayed in place and at work.

Sarah's Part

Sarah's duties at home also expanded in 1863 when daughter Florence joined Freddie, who, at 4, was smart, curious and "on the move." She had to keep him from tipping over oil lamps or dashing onto streets where teenagers raced fast horses at all times of the day. Sarah's other chores included weekly laundry and ironing, each of which required a full day, and mending that never ended. Always frugal, she re-purposed everything she could. However, some relief was in sight. In the mid-1860s Chinese men were streaming into farm towns where they set up creek-side laundries. They charged so little for their impeccable work that Sarah and her friends gave up general laundering, only washing and ironing their intimate apparel. Unlike these younger women, however, senior matron Sophronia Maxson would not let those "foreigners" (as they were referred to) touch her family's clothing.

Although not a great pastry maker like Mrs. Maxson, whom John Bidwell and Charlie Stilson considered nonpareil, Sarah turned out meals in her "cook room," as she called her kitchen, seven days a week. Chico had an ample supply of good food. Fresh produce came from home gardens or John Bidwell's fields and orchards. Families savored "fist-sized peaches, bulging pears, grapes in bunches as large as a three-quart pail ... to say nothing of cherries, apricots, figs and *watermelons* as big as pumpkins and *so* sweet...."[19] [emphasis in the original]. Backyards housed henhouses and John Kempf, the new butcher in town, sold fresh cuts of beef or lamb from local ranches.

Over their first years in Chico, abundance, growing friendships and financial opportunities boosted the Chapmans' confidence in their choice to live there. They settled in—Gus acquired a gold pocket watch, *de rigueur* for successful businessmen, and Sarah filled out her house's furnishings. She also managed to "get out of the house" for church events and visits to friends.

On Sunday, November 2, 1863, a fire broke out at the What Cheer Hotel, destroying Chapman's justice of the peace records.[20] The volunteer bucket brigade's efforts were not equal to the extent and ferocity of flames that destroyed the entire hotel and its stable, including the horses. This was the worst fire since 1853 when Mountain Maidu raiders burned down most of John Bidwell's original ranch headquarters. While Chapman's clerks took up donations at the store and others held fundraisers for the hotel's owner, justice Chapman and the new justice A. M. Barnard had to find and set up a new office and reconstruct their legal records as best as possible. These additional responsibilities led Charles Stilson, a John Bidwell & Co. store clerk, to complain about Chapman's absences from the store.

Deaths All Around

Gus Chapman decided to give up his position as justice of the peace about the time his infant daughter Florence became ill. In addition to the rise of malaria deaths that struck settlers and Indians that summer, a week after the What Cheer Hotel fire influenza claimed Florence's life at the age of four months. Nevertheless, Sarah rallied and produced a full Thanksgiving dinner for her family and friends. However, by December she, Gus and Freddie were bedridden. When Gus rallied and went to check on the store, he was not his confident self. He confided to Stilson he felt "almost discouraged" by his family's bad health.[21]

Florence's demise led Chapman and other residents to join with John Bidwell to form the Chico Cemetery Association. They welcomed his offer to donate more land to the burial ground he first set aside after Mountain Maidu killed his ranch manager in 1852.[22] (The cemetery is located just north of Big Chico Creek, running along what is now Mangrove Avenue.) Some sections were designated for fraternal groups. Although Chapman was treasurer of the Masons, he decided to lay his child under a small marble marker in the Order of Odd Fellows section.[23] Although new to Chico, Gus had joined the Order in Michigan. Membership quickly became important to townspeople like the Chapmans—not only for its fellowship, but also for the life insurance it provided.

In addition to supervising the sales staff at Bidwell & Co., Chapman had to stand in as operations manager for George Wood who had contracted a chronic illness. The buying trips added to Gus's work schedule, sometimes keeping him away from his family for a week or more. However, a side benefit of his journeys was the opportunity to familiarize himself with Northern California. To reach Sacramento markets, he traveled by stage or shared a buggy to Oroville where he boarded the only area train for the rest of the trip. When the Sacramento River was high enough, he boarded steamships at the Chico Landing and sometimes crossed the Bay to San Francisco on ferries. Chapman's talent for general merchandise had been supervision and sales. According to Charlie Stilson, he was also a capable buyer. Although Stilson sometimes fretted about low stock, Gus put off buying trips until he accumulated sufficient cash or absolutely had to keep merchandise at a credible level. After harvests came in and farmers paid down their lines of credit, Chapman went to the cities and bought "a nice assortment of clothing [and] all manner of goods" that made the shelves at John Bidwell & Co. "look great."[24]

Even when in Chico, the strain of working ten or more hours a day did not leave Chapman much energy for social life or, for that matter, an active family life. Sarah, the family's anchor, did her best to lighten the atmosphere during his limited free time. In February 1864 she filled their parlor with guests holding lighted candles for a "sing." On another occasion, she invited company for a winter supper of ham, baked beans and potatoes, with Gus passing around porter beer and brandy, ever his favorites. During the winter months, townspeople had to draw down their wood-piles to keep fires going. Although wood was available, most trees were on private land or at some distance, and, therefore, so expensive that few could afford to buy much at a time. When warm weather returned, Sarah seated her guests under the trees in their backyard where she served the classic Chico dessert: fresh cream splashed over bowls of juicy strawberries. These gatherings had another benefit: they kept Gus somewhat "restrained"—at the store he was known for always dashing around.

Charlie Stilson and the other employees at Bidwell & Co. looked forward to invitations to social events at the Chapmans' home. They missed their families back east; some slept at the back of the store and bathed at a Broadway barber shop. All the male guests appreciated the opportunities Sarah's get-togethers provided them to stay informed and share their opinions with one another in a relaxed, social setting. What was the market for bricks or lumber? Was that freight wagon for sale up the street worth investing in? Would the turpentine demand hold up after the war? When some of the guests brought up the nightly carousals downtown, Bidwell's store employees were careful how they responded because their boss's son Jo Wood was at the center of the partying crowd. Stilson reserved his harsh judgments of Jo for his diary.[25]

Informal conversations at the homes of Chapman and other businessmen became the genesis for Chico's civic agenda. In order to appreciate his management skill in advancing this process, a quick overview of the town's government is helpful. Because Chico was unincorporated in the 1860s, county supervisors in Oroville controlled the amount of tax-based county funds allotted Chico for streets, bridges and policing. Seeking guidance, the supervisors periodically appointed three Chico men to serve as town trustees, later called city council members. The trustees usually appointed their local business and professional counterparts to "citizens' committees" that recommended important town policies the trustees would sometimes implement.

While Chapman never showed an interest in becoming a town trustee, he served on numerous citizens' committees for the next three decades. Later, when townspeople began to challenge the heavy influence of businessmen on the committees, the drive for incorporation was born. Among his peers, who were Chico Village's original leaders, Chapman became a kind of mediator with the even newer arrivals who advocated changes. Chapman's aura of "detachment" gave him an image of independence and built his reputation for balance and integrity.

By the mid-1860s Gus Chapman was well-established and had built a good name for himself. Of greatest practical consequence for his future, he carried the full trust of his mentor George Wood. This well-connected man's confidence in Chapman eventually provided him with access to yet another new start as a pioneer of California's lumber industry.

3

The Civil War As Seen from
John Bidwell & Co.

War issues churning in Augustus Chapman's Michigan hometown in 1861 were also simmering in Chico when he and Sarah arrived. Another recent arrival, housekeeper Mary Silsby, contrasted the Union side's universal popularity in her Bangor, Maine, hometown with Chico's discord in 1864: "There is not that <u>unity</u> of interest that we find in the East…. Society in California is made up of people from all parts of the country…. [Here] we have … even a jealousy of each other, like the [Chico] people of the North and of the South"[1] [emphasis in the original]. Although it was uncommon for California "locals" to enlist, more recent arrivals were eager to champion their home state's side in the conflict.

While fractious townspeople regularly squabbled over squatters' claims and were uneasy about Chinese starting to appear on the streets, the unfolding Civil War kept townspeople "pretty much at each other's throats." In the "bitter strife" over the war, John Bidwell became controversial as the town's most prominent leader of the Union cause.[2]

Census data, memoirs, church records and newspaper accounts reveal how vulnerable the Bidwell & Co.'s trade was to passions over the war. In 1860, 55 percent of Chico's white American-born males were from the North and 45 percent were from the border states and the South.[3] The latter included important farmers like Virginians Allen Henry, Benjamin Strange, William T. Durham, John Guill and John Morehead. John Tatham and Washington Henshaw each brought a young worker to Chico who had been a slave in the South. Although free under California law, both workers remained with Tatham and Henshaw as late as 1860.

George Wood made gestures to neutralize the Bidwell & Co.'s Union identity in order to attract Southern immigrants' trade. This justified his hire of "Secesh sympathizer" Lee Roy, whose presence made no difference in declining Southern patronage and irritated Union man Charlie Stilson until Roy quit in 1864. Southerners were more comfortable a block away at Edward B. Pond's hardware store, where manager George Bush, a member of the Union militia and Stilson's friend, kept the atmosphere strictly neutral.[4] Despite John Bidwell's stand on the war, Southerners still had to use his store for mail, to send a telegraph or buy something not available elsewhere.

Troops based in Chico in 1863 and after to address settler-Indian conflicts boosted the town's economy in general and their trade was particularly important to the Bidwell store. The Army account there made up for some drop-off of Southerners' patronage. Even so, in January 1864 Wood was "quite disappointed with last year's profits as they were $3000 less than in '62," when flood reparations drove up sales. The normal turnover of most store employees continued. Their normal wage was a dollar or less a day. For that, they worked at least ten hours a day and six and a half days every week.[5]

Charlie Stilson, unable to save money on his meager income, took a second job as a teacher, his occupation in Missouri and Iowa. As a member of Chico's first school board of trustees, Gus Chapman was well-placed to help his clerk become the "first assistant" to principal R. A. Allen in the new Salem Street Public School. Stilson also taught Freddie Chapman, Dr. Samuel Sproul's son Jo D. ("Jody") and butcher John Kempf's son John. All three families were already central figures in the community. Another new teacher was Antonia Cosby, wife of the Southern General George Cosby who was struggling as a farmer. She agreed to teach for $50 a month, saving the trustees the cost of a male teacher at $75. She made a start, but resigned because her husband, it was said, was embarrassed that his wife was paid to work.

By 1864 Gus Chapman had joined the local rush to cash in on the state's renewed mining boon. War intensified the federal government's need to buy gold to pay for materiel production which also required resin, turpentine and lumber from Butte County's

Magalia Ridge, about twenty-two miles northeast of Chico. While raw resources were attractive investments, Gus also speculated on mining stocks. People of every rank, means or trade held stock estimated at $50 million (almost $1 billion today). The staff at John Bidwell & Co. were also "players." According to Charlie Stilson, "The great excitement of today has been the call of 150 Ft. in Superior Copper Mining Co.... Allen sold 100 Ft. this morning and Chapman 50 today. I am somewhat interested as I own 15 Ft. Am glad I made the purchase as this advance just makes even on the Samson [mine] where I lost $100."[6]

Politics and Religion

The war also affected religious options. As Baptists, Gus and Sarah hesitated to embrace Methodism, even though it was long the only Protestant denomination available in town. Since the 1850s, circuit riders preached to mixed crowds of Northerners and Southerners in a schoolhouse near Pine Creek. After a preacher's sermon condemned the North for starting the war in opposition to slavery, Northern leaning parishioners headed for different corners of the school yard to discuss how to proceed. This led township Methodists to split into the North and South Methodist churches. That followed the division already established in the National Methodist Church back east. According to Hubert Howe Bancroft, in rural California the Methodist Church South became the chief voice of opposition to the Union, Lincoln and abolition.[7] Northern Methodist farmers built a simple church by Mud Creek. Better-off Southern Methodists built their own in Chico.

In and around Chico, Northern and Southern Methodists were cordial but ardent as they competed for new members. They worshiped and socialized separately. Through the mid-1860s North Methodist Church members still included Bidwell, whose store staff and their friends—the Woods, Chapmans, Hobarts, Maxsons, Gilkysons and Charlie Stilson—became mainstays in that church. In their work to sustain and advance it, the women became "sisters."[8]

Just like Michigan in 1860, when the split in Gus Chapman's home state contributed to his election loss, Chico's Democratic Party split in the 1864 presidential election. In Butte County, pro-slavery Democrat John Breckinridge won 1,173 votes; pro-Union Democrat Steven A. Douglas, 1,552 votes. George McClellan attracted some Butte County Democrats, while about 1,500 voters sat out the election.[9]

John Bidwell led the way for staunch Union Democrats to leave their party and join the newly named Union Party. It carried Butte County for Abraham Lincoln by 622 votes. Chico's most active Democrats, predominantly Southerners, refused to cross over and vote for Bidwell in his run for Congress that year, but he still managed a narrow victory. There is no record on how Chapman voted in that election.

Chico continued to draw immigrants from both sides of the conflict. Direct from battlefields, Union Army veteran Col. Hiram Batchelder headed for Chico, where he became a Chapman family friend, Freddie's teacher and future resident of the home Gus's family occupied during the war years.[10]

Chico's "Little Civil War"

Visions that Chico might become an active battle front in the war seem ridiculous, but suspicions added zest to town life. Bidwell's concern about such rumors led him to plant a spy in Chico's chapter of the Knights of the Golden Circle, a national Confederate group which proposed to expand slave territory. After his mole reported threats on his life, Bidwell retaliated by starting a chapter of the Order of the Union League.[11]

While the Union League membership roster disappeared and Chapman's name does not appear in other fragmentary evidence, common sense indicates he was at least on the membership roll. For one thing, Bidwell expected his employees and close business associates to back his political organizations.[12] According to Charlie Stilson's diary, he joined the militia to get more exercise, but turned into an ardent officer who, as Union League "whip," turned out Republican or Union votes in elections.

Chapman showed good faith toward the Union in other ways. He wrote the 1862 petition Bidwell carried to San Francisco calling for soldiers to protect his Indians against angry farmers the ranch owner characterized as "Rebs."[13] Chapman also prepared Bidwell's application to organize the "Chico Light Infantry" or Home Guard. While the town militia initially attracted about forty men, before long many lost interest in drills and meetings.

As the war continued, Sarah Chapman and other women organized fundraisers on behalf of an Army auxiliary, the Sanitary Commission. This national organization assisted sick and wounded Union soldiers. For example, their proceeds provided water-filled mattresses, tablets for writing letters, iron wire cradles for protecting wounded limbs, dominoes, checkerboards and hospital gowns. In one of their first events, after many planning meetings above the store at Armory Hall (formerly Bidwell Hall), the townswomen greeted a large crowd which made its way there through pouring rain on dark streets deep in mud; the women raised $1,000. Buoyed by their success, they continued to attract Northerners' support of the commission with other events such as the "New England dinner," "Skating Rink from the East" and "Sanitary Ball." Downstairs in the store, Gus Chapman and Charlie Stilson did their part selling tickets and other store help provided physical backup as the women set up their events.[14]

Meanwhile, with these big Union gatherings underway and federal troops in camp across Big Chico Creek, Chico's Southerners considered themselves, in effect, living in occupied territory. They could not gather in big rallies in Bidwell Hall like those that had irritated Charlie Stilson downstairs before the hall was designated the Army's armory. Now, they could only assemble in the privacy of their homes. Constraints like these compromised their emotional attachments to Chico.

During the war, townspeople passed around outdated newspapers from back home for information about the fates of family members and friends. The Bidwell store's telegraph remained the only public source for current war news. Any update it delivered could set off a brawl. At least two men were killed in such fracases. It was also the case that after the ticker delivered word of important Union victories, the local militia members produced smartly executed marches to cheers from some and cursing by others.

The Chapmans watched their mail for news of Gus's younger half-brother George Babcock who had enlisted in a Michigan company. Charlie Stilson, on discovering familiar names, wrote in his diary: "rec'd a paper from home with *sad sad* news of

Charley Strickland's death *killed* in battle!"[15] [emphasis in the original]. One letter delivered news of a Stilson brother's death in a clash. Colleagues and store customers tried to console him at work and fellow North Methodists comforted him after he broke down during a church service. Similarly, wagon builder Dan Sutherland waited for news about two of his Iowa brothers moving across Georgia in Sherman's campaign. Another brother had been injured at Pea Ridge, where still another died. George Wood's wife Caroline worried about her Alabama people. Her husband kept Chapman and Stilson abreast of his correspondence with an Alabama lawyer to whom he dispatched $1,000 in fees to protect his wife's $10,000 inheritance from the Confederate government's designs.[16]

Postwar

On April 10, 1865, word of the South's surrender raced across town from Bidwell & Co. The result was a raucous celebration of the North's victory. Yells sprung up all around, guns were fired, gongs struck, bells rung and anvils pounded. From Chico, travelers spread the news up and down the network of roads that marbled the countryside. Driving the North's celebration in town was the Chico Light Infantry Company's victory parade from Second Street to the plaza at Fourth Street where Camp Chico troops fired a hundred rounds from the Civil War cannon they loaded and reloaded. As night fell, roman candles, rockets and bonfires extended the Northerners' exhilaration into the early morning hours. Jo Wood "got shamefully drunk," along with many others.[17] More reserved people like the Chapmans exchanged embraces and offered prayers of thanksgiving, while Chico's Southerners nursed their losses among themselves. But, somewhere beyond their disappointment, they must have found relief for the end of war.

A New Start

After the war, Chapman shifted his loyalty to the Union Party's successor, the Republican Party, which would flourish in farm towns throughout California's interior valleys.[18] This party suited Chapman's business ambitions even though, now in his late thirties, success continued to elude him. The war cost the

Democratic Party much of its moderate base—men like him-self—and control of it fell to other men Republicans denounced as zealous ideologues. Over decades, Democrats would appeal to the working man by vilifying the propertied. Harsh postwar con-ditions created a large population of dispossessed people who responded to those Democrats' appeal: "The new Democracy [became] heavily weighted with what gentlemen were pleased to call the rabble."[18] While Gus Chapman remained confident he could rise in the world, he would never consider men rabble for being poor.[19]

While Chapman continued his strong interest in politics, he remained focused on earning his fortune. Having gained George Wood's confidence and soon his financial backing, Gus was ready to capitalize on opportunities northern Butte County's postwar years presented.

When Bidwell bought the Potter Ranch in 1860, the ranch gate (bottom) closed off the Oroville-Shasta Trail (center). Old Chico Way (right) and was built as a detour. Rancho Chico (top) was north of the Big Chico Creek.

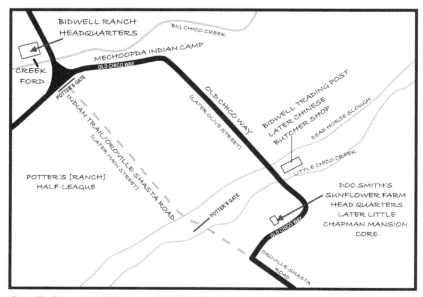

Oroville-Shasta Trail detour, called Old Chico Way (now Olive Street), around the Potter Ranch. The last segment of Old Chico Way became E. 12th St. Connie Ballou, illustrator.

John Bidwell shifted the village in his front yard to the former Potter Ranch across Big Chico Creek. He tore down Potter's gate, reopened the Oroville-Shasta Trail, then renamed it Main Street.

Chapman was manager of John Bidwell & Co. at Front (now 1st St.) & Broadway (left). On the second floor, Bidwell Hall served as a community center. Today, a restaurant occupies the first floor (the second floor was later removed).

When the Chapmans arrived, John Bidwell's first Rancho Chico mansion (and office) was a federal farmhouse, later confused as his mill. The water from the tower behind his house fed the irrigation flume that channeled water over a brick wall (right) in the back to soak his extensive gardens.

In this c. 1871 photo the house was about to be torn down as the current Bidwell Mansion had been built and his office moved downtown.

Chico Village's early downtown.

Wood & Chapman Co. celebrated its grand opening with a celebration ball at the Union House on the southwest corner of 3rd & Main.

OFFICE OF CHICO ENTERPRISE.
ED. HOOLE - PUBLISHER AND PROPRIETOR.

Enterprise newspaper office on the northwest corner of 2nd & Main. Its original editor was a Republican who supported Gus Chapman.

HON. GEORGE H. CROSSETTE.

George Crosette, vitriolic editor of the *Record* newspaper. Although a fellow Michigander and anti-war Democrat, he clashed with Gus Chapman on the country-split campaigns, but otherwise supported him.

PERKINS & CO. ESTABLISHED 1860.
WHOLESALE AND RETAIL GROCERS
OROVILLE, BUTTE CO. CAL.

Perkins & Co. mercantile store in Oroville. George Perkins financially backed Wood & Chapman. He and Chapman backed one another in politics as well.

Powellton hamlet, base of the Chapman & McKay Lumber Co.

The Powellton hotel is on the left. Chapman also kept a cottage there.

Chapman & McKay bought the Chico Lumber Co. at 8th & Main. This was a record-setting delivery of lumber from their Powellton mill.

Chico Lumber Co. is seen in the background at the southern end of Main St. on Eighth St. in the Junction.

Wood's Hall, with its cushioned seats, offered a wide variety of community events such as this tableau, dramas, concerts, debates, circuit speakers like Susan B. Anthony and traveling troupes.

The Idlewild racetrack, west of the Oroville-Shasta Rd., was a popular destination. Charlie Stilson disapproved of the gambling sport and complained about its scandalous activities, including murder.

A ferry at Chico Landing on the Sacramento River. Wood & Chapman shipped lumber from there to other cities.

Deep dust buried streets in the summer, requiring a town water sprinkler.

Chico's Civil War canon was melted down for reuse in WWI.

Sap was extracted from Ponderosa (yellow) pine found in Butte County and elsewhere in California to make turpentine, especially needed during the Civil War.

WE WILL DEFEND IT FOREVER!

NATIONAL UNION TICKET.

For President,

ABRAHAM LINCOLN.

For Vice-President,

ANDREW JOHNSON.

For Electors,

SAMUEL BRANNAN,
J. G. McCALLUM,
W. W. CRANE,
CHARLES MACLAY,
WARNER OLIVER.

STATE TICKET.

THIRD DISTRICT.

For Congress,

JOHN BIDWELL.

NOTE.—The THIRD District is composed of these Counties: Marin, Sonoma, Napa, Lake, Solano, Yolo, Sutter, Yuba, Sierra, Butte, Plumas, Tehama, Colusa, Mendocino, Humboldt, Trinity, Shasta, Siskiyou, Klamath, and Del Norte.

John Bidwell appears on a Civil War election party ticket distributed to voters.

Chapman was an elected school trustee who oversaw building of the Salem Street School, Chico's first public school.

The Chapmans were patrons of James and Selena Woodman's private Chico Academy on W. 5th St. "Better-off" families, including the Chapmans, enrolled their children there to obtain a rigorous education in preparation for Berkeley and eastern colleges.

Travelers on the privately owned Humboldt Rd. The road ran from the Chico Landing to Idaho. Chapman was Humboldt Road's board president for years.

Wood & Chapman relied on oxen-drawn wagons to haul lumber down the Humboldt Road.

The North Methodist Church of Chico, Cal.

Sarah Chapman was an elder of the North Methodist Church in Chico.

The Chico Hotel on W. 2nd St. inspired local pride until it burned down in 1882.

4

The Take-Off:
Lumberman and Merchant

In January 1865, when Chapman decided his lumber under-takings meant he could not do justice to Bidwell & Co., he reduced his role there and Wood promoted Charlie Stilson to replace him as chief clerk/sales manager. However, by mid-March Wood realized his own store work had increased in Chapman's absence and asked Stilson to step back so Chapman could return as manager. Stilson recalled: "Mr. Wood has spoken to me today about the prospect of having Chapman help in the store again—am sure I don't care what arrangements we will make."[1] Chapman agreed to return. With Gus back in charge of the store, Wood worked on other business investments and traveled.

In June that year Sarah gave birth to the Chapmans' second daughter, named Mary after Sarah's elder sister Mary. Her mid-dle name, Euphrasia, most likely came from the Greek word for "welcome," recalled from Gus's college course on classics. (It is unlikely they named her after the herbal remedy euphrasia that pharmacies advertised.) Mary's birth was the family's highlight that year.

With the advent of winter 1865-1866, rain pummeled the valley, drawing Chico trade to a standstill. Heavy snows shut down postal transit and delivery services on Humboldt Road. This meant tons of mail destined for Idaho piled up in every open space at John Bidwell & Co. Boxes and bags arriving by steamships and stagecoaches rose in ceiling-high stacks at the Idaho Exchange Saloon and piled up in a room behind the Chico Hotel's bar. Bored freight drivers and mail carriers drank and gambled while they waited for mud to solidify and roads reopened. Their quarrels usually erupted in the bars and spilled out onto Broadway. Merchants, blacksmiths and owners of stables complained about the collapse of farm and travel trade when the rains created "bottomless roads and bridgeless streams." With the exception of fistfights, the Chico *Courant* ran out of local items. However, idle drivers handsomely rewarded prostitutes. They were among the few women whose independent income kept seamstresses and milliners at work satisfying their yen for fashion. Charles Croissant's new brewery at the southern end of Broadway strained to meet the demand for beer, ale and porter.

The stench from hog pens, always pungent in winters' damp air, penetrated every building. The word "cholera" echoed across town. By contrast, a Mechoopda party from Bidwell's ranch filed along Main Street bearing baskets and bags full of ground squirrels, a delicacy the floods had flushed from their burrows. As the rainy days continued, the Chico library bookshelves at the Bidwell store emptied and private owners' books traveled back and forth among households and boarding houses.

According to *Courant* coverage during this period, Chico businessmen considered the storms the supervisors' excuse for continuing to ignore conditions along the Butte County section of Humboldt Road. As Chico businessmen saw it, the road's deterioration illustrated the supervisors exacting retribution from Chico for its capture of Oroville's lucrative trade. But for the new road, Chico trade bound for Idaho would have had to pass through the county seat.

Optimism returned that April when the rains stopped and roads dried up. Trade again filled the broad streets with pack trains and freight wagons on the move to transport goods between Chico and Idaho.

Good Times

During late 1865 George Wood struck a deal that created a lumber mill partnership between Gus Chapman and William "Bill" McKay, a big, dark-haired man who measured life through clear blue eyes. His bulk and coloring sharply contrasted to Chapman's medium build, short stature, cool gray eyes and fair coloring. In January 1866 they purchased the Morrill mill in

the Sierra Nevada foothills hamlet of Powellton (formerly Pow-
ells), northwest of Dogtown (now Magalia) and east across Butte
Creek from future Sierra Flume & Lumber holdings. They also
put up $3,000 each to buy the year-old Chico Lumber Co. at the
southern end of Main Street and an additional yard on Ninth.
That sale included a large stock of milled wood, heavy equipment, horses, oxen, wagons and carts.[2]

Because nothing suggests Chapman had the means to invest
on that scale, it is likely George Wood helped finance his purchases and retained some interest in the Morrill mill. However,
the exact financial relationship he and Chapman developed eluded discovery here. Wood conferred with Morrill when the sale
was underway; later it emerged he went in with Chapman and
McKay on a timberland purchase. It is apparent that, like in
Addison, Michigan, Chapman's management and sales skills in
Chico had earned him the confidence of an established financial
backer.[3]

Nine years younger than Chapman, McKay had arrived in
California from Massachusetts during the Gold Rush in the
1850s. He soon became a stock raiser in Tehama County, then
switched to lumber production and managed a mill there. Only
a year-and-a-half after Chapman and McKay became partners,
their clear pine won the prize for best lumber in Chico's new
Agricultural Fair and McKay's oxen won the pulling match competition. Teamsters soon considered him a legend because, with
no hint of verbal or physical abuse, he could control oxen pulling
freight wagons stacked with logged trees. They said he only had
to whisper to his oxen for them to respond with perfect obedience and maximum performance.[4]

Although the Woodsum brothers sold their Chico Lumber Co.
yard to Chapman & McKay, they immediately opened a new
identical business elsewhere in town under the same name. A
glimmer of Chapman's years as a lawyer appears in his response
to their effrontery: "The statement … claiming the name of the
Chico Lumber Co. is a BILK! … The undersigned are the only,
and true, successors of said Company, and still occupy and
have possession of said Lumber Yard. …"[5] Although Chapman
& McKay prevailed, the former owners continued to compete
with them in lumber sales for years.

Although Chapman's management role at John Bidwell &
Co. expanded as George Wood's absences increased, he also
had to be at Chico Lumber where he handled sales and managed employees who stacked, sold and delivered fir, sugar pine,
fence posts, shingles, clapboard siding, as well as hay and grain.
Because of his lumber work in Chico and trips to the Powellton
mill, clerks at the Bidwell store had to cover for him and Wood.
Charlie Stilson groused, "Chapman has lumber on the brain."[6]
That George Wood overlooked the strain at Bidwell & Co. suggests his own stake in Chapman & McKay. Bidwell, away in
Washington, evidently was unaware of the extent of Wood and
Chapman's divided time and attention. Ironically, despite the
complaints Stilson made in his diary about Gus's absences, he
also expressed admiration for his boss's drive and the hard work
that getting ahead exacted from him: he mentioned Chapman's
poor health several times and noted that Chapman "returned
[to the store] from the mill about 4 and seems quite fatigued."[7]

In May 1866 Chico residents welcomed a diversion when a
steamship delivered sixty carefully selected horses to the Chico
Landing. For the next few weeks, they daily coursed through
town streets as trainers prepared them to pull four-horse
stagecoaches, "the same as those used by Ben Holladay on the
Overland Route," during the thirty-five-day journeys to Idaho.[8]
One man was so skilled he could "take a wild horse and in an
hour drive him about town perfectly subdued, and [use] the
whip but very little in the operation."

In July Cal Hoose, a Chapman & McKay teamster, delivered
another spectacle. He was admired for his courage in the 1850s
when he transported freight through bandit country and fended off attacks by Mountain Maidu. He was also brave enough
to drive a wagon down the mountains, across the foothills and
into town loaded with 10,330 board feet of pine. McKay had
supervised the placement of every board, shaping the load like a
pyramid. Observers guessed this was the largest load of lumber
a single team "ever hauled in California."[9] Hoose reached Main
Street from Humboldt Road en route to the Agricultural Fair
with not a board or chain out of place. A photographer captured
the scene when the company posted a flag on top; the Chico Cornet Band entertained admirers who flocked to its stop at Chico

Lumber. Hoose allowed as he had "brought that amount to try the road and will bring a full load next time."[10]

Lumber, "the first natural resource [the State] exploited after gold," would prove Chapman's most lucrative investment.[11] Humboldt Road added to Chapman & McKay's value because it opened up additional Sierra Nevada forests to cutting. Chapman soon joined the Humboldt Road Co.'s board of directors; it would elect him president or board chairman for several terms. He also became an early advocate for a direct road to Chico from the Magalia Ridge on the west side of the Sierra Nevada foothills. He predicted such a road would relieve company freight wagons of the eleven miles and two-day drive south to Oroville before turning northwest to reach the Chico Landing. For two decades this vision of a new route would tantalize Chapman and others.[12]

Within a few years Chapman & McKay's twenty employees produced 20,000 board feet of original-growth sugar pine for delivery to the steamboats at Chico Landing headed for San Francisco where Bay Area builders had relied on redwood and Oregon pine shipped by sea. Chapman also entered into lumber contracts with Salt Lake City buyers. Although lumber constituted Chapman's first effort to grow his fortune in California, he was open to an exciting, yet problematic, offer from George Wood.[13]

Wood & Chapman's Beginnings

Caroline Wood's $10,000 inheritance from the sale of her family's store in Alabama arrived in July 1865. As her husband, George had legal control of her money. He "treated" her to marble-topped tables and a suite of furniture for her parlor and reserved the balance to build and stock his new two-story brick building at the northwest corner of Second and Main streets.[14]

Construction began in August and continued through the rainy winter. In January downpours liquefied the ground under the piers of Wood's building, opening a sink hole that imperiled the store's brick walls. Apparently to hide its real purpose from Bidwell, his partner in the Bidwell store, Wood described the rising structure as a "warehouse for a large jobbing firm" suited to projects in the Chico area. This helped him forestall questions from Bidwell, who was too trusting and too preoccupied with plans to leave for his new seat in Congress, to question building a large warehouse on the most important block in the heart of Chico's walk-in retail district. Bidwell had worked in Washington, D.C., for eight months before learning Wood's new building was not going to be a warehouse, but a general merchandise store that would directly compete with Bidwell's supply of goods to Plumas and Humboldt counties and Idaho miners.

When Bidwell found out about the deception in March 1866, he returned to California to confront Wood. He learned that not only was Wood quitting Bidwell & Co., but that Gus Chapman had accepted Wood's offer to make him an operating partner in the new store, Wood & Chapman. According to Stilson, "[It] has been the main excitement in town today. Everybody seems to take an interest in the matter, Chapman has *quit* and there has been some shrewd wire working between Mr. Wood, the town trustees and [George] Perkins" [emphasis in the original].[15] Adding insult to injury, Bidwell found out the rest of his store staff was also leaving for the new store.

The Wood & Chapman building exuded presence. In its corner location, one side extended 120 feet west along the north side of Second Street. On the other side, thirty feet extended north along Main, with its front door angled at the corner. The building began to go up in summer 1865; the store opened for business in June 1866.

The Idaho trade, which drove Wood & Chapman's business, did not disappoint its owners' hopes. On one occasion, a traveler forty miles from Chico spotted thirty-seven supply wagons heaped with lumber, flour and machinery headed for quartz mines at Camp Smith, White Horse, Susanville, Long Valley, Round Valley and Indian Valley. The rider also spotted the former Confederate Army's Major General George B. Cosby, now a hard-pressed Butte County farmer, and his men leading fifty heavily loaded freight wagons.[16]

John Bidwell's Travails

Bidwell had to deal with repercussions from the collapse of his store at the hands of George Wood, principally, and Chapman by extension. Not only had Bidwell lost his entire staff,

Wood took the partnership's account books and his share of the furnishings. Bidwell's anger found sympathizers, but attracted no allies. Wood declared he was acting on his and Bidwell's prior "understanding." Stilson, a stickler about law and rectitude, described Wood's actions as troublesome, but "legal": "whether honorable or not it is per *contract*" [emphasis in the original].[17]

Bidwell had to close his store for a month, then Thomas Bidwell, his younger stepbrother whom he had sent to college, reopened it. However, Thomas was so weakened by advanced tuberculosis that he was often homebound, relying on a Chinese servant and his wife America, "Merrie," the teenaged daughter of a Sacramento River steamboat captain. Merrie also worked at the store in his stead.[18]

Gus must have struggled with his decision to leave Bidwell & Co. and partner with George Wood. Although Bidwell had been one of his employers, he was most indebted to Bidwell's partner for the lumber company opportunity and for his backing at the Bidwell store. Gus and Bidwell had built no discernible relationship of their own apart from both men's reliance on Wood. Now that Wood was turning on Bidwell, Chapman's close relationship with Wood precluded Gus from any future assistance from Bidwell, who would never forget what he considered the perfidy of this trio—Wood, Chapman, and their financial backer George Perkins. All three had to face Bidwell's rage at the time, but only Chapman would live on to experience the full brunt of his later attempts at retribution.

In late 1866, while Wood & Chapman were savoring their store's early popularity, winter weather again shut down Humboldt Road. Snow was piled so deep that some mail only made it through because courageous carriers crossed the Sierras on snowshoes, marking trees on their route. George Wood circulated petitions that pressed county supervisors to keep the road open, but, like the previous year, they ignored the pleas.

Bidwell also discovered that Randall Rice, ranch supervisor in his absence, had somehow compromised the quality of his horse herd and misjudged the financial markets pertaining to crops and livestock.[19] Bidwell had to take out large loans to save the ranch. After attributing to Rice his losses on the ranch side of his operation, he confronted Wood about the store's disappointing annual returns. Stilson summarized the situation at the store as an imbroglio: an "extremely confused, complicated and embarrassing situation."[20]

George Perkins — The New Player

George Perkins's backing of Wood & Chapman initiated a long-term business and political relationship with Gus. Perkins was the leading wholesale and retail merchant in Oroville, where his bank stayed open until his receipts arrived.[21] As a "wide awake" wholesale and retail businessman, Perkins frequently stopped in Chico to call on clients, now including George Wood and Gus Chapman. Perkins had confidence in Wood from his years of wholesale business with the Bidwell store. He had come to know Chapman when he took over much of the buying for Wood. (Perkins's later relationship with Chapman is discussed in a later chapter.) Of course, Perkins was already aware of John Bidwell's importance and reputation in Chico and beyond. His respect for him and Wood in business dealings spilled over into his good opinion of Chico's promise as a town.

Due to George Wood's chronic health problems, Gus Chapman's role in their store expanded. Wood was, in effect, the business's figurehead whose good name and wide reputation enhanced the store's standing. As the principal purveyor of dry goods, groceries, hardware, crockery, boots, shoes, clothing, mining tools and farming implements, Wood & Chapman had a robust clientele for several years. When Wood purchased the Butte Flour Mill, again partnering with Chapman, they moved its granary to Chapman & McKay's lumber yard.[22] With so many arrows in their financial quivers, they had reason to believe they could buffer financial uncertainties.

Perkins was also negotiating a place for himself in a merger between the banks of Oroville's Charles Faulkner and Marysville's Norman Rideout, who were planning to invest together in a Chico bank. For investment purposes, Faulkner and Rideout had to be confident in the quality of Chico businessmen before opening a bank in the new town. Bidwell had literally picked up and moved the community of Chico across Big Chico Creek from his ranch headquarters. Now it was supposed to stand on its own and operate independent of him. Rideout, Faulkner and

Perkins considered George Wood and Gus Chapman the kind of men qualified to build the town and shape its future.

Because in this period Bidwell switched from the North Methodist Church, which Gus sometimes attended, to his new wife Annie's Presbyterian Church, the two rarely crossed paths.[23] However, he and Gus collaborated on Humboldt Road management and other civic projects. Bidwell would never have a chance to retaliate against Wood and decades passed before his attempts against Chapman were successful.

Life at Wood & Chapman

Stilson's remarks about conditions at Wood & Chapman resembled his former take on the situation at Bidwell & Co. After all, the same personnel with the same idiosyncrasies had simply moved from Broadway to Main. Stilson shifted his occasional complaints about "Chapman," his supervisor in the Bidwell store, to complaints about "Mr. Chapman," now his employer. In both positions, Chapman acted for Wood, who continued to pursue investments elsewhere, as his health permitted. Year-round, the younger clerks who regularly partied until 3 or 4 a.m. moaned about their hangovers, a sore point with the senior staff.[24]

Chapman bought and sold for the store and managed the personnel. He oversaw the flour mill and made trips to Powellton to confer with Bill McKay. Travel to solicit lumber contracts or buy for the store made more claims on his time. Throughout this period, Wood counted on Chapman and Chapman counted on Stilson to cover for him at the store. Freed of responsibilities there, Wood bought a Chico saddlery and tinkered with inventions. At the store he showed off his rat trap that was big enough to hold "something less than a bushel."[25]

For George Wood's son Jo, Wood & Chapman became, like Bidwell & Co., a convenient place to pass the time until dark. A regular at the card tables in Allen's Saloon, he kept drinks coming and danced with barmaids, the saloon's unique attraction.[26] While Jo's conduct annoyed Charlie Stilson, Chapman tried to be patient with his partner's derelict son, who considered him a friend. It was Jo who walked over to Sixth Street to sit by Chapman's bedside when the older man came down with his annual bouts of malaria. However, there were times when Jo exhausted

Chapman's patience and he would explode, heaping tirades on the young slacker. Meanwhile Stilson snickered about Jo behind his back at work—and later in his diary. Jo Wood's irresponsibility occasionally roused his father to threats of disinheritance, after which he always broke his promises to reform.[27]

Charlie Stilson's opinion of himself as the backbone of Wood & Chapman had merit because he was a capable, honest and reliable employee. John Bidwell passed his store to his brother Thomas, who urged Charlie to return to clerk for Thomas Bidwell & Co. George Foster Jones, who had purchased E. B. Pond's hardware store, also courted him. George Wood ultimately prevailed, but paid dearly to keep his clerk.[28] Wood had to double Stilson's wages from the Bidwell store to $150 a month.

Stilson had not rushed to join Wood & Chapman, perhaps because of his mixed feelings about both owners. Although he sought and appreciated Chapman's business advice, he found Gus's criticisms, although rare, hard to take. As at Bidwell & Co., he disapproved of Chapman's frequent absences to work on his and Wood's other businesses. To be fair, however, Stilson, too, had bought a partnership in a brickyard and had a stake in a freight team, both of which, at times, also took him away from the store. He complained, "A persistent effort is being made to convince Mr. Wood that I am not doing the fair thing by him."[29] However, once he accepted George Wood's job offer in the new store, he worked with enthusiasm, frequently expressing his desire to aid in the firm's success. At both businesses, Charlie expressed sympathy for Chapman's chronic health problems and praised his skill as a buyer of merchandise suited to each store's varied clientele.[30]

When Wood & Chapman opened, former John Bidwell & Co. customers flocked there in such numbers that Stilson complained about having to ignore the bookkeeping to cover the counters. On occasion he expressed annoyance at all the "ladies" who waited for his personal attention. While he enjoyed the attentions of young women, he also made a point to call on an endearing town elder, Sophronia Maxson, and visited Thomas Bidwell's sociable widow Merrie, both of whom rewarded his after-work calls with a fresh slice of pie or a piece of cake. On lucky days, he stayed for supper.[31]

As the clerks measured out ribbon for one customer or assembled a hay mower for another, they strained to be heard above the din of saws and hammers upstairs where carpenter John Maxson was creating Wood's Hall. Wood had not only driven Bidwell & Co. out of business and challenged Bidwell's flour mill, now he had Bidwell's favorite woodworker building an upgraded version of Bidwell's meeting hall.[32] Meanwhile downstairs the store's owners enlisted a committee of customers to plan Wood & Chapman's grand opening. It began with a dinner party at the Union Hotel, followed by a "grand ball" at which four floor managers led the dancing until early hours.

According to a later recollection, "Perhaps no building served the public as well in the '60s and '70s as Wood's Hall."[33] For one thing, its cushioned seats were more welcoming than the backless hard benches in Bidwell Hall. Its raised stage featured a curtain in colors that complemented the state and federal flags that Charlie Stilson raised and lowered for each event. Although most of the dramas, tableaux and concerts were amateur productions, big crowds flocked there to hear circuit speakers such as Susan B. Anthony, popular essayist Grace Greenwood and lawyer Laura DeForce Gordon. Chicoans regularly streamed up the steep stairs to watch traveling troupes of actors repeatedly perform *Uncle Tom's Cabin*, *Nan the Good-for-Nothing* and Shakespeare's more popular plays.[34]

Chico's cultural rawness presented a challenge to its urbane residents reared in the East and Midwest where colleges and lyceums were established institutions. Since at least the early 1860s townspeople regularly attended lectures and debates, participated in readings and recitations and posed in artistic tableaux. Well after the Civil War's end, the Chico Literary Club discovered the secession debate could still draw a lively crowd. They also grappled with temperance issues and sparred over the justice of Maximillian's execution in Mexico.

The original version of the Literary Club was a Wood's Hall men's group. Eventually, when making the arrangements for their events taxed their enthusiasm, the members offered women the "opportunity" to arrange events, provide refreshments, put out their newsletter and clean up afterward. After women labored in the background for a decade or so, they won approval to recite and, by the mid-1870s, when Wood's Hall closed, men and women were full partners in the club. Until then, club volunteers kept Chico's townspeople somewhat culturally up-to-date, and their events provided welcome traffic to the store downstairs.[35]

Wood & Chapman also donated use of the upstairs hall's large anteroom to house Chico's first free library, in contrast to the earliest version on Bidwell & Co.'s store shelves. The Chico Library Association members' children and their schoolmates moved 352 books from the Bidwell store to the new space. Gus and Sarah Chapman often frequented the library's collection. They and others volunteered books, time and money to keep it afloat at various downtown locations over the decades.

Downstairs, when Stilson took a break from paperwork and sales, customers marveled at his adept use of the latest invention, a "sewing machine," for making door and window curtains that created a "cozy" ambiance in the store.[36] He regularly applied fresh paint to the exterior wood trim and Chapman commissioned a wooden awning over the boardwalk to shelter customers from winter rain and summer sun. Awnings throughout the little downtown presented a jumble of heights, depths, compositions, conditions and orientations to the sun's position or the rain's direction. In 1868, while George Wood was away, Gus had an "express wagon" built for home deliveries. After children set a fire in the store's back lot, he installed a force pump to assist in fire fighting and kept a new water trough full out front for customers' horses.

The Valley Restaurant opened just north of Wood & Chapman and, in 1868, a vegetable market set up business on the West Second Street boardwalk, just beyond its doorway. Alongside the stalls, bootblacks newly arrived from the Deep South set up business. Wood & Chapman's well-established rival Suydam & Jones continued to prosper at the opposite end of their block on Main Street.

At work Monday through Saturday and after church on Sunday, Wood & Chapman staff only took time off for mid-day dinner on Thanksgiving and Christmas. As he had done at the Bidwell store, at Wood & Chapman Stilson unlocked the doors at sunrise to provision teamsters anxious to start for Shasta in the north, the Idaho mines to the east or points south. Once Charlie had them on their way, he swept out the mud they had tracked in, all the time keeping an eye on the door for Chapman's 8 a.m. arrival which signaled his break. On the morning after Sarah returned from her first trip to the East, he noted Chapman's 8:30 arrival because it delayed his breakfast. Although the store officially closed sometime between 8 and 9 p.m., Stilson stayed late to clean up Wood's Hall after events or when the "down" stagecoach arrived late from Red Bluff. Charlie made the best of evening hours when friends stopped in to relax and trade gossip. For example, when he was still at work, a shooting linked to a dispute at the Idlewild racetrack took place in front of Wood & Chapman. As a witness, he fielded questions about it from the curious. He took advantage of this opportunity to expound on his disapproval of horse races and other scandalous doings at the track.[37]

Although Chapman was managing staff, waiting on customers and calling on clients with accounts due, he made time to promote the new Agricultural Fair and lobby the county for better roads. He also attended meetings of the Odd Fellows and the Masons. Chapman and Stilson spent full days working together to prepare the lists and forms they stuffed into the bulging satchel Gus carried on buying trips to Sacramento or San Francisco. En route to the cities, he had time to call on George Perkins and others in Oroville while waiting to board "Binney's Road." This train to Marysville rarely operated according to schedule. Although the *Record* marveled at its "lightening speed," riders recalled how it swayed along the tracks at the "mildest speed imaginable."[38] Drawing on the tradition of steamboat travelers, male passengers sprung to their feet at each stop and moved the freight on and off as needed. After an overnight stay in Marysville, Chapman continued on to city markets.

Because the county supervisors refused to extend rail service north past Oroville, Chapman transported stock by freight wagons to the Chico Landing on the Sacramento River. (The *Victor*, a "splendid and fast sailing steamer" with a Wood & Chapman shipment on board, sank just short of its destination.[39]) The mostly reliable ships also carried passengers and mail on the thirty-hour passage from the San Francisco Bay to Chico. During summers, when reduced water levels shut down river service, Gus shifted back to wagons.

Illness, Death and Hazards

Gus Chapman's chronic malaria reappeared nearly every summer over his entire adult life. Known as "ague" (pronounced **egg** yoo) at the time, it was a common disease in Michigan and California. Sometimes called the Sacramento Fever, in Butte County it was a byproduct of long, rainy winters in combination with the clay soils which held groundwater and bred mosquitoes. Wood & Chapman sold patent medicines like "Ague King" and "Ayer's Ague Cure."[40]

Malarial attacks sent victims to bed with severe, intermittent chills and fever that lasted for days. Chills reduced Gus to helpless shudders. Then a high-temperature fever produced a dry heat that drenched him in sweat and left him in a long, exhausted sleep. As soon as he was awake and feeling fit again, he would head back to the store where Stilson marveled at his quick recovery. But symptoms often returned in a day, sending him home again to fight the next round. When the onsets finally petered out he resumed his normal active life. Although Stilson had issues with his boss, he empathized with Chapman's episodes because he, too, was afflicted with malaria.

One common denominator in Chico was the weather; another was sickness. Whatever their differences, people could always trade health news. For example, bouts with rheumatism (joint, muscle, and fibrous inflamation) left Chapman temporarily "lame" and Stilson's teeth ached so much that Dr. J. S. Morse, Chico's dentist, got him very drunk and pulled out all his uppers. (Morse died from the side effects of alcoholism before Stilson worked up his nerve to remove the lowers.) Silver fillings from Idaho's Black Rock mines relieved and protected a generation of townspeople.

Death was indiscriminate. The regularity of funerals for old and young, well-off and poor surpassed weddings in drawing townspeople from homes, workshops, barns and offices to meet and mourn in common. Women confronted their own mortality with every pregnancy and daily events reminded everyone of potential hazards. Deaths portended not only emotional devastation but also financial collapse.

Chapman, supporting his wife and young children, knew he was all that stood between them and destitution. Perhaps the devastation of each malarial attack heightened his sense of vulnerability and fed his drive to exert himself every moment he felt well. Even though Chico had become a stable farm town, examples of failure were commonplace. On Christmas Eve 1864, in his room behind Bidwell & Co., Charlie Stilson heard "a terrible groaning on the porch, went out and found Mr. Eagan lying in the rain unable to move a limb and without blanket or cover—ah it was a sad sight—a man once wealthy and honored—now a poor degraded brute—we dragged him in the house and he lay there all day unable to rise—has now gone over to Baders as we gave him money to buy food."[41]

As purveyors of farm equipment, George Wood and Gus Chapman knew the dangers it posed to their farming customers. In August 1868 alone, one Chico area farmer fell from a load of hay onto the prongs of a pitchfork; another broke his back and legs when he plunged from a threshing machine onto and under the horses pulling it; a thresher cut off a man's fingers; and a neighbor lost part of his foot. Country life was not just physically dangerous. Chico's sole deputy sheriff earned extra pay for delivering patients to the state's insane asylum in Stockton.[42]

Weather: A Driving Force

Wood & Chapman staff found it a challenge to keep customers comfortable year around. In the summer customers and staff sweltered in the hot, stuffy store. In winter, when Charlie opened the store and found the dipper frozen in the water barrel, he stoked the store's woodstove—but only in extreme weather. Wood was still too expensive to regularly burn in fireplaces or the new invention, woodstoves. Store help wore heavy jackets and, if they lighted a fire, it was extinguished by mid-day or when the deep chill faded inside. Winter sicknesses abounded. One after another, Wood, Chapman, Stilson, clerk George Turner and bookkeeper Frank Titcomb fell ill.

Because the weather was so unpredictable, Chapman's interest in the weather was never casual. When farmers made money, stock flew from his store's shelves and barrels filled the buggies and wagons out front. Seven blocks south on Main Street, his men filled Chico Lumber customers' orders for bags of seed or shingles and four-by-sixes. However, good weather was not an entirely reliable predictor of trade because clear days were good for field work. When drenching rain damaged crops and dissolved the rutted dirt roads, country people were reluctant to spend money even if they could get to town.

Late spring and early summer usually brought relief before the heat set in. But in the approach to it, strong north winds whisked dust airborne, then drove it down, dense and heavy. Some windstorms flattened outbuildings. Wind gusts discouraged travel to town and drove grime and grit into every nook and cranny in businesses and homes. Even glass-enclosed counters could not protect the stock at Wood & Chapman. In a vain effort to keep store goods clean, Gus restricted entry to only one of their double doors.

The summer dust on town streets could reach three to five inches deep, forcing the town water sprinkler to keep refilling the big barrel on his wagon to penetrate it. The search for relief from the heat drew sweaty schoolboys to the creeks. In town, when they found the sprinkler they threw friendly taunts his way, hoping he would shower them with cool spray.[43]

Wood & Chapman's Decline

The store's best days in the 1860s were powered by bulk sales for the Idaho trade. Its business was successful despite the challenges—lack of train service, personnel issues, uncertain wheat markets, struggling customers. When, in the late 1860s, railroad service from Oroville reached the Idaho mines before it reached Chico, the irony was lost on no one. The situation seemed stark as the Republican *Enterprise* predicted in 1868 that "there is no probability that any track will be laid [with supervisors' support] north of Oroville for years to come."[44] Apart from lumber hauling and some immigrant travel, Humboldt Road's freight traffic evaporated. The loss of Idaho mining trade meant Wood & Chapman had to fall back on local agricultural and town trade and left the store dependent solely on personal charge accounts. Stilson's diary observed the steady trickle of downtown store closings by creditors that sent ripples of fear along Chico streets.

At the same time, any survivor who scraped through one more month felt relief and a sense of guilt in hoping they might pick up a failed outfit's customers. Chicoans worried: could their businesses or jobs outlast the onslaught of failures?

Because George Wood's failing health led him to convalesce back east in 1867, Chapman was left on his own. The impact of reduced mining and the loss of Idaho trade was so severe that prominent men like druggist Wesley Lee and Dr. William Tilden gave up and moved back east. Bad as conditions were in California when Lee and Tilden left, even harder times confronted them in their home states and both returned to Chico.[45]

In 1868 George Wood returned to Chico in time for the deaths of his daughter Mary Hallet and her newborn baby. He remained determined to continue to build his businesses. Gus Chapman's own natural optimism was grounded in his lumber business: by June 1868 he and McKay had already sold 125,000 board feet. The *Courant* designated the three richest men in Chico as "gentlemen of fine business capacity, extensive experience and great public spirit."[46] The three were John Bidwell, whose annual income of $16,666 set him apart from his nearest rival; George Wood, who earned $4,265; and Augustus Chapman, who earned $3,000. While the store was in dire straits, Gus was getting ahead with lumber. Even John Bidwell owed him money.[47]

Then, concurrent with the *Courant's* announcement, George Wood's health faltered again and his investments crashed. While he continued to exude the confidence of the professional speculator, reality introduced him to the anxieties of a debtor. To appease his creditors, he borrowed from daughter Mary's widowed husband Harry Hallet and his older brother Andrews Hallet.

As the 1860s closed, Wood had to sell the flour mill he and Chapman owned. Chapman & McKay bought his share of their timber lands. Frank Titcomb and George Bush purchased Wood's share of the Main Street store, now called Chapman, Titcomb & Bush. Titcomb, an insurance agent and lawyer by training, had been the bookkeeper for John Bidwell & Co. before he left to join Wood & Chapman. Titcomb was personable, but Stilson worried that he drank too much and, like Chapman, he had malaria. Chapman & Titcomb's new partner, George Bush, had managed the Suydam & Jones store up the street. Like the pharmacist Wesley Lee and Dr. Tilden, Bush briefly left Chico after the Idaho trade collapsed. Like them also, Bush returned and partnered again with Chapman & Titcomb.

Despite the changing winds, general merchandise stores were still considered good investments because they were central to business and domestic life. They even rivaled churches and schools as community centers. Township residents mingled at Chapman, Titcomb & Bush where they opined on the loss of Idaho trade and deterioration of Humboldt Road. They also puzzled over how to circumvent the county supervisors' opposition to a railroad connection to Chico and still grumbled about needing fences to keep cows and pigs, still grazing on the streets, from invading their gardens. For six-and-a-half days each week, Chapman, Titcomb & Bush resembled what John Bidwell & Co. had been—the place where "families residing within a circuit of a dozen miles procure nearly every article they desire [for farm, workshop or home] which is not produced by their own industry. To conduct such an extensive enterprise profitably requires a large capital and a knowledge attained only by careful observation and study."[48]

However, to make up for the marked drop in trade, Gus and his partners let all their employees go and divided the store work among themselves. In 1868 Charlie Stilson and his pal Charlie Pond opened up a hardware store on the "wrong [east] side of Main Street," across from Chapman, Titcomb & Bush. Businessmen hoped improvements to Humboldt Road would again draw freighters from "somewhere" to Chico. Meanwhile, the wet winter of 1867-1868 flattened heavy wheat crops in the fields of the store's farm clientele whose spending they had counted on to carry the store.

In April 1869 the *Courant* reported: "We called in upon Chapman, Titcomb and Bush, the other day. It was a change in all its surroundings. Titcomb at books, Chapman behind the counter, almost ubiquitous—one moment with the ladies, up to the eyes in dry goods—the next across the room waiting upon gents, weighing sugar and coffee. They do their own work, and have no expense for clerks, bookkeepers and general attendants; and selling only for cash they incur no risk; and are not required to pay tax upon the profit margin heavy expenses, dead [sic] letters of credit, and waste of time in fruitless efforts of collection. They sell low, and if you have the cash they will sell lower—until every complaint of high prices shall be hushed. Their desire is to sell only for cash."[49] However, before long Wood & Chapman had to relent on their demand for cash and permitted customers to open charge accounts. Stilson considered this "the besotting sin of credit in California."[50]

The Decline of George Wood

While the sale of George Wood's properties satisfied most of his debts, Reverend James M. Woodman, his last creditor, refused to negotiate a settlement.[51] Wood blustered, "I won't allow myself to be trampled to the dust by him or any other living man."[52]

The quarrel between Wood and Rev. Woodman, whose role is further explored in the next chapter, must have troubled the Chapmans. They owed every advance they had made to George Wood's trust in Gus. At the same time, as backers of the Chico Academy, they were close to the Woodmans, its founders. But they had depended on Wood's favor, so they must have felt anxious when he eluded the wrathful, stubborn cleric by returning to his East Coast home—without his family. He left unfinished business in Chico; in Massachusetts he stewed in bitterness. Feeling abused, he remembered his handsome Christmas donations to Chico's destitute Southerners and their poor children. Wood blustered, "If I get back to Cal … he [Woodman] will find me less willing to contribute to his support than of old. To say the least, he was sycophantic … when I was paying him $150 to $250 a year to bolster him up his way."[53]

To make matters worse, Wood and his wife Caroline were at loggerheads when he left for the east. He left her with no money to pay their mortgage; he had spent her inheritance; she had to go to her hard-pressed son-in-law Harry Hallet for cash; their daughter Mary had died; and son Jo was a deadbeat. When their former son-in-law eventually wrote George that Caroline's health had improved, Wood responded: "I will not say I am glad to hear Mrs. W. is better."[54] Help came when George's brother in New York satisfied the debt to Rev. Woodman with gold drafts sent to Henry Hallet via Wells Fargo. The brother also paid down Caroline's mortgage and paid off her grocery charges at Chapman, Titcomb & Bush.

Now paranoid, George Wood became suspicious of Gus Chapman's management of their business ties. Despite having no shares in Chapman, Titcomb & Bush, he wrote Hallet: "Please let me know if Chapman is doing business in his own name or what?"[55] Since subsequent correspondence did not again raise this concern, Hallet apparently reassured him that was not the case. For years to come, Caroline Wood remained dependent on her remaining daughter's help and her son-in-law's income. Her shiftless Jo would come and go, leaving her in despair. While Wood wrote he wanted to return to Chico, he realized his health could not tolerate the brutal summer heat. Rev. Woodman's actions occupied his thoughts until he died alone, a blind pauper in Massachusetts in the 1880s.[56]

In the mid-1870s, with little cash in circulation, the calls Chapman, Titcomb & Bush made for customers to pay off their accounts "in cash or produce in hand" were often futile.[57] The cash drawers were near empty and customers' complaints about dwindling stock embarrassed the clerks. The staff knew there were problems, but the partners remained closemouthed about the store's financial condition.

Although the loss of Idaho trade shocked Chico's economy, Chapman's cushion remained lumber sales. But, for another year or so, the store gave him a good base in town and subsequent actions reveal he disliked the operational side of the lumber business. And now that his partners covered the store, he was free to branch out again. It must have become clear to Sarah, if to no one else, that, like George Bush, Chapman was never contented with any one business or project.

Town trustees backed forward-thinking citizen committees that recommended policies for public education and improvement of roads and bridges. However, any recommendations to supervisors were still destined to fail if they challenged Oroville's interests. The supervisors' successful attempts to subvert Chico's Humboldt Road trade had made that clear.[58] In order for Chico to attract investors and build trade, it had to escape Oroville's clutches. It was time to incorporate the town.

Unless the town acquired railroad service, it could never build solid economic roots. This meant that Chico's financial prospects were at risk to a distant railroad company's decision, which, in turn, depended on federal government influence. Only John Bidwell could work at that level of politics.

5

Chapman Tests Chico's Political Waters

Although a steady paycheck and promising investments deepened Augustus Chapman's commitment to Chico through the mid-1860s, he generally avoided party politics. He left Michigan in 1860 as a Democrat, but that party's divisions over the war had doomed his first run for public office. In Butte County he found the Civil War had also fragmented Democrats there, while Whigs hovered at the margins. As explored in Chapter 3, his support for the Union League and role in starting the Chico Light Infantry influenced the shift in his political identity from Democrat to Republican. However, his ambition to rise in the business community was likely the most important ingredient in his change of party.

Although a recent arrival, Chapman became a volunteer in popular public causes. As previously mentioned, he drafted Chico's 1862 petition to secure state help against Mountain Maidu raiders. In 1863, he wrote Bidwell's application to launch the Chico Light Infantry. While both tasks were at the behest of Gus's employer Bidwell, they also served as a credit to Chapman in his new hometown.

Only months after the Chapmans' 1861 arrival, town leaders agreed to "secede" from Butte County. Their goal was to leave the southern and eastern townships in place and form a new county comprised of those remaining in the north and west. Northern county leaders in the campaign included John Bidwell; Dr. Sam Sproul, the Kentucky-born physician whom Chapman knew as a fellow Mason; the former Massachusetts sailor and justice of the peace Andrews Hallet; and then-rival merchant E. B. Pond.[1]

Prominent farmers in support of the split included the Chapmans' fellow Michigander Alfred D. Nelson, ranchers Thomas Wright and Robert W. Durham and James Tormey. (Gus and Sarah Chapman would eventually occupy the Tormeys' house, originally J. B. Smith's "Sunflower Farm" house, south of Little Chico Creek.[2]) Chapman contributed to their mission the political savvy he had learned back home.

Oroville's *Record* caught on to their intentions immediately and branded their claims as the northern county's "secession work."[3] The county-split plan provided a fleeting but precious moment of mutual purpose between Chico's Northerners and Southerners. Despite their differences over the war, they agreed economic development in the valley would never receive county investment as long as miners in more heavily populated foothill and mountain areas continued to control the Board of Supervisors.

Oroville leaders recognized that, because the county's gold mining-based economy had weakened, the population of miners was subsiding, along with their financial contributions to the county coffers. To counter this loss, the supervisors counted on taxes from the increasingly lucrative valley farms and ranches carved out of vast Spanish land grants the Mexican owners had sold to a few immigrants in the late 1840s. Oroville leaders understood that, should those great ranches shift to a new county centered in Chico, Butte County would shrink to comprise largely government-owned mountain lands populated by non-taxpaying hostile Mountain Maidu and impoverished miners who were becoming aged candidates for expensive care in the new county hospital.

Chicoans resented the supervisors' use of their taxes to support the new hospital in Oroville, since, on a good day, it was at least six hours from Chico by carriage and, therefore, useless to most valley residents. They also seethed when supervisors used county tax income to extend railroad service to Oroville but denied every Chico appeal to extend it to them. This was the political talk that immersed Gus Chapman at the store and as a justice of the peace.[4]

After the supervisors, as expected, dismissed the Chico men's demands to "free" northern and western townships to form a new county, the contest moved to the State Legislature. Chapman and other staff at the Bidwell and Pond general stores gathered customers' signatures on petitions that accused Butte County supervisors of favoritism toward Oroville in school budgets and road and bridge construction at Chico's expense.[5] Even though county governments had little income and few responsibilities, residents still demanded that roads and bridges be repaired and new ones built.

Disparagements by Oroville's businessmen and public officials rankled in Chico where residents, staking their futures on its potential, read potshots by Oroville's *Record* editor George Crosette. He railed against "Cheek-o ... this remote corner of ... unfortunate Butte," equating it to places like Hog Hollow, Cutthroat Canyon and Dogtown.[6]

Even though the county division issue introduced Gus Chapman to Crosette's vitriol, the two men still developed a complex friendship initiated by their shared formative identity as Michiganders and anti-war Democrats. Those identities surmounted later differences on other issues.

In 1864 Chico's county-split committee headed for the State Legislature in Sacramento carrying the division petitions. In committee meetings they vied with their Oroville counterparts for Assembly members' support while Bidwell carried their appeal to the governor. Although the Oroville lobby prevailed, they went home resenting Chico even more. Chico's charges against their integrity had embarrassed them and they realized the outliers were determined to destroy their control of the county—or even the county itself—as they knew it. While a train delivered the Oroville men practically to their doorsteps, the exhausted Chico men still had to endure six more hours of travel in buggies or a stagecoach to reach home. This gave them ample time to further fan their anger at the county supervisors' denial of train service to their town.

In 1866 Chico's leaders tried again to split the county. Chapman, now steeped in town affairs, and his cohorts on the county-split committee had given up on appeals to the supervisors. They pronounced themselves "empowered with full charge and control of the matters and subject of division of the county...."[7] This time they had help from Chico's new newspaper, the

Courant, which publicized their claims. Its editor portrayed Oroville as "a big pot-bellied spider whose legs in the shape of roads will spread out in every direction, and lead only to itself."[8] By contrast to Chico's steady growth, fluctuations in mining taxed Oroville's leaders' confidence in its future.

In this county-split campaign, outlying farmers shifted to a largely auxiliary role. The exception was J. C. Mandeville, whose ranch adjoined Chico. He represented rural interests on the ad hoc committee and became important to Chapman's future. Even though Gus was completing his last term as justice of the peace, had co-purchased Chico Lumber, the Powellton mill and the Main Street store, he was poised for another acquisition—Mandeville ranchland south of town across Little Chico Creek.

In this latest split attempt, Gus Chapman worked with rival merchant E. B. Pond and A. W. Bishop, publisher and editor of the *Courant*.[9] Also active was Chico's R. A. Allen, later elected county school superintendent. County supervisors regularly allotted this one position to a Chico resident as a concession to regular complaints about their exclusion from "important" county positions—those that controlled budgets and appointments.

Chapman brought to this round his former work as a lawyer and his lumber company's connections to Oroville businessmen. Despite the tensions between the two towns, Chapman remained on good terms with Oroville merchant George Perkins, who had backed him and Wood and remained a wholesale supplier to the Chico store.[10]

The county-split committeemen again looked to the State Legislature, counting this time on their "ace," Assembly member and fellow Chico resident Dr. William Tilden. Because Dr. J. B. Smith had died and Sam Sproul could no longer cover all the medical needs of the growing population, Bidwell had persuaded Tilden to move from Oroville to Chico early in the decade. However, Tilden, a dynamic physician and a popular Oroville Democrat, almost immediately won election to the State Assembly. (He left his first term in the Assembly to become superintendent of the State Insane Asylum in Stockton. However, asylum directors fired him for drawing his pistol to bring an unruly staff member under control. Irate at such disrespect for Tilden, Chico and Oroville voters sent him back to the

Assembly.[11]) Despite the Chico committee's efforts and Tilden's backing for the county split, this attempt also failed. (William Tilden's daughter, Isabelle, would marry the leading split opponent, widower George Crosette.)

Between the 1862 and 1866 county-division attempts, another issue loomed. Chico could no longer ignore its need to replace the one-room building its committee rented for a public school in 1861. Few children had the privilege of private tutors or could attend R. A. Allen's private classroom on the second floor of his home. Because the Chapmans' son Freddie had reached school age, Gus campaigned on behalf of a school bond campaign to build a new public school. Proponents eked out a win over the "no-taxers": feisty bachelors, many former gold miners, living in Chico boarding houses but feeling little commitment to the community. With Gus Chapman an elected school trustee, Chico erected a brick school on Salem Street and R. A. Allen closed his own school to become its principal.

Freddie Chapman became one of its students. His teacher Charlie Stilson taught a class in the new building, working for Wood & Chapman before and after school. Although the bond money ran out before the building was complete, the trustees opened the school in time for the fall semester. This meant the faculty and students had to navigate partially completed floors and dodge chunks of ceiling plaster that crashed without notice. Stilson, exasperated, went to a trustees' meeting where he threatened to quit unless they finished the building.[12] They obliged, calling for a supplementary bond that voters begrudgingly approved. Soon complete, the Salem Street Public School became an object of civic pride.

Town education also improved as a side effect from an exodus of Oroville leaders to Chico in the late 1860s and early 1870s. This took place in conjunction with the serial county-split controversies, which evidently led some residents to compare each town's relative prospects. Oroville leaders who moved to the Chico area included bankers Charles Faulkner and Harmen Bay and Methodist minister Allen Hobart.

Among the newcomers to Chico were Reverend James and Selena Marie Woodman in 1868. He was a Congregationalist minister on the Oroville committee that thwarted Chico's efforts to split the county in 1862. Typical of pastors' circumstances, the Woodmans were financially strapped upon their arrival. As Gus Chapman, Charlie Stilson and George Wood moved about the Chapman, Titcomb & Bush store, they could hear Rev. Woodman proselytizing on the boardwalk out front. Charlie Stilson was indignant: "Mr. Woodman was around with a subscription [to sign an agreement] today and it gave the miserable loafers & the grog sellers a chance to vent their ignorant spite by refusing to sign [up for his new church]."[13]

George Wood offered the Woodmans more than sympathy: he donated the modern equivalent of thousands of dollars over several years to build a combined church for James and school for Selena, the Chico Academy, on West Fifth Street.[14] John Bidwell must have helped the couple acquire their posh site west of downtown. After a year or so congregants gave up on Rev. Woodman's fulminations; he closed his church and the couple joined the North Methodist Church, where they played modest roles over the years.[15]

Gus and Sarah eventually transferred Freddie from the Salem Street Public School to the private Chico Academy. Although the Chapmans remained public school supporters, they, like other better-off families, sought rigorous academic standards and wanted to separate their "promising" children from "undesirable" schoolmates. From its opening, the Chico public school contended with overcrowded classrooms and occasional disruptions by unruly students. The Woodmans, at least partially out of necessity, soon acquired reputations as stern disciplinarians.

With one public and one private school and the county split ever elusive, attention turned to the need for railroad service. Customers who bought Chapman's gang plows and grain lifters for their enormous wheat fields worried that, even if Chico expanded to the Sacramento River and became "a seaport town," steamships' capacity would be inadequate to carry all the grain and lumber to market.[16] Wheat production alone reached 15,000 tons in 1866. As a shipper of lumber, Chapman found common cause with farmers in their call for a train routed through Chico, well east of the Central Pacific Railroad's more economical preference: a route straight up the Sacramento Valley where towns like Williams and Orland had been established.

Local businessmen pinned their hopes for railroad service on Congressman John Bidwell. One of his major objectives in Washington was to secure the U.S. mail contract for himself along Humboldt Road between Chico and Idaho. No less important, he convinced the federal government to demand the railroad move its planned track east to Chico. Neither diversified crops nor new industries could guarantee Chico's future without it. It was common knowledge among recent immigrants there that once lively trade centers back east turned into ghost towns when railroad service bypassed them. Gus Chapman recalled that when the railroad failed to lay tracks through Spring Arbor, Michigan, his entire college campus packed up and followed the new railroad line to Hillsdale.

Bidwell's lobbying was successful. On July 25, 1866, President Andrew Johnson signed his bill mandating the Central Pacific Railroad swerve its north-south tracks to serve Chico. As residents celebrated Bidwell's victory, they shared in his hopes for the town's future. They did not criticize him for self-dealing the mail contract, which only became illegal later. It was common for nineteenth-century office holders to serve their own interests because no explicit ethical or legal restraints inhibited them.

Because trains now connected Idaho trade to Oroville to eastern sources, Chico merchants lost the trade they recently gained via Humboldt Road.[17] Their only alternative was to press for tracks to link up to other markets as soon as possible. The new hope was that, once railroad service arrived in Chico, an influx of immigrants would follow and revive the economy. Gus envisioned customers patronizing not only Chapman & McKay, but also Chapman, Titcomb & Bush. Ever the optimist, Gus Chapman turned his attention to developing housing for the anticipated arrivals by train.

Valley cattle ranches were in decline but winter wheat planting was on the rise. Even so, merchants like Chapman remained uneasy about dependence on the one-crop economy, vulnerable to floods, droughts and the vagaries of European and Australian markets. Searching for alternatives, in the late 1860s town leaders urged farmers to introduce hops, barley, oats, castor beans and corn; Chapman later advocated jute. Rumors periodically circulated that one investor or another was ready to build a sugar beet processing plant. Chapman named a street "Mulberry" for the trees he and others planted in the hope of developing a silk industry.[18] Talk of a grain-sack factory for the farmers or a woolen mill for sheep farms tantalized Chicoans for decades.

Because so many Chico residents were still new, local investors like Gus Chapman became anxious when some gave up and left for other states; current talk focused on the appeal of Arizona. *Courant* editor Bishop surmised that, between 1861 and 1867, California's population declined. He blamed state residents' "nomadic habits and natural love of adventure."[19] Some, who originally left their home states to earn their fortunes, went home when they had saved enough — or lost everything.[20]

Unwilling to leave their futures to fate, Chapman and others decided Chico's problem was that it was unincorporated. The town could only provide limited services allotted by county supervisors. Despite the scattering of attractive cottages and a few handsome brick buildings, ramshackle frame stores and random, garbage-strewn lots were not uncommon. The trustees repeatedly had to explain that the supervisors granted them no power to intervene in private property matters, even for safety, let alone appearance. Owners could build where and how they chose. Without increasing the street sprinkler's hours, the town water wagon's spray could only temporarily keep down summer dust on roads.

However, the town trustees concluded their power was sufficient to order the constable to round up wandering animals. Although most front yards were protected by picket fences and, in back, high board fences shielded chickens and gardens from roaming pigs, public thoroughfares were open. The trustees erected wooden barriers around street trees to stop cows from nibbling on their lower limbs. Volunteers built a corral to hold domestic livestock the constable rounded up; their owners' fines went to the public school. Calls also went out for residents to remove piles of trash they couldn't discard in their outhouses. In one day, the conscientious constable ticketed each of the three town trustees for letting their cows graze on side streets. The news of their violations sparked derision from the townspeople, but compliance improved.

For Chapman, growth promised more customers and an

ample labor supply. With thirty employees at his lumber operations, even a modest surplus of working men would tamp down wages. The *Courant* spoke for businessmen like him: "In Chico labor is most informally aristocratic ... a man who wants anything done in this section has to petition for it on his knees as well as pay for it roundly when done."[21] When local carpenters got together and raised their hourly rates, the *Courant* sent out-of-town papers an appeal for one hundred to move to Chico. To the employers' dismay, only fifteen men arrived while others left. For the present, Chico carpenters held their own.

Employers, determined to depress wages, turned to "some of the wealthiest men in the state" who had created the California Labor and Employment Exchange and the Immigrant Aid Association. The groups intended to lure large numbers of eastern workers to compete for work in the factories expected to open at the completion of the Union Pacific Railroad (part of the first transcontinental railroad).

Confident that a population boom was coming to Chico, Chapman readied himself to sell lots, lumber and merchandise.[22] However, in 1868, of the 50,000 workers who moved to California, most who arrived in Chico were Chinese. In reaction, the *Courant* renamed itself the *Caucasian*.[23] The frugal Chinese bachelors' influence on trade proved insignificant, but employers snapped them up for their experience, talents and willingness to work hard for low wages. Even so, the businessmen were disappointed: in their call for residential growth, they had envisioned European workers and their families, not Chinese.

For example, they particularly hoped to attract Germans, "a hardy, working, intelligent, educated class, the 'mudsills' of society, the true wealth and substantial basis that makes the nation great and powerful."[24] One rumor emerged that a colony of Danes "now on their way" would create small farms out of Bidwell's ranch or the vast ranch of J. C. Mandeville, the speculator on mining stock and farm land who worked with Gus Chapman on the 1866 campaign to split the county. Decades later, in his essay on California prison reform, Chapman linked the state's vast land grant ranches to constricted opportunities for "lost" young men.[25]

Chapman purchased 1,000 acres of Mandeville's working

ranch, along the Oroville-Shasta Trail just southeast of Chico across Little Chico Creek, to lay out a subdivision—the only side of town John Bidwell did not own. Because Bidwell expected the pending railroad transportation would deliver his farm produce to urban markets, his plan was to keep his remaining farmland around the town to meet the expanded demand for food. As recently as 1867 he had sacrificed creek-bottom cropland to expand residential housing west of Broadway.[26] Businessmen grumbled that Bidwell's expansion, while welcome, would not satisfy the expected demand for housing; in effect, Bidwell's land had Chico "surrounded." Even though rumors about in-coming Danes faded as the 1860s came to a close, the *Courant* remained hopeful: "Every day brings to our section persons seeking for land upon which to establish homes. All the qualifications for pleasant and profitable homes can be found but no land for sale or rent."[27] Chapman was convinced his development on the Mandeville land would change that. While still attending to lumber sales and the store, Chapman's focus was shifting to real estate, the subject of a later chapter.

Charlie Stilson, who had griped about Chapman's distraction in the days of his and McKay's lumber company purchase, noted the same during his subdivision planning: "Heavy customer patronage—more than for months. Keeps us all busy and I regret to note that Mr. Chapman places too much confidence in us clerks and often leaves a customer with us that he ought to attend to himself and if he is not now particular it will affect the trade very materially."[28]

While the cuts for streets and alleys in Chapman's subdivision were becoming visible, town talk was that railroad service would draw rich Bay Area investors to Chico where their handsome offers would overcome local big ranchers' sales resistance. Those purchasers with major businesses on the coast, it was said, would break up the huge ranches and divide most of the countryside into family-sized farms. Local men hoped the out-of-towners understood how much San Francisco's prosperity "depends upon the building up of the interior." They projected such men would reserve the choice land for building second homes for their own families during "the pleasant part of the year."[29] Gus believed he was ahead of the game.

The Train Arrives

A celebration greeted the first train's maiden arrival in Chico on July 4, 1870. Its exuberance impressed northern Butte County residents of every description, location and condition.[30] A committee of businessmen, including Gus Chapman, launched the day's events at sunrise with the militia firing blasts from the Civil War cannon, while blacksmiths picked up the rhythm on their anvils. Morning and mid-day military parades took place. Long lines of farm families' buggies and wagons reached town carrying hay for the noon feeding of their horses. Livery stables could not accommodate all the calls for services, hotel rooms were booked and Union Army veteran Charlie Wood sold out his entire stock of straw hats. Extra saloon bartenders were at the ready to keep customers happy all day and through the evening.

Chapman waited on customers until he could slip away to shepherd Sarah and the children through the throng that flowed west along Fifth Street to a shed the railroad designated as the depot (rebuilt and still in use today).[31] Keeping an eye on Freddie and a firm hold on Mary, Gus and Sarah shared the crowd's excitement when the engine pulling two coaches and a pair of freight cars slid to a stop, enveloped in steam.

Guns fired and the Chico Cornet Band played, competing with bells ringing at the Salem Street school and the Methodist Church South. John Bidwell, flanked by Charles Faulkner, the new banker in town, and farmer John Guill, welcomed the railroad officials and influential passengers. Happy shouts punctuated the event as local businessmen took possession of their products. Gus Chapman and William McKay stepped forward to collect ten tins of iron nails. Gus was particularly grateful at the prospect of reaching San Francisco lumber outlets in only eight hours. Despite the arrival of this fast new mode of travel, through the century's end, the family continued bouncing along in bumpy, slow, dirty stagecoaches on trips between Chico and the Chapman & McKay mills in the mountains.

From the unshaded depot, the crowd drifted to Bidwell's Oak Grove in the wooded area west of the tracks, where they found barrels full of tin cups to dip in tubs of ice water scattered throughout the grounds. Further west, down Big Chico Creek, bronco-busting was the big attraction. Talk, laughter and beer mixed as 3,500 guests devoured as many pounds of roasted beef, mutton and pork. Parents danced, sang along or listened as the band played popular songs. Their children waded in the creek and chased each other through the trees. The Idlewild racetrack, west of the Oroville-Shasta Road (formerly Trail) and in sight of Chapman's new subdivision, was, as usual, a magnet. With a wet spring behind them, the Indians subdued, train service in place and heavy crops in the fields, this was, at long last, a moment for everyone to savor.

As the day faded behind deep shadows cast by oaks, syc-amores and ash, skyrockets fired until the third gun salute signaled children's bedtime. After bedding them down, grownups returned downtown for the Chico Light Infantry's Grand Ball, where they danced and enjoyed the concert. There was much to say about the day's balloon launch and the purse race for three-year-olds.

The Developer

Immigrants like the Chapmans measured Chico's promise by its development. Plans for new housing were a key indica-tor of steady growth and the arrival of railroad services was a breakthrough. The railroad connection vindicated Chapman's land purchase.

The men who carved out streets and alleys from raw land were admired figures. Town and county clerks who recorded sales and oversaw permit papers filed building projects in the names of the developers. Following this practice, the county name "Chapman's Addition" became the County Recorder's 1870 place name for Chapman's 120-acre subdivision, carved out of his Mandeville land purchase.

In the early 1870s, when businessmen were anxious about wheat market fluctuations and the new railroad's freight prices, incorporation became the issue of the day. While "incorpora-tion" is a cold, legal term, debate about it kept Chico politics running hot for two years. Whom would it help? Whom would it hurt? Opponents were convinced it would turn trustees into politicians who would become corrupt and abuse their power by raising taxes and wasting revenue. Supporters envisioned that, as an independent legal entity, Chico's elected leaders would no longer have to beg county supervisors to fund roads and bridges, add constables or improve insurance terms. Supporters like Chapman expected locally elected officials would create a more orderly and inviting town which would, in turn, attract new residents.

Now that Gus Chapman was heavily invested in real estate, he had a stake in the town's incorporation. Between downtown Chico and Chapman's Addition there was a colorful and lively, albeit sometimes tough, section called "the Junction." Chapman knew the Junction well because his lumber outlet, adjacent to it, was located on the east side of Main Street, between Seventh and Eighth streets, just north of the creek and Chapman's Addition. Riders and freight drivers arriving daily from the Oroville-Shasta and Humboldt roads entered Chico at the Junction.[32] And its blacksmiths, stables, wagon builders, brewery and brothels, as well as the saloons and rooming houses, serviced their needs.

Chapman was close to other businessmen there. Like him, brewer Charles Croissant belonged to the North Methodist congregation. N. B. Gardner, who operated the Junction Hotel, built his home in Chapman's Addition. Other Junction businessmen regularly stopped at Chapman's office, the official polling place, to talk over election issues or town controversies. Teamsters who patronized Junction-based businesses included the Chapman & McKay drivers en route to the firm's lumber outlet on Main, the Fifth Street depot or the Chico Landing.

Gus Chapman also would benefit from incorporation in another way. For example, when the footbridge across Dead Horse Slough next to the Chapman & McKay's Chico Lumber Co. began to rot, town trustees could order repairs that county-appointed trustees in Oroville ignored.

In addition, supporters like Chapman claimed a fully empowered town government could take some of the "edge" off unlawful conduct in Chico. Town trustees could finally hire enough constables to end criminals' free rein. Most annoying were the ever-changing mixtures of hoodlums and unemployed drunks who sprawled along the boardwalks and simmered with resentment as they harassed hard-working Chinese scurrying around them. Advocates claimed offenders' fines alone could pay for all the town services.[33]

An additional aggravation was bands of boys as young as seven who roamed through the town's pitch-dark streets. Rarely at home or in school, some were orphans or had parents who wouldn't or couldn't control them. They shoplifted, hung around the saloons, raced along boardwalks, frightened horses and generally annoyed pedestrians. One of their malicious pastimes was to throw rocks at the Chinese. Newspaper reports suggest residents were resigned to their pranks because "boys will be boys."[34] One cynic looked to the bigger picture: Chico's "principal streets were used as race courses; the only protection a peaceable citizen had against the toughs that infested the town and could not be gotten rid of was a club...."[35]

Some of the town's problems were spillovers from "toughs" or "rough trade"—the freight drivers and laborers concentrated at the Junction, Wall Street boarding houses just east of Broadway and Main Street saloons. While saloons dotted the downtown, their concentration at the Junction impinged on Chapman's ability to sell house lots in his subdivision near it. Spanning Main and Broadway, the Junction was on the corridor between Little Chico Creek and downtown stores, the post office, library and churches. In the Junction, teamsters passed the time with casual acquaintances such as idle drunks and gamblers like Jo Wood and his sketchy friends on the lookout for easy marks. In 1870 Chapman was still preparing his plat map when a local "gang" member shot Thomas White at the Idlewild racetrack.

Meanwhile, the approach of a national depression accelerated Chico's unemployment. Some of these individuals, along with vagrants, were responsible for an upsurge in thefts. When the county sheriff declined to restore "order," talk of a "vigilance committee" began. These problems solidified support for Chico's incorporation.

Incorporation opponents dismissed the appeal of supporters for enhanced fire service, arguing that Chico had not seen a major fire since the What Cheer Hotel burned in 1863. They claimed that residents' homes and their safety would be ensured if they would only be more responsible about their own debris removal and control the overgrowth on their property.[36] Another defense against fire was to build with brick—the stores of John Bidwell,

Gus Chapman and Jones & Reilly were among the few relatively fire-resistant downtown structures.[37] Of course, stacks of fir and pine at Chapman & McKay's lumber yard posed a risk. Even the grand residences under construction along West Fifth Street, the town's fashionable entryway from the train depot, were built of wood. Buildings were at risk from ash piles produced by fireplaces and wood stoves. Boards, brush, empty boxes, barrels and leaf piles were scattered at random along streets and yards. Tinder-dry thistles and weeds along the major thoroughfares posed another danger each summer.[38] The fears were realized when, on a single night in 1872, a spectacular fire demolished Hallet & Loy's planing mill and the home of pharmacist Wesley Lee. After that, resistance collapsed and petitions urged the Board of Supervisors to approve incorporation.[39]

To the consternation of incorporation supporters, John Bidwell suddenly presented an obstacle. He had been a supporter, but turned against it when proponents defied his instructions and prepared to submit a proposed town map with its northern boundary at Big Chico Creek. This meant acres of Bidwell's Rancho Chico between Front (now First) Street, and Big Chico Creek would be subject to town taxes. Word of Bidwell's objection split incorporation supporters. Tempers erupted, but Gus Chapman was among the businessmen who believed it was necessary to keep the boundary he wanted because incorporation would fail without his support. To back Bidwell in this controversy likely struck Chapman as an opportunity to soften the ill-will Bidwell had harbored toward him since he left the rancher's store and became his competitor. In addition, as political realists, Chapman and his cohorts expected the supervisors to align with Bidwell because they usually had done so in the past. And that is what happened. Despite opposition, the proposal Bidwell objected to was sent to the Board of Supervisors. He drove to Oroville where he convinced the supervisors to deny the townspeople's petitions to include—and tax—his land within the proposed border.

Determined not to let Bidwell prevail, incorporation supporters took the issue to Sacramento where they asked the State Legislature to nullify the supervisors' support for him to keep his property outside the town boundary.[40] In February 1872 the Assembly, which also heard from Bidwell, excluded Rancho

Chico land from incorporation but approved it for the rest of the town.

With Chico now incorporated, town leaders began organizing their first municipal election.[41] Deep divisions arose when the election produced 217 ballots, even though only 139 men were registered to vote.[42] Nevertheless, the election stood and Chico's new town trustees rented a meeting room above the Hibbard & Sommer store at Second and Broadway. One of their first ordinances dealt with fire protection planning. It required every resident to keep on hand sixty gallons of water in barrels or tanks. They also had to keep at the ready a pair of two-and-a-half gallon empty buckets labeled "FD" for Fire Department.

The success of the incorporation campaign and the first trustee election made it unmistakable that Chico businessmen continued to be the town's financial and political establishment. This attracted the later notice of historian Clarence McIntosh: "Second Street businessmen and the lumber company officers became the most important leaders of the town at least in a political sense" after 1872.[43] The present account of Chapman's experience establishes that their influence was already in place well *before* that. Bidwell, Chapman and other business leaders had succeeded: there was train service, incorporation, Bidwell kept his land out of town and Chapman had his subdivision.

And finally, in the early 1870s, with railroad construction complete and mining played out, the number of Chinese on Chico streets accelerated. Once in Chico, they snapped up grueling work in town and on farms at wages that undercut white labor. This initiated a conviction by a growing group of townspeople that they had to unify against the Chinese.[44]

6

Sarah Chapman Makes Her Place

For more than a hundred years glimpses of Sarah Sickley Chapman's life have survived in newspaper items, a diary and random documents. From these, it emerges that her husband's long hours at work in Chico and frequent business travel over decades rendered her the equivalent of a single parent. Other items reveal her family's individual travails as they evolved in uncertain times. Taken together, it becomes clear that this tiny, proper woman embraced her role as a trusted arbiter and responsible financial manager, as well as the principal source of consolation and encouragement to her driven husband and their lively children. Through it all, she stayed committed to support the North Methodist Church where she and others in the women's auxiliary raised money to pay the pastor and improve and maintain church property. Along the way, the women built enduring friendships. Sarah's 1899 diary entry affirms she embraced her faith's demand that she serve her family and, beyond them, her close friends and the community.

Sarah arrived in Chico, a town of bachelors, as "Mrs." Chapman. Her title conferred a life status equivalent to a well-remunerated profession. To be "Mrs. ---" was a credential so respected women even used it to address one another. For example, although Sarah became like a sister to Mary Deal or Rebecca Ball and like a second daughter to Sophronia Maxson, they all called her "Mrs. Chapman." Even in the intimacy of her diary, Sarah referred to her closest friends of thirty years as "Mrs. Camper" and "Mrs. Chandler."[1] Their husbands also observed this custom in public from their wedding days forward. Gus inscribed "Mrs. Sarah A. Chapman" on the front leaf of the book that was his wedding present to her.[2]

In contrast, use of first or full names such as Emma Tolliver,

Mary Evans and Lizzie Adams was proper until the women married.[3] After a time, women who did not marry but held acceptable positions—teachers, for example—won the addition of "Miss" to their full names. Miss Emma O'Farrell supported herself as a postal clerk, a job which passed to Miss Alice Sproul before she became a teacher. Similarly, bachelors and young men used one another's first names—such as Jody (Sproul) or Freddy (Chapman)—until they married or had a business. After that, initials often replaced their first names. For his entire life in Chico, Augustus was A. H. Chapman or Aug. H. Chapman. The Camper family's children, to whom Gus and Sarah's family were particularly close, called him "Uncle Gus." This suggests that closest friends and family called him "Gus" in private. In the intimacy of this biography, each of the alternatives has been useful.

For most of Sarah's adult life, Gus provided for her and their children at a decent to ample level. Her role was to make him and their children her highest priority every day. During their first months in Chico she went without domestic help, which she had in Michigan. While they became established, she stretched the income of her chronically harried and exhausted spouse by parenting their young children alone and making a comfortable, welcoming home anytime he could be there. Even when Gus was working in town, his routine ten- or twelve-hour days left him exhausted. For the days or weeks he was away on business trips or staying at the mill, she navigated all school, home and church matters.

Of course, personal crises interrupted routines. In early fall 1863, when their baby Florence was sick from a severe influenza that swept through Chico, seasonal malarial attacks were already even more intense than usual. Gus, who was malarial and expected his own seasonal attacks, stayed home to help Sarah tend their suffering child. However, both parents and four-year-old Freddie also came down with the flu. They had only recently recovered when Florence died in early November.[4]

Gravestones in the pioneer sections of the Chico Cemetery illustrate the nineteenth century's roll of dead young women and their babies. Sarah Chapman no sooner came to terms with her own loss than she consoled and assisted her grief-stricken friends in turn. Trunks and chests across town yielded folds of black crepe ready for use as armbands or to drape as bunting over doorways and buggies. Mourning dresses moved from back corners to the centers of wardrobes, subject to emergency alterations by friends and dressmakers.

For a few days, survivors forestalled the full onset of grief by arranging for the funeral at home, where flowers from friends' gardens surrounded the coffin in the parlor or sitting room. Carriage windows were sometimes draped to shield grieving passengers from public display in the buggy parade to the cemetery. Over the rest of their lives, women, on visits to their family graves, sometimes brought a bucket of tools for weeding the plots and scrubbing the stones. Then they left a flower arrangement made up of the azaleas or hydrangeas in their home gardens.[5]

Expenditures attendant to death added to Chico's economy. Black crepe and coffin trimmings were always available at Wood & Chapman. One local merchant advertised clothing that opened down the back to make it easier to dress the dead; another offered the "New Combination Corpse Preserver." The basement mortuary of Hallet & Loy's furniture shop on Broadway stacked coffins of various sizes and rented out funeral carriages: black for adults, white for children. Pastors and hearse drivers picked up extra income.

In the two weeks after Florence died, while the family grieved, Sarah put away her baby's clothes, bedding and rattles. That year the death toll also rose from malaria, which meant more funeral cortèges than usual were crossing the bridge to reach the cemetery. At the temporary federal camp on Bidwell's ranch, Mountain Indians awaiting removal fell at the rate of three a day. Sounds of wailing at their burial ceremonies pierced the quiet nights.

The Chapmans conformed to the common expectation of stoicism in dealing with grief. They invested their energy in trying to forget. When they resumed routines, they avoided talk about the dead and counted on time to ease their private pain. However, in his anguish the merchant Carl Sommer took a different course. He struggled over the death of his four-year-old daughter Edith. Each afternoon he left Hibbard & Sommer, his fancy goods store, and walked alone up Big Chico Creek to the cemetery where he crouched by Edith's grave until the sun went down. She feared the dark, he explained. Carl and his wife Wilhelmina "Willie" Pratt Sommer had also lost their little boy. Carl would die early, leaving his wife and a surviving daughter.[6]

In November 1864 Sarah was pregnant again. While this was good news, pregnancy was dangerous and even life threatening. Sarah enhanced her chances by prayer and took hope from her history of successful deliveries. Looking beyond health and sentiment, she was fortunate her husband was a good provider and loyal companion. While most of her friends also seemed well married, this blessing eluded other expectant mothers visible on Chico's streets.

Those were the frail and destitute women who were workingmen's widows. Others had derelict husbands whose meager, irregular wages meant empty food bowls and shabby hovels. When women became desperate to relieve themselves of pregnancy, they looked to obliquely worded advertisements for mail-order contraceptives and abortifacients in the *Record* or *Courant*. As early as 1866 the *Courant* regularly ran ads "To Females" offering "Female Monthly Pills." Company products treated "irregularities" and relieved [menstrual] "suppressions"—that is, by abortion. A common appeal urged women to "let no false delicacy prevent you but apply immediately and save yourself from painful sufferings and premature death."[7] While abortion was discretely advertised, it was understood to be a private transaction and was closely guarded by buyer and seller of the service.

Sarah's pregnancy was successful and their daughter Mary was born in summer 1865. While Mary was an infant, Sarah decided to rent a room in their house. While it was socially unacceptable for middle-class married women to work away from home, families, including the Chapmans, often needed money beyond what husbands earned (or would share with their wives). It was considered respectable for resourceful women to generate cash from home as long as they adopted acceptable enterprises. Some sold eggs and chickens; one widow fitted lengths of canvas over the wooden porch floors of houses each fall to fend off wood rot; another sold books door to door. Widow Lavinia Sproul gave up her private schoolroom and taught in Chico's public school for decades. Sarah's choice was another common one.

Rooms with home-cooked meals were in demand because Chico, still the takeoff point to Utah mines and still a bachelor town, was becoming the "Gateway to Lumber." Teamsters, miners, traveling salesmen and tradesmen packed the boarding houses. While rental housing was considered the business of husbands (when there was one), the nature of the work left no doubt a woman was in charge. For a year or so, Sarah Chapman rented a room to hotel clerk Jo Cramer, who subsequently left for the Colorado mines, where he became rich and, by 1879, a "pillar of the Leadville community."[8]

Time for Church

Perhaps because Gus and Sarah assumed other Baptists would come to town, they were slow to accept Methodism, but it remained their only option through the 1860s. Therefore, they attended the sermons of circuit preachers north of Bidwell's Ranch at the schoolhouse near Pine Creek or at a building that farmers erected on Mud Creek, both north of town.

Sarah waited five years before she accepted a Methodist pastor's call for church members to embrace "faith in action." That suited Sarah's belief that her work for family, church and community gave spiritual meaning to her life.[9] Gus did not formally become a Methodist, but he agreed to help out when needed. On November 25, 1866, Pastor Hobart of the North Methodist Church baptized Sarah by sprinkling water over her head—her other option was immersion in the frigid waters of Big Chico Creek. With this, she joined the church's sisterhood to provide whatever it needed, whether maintenance, recruitment or funding.

Methodists paid ministers no regular wage and their wives lived in anxiety about when—and if—compensation would arrive. Wives were expected to tend the congregations for free. Month after month, year after year, the women's auxiliary raised money or assembled in-kind donations to pay their pastors' wages. Oroville pastor James Woodman's first wife must have despaired when he turned down his wage one month because church women raised it by holding a dance. So the women donated his wage money to benefit soldiers in the Union Army. A young woman from the McIntosh farm family, prominent in Chico's Methodist Church South, was aware of the hardships of pastors' wives. Therefore, when she received a minister's marriage proposal, she was ready: "He [stipulated] that she would be expected to raise a big family, do the cooking, washing and housework, lead the choir, play the organ and teach Sunday School." Her suitor was astonished when she replied, "No, thank you."[10]

North Methodist women competed with their South church counterparts for new members and both navigated conflicts which imperiled every congregation at one time or another. For example, men and women called on their own interpretations of Scripture to advance intense "theological" — or pseudo-theological — discussions which sometimes turned into disputes. These often grew out of disagreements about pastors, whose personal and professional conduct was usually subject to church women's scrutiny.[11] All in all, churches were the only significant institutions that men, for the most part, allowed women to control. Sarah Chapman and her friends found satisfaction in church work because it nourished their spiritual needs, provided meaningful responsibilities and helped satisfy their social needs in a significant adult organization outside their homes.

The women realized, of course, the value of their unacknowledged contributions to the community. Most of them also understood how much more they could accomplish with greater authority — or even a vote. Having neither, in Chico or elsewhere, they mastered subtlety and manipulation in dealing with their pastors or husbands to advance their goals. Such women provided a reliable audience for traveling speakers who called for female suffrage and equal rights in appearances at Wood's Hall. As early as 1865, when such causes were considered exotic, attentive audiences showed up to consider what changes might be possible.[12]

By the 1870s the Methodists and new Presbyterians in Chico advanced a few women to seats on their local governing boards. Sarah Chapman and Rebecca Ball joined the board of their North Methodist Church; Annie Bidwell initiated the placement of women on governing boards for the Presbyterians.

Because, among the women in her circle, Sarah was more at ease dealing with money, she often handled their cash box at fundraising events. While the Methodist South congregation was financially better off than the North members, both churches' women struggled to maintain or improve church property and to keep Chico an attractive stop on the schedules of circuit-riding pastors. Decade after decade these women's careful plans and imaginative events met every demand. As they sustained their churches, they tested and deepened the friendships they built along the way. No one in either group, however, enjoyed the relentless quest for money which forced them to compete for cash with one another, the racetrack and saloons.

Because it was distasteful to make continuous appeals to people they knew had already given or were hard-pressed, they created social opportunities, entertainments and home-cooked food from their kitchens to earn what their churches or other causes needed.[13] Nostalgia worked for them in the 1860s because townspeople, still lonesome for their former homes, warmed to church "sings" which featured such hits as "Pining for Old Friends," "Faces to the Memory Dear" or "Home Again Returning." In March 1868, when the Methodist Church South's mortgage holder suddenly called in his loan, the women announced that they would hold a two-day fair. With the proceeds and other donations they managed to meet his demand. Only a month later, Sarah and her North Methodist friends found a similarly compelling need for $300 to remodel their parsonage which was so shabby it attracted criticism in the newspaper. Although the women sighed and grumbled, they successfully tackled each crisis—and paid every bill.[14]

In the competition for financial support through the mid-1860s, the North Methodist Church's advantage was John Bidwell's membership. However, his marriage to an ardent Presbyterian sidelined his years as a Chico Methodist. The message Annie Kennedy sent him from her parents' Washington, D.C., home decided it: "I have attended the Methodist Church a few times and with profit, but the rejoinders, and unrestrained expressions so excite me that I believe I should lose my reason were I regularly to attend that church."[15] Bidwell gave up and joined twenty or so other Chicoans, many of them also recent

Methodists, in the Presbyterian Church. Bidwell built them a handsome church, but he would maintain the North Methodists' goodwill by occasional donations, some substantial, over many years.[16]

Despite searing heat, women of both Methodist churches joined forces to organize summer camp meetings or "revivals." In 1873 Sarah worked with the venerable Sophronia Maxson, the pastor's wife Millie Hobart, the beauteous Mary Deal and Rebecca Ball, the church's first female trustee. Bidwell allotted them the leafy oak grove a couple of miles north of town where all the Methodists had gathered before the war. The grove offered plenty of space for creek-side bonfires, as well as open fields for "parking" the horses and buggies that delivered large crowds for evening sermons. In order to fend off visits from local rowdies always in search of a crowd, the women banned alcohol from the grounds and expelled "huxters' shops" from the periphery. When eruptions threatened, the pastors exhorted participants to behave in the camp as if they were in church.[17]

The women cooked and sold food at the "boarding tent," provided childcare, chose the hymns and ordered programs that set out prayers and lyrics of favorite hymns. Such events drew on their creative and business talents. This was all necessary because their circumstances in Butte County were unlike those in their home states where, since the 1840s, changing protocol had turned such gatherings into formalized and "decorous" assemblies. By contrast, from the 1850s through the 1870s in Butte County, the lingering traces of frontier conditions meant the camps' earlier rustic style of worship was still in place.[18] Sometimes the women's efforts were lucrative. At one camp meeting's close, their pastor jotted down his satisfaction, both in the converts and in the "quickening" (financial proceeds) their work produced.[19]

Methodist preachers who traveled to Chico for camp meetings or regular stops on their circuits were articulate men of broad experience whose elders dispatched them from one far-flung circuit to another every two years or so. This inspired a joke in Chico: "A young lady being asked where her native place was replied: 'I have none; I am the daughter of a Methodist preacher.'" In their sermons, preachers employed simple but vivid rhetoric to interweave a dark view of human nature with calls for repentance.[20]

The emphasis on order and authority reassured parishioners and other newcomers whose California lives were otherwise steeped in uncertainty. Methodism particularly suited them because conditions in the 1860s resembled those of the pre-Civil War Midwest and the interior South where their parents had settled. As additional denominations established roots in Chico, the cultural dominance of its more hedonistic residents from the Gold Rush days receded. Decades would pass before the steady exertions of church women like Annie Bidwell, Isabelle Tilden, Selena Woodman and Sarah Chapman would erase the frontiersmen's rough imprint on Chico.

While Gus Chapman never became personally committed to any Chico church, he followed his wife in centering their social life around members of her North Methodist congregation. Through this, the Chapmans developed ties to the families of other small business owners, skilled craftsmen and farmers.

School Days

Around the corner from the Chapmans' place, the Woodmans' Chico Academy became their children's second home. The young children shared the large schoolhouse with their schoolmates boarding there. James and Selena taught classes by day; at night they supervised the ranchers' children. When school was in session the school's orchard, garden and chickens contributed to their daily fare. Tending them was an everyday responsibility everyone shared.

Reverend Woodman, once a physician, was headmaster and taught science classes. He became a familiar sight as he chauffeured children at the reins of his "shiny black horse" that pulled the high carriage townspeople dubbed "Noah's Ark." On the side, he could be ruthless, driving hard deals in his real estate sideline.[21]

Selena Woodman oversaw the school curriculum, tended to the student boarders, was responsible for general upkeep and looked after her two boys. At the same time Charles Woodman, son of the pastor and his late first wife Martha, was nearing graduation. In the Woodmans' fundraising, Selena handled the planning and production of ambitious student performances. She taught, counseled and disciplined students and conferred with their parents. A strong-minded woman, her intellectual standards and proud demeanor reassured and sometimes intimidated parents and regularly irritated critics. They considered her overbearing and haughty and her school a place for the benefit of "rich" children. Although the Woodmans welcomed E. C. Wilson, a lumber worker, to attend classes while he waited out winters in Chico, the couple received no credit for their outreach to him and others.[22]

All in all, Selena Woodman was rigid, but more adept than her prickly and stern husband in handling public relations. The Chapmans were loyal patrons of the Chico Academy because they wanted their children to be adequately prepared for college. They rallied behind the Woodmans not only in financial crises, but also in recovery from an arson discussed later in this chapter.

Home Nurse

While Sarah Chapman's church and the children's school regularly claimed most of her attention, she was also her family's nurse, ready to turn a bedroom into a sick bay with the flick of a sheet. Daughter Florence's early death had impressed on Sarah how fast an illness could turn mortal. Freddie's scrapes and Mary's close calls as a one-year-old, and again at four years, tested their mother's understanding and resources.

Medical problems periodically threatened the young family's sole wage earner. Gus Chapman went to work even when rheumatism left him limping and the onset of facial pains (perhaps shingles) mired him in misery. On occasion, acute "gut problems" kept him at home. Cholera and dysentery regularly struck residents throughout town because of wells' proximity to outhouses. In addition to all this, Gus's yearly bouts with malaria meant home stays when he was helpless and totally reliant on Sarah's ministrations for a week or more. Meanwhile, employees stopped in to stack wood for the family and brief Gus on the store or the lumber outlet. With even one man off duty, the rest strained to keep up. Sarah worried about Gus's myriad illnesses and was keenly aware she and the children would be destitute without him.

It seems Sarah was also Gus's general counsel when he grappled with reverses and complications during their decades together. This speculation stems from descriptions of Chapman in Charlie Stilson's diary, newspaper accounts and his obituary. Taken together, they indicate that Gus was not given to socializing with "the guys" after hours. They suggest he strictly divided his time between home, civic duties and long days at work. He maintained privacy about his personal and business circumstances.

For example, although Gus sometimes tossed a business tip Stilson's way, that was not his regular practice and he never confided in his principal clerk or sought his counsel. He was always attentive to his mentor George Wood who left full management of the store to him during his frequent and extended absences. With long hours and only one-half day off every week for everyone, there was little time to relax. This is why, in the 1860s and thereafter, his principal listener and adviser must have been Sarah.

Hazards and Celebrations

Henry David Thoreau could have had Chico in mind when he queried, "But why go to California for a text? She is the child of New England, bred at her own school and church...."[23] In other words, California did not offer a novel example for others to copy. Rather, state residents wrestled with the same problems as others elsewhere and established similar institutions to address them. Alcohol abuse impoverished and destroyed families throughout the rest of the century and after. The effects of this affliction were visible in Chico's downtown and the Junction. In both areas roughnecks regularly passed out on boardwalks and collapsed in gutters. Alcoholism also afflicted some better-off men for whom liquor delivered momentary relief from the strain of being the sole support for large families in the constantly shifting economy.

The ranks of drinkers found reinforcements with every wave of new residents. But so did temperance advocates. In 1867 fifty dedicated believers ignored a downpour and slogged across coal-dark streets, ankle-deep in mud, to attend a winter temperance meeting at Wood's Hall. Once upstairs, they prayed, sang and counseled one another. Packed houses listened to itinerant speakers or were entertained by touring companies that periodically performed *Ten Nights in a Bar-room*, based on the 1854 novel *Ten Nights in a Bar-room and What I Saw there*. In 1868 parents delivered forty-seven children to the first meeting of the Band of Hope which warned them away from alcohol and tobacco. Some youngsters began to annoy smoking grownups with their chant: "Tobacco is a filthy weed / From the devil came the seed / It robs your pocket, stains your clothes / And makes a chimney of your nose."[24]

Whether the temperance campaigners worried about the alcoholics in their own families or shuddered at the sight of strangers who stumbled along public streets, then slumped over barrels, they yearned to end the misery of the victims and their own disgust. Gus Chapman stepped over and around such men near his lumber business at the Junction. He encountered them uptown outside Bidwell & Co. and, after that, near Wood & Chapman. Everyone at both places knew Jo Wood and Frank Titcomb often arrived late at work hung over.

Despite all this, Gus and Sarah Chapman never joined temperance groups. While upstairs, above the store, Band of Hope members inveighed against drink, downstairs George Wood and Gus Chapman were conducting a lucrative business as general merchants and wholesale dealers in bottled liquor, kegs of beer and local wines. In addition, they owned the building next door that housed the Black Rock Saloon. Every week or so, Gus took home beer and porter or brandy to enjoy with Sarah and never shrunk from liquor sales. For example, on a hot July day in 1869, the *Courant*'s editor rewarded Chapman with a plug: "The boys of Chapman, Titcomb and Bush's store know well how to treat an editor. We acknowledge receipt of a large pitcher of Philadelphia lager. The firm always keeps the Philadelphia lager on hand, and saloons will do well to call upon them. Many thanks!"[25]

Residents new to Chico were nostalgic for their native regions' preferred drinks. An exhibit at the town's new Agricultural Fair in 1868 reflected the townspeople's cosmopolitan palates. The popular display that year featured Irish whiskey, Holland gin, London porter, French champagne, sherry, grape brandy, stock beer, stock ale, claret, red wine, Los Angeles Angelica dessert wine and Isabella port, as well as the particularly popular New England spruce beer.[26]

John Bidwell brought his new wife Annie Kennedy, a temperance advocate, to Chico in late 1868. Bidwell, a former saloon owner and active wine grape grower, pulled out his grape vines and pleased his wife by helping to fund the town's already popular temperance work. While two temperance groups, one for young people and one for adults, met in Wood's Hall, the wholesale liquor trade downstairs likely incurred Mrs. Bidwell's disapproval.

Chico's Bavarian brewer Charles Croissant and his wife Bertha were the Chapmans' associates in the North Methodist Church. While Bertha's husband had a unique status in the community, she pursued a home life typical of Chico wives. She and Sarah's other friends entered their crafts in the Agricultural Fair's popular contests, which became a highlight each year. Even Selena Woodman—Chico's "bluestocking," as intellectual women were known—entered her jams, jellies, pickles and catsup. Her brandied cherries won acclaim.[27] Wood & Chapman exhibited a plaster bust one year, then entered lumber and women's dress goods in another. Freddie Chapman displayed the miniature log cabin and other toys he made. Sarah Chapman, whose name does not appear on any of the long lists of contestants, was evidently content to be a spectator and cheerleader. She was not confident about her needlework, although she sewed "cozies" and "tidies" nice enough to give as wedding presents. Whether on the temperance issue or in crafts, she was independent enough to go her own way.

Throughout the 1860s Sarah milked both cows, gardened, cooked, cleaned, washed clothes and carried countless buckets of water she drew from their backyard well.[28] Gus made her one of the lucky women who owned a sewing machine, which he hoped her many women friends would covet enough to buy from his store. By 1863 Sarah had acquired enough furniture to equal the value of their cow. In 1864, another good year, Gus treated himself to a gold watch and Sarah shopped for more furniture. In 1867 the Chapmans, like other Chicoans, cut back on wax-dripping candles in favor of newly affordable kerosene lamps. Still, Gus invested most of what he made in real estate to develop the lumber company.[29]

By and large, women hesitated to leave their eastern families to migrate west. In 1864 Lydia Steward complained to her distant family, "Oh, how I wish we could start for Maine right away. We would go now if money could be had. Times are very hard and we know not when it will end."[30] This may explain why Chico's Methodist women, so removed from their mothers and sisters, virtually adopted one another—friendships softened their losses. In Sarah's circle Sophronia Maxson, a motherly woman, became a Chapman family friend and mentor. John Maxson, her husband, was a North Methodist Church steward who owned a small sash mill and built much of downtown Chico, including the Wood & Chapman store. Mrs. Maxson's warmth and helpfulness inspired affection. Her cakes and breads reminded young Charlie Stilson of his mother's pastries in their Wisconsin home. John Bidwell was another fan. When his new wife hired a cook in 1868, he suggested Annie have Sophronia Maxson train her how to can peaches.[31]

Chico women grew close as they exchanged visits or lent a hand at one another's homes. On warm summer evenings they strolled downtown for refreshments. They also met at their gates for the walk to a Wood's Hall church service or, later, to their cramped church at Fifth and Broadway. Ledgers suggest she was not a frequent visitor either to Bidwell & Co. or later to Gus's store, probably because she relied on him to bring home what they needed. However, when he was away on business, Charlie Stilson spoke of Sarah Chapman's shopping at the store as a welcome event. As a very speculative aside, John Bidwell's successful marriage to tiny Annie Kennedy suggests he appreciated petite women. As the only evidence, when his path crossed Sarah's he simply entered the name of small "Mrs. Chapman" several times in his diary, discretely separate from his lists of people he noticed.[32]

In 1865 Stilson noted in his diary that Sarah stopped in to pick up trimmings for the community Christmas celebration. Every settler was far from family and many lamented missing the decorated tree tradition. In Chico this posed a problem because few valley homes could secure fresh cut fir trees. Arduous trips to

the high country to cut them took days and still felt potential-
ly dangerous because the memory of hostile Indians there was
still fresh. The *Courant's* account covered one year's celebration
when Sarah Chapman, Rebecca Ball, Sophronia Maxson and
their friends had trees brought down for a celebration the whole
community shared:

Christmas at Chico.—The Christmas arrangements for
our town were well-conceived and successfully carried
out. Two large pines that reached from floor to ceiling,
with wide spreading branches were loaded, literally covered with gifts of all kinds, sizes and Monday, Armory
[Bidwell] Hall was flooded with packages, the ladies arranging order, beauty and form from chaos, and at night
the trees, lighted by colored tapers, presented a magnificent appearance. The large Hall was crowded at an early
hour, and before the time for distribution of gifts, not a
foot of unoccupied room remained. When the time arrived, Old Santa Claus himself, clad in his unique cos-
tume, with ancient beard and long silver locks, made
his appearance among the cheers of the audience and
screams of terrified little ones, and commenced the delivery of the thousand gifts on the right hand and on
the left. Everybody, from the oldest to the youngest, received one or more Christmas gifts. The Sunday School
children were remembered by the patrons of the Sunday
School, and each received a pretty book besides the other
gifts distributed. After the distribution of gifts, the ladies
brought forward a beautiful "Guess Cake," which was
won by Mrs. Chapman. Then came the "Grabbag" and
fun, from which was realized many a twobit piece, all
of which will be appropriated to a worthy object by the
ladies. After the Hall was cleared, a merry dance wound
up the festivities of the "Merry Christmas." It was one of
the most pleasant gatherings we ever attended, and everybody seemed highly pleased, old and young happy
alike.[33]

Sarah left her guess cake at the store overnight for the staff to set out with fruit and wine for customers. Stilson's references to Sarah and later sources suggest the affectionate, even spontaneous, side of her nature. She became Charlie Stilson's matchmaker on the young store clerk's leisurely stroll toward marriage. Emma Tolliver, in the front rank of Stilson's many girlfriends, often arrived from San Jose for stays with the Chapmans, ostensibly to visit her brother.[34] Fifty or more years later, Marjorie Pingrey recalled Sarah as the dignified elderly woman who once impulsively kissed her adorable baby after church. Mrs. Pingrey noted her surprise and concern because, as a young mother, she worried about contagion.[35]

Sarah did her best to maintain ties with her family in Michigan and made two lengthy visits to see them. Her first trip took place in 1866 when she, Freddie, 8, and Mary, 2, sailed from San Francisco to New Orleans, then continued up the Mississippi to Michigan. While on board she must have recalled her Sickley family's treacherous crossing of Lake Erie when she was a teenager in the 1830s. While visiting in the spring, Mary survived a dangerous sickness. Sarah and the children remained with her family for three months. In 1869 she and the children returned east by train out of Sacramento on one of the first cross-country trips on the new Pacific Railroad.

Such visits to cherished "home states" caused unease in family members who stayed behind. Would the travelers be willing to return to face the hardships of the new state? However much most Chicoans appreciated California, they missed the emotional and familial attachments, the material comforts and the established cultural life of their native homes. That explains the *Enterprise*'s wistful message when noting Sarah Chapman's departure with her children and companions: "May the endearments of the older home have no influence to lessen by comparison those of the new for we cannot spare any of them."[36] Secure in knowing that her Michigan family remained part of her life and that, in Chico, she was among dear friends, Sarah returned, ready to consider it her own true home. Meanwhile, Gus had determined the location of their family house was about to change.

7

Family, Real Estate, and Politics

By the late 1860s lumber remained a healthy contributor to Chico's economy, but anxiety about housing tempered optimism about the town's further expansion. If new people descended in large numbers, as hoped, where would they live? When rumors circulated in 1867 that about fifty Danes were on their way to Chico, the newspaper lamented: "Every day brings to our section persons seeking for land upon which to establish homes. All the qualifications for pleasant and profitable homes can be found but no land for sale or rent."[1]

The problem was that land surrounding Chico on three sides belonged to John Bidwell, who counted on pending railroad transportation to deliver his farm produce to urban markets. He also believed he had already given up enough cropland to establish Chico, including the lots he was then preparing for houses west of Broadway between Chestnut and Hazel and Front Street south to Fifth Street.[2]

Therefore, in the September *Enterprise* the editor set out the problem and affirmed Chapman's solution to it: "No [one should] think of extending beyond the bridge over Big Chico Creek, as no more land in that direction can be had for town lots. No one will think of carrying the town over the railroad, as roads of this kind do not permit to follow streets. This [Chapman's plan to open a suburb] then is the only direction left. Chapman will give fair bargains." Gus planned to turn some of the land he purchased from the Manderville farm in 1890 into lots of five to twenty acres. By creating house lots for Chico's growing populace, Chapman meant to do well by doing good.

Gus sold 400 acres of his Mandeville land to ranchers. From the 600 acres he retained, he carved out six residential blocks along the Oroville-Shasta Road on 120 acres of the land closest to Little Chico Creek, Chico's southern boundary. While the county recorded it as Chapman's Addition, Gus leaned toward "Chapmanville." Within a few years popular usage settled on "Chapmantown." Chapman intended to develop only land extending east from the Oroville-Shasta Road to present Boucher Street and south from Old Chico Way and later East Twelfth Street to later East Sixteenth Street. He kept the remainder south of present East Sixteenth Street open for future options.

In June 1871 J. R. Woollen sold Gus a second parcel, a long strip of about thirty acres that nudged the northern border of his subdivision closer to Little Chico Creek.[3] Called Chapman's Addition North, it ran parallel to the creek, between the Oroville-Shasta Road and the Boucher Ranch. Its southern border was Old Chico Way (which he renamed Bidwell Avenue and now is East Twelfth Street). This addition pushed the border of Gus's suburb nearer the Junction. On the Chapman's Addition North map he inked "Chapman st" or perhaps "Chapman site" near a tiny squiggle approximating the shape of Bidwell Mansion.[4]

This land, dubbed "Sunflower Farm," had previously belonged to Irish physician Dr. J. B. Smith. He built a substantial, but simple cottage standing on brick piers and covered with oiled clapboard siding. The bachelor doctor and a few hired hands bunked upstairs under the eaves. After Smith lost his ranch to bankruptcy in 1863, widower John Woollen lived there with his teenaged daughter Rebecca and several hired hands until his remarriage. Nothing about the house suggested it could be a model home for the desirable dwellings Gus envisioned on the lots he laid out.[5]

Finally, in June 1872 Gus completed his third and final purchase called Chapman's Reserve. This was Woollen's narrow strip of deep forest between the Boucher Ranch and Little Chico Creek, "a popular trout stream." The addition of the contiguous reserve acreage, intended to be his family's park, completed Chapman's subdivision, which now reached the creek bank. Gus wagered his new subdivision's natural beauty would appeal to buyers. For him to reshape its rolling valley swales into level streets and uniform lots mustered every talent he had and every cent he could raise by sales and mortgages. The six large residential blocks were neatly divided by wide streets. Chapman had surveyor James McGann designate another whole block for an eventual school whose grounds would double as a park. As sole investor he no longer had a "George Wood" to guide, fund, rescue or pester him. This was a period when Chico, like the nation, celebrated "the businessman and the Chamber of Commerce and the sub-divider." Gus Chapman was all of that.[6]

With such a considerable project underway, Gus could not yet afford the grand house he required to declare his place in the community. In the meantime, after conferring with San Francisco architect Henry Cleaveland, Gus decided to remodel the Woollens' farm house on Chapman's Addition North. Its purpose was dual: a family home and a model home for the subdivision.

It is likely Chapman hired Cleaveland to expand and remodel the house. Since his design of John Bidwell's elegant home, the architect frequently stayed at Rancho Chico while he consulted with area clients. In 1870 and 1871 Cleaveland was working with Bidwell and his crew to landscape the grounds where the rancher had recently demolished his former home, a large federal farmhouse, and the nearby adobe hotel. For the Chapman job, Cleaveland attached a wing across the house's south end to add living space and a formal front facing Bidwell Avenue. After the Chapmans' house was completed, an *Enterprise* journalist asked to do a story about it; Cleaveland was likely his guide. The journalist reported the house as only one-story because its high, peaked roof obscured the attic floor, which Cleaveland considered an additional half-story. He elsewhere described such houses as "story-and-a-half" cottages.

In remodeling the Chapmans' house, Cleaveland retained the low ceiling in the original attic room. Then, in adding the decorative front wing he kept the new roof the height of the original one behind it. In the new space, however, he framed the ceilings higher within the gables and added a bath room and two bedrooms. Two sets of French doors opening on to balconies extending from two sides of the extension gave the house the appearance of a full two-story home from the front. He had turned the nondescript farm house into a classic "Downing" cottage, a type of housing originally designed by Andrew Jackson

Downing.[7] His cottage designs became associated with Henry Cleaveland in American architectural history.

The *Enterprise* article described the Chapmans' remodeled house as a "German cottage." While the Chapman house's finishing does not resemble a usual German style, its expanded shape reflects an Andrew Jackson Downing illustration the architect called "A Cottage in the Rhine Style."[8] This distinctive reference supports Cleaveland as the remodel architect and interview source. In the case of the Chapmans' house, the architect created a Gothic Revival style with Eastlake influences and Italianate trims on verandas lining the corner house's two street sides. The tax record gave this improvement a value of $2,750.[9] (In the 1880s, Cleaveland bought property in the countryside and designed a house for Chico's Presbyterian minister, courtesy, no doubt, of the Bidwells.)

In late 1872 the Chapmans moved in. Sarah observed the local tradition of placing a long-handled brush at each of the house's five entry doors for visitors to sweep dust and mud from their boots. While a graceful model home, it was only a step to the grand house on a new street Gus inserted on the planning map after it had been submitted. Later named Chapman Street (now East Eleventh Street), it ran from the Oroville-Shasta Road east to Nelson Street.[10] The tiny library (a Cleaveland must) that fitted into space off the sitting room doubled as Gus's real estate office. While sales were initially strong, he found himself worrying about future sales because his subdivision—nine blocks from Chico's prime business street, West Second—was considered "out of town." As he feared, sales began declining.

Fallout

The Chapmans were only in their new home a few months before Gus realized no Chico real estate boon was imminent. The arrival of train service in Idaho meant eastern companies replaced western ones as suppliers to miners. The bet he and his partners had made in Chapman, Titcomb & Bush had rested on railroad service making up for the loss by attracting new residents whose investments would make up for it. Skeptics blamed well-off residents for squandering their fortunes on local mining speculations. In the main, however, complaints reverted to the standard explanation that Chico's chronic shortage of funds was due to farmers' insistence on wheat as their single crop.

Chapman & McKay's robust lumber sales cushioned Gus's disappointing lot sales because Sierra Nevada lumber was becoming competitive with Oregon lumber in the coastal market.[11] A steady line of Chapman & McKay's oxen-drawn wagons continued hauling logs down Humboldt Road to the train depot and the Chico Landing. Gus contracted as much as 125,000 board feet a month to clients as far away as Salt Lake City and San Francisco.[12]

In contrast, the Chapman, Titcomb & Bush store was "running before the storm" and "[sailing] under bare poles." With store patronage in steep decline, the partners abandoned their cash-only policy and reinstated charge accounts, all for naught. The partners posted the store for sale and called for customers to pay off their bills. Chapman focused on collections and negotiated debts the store owed suppliers like George Perkins.[13] Charlie Stilson observed Chapman, Titcomb & Bush's struggle from the vantage point of his agricultural implement store across Main Street. He also remarked on Lee Pharmacy's financial peril and noted the fire that demolished Hallet & Loy's planing mill. As he put it, "Everyone looks as if they are afraid someone would present a bill."[14]

When Charles Harker, a former gold miner, and George Dorn, a mining store merchant since the 1850s, bought the partners' store at Second and Main, they renamed it Harker & Dorn. George Bush left for West Virginia and Henry Titcomb headed for San Francisco where he became an agent for the Ghirardelli Company. Still committed to Chico, Gus Chapman continued in the lumber business but concentrated on developing his suburb.

However, Gus was so often seen at Harker & Dorn some guessed he had second thoughts about selling it. Trade picked up with Dorn's expansion of the groceries section. Upstairs, Dorn and Harker partitioned Wood's Hall into offices rented by the *Enterprise*, Dr. Carnot Courtland Mason and the new law firm of Albert J. Gifford, who partnered with Franklin Crawford Lusk. Junior partner Lusk immediately attracted curiosity about his elaborate office furnishings which seemed ostentatious and better suited to a St. Louis or Chicago firm.

Since Chapman only drank in moderation, when he owned the store the saloon next door on Second Street was nothing more to him than a valuable rent-paying client. In contrast, Charles Harker found the liquor there an irresistible lure. Drink gained such a grip on him that, in a rage, he stabbed his wife's brother who had come to their house to help her leave him. Then Harker's knife cut his wife as she tried to grab it from him. The victims survived and the sheriff delivered Harker to the Napa Insane Asylum. George Dorn, now sole owner, made his store a downtown mainstay for decades. Dorn and Chapman became personal friends who went on to collaborate in developing Chico's gas and water services.[15] Both would support incorporation and lead in the 1877 response to anti-Chinese violence.

Lumbermen and Farmers Unite

Like George Wood, when Gus traveled in search of lumber contracts he left store operations to the employees and lumber yard management to senior employee George Turner. With his focus on sales, Gus agreed with his farmer friends—James Morehead, Daniel Bidwell and George Miller—that railroad freight charges were exorbitant. However, unlike the big farmers, lumbermen had no organization to represent them. Therefore, Gus combined forces with farmers of the Upper Sacramento Valley Agricultural Society which elected him treasurer in 1870.[16]

Society members objected to the Central Pacific Railroad's arbitrary regulations that inflated freight rates. For Chico Lumber deliveries, Chapman had to pay in gold on invoices calculated for an arbitrary destination well beyond Chico. The price for that added-on segment could cost half again as much as the whole bill and, if refunded, it arrived as paper money, not gold. Men of the society and their counterparts objected and lobbied to expand the volume, speed and reliability of railroad services. As early as 1872 the usually mild *Enterprise* accused the Central Pacific of "designs ... to absorb the whole carrying trade of the State and hold the country at its mercy."[17]

In support of Chico's new identity as the "Pine Capital of California," it sprouted five lumber yards, a factory for sashes, doors and blinds and two planing mills. By 1875, according to the *Enterprise*, lumber's influence rivaled that of wheat: "The great land leviathans, with their ten or twelve mules attached as motive power are constantly arriving from the mills with their thousands of feet [of lumber]."[18]

Freight wagons stacked high with Chapman & McKay's pine remained a familiar sight as drivers such as Peter Munjar guided them down Humboldt Road.[19] Riders heading north along the steep Sierra Nevada foothill passage listened for the lead animals' bells to announce their approach around blind bends. Because the oxen could not make sudden stops or shifts, other riders and drivers along the way had to move to the side. On approaching a steep descent, a driver would find a stopping point. To create a drag sufficient to brake the wagon, he would cut down a small tree and chain it to the rear of the wagon.

Trees, seemingly everywhere, frustrated American farmers. Most considered them obnoxious, giant weeds—an impediment to growing crops. Therefore, Chapman & McKay, like other lumber firms, were celebrated for felling countless original growth trees, some of them 25 to 50 feet in circumference and 250 to 300 feet in height. The eastern practice Thoreau deplored was evident in Butte County: "If a man spends his whole day as a speculator shearing off those woods and making earth bald before her time he is esteemed an industrious and enterprising citizen. As if a town had no interest in its forests but to cut them down."[20]

At the Powellton hamlet, where Chapman & McKay's main mill was located, the *Enterprise* captured the fervor: "Notwithstanding the vast amount of timber that for years has been cleared away for lumber purposes, these pineries still have an abundance, and it seems as if their stores were inexhaustible. Chapman and McKay's mill is the best and cuts an immense amount of lumber."[21]

As an example of the firm's productivity, by October 1870 its mill had cut 500,000 board feet for their Chico Lumber retail outlet and shipped an additional 1.2 million board feet primarily for mining construction. But even this quantity could not satisfy the demand. During the same month that year, when Chapman & McKay sent 200,000 board feet from their Powellton mill to San Francisco, they had to purchase an additional 100,000 board feet from a rival mill to satisfy their retail customers in Chico.

Yet even that failed to meet local demand. The sight of pine loaded on wagons lumbering through town to the Fifth Street depot irritated Chicoans whose own lumber requests remained on back order.[22] By 1873 Chapman & McKay was the third most significant landowner in Butte County; even so, they ranked well behind John Bidwell and George Perkins.[23]

During the production season—roughly April through November—Butte County mills employed 300 to 400 men at "fair" wages. Together the mills maintained about 300 oxen, as well as horses and mules which also hauled freight.[24] County production had soared from 6 million board feet in the mid-1860s, when Chapman & McKay first went into business, to 62 million board feet by 1873, when the economy weakened and they made their first unsuccessful attempt to sell Chico Lumber at Eighth and Main. (That attempt may also have reflected Chapman's absorption in developing his subdivision.) With such a demand in the cities and new valley towns along the railroad, Chapman and McKay were finding it stressful to work with one another. McKay was committed to traditional production and delivery methods like his oxen-drawn freight wagons. On the other hand, Chapman was seldom content with comfortable, traditional methods; his focus was speed and the ease of bulk delivery that railroads provided.

Frustration with the Central Pacific Railroad led Chapman to back Bidwell's call in 1873 for a locally owned narrow-gauge rail line between Chico and Colusa.[25] The *Enterprise* and *Record* noted Chapman's involvement in this pursuit. From Colusa, on the Sacramento River, south, steamboats were still a reliable option for shippers of wheat and lumber to tidewater ports.[26] The narrow-gauge design was not only cheaper to build and operate than the standard-gauge tracks, it was exempt from county taxes. With such incentives, Chapman and Bidwell overcame their present tensions over a school site issue and joined with others in plans to bring narrow-gauge railroads to the Sacramento Valley.

After an 1875 meeting, lumbermen shared their concerns about weakening construction trends in the San Francisco market. Chapman & McKay was increasingly dependent on orders from mining speculators.[27] In response, Gus expanded his sales campaigns in Colusa, Yolo and Sutter counties, where towns were springing up along the new train tracks. Sales of construction materials to build Orland, Woodland, Gridley, Biggs, Williams and other towns compensated for some of the downward trends in cities such as Sacramento and San Francisco where the national depression first reached California.

Chronically hard-pressed farmers welcomed the lumbermen's positive thinking. According to Chapman, once the narrow-gauge railroad line was in operation, its profits from the volume of lumber business alone could finance train operations and reduce farmers' shipping costs. While information about this claim is sparse, the spirited collaboration suggests a strong bond between farmers and lumbermen.

As a big farmer, John Bidwell must have listened with wry interest as he heard Chapman, once his "disloyal" chief clerk and now a lumberman, proposing to financially "carry" agriculture. On behalf of the county's narrow-gauge railroad backers, Chapman set off for the Bay Area to observe their operations. On returning home, he and Colusa County leaders delivered glowing reports to Bidwell, who offered $10,000 toward the construction of a narrow-gauge track. That same evening, however, the visitors watched a roaring fire consume the huge hay barn Bidwell had just erected on Rancho Chico. This arson attack by opponents of Chinese labor "disheartened" Bidwell, who explained to the men that he had to withdraw his backing of the narrow-gauge tracks in order to rebuild his barn and replace the hay.[28] The narrow-gauge idea lingered on for about a decade and arson threats weighed on Bidwell for another twenty years.

Lumber had rewarded Chapman with a small fortune since the mid-1860s, but he not only had no interest in the mill, it seems he loathed the business itself. Every trip to Powellton and endless trips to distant contractors removed him from his real estate development and other promising ventures. By contrast, Bill and Mary Ann McKay were content to live in Powellton from late spring to early fall, where she kept house and he managed timber cutting, processing, transport, livestock, machine maintenance and personnel. Although the McKays lived in Chico every winter, Bill never appeared in press items about the Chico Lumber outlet, which suggests he avoided Chapman's bailiwick.

Despite personal tensions and the arrival of the great depression in the mid-1870s, McKay and Chapman had to consider how structural changes underway in the lumber industry would affect their business.[29] They were aware that monopolies were developing on the West Coast like those in eastern industries. Investors were buying and consolidating independent mills into expansive operations under central management. North and east of Chico, investors in Red Bluff-based Sierra Flume & Lumber had bought up vast tracts of timberland to the edge of Butte Creek across from Chapman & McKay's land and their Powellton mill.[30]

Sierra Flume & Lumber's actions revealed its investors' ambitions. The company erected giant wooden V-shaped flumes (channels) through which they piped creek water that floated logs from the mountains to the Sacramento Valley floor for processing. In August 1874 a flume reached the company's new mill at the intersection of Chico's East Eighth Street and north-south Pine Street, which bordered the entire west side of the vast mill. On the east side of its yards, a rough settlement housed workers who called it "Oakvale." When that didn't catch on, they tried "Buttermilk Flat," but most Chicoans settled on calling it "The Dump" or "Dumpville," for the giant log piles the flume emptied there. Flumes, a state-of-the-art technology, flooded the market with so much lumber that prices plunged. With this, Chapman & McKay and their rivals reduced their cutting and milling. Teamsters' job losses doomed at least two Chico saloons and the unemployed commiserated at "hard time" parties.

A Sanborn fire insurance map shows that Bidwell had built his own water flume that entered Chico east of Chapmantown, crossed Little Chico Creek and veered west to follow Pine Street where it paralleled the Sierra Flume & Lumber factory and emptied into Big Chico Creek near his flour mill.

To McKay's dismay, overproduction linked to the flumes also reduced the demand for oxen. Despite the efficiency of the flumes, the devoted livestock man insisted Chapman & McKay continue to use the beasts for lumber delivery. He argued they were cheaper to maintain and more dependable than flumes, which sometimes rotted and fell apart, burned or just broke down. But livestock also presented problems—in 1874 a "mad bull" rushed a Chapman & McKay employee's horse, seriously goring its rider.[31]

Despite all this, by the mid-1870s Chapman still earned a steady, if not always, ample income from the lumber business and enjoyed his freedom from the general store. With George Turner on the job at Chico Lumber, Chapman indulged his chronic entrepreneurial restlessness. He focused on his subdivision sales and expanded buying and selling or renting town buildings.

Chapman and Bidwell at Odds

In late 1872 several new houses were going up in Chapman's Addition east and south of the Chapmans' remodeled farm house, but prospective buyers were not snapping up other lots. He launched an advertising campaign laying out choices of five- to twenty-acre lots—big enough to accommodate any combination of house, garden, family orchard, woodshed, barn, stable, chicken house and, for some, a freestanding summer kitchen. When Gus delivered to *Enterprise* editor William N. DeHaven a juicy blood orange plucked from the tree in his yard, DeHaven slipped in a news item that Chapman ordered 500 trees and shrubs to line the streets. He also planted them in a community park he created across from his house, where he planned to build a school. He also published items about his plans for alleys and boardwalks. Then Gus made a gesture to ingratiate his adversary by naming the principal street "Bidwell Avenue."[32]

By 1874 Chapman associates had built family houses, many on two or more combined Chapmantown lots. Purchasers included the Chapmans' friends, rancher James Morehead and Schuyler Walker, who, along with carpenter William Bradley, had remodeled the Chapmans' farm house, perhaps in trade for his labor. Another early buyer was Gus's partner William McKay, who fronted his family's house on the Oroville-Shasta Road for winter sojourns when the mill shut down. While such sales were gratifying, Gus was not satisfied. So he further reduced some lot sizes to make them more affordable.[33] Meanwhile, occasional improvements in fluctuating lumber sales and rents from his various Chico properties kept him afloat.[34]

Even Gus's family found Chapmantown's country location

inconvenient. Nine blocks separated it from the heart of Chico.[35] Their former home at Sixth and Chestnut was only about a minute's walk to the public school and the Chico Academy and a reasonable stroll to Second Street stores. Now, when a quick trip was necessary, they had to hitch up their horse and buggy to drive to town. The move transformed Sarah into a familiar driver on Chico's streets. With her husband often away and a hired driver impractical and too expensive for daily life, Sarah dispensed with the demure image a lady was expected to cultivate and took the reins.

Gus's experience differed. Although his walk to Second Street stores or the bank was a "stretch," their new house was only a few blocks from Chico Lumber in the Junction, where he was accustomed to its lively, workaday grunge. He ignored its rough ambiance—teamsters, mechanics, wainwrights, prostitutes, boarding houses, saloons and the like. Sarah must have made him aware, however, that Junction sights and sounds discomfited her personally and as a parent. She could not prevent Mary, 6, and Fred, 12, from discovering colorful characters and learning "forbidden" vocabulary when their mother drove them through the Junction or when young Fred and his pals were old enough to navigate its boardwalks en route to school or for visits with friends.

Gus and Sarah had to caution their children to be careful approaching or crossing the busy Oroville-Shasta Road on their way to town. Drivers had to be careful about merging onto the road with other buggies and wagons, as well as horseback riders, reluctant to slow their speed. Once across the bridge over Little Chico Creek, they had to navigate the Junction "roundabout" with feeder streets on four sides. Freighters and townspeople alike patronized its jumble of services and amenities—all moneymakers for Chico residents.

Unfortunately, the Junction reeked. The seasonal odor came from Dead Horse Slough, which became Eighth Street after the slough was rerouted. Until then it ran alongside Chico Lumber and crossed Main on its way to the distant Sacramento River. The slough alternately flowed and stagnated. Each summer, when its green-tinged water shrunk to puddles of slime, the odor combined with the smells from horse corrals to create a particularly noxious stench. The slough bridge was also an "attractive nuisance." It was a rickety magnet for exhibitions by gangs of bored boys who could not resist the "ague dance" — they stood on the bridge and made it shake by jumping together in the rhythm of malaria victims' shivers.

Sarah had no sooner settled into their remodeled farm house facing new Bidwell Avenue and registered the complications of living out of town than she became pregnant. On January 4, 1873, in a winter of regular downpours, she delivered the couple's fourth child, Augustus Jr. — "Gussie."

Gussie's birth put Gus Sr. on double duty that month. In addition to increased demands at home, he had to participate in annual boards of director meetings. Still a leader in Chico's serial attempts to form a new county, Gus now had a place on the boards of directors of the Bank of Butte County, Humboldt Road Co. and Chico Water & Gas Works. Augustus H. Chapman had "arrived."

Despite their differences as the 1870s evolved, town trustees appointed businessmen like Chapman and Bidwell to serve on citizens' committees and consult with other businessmen for various kinds of expertise. Therefore, Bidwell and Chapman found it necessary sometimes to stop at one another's home or office to discuss civic concerns. Committee memberships should not infer either man pursued a private friendship or patronized local venues for birthday and anniversary celebrations where they might have developed one. Neither did either man have more than one close friend at a time. On Fridays, the well-lubricated Chico Jockey Club members did not save chairs for Bidwell or Chapman at Tom Dooley's oyster suppers. Nor did either man join hobby groups such as the Chico hunters who traded rumors in August Thiel's news and tobacco shop, their informal "clubhouse." (Thiel's budding leadership ended when, during a hunting party, his gun discharged, killing him as he climbed over a farmer's field fence.[36])

When in town, long workdays meant Gus ordinarily made it home late, often tired and soiled from travel. While he and Sarah attended events at friends' homes, he must have savored his few waking hours at home with Sarah and found comfort in a glass of port. Chapman was too driven, too puritan and too exhausted to invest himself in most social events.

Therefore, when Chapman and Bidwell met to consider business, political and civic matters of mutual interest, such as Humboldt Road or the narrow-gauge railroad, they strictly observed civility and propriety. Other Chico businessmen also had strained relationships. *Enterprise* editor DeHaven observed: "Petty jealousies among even the best businessmen of the place could chill relationships.... If [Chico businessmen] would more frequently meet in a social capacity they would be less distrustful, know each other and oftener unite for common support."[37] Therefore, civic leaders attempted to avoid turning personal differences into overt alienations that would obstruct progress on projects important to everyone. In Chico, as in the country at large, common need led to cooperation that periodically softened the economic struggles that pitted each against another.

For example, in Chico's civic life, the county split was the perennial cause that united residents. In 1873 developer Chapman, merchant Charles Stilson and farmer B. F. Allen raised funds and produced petitions signed by half of Chico's voters. When they presented the petitions to a chilly meeting in Oroville, the Board of Supervisors, as expected, denied the split again. Unfazed, the Chico men immediately headed for the State Legislature in Sacramento. When that county split failed there yet again, they rallied anew and secured a State Supreme Court hearing where judges ordered a county election, finally giving them hope. Chapman offered $1,000 toward construction of a county building near the Chico Plaza on a downtown block Bidwell was ready to donate with his cash gift of $10,000. As in the previous county-split campaigns in Chico, this vote also produced high emotion, slippery ethics and another narrow loss.[38]

A Try for Office

During the early 1870s Gus's longstanding ambition for a career in politics resurfaced. He had lost his try for election in Michigan, but became a justice of the peace in Chico and then stepped back to bolster his finances. Now that his record of public service had earned bipartisan goodwill and he had income from lumber and real estate prospects, he ran for an open State Senate seat. During the later 1860s the Butte County Republican

Party had considered nominating Chapman for that position, but he could not gain support from Oroville. By contrast, in the party's 1873 convention, Oroville delegates backed him, despite his support for the county split and their usual view that any important county position should be reserved for one of their own. This time Gus won the nomination to run against an Oroville Democrat. Goodwill from Chapman & McKay trade with Oroville businessmen, including wholesaler George Perkins, most likely helped him.

Although Chapman won positive notices during his campaign, he lost the election by 186 votes. Despite this narrow defeat, he drew more Oroville support than Oroville Democrat William C. Hendricks drew in Chico. There, townspeople grumbled that some Oroville Republicans had crossed party lines and voted for the Democrat Hendricks in order to keep the position away from Chico.

In other words, if Oroville prevailed because a few residents placed town loyalty before party, Chico lost because a few voters placed party before town: "We talk but never act. Oroville does not talk but always acts as a unit. Every two years we talk self-interest, concert of action, disregard of party lines and etc., to offset the favored object, speak it loud and long so that everybody knows it, and then go to the polls and cast a party ticket."[39] The Oroville paper incorrectly reported that Chapman was elected to the State Senate "by a very large vote." All other contemporary accounts spoke to Chapman's loss. This outcome not only gave Chico one more grievance against Oroville, it deepened the strains at home between Democrats and Republicans. Divisions anchored in the Civil War lingered on and occupants of California's small towns dwelled on all manner of new grievances.

How could Chapman suddenly become the Bank of Butte County's vice president with a seat on the board of directors? The reason may have been political. In those years, because George Perkins was to Oroville what Bidwell was to Chico, Perkins must have resented the rancher's leadership role in Chico's serial attempts to split the county, which would have devastated Oroville's economy. Their strains on that issue, at that time, explain why Perkins backed George Wood to leave his and Bidwell's store in 1864 and launch Wood & Chapman and causing

Bidwell & Co. to fail. After Wood moved to the East, only Chapman remained to absorb the brunt of Bidwell's resentment of Wood and himself for disloyalty. In 1873 Perkins left Oroville commerce to enter political office and build a fortune in shipping. Apart from catching up at annual bank meetings, Perkins and Chapman moved in different orbits for several years as Perkins focused on his Oakland shipping business. Later, the men's relationship would significantly develop at the state level (the subject of later chapters).

Meanwhile, in that same year there were portents of bad times, including severe weather, approaching Northern California. At Chapman & McKay's lumber yard a downpour funneled water into Gus's office via a large hole it drove through a rotted spot on the wood-shingled roof. On the bright side, the waterfall extinguished a stovepipe fire.[40]

This incident was a prelude to the April 4 conflagration that obliterated an entire block-and-a-half of buildings between Main and Broadway. The flames were so high their brilliance was visible beyond Redding to Shasta Village, more than 75 miles to the north, where residents thought the town of Red Bluff was on fire. The most prominent casualty was the Bank of Butte County's frame building, which the bank replaced with an ornamented brick edifice at the southeast corner of Second and Broadway. (Although stripped of most of its elegant exterior trimmings, the building stands today.) There, at its long, semi-circular counter, Chapman handled his business in company with friends, clients and rivals. Light from its tall windows along Broadway overlooked the counter, warming or chilling the occupants according to the season. Gus became a good friend of Charles Faulkner, the tall, genial Wells Fargo agent whose title as cashier belied his actual role as bank manager. As mentioned earlier, he and his brothers sold their Oroville bank to George Perkins and his new partner Norman Rideout from Marysville, who then dispatched Faulkner to run their Bank of Butte County.

Faulkner brought along John R. Robinson, a quiet man of impeccable integrity. He managed Faulkner's Wells Fargo desk and soon became a bank officer as Faulkner's assistant. Faulkner and Robinson dealt with Chapman almost daily in his business dealings, as a board member and when he attended school trustee meetings in Dr. Carnot C. Mason's office. The Chapmans' friend, he had moved his practice from the former Wood's Hall to the bank's second floor, where he, Chapman and various associates met to manage Chico's Republican Party and the public schools through a couple of decades.

The aftermath of the 1873 conflagration led to other upgrades downtown and finally sparked the city to shift fire protection from private individuals who showed up with water buckets to units of organized volunteer firefighters. Using their new authority and taxes from Chico's incorporation, town trustees sunk cisterns for a water reserve under public streets. Following their lead, Gus and Sarah hired Chinese workers to dig a wide and deep brick-lined cistern next to their kitchen porch. That location would prove useful when the next owner and a deliveryman used it to dowse a roof fire. While the Chapmans did not regularly hire Chinese, they called on them for projects such as laundry and digging outhouse holes (which better-off owners lined with brick).

While Gus Chapman remained ambitious about elective office, his loss of the 1873 State Senate seat meant, for one thing, he could no longer avoid his never-ending problems with his partner Bill McKay and the ongoing need to sell the rest of the lots in his subdivision. Both concerns deepened with the depression's full onset. While the most dramatic effects appeared in cities, Chico did not escape. In September, upon word that San Francisco's Bank of California closed, the *Enterprise* noted that "the terrible effect on the commercial interests of the State can hardly be estimated at the present writing." Some said William Ralston, the bank's president, drowned himself in shock and anguish while others claimed he died by accident. The Bank of California's financial reach extended to Butte County. On a minor note of interest, word arrived that Harry Reed, Daniel Bidwell's son-in-law and a member of Ralston's immediate staff, had lost his job. This led to another loss, the Reeds' use of Ralston's private railroad car. The Reeds and their daughter became dependents of Daniel Bidwell thereafter. The Bidwell-Reed situation presented a stubborn reminder of how capricious success can be.

Other closures that followed included the Odd Fellows Savings Bank and the Masonic Savings and Loan, both in San

Francisco. Chapman was a member of both clubs. While the Bank of Butte County and the Bank of Chico both escaped failure in the depression, other repercussions ensued.

Store cash boxes began to empty because each time local merchants paid their San Francisco or Sacramento suppliers, Chico's currency diminished. Although San Francisco banks reopened, for some time they locked up most of the cash that crossed their counters in order to forestall new runs on their holdings. Almost no currency flowed to Chico to replenish what had been lost. The drain of currency out of the Sacramento Valley left "the entire interior exposed to want [and] to actual danger of bankruptcy."

According to the *Enterprise*, "Money, the greatest necessity of the times … can no more be seen than had. It is no essential use that we have property in abundance; that our crops, undisposed of and of great value … none can bring money because there is no money in sight, and money is the only thing that will pay debts…. So long as [businessmen's] city backers let them alone, all is right; But, once pushed themselves, they must in turn push those whom they have accommodated."

In 1875 the depression's effects deepened with the onset of winter rains that brought most construction to a halt. When neither the latest buyer of Chapman & McKay's Chico Lumber Co. nor the buyers of their mill could keep up their payments, McKay and Chapman recovered those businesses. While they both wanted to dissolve their partnership, they were, by necessity, forced to work together again. McKay started up production and Chapman tended to debt collection. Few residents were in a position to buy lots in his subdivision. In addition, while he and Bidwell had seemed to work out a "modus vivendi," Chapman soon learned that Bidwell was launching a project that threatened the future of Chapmantown.

1870s

The Chapman and Bidwell Rivalry

The year 1874 was hardly underway when a fire threatened one of Chapman & McKay's mills. Only McKay's rapid response in extinguishing it preserved the partners' position as "the heaviest of [Chico's] lumber men."[1] The next low point for Gus Chapman came that spring when John Bidwell announced his new housing development, Bidwell's Addition. Workers began carving out lots and streets from Rancho Chico grazing land south of Big Chico Creek along the eastern edge of downtown. While its location right behind the bustling Chinatown on Flume Street could be a problem, its convenience to downtown was a plus. Chapman must have been alarmed; with that advantage, Bidwell's Addition would directly compete with his subdivision.[2] Overt competition between Bidwell and Chapman on subdivision issues provided rich fodder for town gossip. Gus had to make his more appealing than Bidwell's.

As previously mentioned, Chapman had started work on Chapmantown in the late 1860s when Bidwell declared he would not sacrifice more land for Chico's development. In that prosperous time, his decision made sense. However, by the early mid-1870s the economy, local and national, had weakened and he changed his mind.[3] Like everyone else, Bidwell needed money—on a large scale. Still Chico's wealthiest man, he had to meet a big payroll. He also supported an entire village of Mechoopda Indian families, juggled an uneven cash flow and had just borrowed $90,000 (over $2 million today).

The Gas and Water Tactic

Chapman could not ignore what was happening east of Flume Street and just north of Dumpville (Buttermilk Flat). Teams of horses were pulling grading equipment to carve out flat subdivision lots and streets from the swales rolling across Bidwell's grazing land. While Gus had limited options for encouraging lot buyers to buy in Chapmantown rather than Bidwell's Addition, his presidency of the Chico Water and Gas Works provided him some advantages.

The original local gas company had led the way in 1871 after town trustees rejected an outside entrepreneur's proposal to provide the fuel and equipment for streetlamps. Chico streets had only seen lighting when participants in occasional night parades carried torches while escorting important visitors to and from the train depot and the Chico Hotel. While the trustees were curious about gas lighting, they had heard of swindles elsewhere and wanted to keep the work local. They contracted with Adin Bullard, John W. Gilkyson and Charles Stilson to form the first gas company. Despite public resistance to this "newfangled" invention for street and home services, in 1872 the trustees gave permission for enough gas piping that, in two years, the company had installed a scattering of dim lights downtown. To the company's disappointment, the public was indifferent and the investors' confidence foundered.

Then, when Chapman and other backers bought a majority share in the gas and water companies, they decided their priority was to update the water service and postpone expanding gas service. (Although legally separate, the two companies were administratively treated as one and shared the same board of directors and thus are treated as one hereafter.) In November 1874, after the board of directors elected Gus president of the company, the members proceeded to build large capital stock for improvements.[4]

Gus hired laborers who dug down 35 feet to tap into an artesian well west of downtown. Above it, carpenters built a towering 110-foot frame structure to support the tank holding 60,999 gallons of water. Viewers who braved a climb to the handsome observatory's peak claimed they could see Cherokee, Mt. Shasta (over 130 miles to the north) and Marysville to the south on a clear day.

When Chapman and the board authorized their company manager John Gilkyson to buy water pipes, they discovered a building boom in the Bay Area had already laid claim to the entire iron pipe supply. So the company met its promise of service to townspeople by installing temporary wooden water pipes. They began laying them in 1875 and reached Chapmantown in April 1876, which happened to be the year Gus Chapman was faced with the development of Bidwell's Addition. Two more years passed before water pipes reached Bidwell's Addition.

The delayed delivery may, of course, have been related to a repeat of the iron pipes shortage. It is also possible that Chapman slow-walked the delivery to Bidwell's Addition to advantage his own subdivision. Or the delay may have been Gus's retaliation against a new proposal by John Bidwell that was so clever and dangerous to Chapman's lot sales that, within seconds of learning about it, Gus had no time to deal with the water and gas company. When Chapman retaliated to save his suburb, he risked his reputation to make sure John Bidwell "got the message."

The Rivalry Becomes Public

By 1870 tensions between Chapman and Bidwell seemed to have been forgotten. Chico's population of about 4,000 was small enough that anyone paying attention believed the problem started five years previous when Chapman left with Bidwell's partner George Wood to open a competing store. However, Bidwell and Chapman were discreet by nature about their personal affairs and neither fed the gossip about their relationship. Evidence suggests they never named one another when they differed, but they could not disguise their rivalry now that each had so much at stake in their competing subdivisions. While Chapman's water improvements were underway and, until Bidwell issued the suburb challenge that shook Chapman, each had been competing for lot sales in conventional ways.

While they remained closemouthed, their rivalry became clear in the pattern of newspaper advertisements each used to tout his subdivision. For example, Bidwell intimated that his addition was yet another of his countless sacrifices for the town's benefit. In other words, he was not a crass financial speculator like Chapman. When Chapman predicted buyers would see a 100 percent appreciation on the value of their lots in a year, Bidwell countered he would provide seven rental houses and affordable lots on which working men could build family homes. As if engaged in a stylized dialogue, Chapman replied that large lots suitable for families were available at low prices in his subdivision.[5]

Another issue percolated in the background. Chapman had reserved most of a block in Chapmantown for a park and a school. The existing Salem Street Public School was roughly equidistant from the Chapman and Bidwell additions. However, by 1874 there were 600 school-aged children and residents grumbled that Chico's growing population had overwhelmed its only public school.

Supporters of a second public school for first through sixth grades made a compelling case to overcome citizens' objections to higher taxes. In their appeals, they assured that new facilities would improve education, making it possible for young toughs to better themselves and find gainful employment. The school trustees' bond campaign to fund a new school took place while Chapman and Bidwell were competing to sell lots in their additions. Bond backers gambled that, because both men were reliable supporters of Chico improvements, civil by nature and needed the proposed school site near his subdivision, they could collaborate on the new school's location. When the trustees approached Bidwell, Chapman and big rancher David Reavis to build support for the bond, they all agreed to help promote it.[6]

Chapman briefly interrupted his work on the bond campaign in mid-March. Downtown and thirsty, he ducked into Charlie Stilson's Main Street store and headed for the company water bucket in the cooler, dark area by the basement door at the back. When Gus reached for the dipper, he took "one step too far" and plunged down the stairs. Despite contusions and a broken left wrist, he did not slow his rounds for the bond campaign. On election day, a majority voted in favor.[7]

With the bond passed, the three school trustees were to meet and choose the site, select the design and plan the construction. However, when one trustee resigned, voters had to elect his replacement before decisions could be made. Augustus Chapman became the only announced candidate for this third seat. If selected, he would vote on a location for the new public school. Despite the obvious conflict of interest and risk to his reputation, Gus was desperate and decided to leave nothing to chance.[8] The stakes had risen even higher because, while the Bidwell Addition was the biggest threat to his subdivision, a third bidder proposed a school site two miles from Chapmantown.

As the only candidate for the third trustee slot, Gus was preparing to take office. However, on June 27, 1874, election morning, word spread that two more candidates had added their names to the ballot, John Gilkyson and lawyer James F. Hutton. According to the newspaper, Chapman supporters passed the news around town. Voters surged from their homes and stores and converged on the polling place by foot, omnibuses, wagons and carriages. There, they cooled their heels in a lengthy line to cast their ballots. The result was a victory for Augustus Chapman who garnered 228 of 284 votes, 80 percent of the ballots cast.[9] He must have been grateful and relieved by the vote and its wide margin. While the outcome not only "saved the day" for him and nurtured his lingering dream of a career in politics, he recognized the whole town knew he had a conflict of interest and, by rights, should not have run for that office.

Why had voters surged to the polls to help Chapman despite his conflict of interest? Circumstances suggest his supporters suspected John Bidwell was behind the sudden appearance of the two new candidates. One candidate was the well-liked John W. Gilkyson, by turns a minister, farmer, insurance man, miller and the gas and water company manager; the second was lawyer James Hutton. Voters could be expected to split their votes between the popular candidates, Chapman and Gilkyson, son of the pastor who brought his family from Oroville in the early 1870s. With this split, the rest of the votes would likely favor lawyer Hutton. Chapman's allies may have still resented Bidwell's role two years previous when he convinced county supervisors to crush the townspeople's intent to place a slice of his land within Chico's municipal boundary.

In addition, townsmen may have picked the prosperous Chapman because they still saw him as one of them even though he had "made it." Many knew him when he worked behind the counter at John Bidwell & Co. and later at his own businesses. (Few were still around who could personally recall Bidwell's difficult years establishing his ranch in the 1850s.)

The secret ballot in the school trustees election allowed residents to put the town's richest man "in his place." A comment by Alexis de Tocqueville captures the apparent feelings of some in Chico about Bidwell in the 1870s: "In the United States people do not hate the higher classes of society but are not favorably inclined towards them and carefully exclude them from the experience of authority.… In general, everyone who rises without their aid seldom obtains their favor."[10] Although Bidwell noted the election result in his diary as if it were of no consequence, his response was aggressive, immediate—and shrewd.

The School Clash, Part 2: Bidwell Retaliates

Gus Chapman returned to the school board, bringing expertise from his terms as a trustee in the 1860s, when members built the Salem Street School. For the 1870s term, the board met in Carnot Mason's office in the former Wood's Hall above George Dorn's general store. Trustees Rufus Cochran and Dr. Mason, Chapman's closest friend, immediately elected Gus their board chairman and clerk. Therefore, he ran the meetings and wrote up each summary of their actions.

When Chapman arrived for his first board meeting, Mason and Cochran passed to him the sealed envelope from John Bidwell. If Gus opened it with trepidation, his instinct was prescient. Its content was meant to stick Gus Chapman's conflict of interest in Chico's collective craw.[11]

He scanned the content, then read them Bidwell's offer to sell the trustees a full block of his new subdivision on the east side of Orient Street ("Old Chinatown") east of Flume Street between Fifth and Sixth streets for one dollar, forcing Chapman to deal with his conflict of interest in this vote. On the one hand, would he respect his responsibility as a public official to vote in the public interest—that is, to save the public money by choosing the site near Bidwell's Addition? Or would he vote in favor of his own financial interest—that is, force the board to pay more for property near his subdivision? Cochran voted to accept Bidwell's offer; Chapman and Mason voted it down. No explanation for their vote was necessary. Chapman voted for his own financial survival: had he lost the south Chico school site, he faced financial ruin.

Chapman and Mason voted to pay $2,000 for four acres on the Oroville-Shasta Road at Chico's south end. The lot began at the

Little Chico Creek bridge and extended west along the creek's southern bank in full view of the empty block across the road that Chapman had reserved for his family's future house. In 1861 the school site had been the farm where widow Lavinia L. Sproul had started her short-lived school.[12] Chapman and Mason then accepted Chapman's offer to donate half the amount, $1,000. Bidwell could do nothing to stop this transaction. Instead, as a man of iron self-discipline, he would wait to satisfy his appetite for quiet vengeance, or justice.[13]

A schoolboard member today who did what Chapman had done would be indicted. However, nineteenth-century government, in general, enforced no business standards or public ethics. The country's changeable economic climate meant that Chicoans, like other Americans, could sink into bankruptcy and impoverishment without any recourse. No safety net programs softened their falls, no grants helped them rise. In response, desperate people bent rules or disregarded ethics and "gave fate a nudge" when their future or their honor depended on it. Therefore, by the standards of his day, Chapman's conduct, albeit unethical, was legal.

Did John Bidwell remember how he had stretched ethical standards to protect his ranch when it was at risk?[14] In 1852 he had secretly urged members of Congress to reject the very same Indian treaty he had strenuously urged local tribal leaders to endorse when he hosted a week-long meeting on his ranch. Additionally, as a member of Congress during the mid-1860s, he campaigned for and won the mail route to the Idaho mines, benefiting his store and ranch products. In doing so he provoked his other constituents, Oroville businessmen, who claimed their elected representative had sold them out, that he had stolen "their" mail route, a major revenue for their town. Then, again a Congressman, he persuaded Congress to successfully pressure the Central Pacific Railroad, which was about to install the first north-south route through California, to divert tracks east to run alongside his own property. This route benefited his business and "saved" Chico, but it circumvented the straighter, more efficient alternative the railroad company preferred.

The *Enterprise* reported on the school site drama with delicacy. Because Chapman and Bidwell were valuable clients, publisher

Major Ed Hoole and editor Captain William N. DeHaven printed mild affirmatives about Chapman's and Bidwell's new subdivisions. While DeHaven had preferred the Bidwell Addition's downtown location for the school, now he endorsed Chapman and Mason's rationale for the site at the south end of town. This choice, he said, would obviate the concerns of those who thought Bidwell's site was dangerous because it was only one vacant lot away from "Old Chinatown," where opium dens were popular for its residents and a broader clientele. Children would have had to walk through or near there to reach the proposed Bidwell site. In addition, the editor acknowledged that "the lower portion of town [Chapmantown] is as much entitled to consideration as the upper" because most students already lived along the streets in that direction.[15] DeHaven did not ignore Chapman's awkward position.

> Mr. Chapman is aware that his motives will be impugned, and while he feels the delicacy of his position, he is conscious that he has faithfully done his duty, looking solely to the interests of all concerned. His contribution was the result of his hard-won knowledge that he would be personally benefited and in consideration of which he has endeavored, so far as he could, to render an equivalent. Our people must remember that Chapman's Addition is a matter of importance to our town. That its improvements add to the value of the property of the city proper, and that when our lots shall all be utilized, this new town is to take up and extend our privilege for building.[16]

Perhaps out of guilt, Gus Chapman worked all the harder to produce an outstanding school building.[17] Well before his election, when he went to San Francisco to consult with Sutro Company brokers about the bond sale proposal, he toured Bay Area cities to view school buildings and met several times with architects. Trustees Chapman, Mason and Cochran settled on a brick building in an "Americanized Gothic" style which featured a bell tower over its three stories and a full basement.[18] Every detail mattered.

Enlisting Chicoans' interest in the new school, Gus invited

the public to stop by the Chico Lumber Co. office where adults could squeeze into sample school desks. No records state which businesses furnished construction materials for the new building. Cynics suspected Chapman & McKay's mills sold lumber to the $30,000 school project, but, according to the *Record*, the lumber came from an out-of-town firm. Like the Salem Street School construction problems, this new one suffered delays when heavy storms caved in the unfinished roof and undermined the framing, causing the builder to insert heavy metal rods in the replacement walls.[19]

Criticism died once the dignified brick building, Oakdale School, overlooked Little Chico Creek. Its school bell's tone, distinct from those of the Methodist Church South and the Presbyterian Church, became integral to the sounds of Chico. Two additional bridges over Little Chico Creek were built: one west of Broadway and the other on Olive Street (formerly Old Chico Way), enabling teachers and children from central Chico to circumvent the roughness of the Junction. While the school went up, interest deepened in two additional housing developments starting up west across from Chapmantown.

When Chapman extended water pipes to his subdivision, "that provincial town [became] a part and parcel of Chico."[20] To his earlier school donation, Chapman contributed its landscaping: all its trees, shrubs and flower beds.[21] With such financial and material contributions, Gus, in effect, gifted the Oakdale School with the equivalent to what Bidwell had offered. Several generations of Chicoans would cherish memories of that school's long blackboards, tall windows that lighted the schoolrooms and the rich smell of oil student workers used to buff its wooden floors.[22] The school's first class met in 1875 and succeeding generations of students in grades one through six continued there until 1950 when its later replacements there were torn down. Other schools have occupied the building site since then.

With the introduction of water piping to the school, its grounds greened. Lawn irrigation throughout Chapmantown inspired the neighborhood's home gardeners to plant camellias, azaleas and roses around their homes. Fencing already surrounding front yards protected the new plants from grazing cows that, while annoying, kept weeds low in the streets. For decades it was a popular Sunday outing to take a drive to admire the gardens of Chapmantown.[23] As it turned out, the Oakdale School's location did no harm to Bidwell's Addition, where, by October, lots were "selling like hotcakes."[24] And Gus's lots sold out too. But an unruly teenager stirred up new problems for Chapman.

Hot Times

The winter of 1875-1876 was relentlessly dreary. Three destitute Chinese committed suicide, no one was house hunting, desperate transients were filtering into town, lumber sales were flat. And repercussions from a dramatic event on November 9, 1874, carried over into the new year. After a fifteen-year-old boy, a student at the Woodmans' Chico Academy, burned it down, the boy's parents quickly sent him away to avoid arrest. Fearful of another fire, from then on, when the couple caught young culprits smoking or swearing on campus, they sent them to cut a switch from a tree on the playground and then used it to whip them.[25] After that, on New Year's Day, while John Woodman and his son Charles visited with Constable Ben True in the schoolyard, two Academy seniors stoned them, then fled.[26] The assault was outrageous, but attention stayed fixed on the destruction of Chico's only high school.

Gus Chapman was a central figure among Chico Academy parents who immediately launched a restitution plan. The school's loss had affected better-off families who planned to send their children to competitive colleges after graduation. Among those were Fred Chapman, a junior who was approaching graduation, and Mary, just starting high school. They could not expect help from the general public. For years skeptics had been fending off calls for a free high school as a ploy to raise taxes.[27] Opponents, claiming they spoke for poor families needing the wages of their children, labeled high school a frill, only appropriate for pampered children of "rich" parents like the Chapmans or trustee Cochran, whose son graduated just prior to the fire. Therefore, the new Oakdale School had hardly made its start when Chico Academy parents called on it to rescue Chico Academy students needing to complete their requirements for college admissions.

All three trustees, Chapman, Cochran and Mason, had links

to the Chico Academy. Moving fast to get ahead of criticism, they turned over an entire floor in Oakdale School for the high school students from the Academy. To accomplish this, the trustees transferred the public school students from their third-floor classrooms to a rented building. Then they hired Col. Hiram Batchelder, at a higher wage than other teachers, to instruct the Academy's senior class. They also ordered him to maintain his charges' activities at some distance from the younger students. However, once on campus, Fred and his classmates commenced to tease, ignore, patronize and fascinate the younger children. No apparent harm resulted.

With that in place, Chapman and other parents focused on restoring the Woodmans' finances and replacing their school. This led them to take a new interest in the looming election for Butte County's superintendent of education. Because Oroville politicians regularly "tossed" this position to Chico candidates, reserving more powerful state and local positions for their own residents, any candidate from Chico had a better than average prospect of winning. Taking that into account, as well as a new state law that made women eligible for the post, Academy parents persuaded Selena Woodman to run for the position. Her husband was likely not a contender because his reputation, even harsher than hers, made him unelectable. In addition, Chico's biblical literalists took offense at John Woodman's conviction that evolution and science are compatible expressions of God's will.[28]

For Gus Chapman to back a woman was no stretch. His widowed mother had done her and his share of farm work so he could stay in school. At Michigan Central College he had competed with women. When he traveled he never worried because he respected Sarah's judgment about their children, money and property.

Selena Woodman became an active candidate. A stern woman, she had driven herself to manage the school and oversee the live-in students. She led the faculty and taught classes. At work and in school productions, she immersed her students in the "high" culture she embraced but Chico's "plain" people disdained. When she issued an edict that her students could not perform in public entertainments whose dates conflicted with

Chico Academy performances, even some supporters were uncomfortable. From the Woodmans' point of view, proceeds from student performances in debates, readings, theatrics and music were essential for their small school's survival.

One reason parents longed for the Chico Academy to start up again was because they could count on the Woodmans' reliability. Every school year, between late August and June, Academy mothers did not have to supervise their children during the daytime or cobble together daily lessons. In contrast, Chico's public schools sometimes opened as late as November and turned away children and cut off teachers' pay as early as April or whenever the tax funds ran out. The Woodmans' school was at a peak of importance for the Chapmans in 1875, not only because of Fred's college plans, but because they intended to provide an equal education for Mary, an exceptional student according to the published rankings in Chico's newspapers. Over the years, Chico Academy graduates were admitted to the new University of California at Berkeley, as well as Yale University in Connecticut, Vassar College, Mount Holyoke Female Seminary and Wellesley College in Massachusetts, and West Point (United States Military Academy) in New York.

By April 1875, Chapman and D. M. Reavis had launched Selena Woodman's campaign. In order to protect her from the allegation that she was an "ambitious" woman, the Chico Academy's male parents publicly called on her to run for county superintendent. Bowing to their "plea," she started canvassing for votes. She had reason to believe her years as a teacher in Oroville and Chico, as well as her reputation for high academic standards, would overcome the all-male voters' prejudice. To allay their doubts, she crisscrossed the daunting county terrain by stagecoach to garner support. The recently elected incumbent Jesse Wood, her only rival for superintendent, felt secure enough to skip campaigning.[29]

Despite Selena Woodman's efforts, her opponents labeled her "The Ring's" candidate, a reference to Chico's cluster of business owners like Chapman, George Dorn and Frank Lusk who, for years, had shaped town policies in repeated appointments to citizens' committees. Because Mrs. Woodman's backers were well off, her run tapped class resentments that periodically poisoned

Chico's public life. For example, a writer characterized her as having "opposed by every act, look, and word of sarcasm in her power, the development of the public school system...." Then, addressing her supporters, "Take her to yourselves, gentlemen, give her a private school and patronize her generously. But we patrons of the public school do not want her and will not have her thrust upon us."[30] Opponents also denounced her as a selfish woman for seeking a county office, the rightful preserve of men with families to support. Characteristic of *Record* editor George Crosette's anti-Semitism, he suggested that only Oroville Jews supported her. None of Selena Woodman's qualifications, efforts or endorsements could overcome the antagonism.

The victor was a no less worthy candidate: incumbent superintendent Jesse Wood had moved to Chico to serve as the Methodist Church South's pastor. He had a full background in school management and, as the sole support for his wife and ten children, he needed the job as much as Selena Woodman.[31] Although Jesse Wood and Gus Chapman were on different sides of this contest, closer links would follow.

A Welcome Distraction

Townspeople happened upon an incident that diverted everyone from the school controversy. That July, when the annual cattle drive plodding south on the Oroville-Shasta Road crossed the Big Chico Creek bridge onto Main Street, cowboys kept the cattle moving while Bidwell's men gradually added his herd waiting in the Front Street corral. This created a long "parade" of cows slowly moving toward the Junction where the cowboys would turn them onto Humboldt Road toward summer pasture in the high country. In the 1875 drive, however, the cattle had no sooner crossed the Big Chico Creek bridge than the *vaqueros* lost control. Animals wandered off and casually turned in all directions to explore side streets where they spooked horses and sauntered along boardwalks. Watchers fled or enlisted to help gather the strays. One steer took particular interest in Hattie Finnegan and chased the dressmaker every which way until she reached a sturdy tree. There, she darted from side to side to fend off its lunges until herders rescued her.[32]

Money for the "Big House"

As the heat of August descended, townspeople wondered why Gus Chapman, who never lingered in the mountains, remained unusually long at the Powellton mill. Curious, they plied his Chico Lumber manager with questions, but George Turner had nothing to offer. However, they were onto something: this stay was different. He was working on a new speculation, moved, in part, by his growing family's pressing need for space. Keen to make some "fast" money, he recruited Ridge businessmen and valley counterparts, including Carnot Mason and John Bidwell, to join him in a mining venture. Ignoring frequent press exposés about corrupt mining speculation across the West, they formed the Chico Consolidated Silver & Copper Mining Co. in November 1875. So eager were he and company president Ed Aldersly, mining veteran and fellow lumberman, they made ready to head for Oregon mining sites that winter.[33]

However eager Gus was to get underway, he delayed their departure to be with Sarah when she delivered their last child, William "Willie" Winthrop Chapman.[34] With a baby, toddler, grade schooler and teenager, the Chapmans' family home was bursting. Sarah was also organizing the house and family to host the January 1876 wedding of George Turner's daughter Olive to mill worker Alonzo Curtis in their parlor. Sarah's wedding arrangements for Olive, a family favorite, fascinated Mary, 11, and Fred, 17, by now an accomplished musician.[35]

Chapman and Aldersley finally departed in February 1876. Despite rough weather at the Gallico Creek mines in southern Oregon's Rogue River Valley, the men collected handsome rock samples and hastened home. Even though Gus arrived sick from the labor of travel and mining through snow and ice, he and Aldersley headed to the Bank of Butte County where they showed their "take" to partners and friends, assuring them they had found great quantities. However, when Chapman took the rocks to a San Francisco laboratory for testing, they were declared not valuable.[36]

No other rescue from the men's various financial crunches was in reach. In Chapman's case, it meant he had no windfall to fund the "big house" he envisioned. Although Chapman's healthy ego played a role, the house represented more than that. Since the colonial period, businessmen understood that, since credit was based on reputation, appearance was everything. Any doubts about a borrower's ability to pay his debts could mean the call in of other debts, unraveling the precarious structure of credit.[37] As an ambitious businessman, Chapman needed to count a very substantial residence among his assets.

Of course, more prosaic duties continued. Gus Chapman and John Bidwell resumed their reserved civil collaboration on community projects. Notwithstanding their bitter competition over Oakdale School's location and their shared embarrassment over the mining debacle, Chapman, Bidwell and John Gilkyson agreed on another strip of Rancho Chico, including the Edgar Slough, for an addition to the pioneer cemetery.[38] Once again, Bidwell would give up farmland for Chico's benefit.

Without the hoped-for windfall needed to build the new house, Gus raided his assets. He looked first to his most significant and least liked asset, Chapman & McKay. Because flumes were dumping huge amounts of lumber on the market and flattening prices, he convinced McKay to sell their company. Chapman also sold the large parcel of ranchland he still owned south of now East Sixteenth Street. In April 1876 Gus and Sarah sold their Bidwell Avenue (now East Twelfth Street) home, the farm house remodeled by Henry Cleaveland, to master carpenter John Maxson, 68, and his wife Sophronia. No longer able to work in heavy construction, Maxson was finishing desks and chairs for Annie Bidwell's Indian school.

The money went to their new, big house and, in 1879, he had enough left to purchase the controlling shares in Chico's gas and water startup company. He appointed the same directors for both—his close associates Charles Faulkner, George Gilkyson and George Dorn. Charles Stilson had served on both boards, but decided to move on. Just as when they worked at Bidwell & Co., he and Chapman had a strained relationship and, while they were civil, they never reconciled.

The Chapmans' Bicentennial Trip

Gus delivered the Chico Academy commencement speech at Fred's high school graduation in May 1876. Mary, 12, presented her class's present to their teacher and Fred sang "Jersey Blue." Then he and another student read a dialogue, "New Englanders in San Francisco." Now that school was over, it was time for a cross-country trip to visit their Michigan families and deliver Fred, 17, to his New York college.

Once the family reached Sarah's Sickley family in Michigan, she, Mary and the little boys settled in for the summer. Gus, on his first trip home since 1861, visited his half-brother George Babcock and then entrained with Fred to Philadelphia.

There they joined in the centennial celebration of the Constitution.[39] A Chico traveler's lengthy and finely detailed account of the exhibits there, which the *Enterprise* published during their sojourn, may have come from Gus. Its smooth style resembles that of Chapman's in his later extended reports while in state service (treated in later chapters). In addition, Gus's mercantile experience informed him for the account's focus on exhibits of fine furniture and woven goods. The writer also admired complicated laundry ironing equipment that struck him as suited to undermine the Chinese hold on Chico's laundry business. The writer particularly admired a machine that turned out pins for dressmakers. One appeal was its simplicity—it was suitable for a worker with the skill level of a twelve-year-old girl. (Chico's public school teachers were in a constant quandary because many adolescents girls only showed up for classes in-between jobs as laborers or domestic servants.)[40]

When Gus and Fred reached New York City they attended a rally for Democratic presidential candidate Samuel J. Tilden. The politician's remarks reawakened Gus's old fervor for the Democratic Party, an enthusiasm he knew Chico publisher George Crosette would appreciate. Although Gus had become a solid Chico Republican, he wrote to Crosette's *Record* that he had just seen "the next president."[41] Tilden's popularity for his successful prosecutions of New York's corrupt Tammany Hall politicians, led by William "Boss" Tweed, had raised Democrats' hopes and Republicans' fears.[42]

However, once Gus returned to California, he slipped back into his Republican mode and supported Rutherford B. Hayes. The fight between Hayes and Tilden mobilized every ounce of political passion from the already competitive, even combative, party men who organized Chico voters. Passions remained so intense that the Republican State Central Committee, for "the peace and tranquility of the community being paramount," forbade all local party men to participate in demonstrations regardless of who won.[43]

Their concern anticipated conditions in Chico on November 11, 1876, election day, when downtown streets, usually quiet at 7:30 in the morning, coursed with voters and party volunteers. Farmers checked into hotels for overnight stays to vote and follow local results; others planned to stay even longer to catch the national results. Before the Chico polls opened, party volunteers scoured the town for every voter they could claim for their side. They roused men from their sickbeds, "sometimes almost against their will, in order that not a vote should be lost."[44] Teams of Democratic and Republican poll watchers grilled each voter to spot any technicality that might eliminate a vote for the other side. For example, suddenly suspicious of Thomas Walsh's citizenship, Republicans questioned him intently, even though he had been a registered Butte County voter since 1860.

When the polls closed at 5 p.m., "Democrats and Republicans alike crowded that room, each holding his breath for an instant as a [ballot] ... was picked up to be read. When the name [of presidential elector] Sherb was uttered by [the vote counter] a sigh of relief would fall from the mouths of the Democrats, and as [presidential elector] Miller's name was announced the Republicans would heave a sigh of relief."[45] While no evidence places Chapman in the room, his keen interest tells us he would not have missed a second of it.

For Chapman and his Republican friends, Hayes' Chico win was even more exquisite for its slim margin. In Butte County their man won by thirty votes. Similar margins appeared in Placer, Yolo, Trinity and Shasta counties.[46] While Tilden had narrowly lost in Chico and Butte County, for a day or two the news wire continued to project his imminent national victory. Chico Democrats savored their first presidential victory celebration since before the Civil War. By the third day, when the national vote count projected Hayes' victory, Republicans cheered and Democrats stewed. When that result did not stand, country farmers extended their political sabbatical from chores. Waiting for the final tally, partisans on both sides laid heavy bets at even odds. According to the *Record,* Chico wagered approximately $20,000 (over $500,000 today). The payoffs were months in coming. On March 6, 1877, a historic cross-party deal in Washington, D.C., finally handed Hayes a "victory." The drama had exhausted everyone. Chico Republicans ran up a flag, Democrats groused.[47]

The House Goes Up For Sale

While Fred acclimated himself to his freshman year in New York and the Maxsons settled into the Chapmans' former farm house, Gus and Sarah and the younger children lived in temporary quarters. Over the long, rainy winter of 1876-1877 they savored the quiet and planned their new house. It was meant to be the visual focal point of their now successful subdivision, full of attractive cottages housing families with young children they could see twice daily walking past their home to Oakdale School. To achieve this vision, however, they had to wait out another stormy winter like the ones that plagued Gus in the erection of both the Salem Street and Oakdale schools.

Construction waited until early spring 1877. Then the sale of Chapman & McKay and Chico Lumber fell through that summer and the old partners had to gear up again. Despite disappointment and frustration, Gus, helped by a bank loan, was going to have the house he always wanted. That, along with a belief in Chico's growth to 5,000 residents, may have softened the blow of having to work with Bill McKay again.

The Chapmans' canvas for their new home was the entire block Chapman had reserved between the Oroville-Shasta Road and the site of their former remodeled farm house, now occupied by the Maxsons. From that house they had learned what they didn't want. It was set so far back on two sides that, on rainy days, visitors were drenched by the time they reached a door. In his design for the new house, Gus placed the house eastern style: its formal front door was only a few steps from Chapman Street (now East Eleventh Street). Sarah realized her dream, a summer kitchen or, as she called it, a cook house, at the east end of the main house, which avoided summertime cooking heat there.

By October 1878 the new house's interior finishing was well

underway. A reporter was impressed:

> The new residence of Mr. Chapman is now being erect-
> ed. The house is more than a common dwelling house, it
> is a palatial mansion, built in the most approved modern
> style of architecture with several large bay windows and
> each opening so situated as to have a current of air pass-
> ing through the opposite direction. The building proper
> is 28 x 65, two stories and contains fourteen rooms, be-
> sides bath room, pantry and each is supplied with gas
> and water. The finish of the building is the best we have
> seen, and with beautiful grounds surrounding, some
> ten to fifteen acres in extent, all beautifully laid out. Mr.
> Chapman will have the prettiest place in this section,
> next to the Rancho Chico.

According to the *Enterprise*, it was a "dwelling that will be the
largest and finest house in this section, next to Rancho Chico." In
a similar vein, the *Record* deemed it "the largest and finest house
in this section." A hundred years later, Elsa Boydston Brooks,
who lived there as a child in the 1890s, recalled the dwelling as a
long, white house with beautiful rooms. A narrow lawn separated the house from Chapman Street, where a high curb facilitated
graceful entry to and exit from carriages. When the Chapmans
moved into the new house across the street from their previous
one, Gussie, 4, and Willie, 2, would remember no other childhood home; as an adult, Gus Chapman Jr. erroneously declared
it his birthplace.[48]

Unhealthy Water

By the end of 1878 the Chapman children were enjoying their
spacious new home and, as usual, their father, spared trips to
Powellton during the winter, was absorbed by other work. The
mill sale having collapsed, McKay planned for its spring 1878
reopening. Chapman was again in charge of the Chico Lumber
Co. Gus also was preoccupied with conditions at the water company, which had yet to replace the temporary wooden pipes.
The company had earned praise for its purchase of Holly system pumps capable of delivering 43,000 gallons of water per

minute and the large building the company erected to house them. However, community members continued to criticize the company that summer because there was a severe upturn in diphtheria—"brain fever"—and cholera, which clustered east of Main Street near Chapmantown and along Dead Horse Slough running the length of East Eighth Street.[49]

Townspeople were convinced the water company's decaying wooden pipes were delivering outhouse-polluted water to their homes and businesses. The peak of sickness saw Chapman's fellow Republican leader Park Henshaw and his wife bury an afflicted child, only to return home and find their only other child had just died from the same cause. Henshaw's wife left him for her family's home in the east and refused to return. The Fox family lost three children, 3, 9 and 12, within two months. Over May and June fifteen children and three adults ("one a Chinaman") died.

Chapman found the company could not replace Chico's wooden water pipes because it could not afford new iron ones without help from the town trustees who, once again, refused. In the meantime, he began commuting to Sacramento to work at the constitutional convention (the subject of a later chapter). Chico residents might have been impressed by this, but they were more consumed with worry about their families' safety from water-borne diseases. Despite pressures from all sides, Chapman's company still lacked town backing to buy iron pipes. He ignored complaints about the unreliability of Chico's gas streetlights: while the lights only aggravated townspeople, the water problems threatened their lives.

While Chapman and the company board grappled with the pipe replacement problem, they decided to give gas-lighted streetlamps another try. Done well this time, they might sub-due public frustration and generate capital to buy the iron pipes. However, the company also needed a public subsidy for the lights. Chapman again found resistance from residents suspicious of higher municipal taxes to pay for street lighting and those who considered their occasional positioning of kerosene lanterns or a mass of candles sufficient. To win over naysayers, the company installed a few more streetlights downtown and along Salem Street. Chapman met with John Bidwell to explain the value of gas pipes to the Presbyterian Church. In response to Bidwell's concerns, Chapman's employee set up a gas lamp at his front gate. While the skeptical rancher admired the bobbing little light, he dismissed it as a novelty. Because others also remained skeptical, the company stopped at a few lines. Full gas service would not arrive until the mid-1880s when the company laid iron pipes in the town.

While the arrival of a gas option eventually became attractive, Chapmantown residents' attention was diverted by a prospect that disturbed them more: a liquor store was going to open across from their homes on the Oroville-Shasta Road. Gus responded to the frenzy with assurances that no "whiskey shop" would find a place there. Resistance to that affront prevailed for decades.

Chapman had turned rough ranchland into a subdivision for close to 500 Chico residents.[50] In order to accomplish that, he had dealt with its disadvantageous location, competition with John Bidwell for a new school site, embarrassment at how he accomplished his victory over Bidwell and ongoing tensions with William McKay. However, he still had to secure those iron water pipes.

9

The Depression Hits Chico

As 1878 opened, the Bank of Butte County's leadership—President Park Henshaw, Vice President A. H. Chapman and Treasurer Charles Faulkner—launched the latest attempt by Chico businessmen to free northern Butte County from the Board of Supervisors' control. County budgets continued to ignore Chico and its surrounding area's rotting bridges, rutted rural roads and understaffed constabulary.

This time the "split committee" skipped the usual round of local public denunciations and on its own, dispatched three of its members with the usual petitions to add northern-county men to the Board of Supervisors. In Oroville, they placed their proposal on the agenda and fanned out across town to lobby friends and business counterparts. Lawyer Henshaw sought out clients he worked with before his move to Chico and Faulkner approached commercial leaders he had known when he was a banker in Oroville. Chapman called on businesses his mercantile and lumber companies patronized.

Each man tried to assuage the entrenched concerns of the supervisors and other southern county leaders. The Oroville leaders feared that the Chico township's population growth would inevitably shift power from Oroville and the mountain mining districts to the Valley. That shift would create a loss of tax revenue the supervisors counted on from the agricultural wealth centered around Chico. In this round, Henshaw, Faulkner and Chapman tried to persuade their Oroville contacts that, if the supervisors would only add northern-county residents to the board, it would be fair to Chico, all the while assuring the Oroville leaders that their area would remain powerful.

The Chico representatives declined to mention that, if they could win Oroville business leaders' support, new supervisors from Chico would use their majority on the board to split Butte County in two. Henshaw, Faulkner, Bidwell, Chapman and others in Chico planned to initiate a "secret" third phase they omitted from their pitches: once the split was in place, their new county's Chico-based Board of Supervisors would merge their county with a proposed southern Tehama county where agricultural interests also prevailed.

The three men spent several weeks lobbying in Oroville before calling home for backup. John Bidwell, Alexander H. Crew of the Bank of Chico, and merchants Charles Stilson and George Dorn arrived to help them lobby Oroville's skeptical leaders. In the end, they all gave up and went home, chastened by the universal resistance and repudiation that won them the Democratic *Record*'s dismissal as "a few discontented soreheads."[1] On their long drive home, they compared notes and worked on their next approach.

The Long Depression

In May 1876 the lumber market was weakening from the depression and the increasing impact of water flumes led Gus Chapman and Bill McKay to sell their "first-rate" Chico businesses. Their retail lumber yard at Eighth and Main and the Magalia Ridge mill in Powellton went to Charles Holbrook and J. N. McCormick for $22,500 (over $600,000 today).[2]

In the winter of 1876-1877 torrential rains melted six feet of mountain snow. Within hours, valley creek banks overflowed, inundating wheat crops and dissolving roads. Large parts of the valley resembled a lake. Downtown Chico flooded and stagecoach services shut down; with no travel there was no mail. Between May 1 and June 6 fifteen children and three adults died. Of the eighteen, diphtheria took fifteen, among them a son of Sarah's friend Isabelle Crosette and her husband George. By late summer, grain crops failed, bankrupting not only farmers but also their Chico creditors.

Gus's focus was to sell off the lumber company's towering stacks of fir and pine before the transfer to new owners was complete. However, construction had shut down and debtors strained to make payments on their accounts. In a trip to San Francisco that summer, Gus negotiated with a contractor who owed the company for 300,000 board feet of sugar pine. By December, he still had not managed to collect the entire balance.[3] Although Gus Chapman and Bill McKay had sold their businesses and were free of one another, within a year the sale to McCormick and Holbrook fell through, forcing them to revive their partnership.[4]

Compounding their problem in resuming the lumber business, they had to deal with the effects of flumes, which had proved so efficient in the transport of logs that lumber swamped the market just as demand plunged.[5] The Chico flume crossed mountain ridges and swooped down to the valley floor, then crossed Little Chico Creek at Ninth and Pine. There, the trough in Dumpville spewed a waterfall that expelled the log sections into huge, random, unstable and dangerous dumps.

As the excess lumber supply battered prices, Jason Springer & Co., a significant buyer of Chapman & McKay lumber to supply its retail outlets, went bankrupt. When its sash and door factory near the flume closed, fifty Chico men lost their jobs. The Springer Co.'s stores in San Francisco, Oakland and Portland hung on until 1879 when a sheriff's sale dispersed the last of its business property.[6] It was even a struggle for Sierra Flume & Lumber, the new giant of the area, to keep its 50,000-acre operation afloat. When it reorganized as Sierra Lumber in 1879, it had closed all but three of its eleven mills. Its Red Bluff-based owners blamed the economy and restrictive federal land laws for thwarting their efforts to become an even larger integrated operation.

Growing unease about flumes eased some of Chapman's skepticism about McKay's refusal to use them. His ongoing deliveries by oxen-drawn freight wagons had turned out to be a cheaper, more reliable system than the flumes, which were often out of commission from wind damage, fires or rot. The process of flume transport also damaged logs. They constantly battered one another in the flumes' narrow channels as they raced to the valley. Therefore, mountain workers had to cut them into extra-long sections before loading them into the flume's rushing water. Then, when the beaten-up logs arrived at the dump site in Chico, workers had to cut them again, this time to size, creating more waste.[7] (The flumes also transported people and goods to Chico.)

At the height of the flume system in 1879, a Humboldt Road traveler observed fifteen lumber wagons one-half mile from Chico. While William McKay had their mill back in operation and their freight wagons on the road, Chapman still struggled to sell the lumber. Nevertheless, an optimist by nature, he continued to buy new timber stands for the company.

The Family

The Chapmans remained healthy and active. While Fred was away at college in New York, Sarah, 44, was busy caring for Mary, Gussie and Willie. There seemed no end to the furnishing and maintenance of their fourteen-room house, a considerable contrast to what her smaller previous homes required. She was also responsible for supervising fifteen acres of grounds around their house and across Chapman Street where the family's park extended out-of-sight along the creek. On the other hand, her new summer kitchen at the east end of their home was the godsend she had wanted to relieve the house from the kitchen's summer heat.

In the late 1870s Mary's adolescence unfolded in three places: the new house, the North Methodist Church, where she became a Sunday School regular after her brief rebellion, and the Chico Academy where she continued to be an honor student. Always close to her parents, she inherited her quiet personality from her mother and her independence from her father.

Despite the hardships surrounding them, Gus's various investments kept the family comfortable during the depression. Sarah's friend Eliza Camper was also fortunate. Hard-up townspeople who could not afford a new buggy or carriage brought their old ones to her husband Henry's Junction shop for repairs.

Likewise, fellow Methodist John Maxson had bought the Chapmans' remodeled farm house in Chapmantown, even though the depression cost him farm and carpentry jobs. He and his wife Sophronia were elders about the same ages as parents much missed by Chico's new residents. The Maxsons' kindnesses had earned them great affection. They had also garnered sympathy because they had loaned their life's savings to their only child Jane who moved with her husband to Chicago and never visited or repaid them. In a couple of years, when John was no longer able to work, the elderly couple sold the former Chapman house to live in the Odd Fellows Rebecca House near San Francisco. Friends and neighbors helped them pack and then waited for the train with them. John Bidwell, a fan of Sophronia's pies and long a patron of John's woodworking, joined the group to bid them well. William McKay's wife Mary Ann missed Sophronia so much it was not long before she left for a visit.

Ruth Hobart Gilkyson was a North Methodist stalwart close to Sarah. Her devoted and hardworking, but regularly unlucky, husband John struggled to support their eight children and her elderly parents whose years in the Butte County's Methodist ministry had left them impoverished. Even with Gus Chapman's help finding jobs, John struggled from one job to the next. Mrs. Gilkyson packed boarders into their small but well-appointed frame home. Other friends and acquaintances of Sarah supplemented their husbands' wages by selling chickens and eggs. Some offered voice, sewing or painting lessons. Maude Blood sold French lessons to Mrs. Bidwell and others after eyesight problems compelled her to leave Wellesley College in Massachusetts.

Sarah and her friends worked for the church, visited one another at their homes and took walks downtown for sodas. Sarah hosted "socials" that helped the church pay its bills and were also valued by the women for the pleasure they found in companionship. When Fred, now an accomplished musician, returned from college for summer breaks, he played his trumpet with the Neubarth Band. He partied with friends who spread out in the Chapmans' double parlors, or on the verandas in summertime, to perform popular music and hymns. A favorite option was to bring their private concerts to picnics in the family's park along the creek. The company, food, music and setting of the Chapman gatherings were well worth their guests' efforts to hitch up and drive across town.

The Chico Relief Society

The North Methodist church assigned men to the positions that managed finance and budgeting. North Methodist Ladies Aid, the church women's auxiliary, tended to fundraising, children's programs and other projects of their choice. With the depression in place and Ruth Gilkyson in the lead, the Methodist women launched the Chico Relief Society. Capable and compassionate counterparts from the Presbyterian and other churches were also troubled by the suffering evident around them. Tasked to raise money for services to the poor, the Relief Society approached businessmen for monthly contributions of 25¢, but Chico's impoverished population outpaced the women's ability to meet all their needs for food and housing. When businessmen began to feel tapped out and donations slipped, pairs of women called on them at their stores and offices. Despite such transactions' discomfort for everyone concerned, business owners understood the Relief Society's value for them as well: when the needy approached them for help, they referred them to the women.

The ongoing homelessness and hunger began to harden people's attitudes, but Susan Heath Crew, Rebecca Ball, Katie Kempf, Sarah Chapman, Annie Bidwell and others continued their social work. They negotiated with town officials for the use of available jail cells for sick single men. They "borrowed" empty houses, spaces in barns or offered their own sheds to shelter families living on the streets. They hired sick nurses and donated garden produce or canned goods. They comforted poignant victims in despair. Women of the African Methodist Episcopal (AME) Church provided similar aid to hard-pressed members of their community.

While Chico had long been a town where drifters and grifters were a familiar sight, some turned aggressive. With a rise in thefts, sympathy for the destitute turned into fear of hoboes or "bums." At bedtime Eliza Camper's husband Henry began to tuck his valuables in his pants which he rolled up and placed under his pillow. One night a thief quietly broke into their house on West Fifth Street and found nothing on the bedroom chest of drawers. Then he reached under Henry's pillow, snatched the pants and ran off.[8] A year later, in 1877, the *Enterprise* reported that "the increase in hoodlumism and gambling as of late assumed mammoth proportions, and the crowds of loafers who hang around the street corners and in some localities monopolize the sidewalk to the annoyance of the ladies as well as the business community. [These have generated] calls for prompt action from authorities."[9]

Homeowners began locking their houses—the Chapmans among them—after trips to Charlie Stilson's store where they bought out his entire stock of slide bolts. This rise in thefts and violence reflected a trend across the state's interior. Walter Fisher noted the anxiety during his California travels: "There is not difficulty in accounting for the fact that a majority of rural Californians sleep with the rifle in the bedroom and travel revolver in pocket."[10]

By January 1876 W. C. Hendricks, the Oroville Democrat who had narrowly defeated Chapman for the State Senate seat in 1873, tried to appease his uneasy constituents by introducing a bill to make highway robbery punishable by a life sentence or death.

Once the rainy season arrived and downpours destroyed the winter wheat, desperation became so deep it took Chico in a dire direction. While anti-Chinese sentiment had persisted around the margins in town since the late 1860s, in late 1876 the frustrated populace erupted and formed a full-blown campaign to drive them out. That morally troubling development confounded many of Chico's traditional leaders. For one thing, farms and town businesses relied on Chinese laborers, whose wages were about half that of white workers. As he had done with respect to both sides in the Civil War, Augustus Chapman walked a fine line between the anti- and pro-Chinese leagues. Since the regular employees in his home and businesses apparently were Whites, he escaped anti-Chinese antagonism.[11]

In early 1876, after anti-Chinese men burned down his new barn, Bidwell appealed to town residents to join him in standing up to the anti-Chinese. However, no one publicly came to his side and anti-Chinese sentiment intensified and spread. Chapman's associates who employed Chinese labor were cautious about taking a public stand and attracting attention to themselves. However, when they crossed paths at the bank or relaxed over oyster dinners at Tom Dooley's, they complained among themselves about the anti-Chinese "troublemakers."

The issue became personal for Chapman when arsonists started torching Chinese buildings and those of their employers. As the owner of his new "stick" home and a lumber yard, he could not ignore his vulnerability. He lodged his watchman R. T. Carter in a room above his Chico Lumber office. While Carter never saw an arsonist, in February, when he heard glass break below, he crept downstairs, flung open the office door and fired his IXL five-shooter at the window, narrowly missing the intruder who escaped.[12]

The Chico anti-Chinese organized a "camp" or chapter of the "Order of Caucasians" in 1876. Its 200 members made it Chico's largest fraternal organization.[13] Because members included "some of our very best citizens," non-members like Gus Chapman didn't consider it dangerous. Chico's small size meant that, in their daily lives, the Chapmans and their children ordinarily associated with Order members or their families, including Fred's teacher Hiram Batchelder and two other faculty. The president of Gus's Odd Fellows Hall was on the Order's board, as was their butcher and fellow Methodist John Kempf, whose wife was Sarah's friend. In addition, members included at least four lawyers, a minister, two important builders, a farm manager, a newspaper publisher, the county recorder and eight other respected businessmen. Prominent farmer and Chapman friend Dan Bidwell, John Bidwell's half-brother, was sympathetic to the new cause until John brought his influence to bear. Democrats and Republicans were active members.[14] Because numerous laborers were also members, later historical accounts erroneously discounted the Order, as if it only spoke for poor, new arrivals—outsiders and "radicals."

In fall 1876 Sierra Flume & Lumber opened a major sash and door factory in Chico. Since June, Chicoans had counted on the company president's promise to employ over 200 white men. By December, however, the company had hired few white townspeople and instead brought up a trainload of Chinese workers under contract from the Chinese Six Companies in San Francisco.[15] A protest meeting at the town hall on December 9 drew hundreds of small business owners, skilled and unskilled workers and professional men. No sources place Gus Chapman there. If not, he had plenty of sources who were present and informed him about a violent faction that was supposedly "secretly" organized later that evening to attack the Chinese. Soon labeled the

"Labor Union" by opponents, it bore no relation to the purpose or organization of worker unions forming back east. It became, in effect, nothing more than a violent gang made up of mainstream members.

No authority stepped forward to investigate, let alone prosecute, the perpetrators of the ongoing Chinatown arsons and attempted killings of Chinese. The only resident with the courage to object and call for action against such criminals had been John Bidwell the previous spring, when his new barn was burned down. Finding no support, he had stepped back and stayed home from church and travel to guard his property.

Because Gus had a broad range of business, civic and family contacts throughout Chico, he was well placed to glean information about anti-Chinese actors and incidents as they unfolded. Among those well-placed to inform him "on the street" was his former lumber outlet manager George Turner, now a supervisor at Sierra Flume & Lumber. Another was anti-Chinese Hayden Jones, a carpenter and Chapman & McKay customer who lived behind the lumber yard. Jones railed against the Order of Caucasians because they refused to employ violence to drive out the Chinese. Despite the demands by Jones and others to use violence to expel them, Order leaders refused to endorse such methods. Chapman was well-acquainted with the very large and charming Constable York Rundel who became controversial as he navigated pro- and anti-Chinese labor politics.

When the anti-Chinese so-called "Labor Union" assembled in "secret," the members' random shootings led to multiple killings that the town marshal and the anti-Chinese sheriff declined to investigate, they crossed Gus Chapman's personal "red line."

10

Chapman: Chico Vigilante

In December 1876 intermittent meetings and public rallies sprung up in response to the past year's arsons on Chinese buildings and assaults on Chinese workers. By March 1877 none of those crimes had been investigated. On March 14 a party of six armed white men walked after dark to Christian Lemm's ranch east of Chico and shot-to-kill six Chinese workers at rest in their hut after clearing brush for him. (The ranch was located approximately at the intersection of today's Highway 32 and Forest Avenue.) Four lay dead, one was gravely wounded. The injured sixth man played dead and escaped to Chico's Old Chinatown on Flume Street, about two miles away. Men there took him across town to New Chinatown next to the railroad tracks, where leaders sent for Constable Ben True.[1] He was the only official they trusted because he treated them with respect and mediated between them and employers. True and a Chinese went alone to the Lemm Ranch where he protected the crime scene from gawkers and prepared for removal of the four bodies by wagons to the morgue in the basement of the Fetters & Williams furniture shop on Broadway. True found the fifth victim alive, but he soon died.

On March 17, three days later, three men set fire to an Old Chinatown building on Flume Street at 2 a.m.[2] At 3 a.m. they set fire to a New Chinatown building near the tracks on Orange Street. Chinese watchmen, with water buckets at the ready, quelled the flames at both locations.

Chico Chinese leaders agreed they could not expect aid from anyone other than Constable True. Once again, there would be no town or county investigation, let alone protection. They sent emissaries to the Chinese Six Companies in Sacramento and San Francisco to plead for help.

Later the next morning word of the Lemm Ranch killings had spread and law enforcement headed out to assess the scene, but no town or county investigation ensued. Meanwhile, it became known that the Chico Chinese had sent for help from their Sacramento and San Francisco leaders. News of the killings had spread throughout the Chico township which withdrew from downtown in a heavy silence, according to reports.

With news that information about the killings had reached the big cities, Gus Chapman formed a private vigilante committee of business leaders—the Citizens' Executive Committee on Anti-Chinese Crimes—to circumvent Chico government's refusal to act. (It will be known here as the Chapman Committee, imparting ex post facto credit for his role.) Chapman's appeal was stark in its declaration that the actions at issue were not justifiable as partisan politics—they were crimes. He recruited men who, like him, objected to the unspoken policy of town trustees and police to ignore *every* crime against the Chinese and their employers. Although many in Chico were uncomfortable about the rising level of violence, it was Gus Chapman who stepped forward and rallied them into action. The text of his call has not survived, but its message resonated with businessmen and farmers who showed up, ready to restore justice to Chico.[3]

Among the motives that drove the recruits were anger and fear. According to the *Record*, reason also played a role. The men who answered Chapman's call recognized it was imperative to reassure their Sacramento and San Francisco insurance brokers and investors that they could count on the responsible businessmen of Chico to restore order and protect property. The speed with which they met and embraced the role of vigilantes suggests Chapman underscored the imperative for immediate, direct action. Had there been a debate about what justice required, it would have continued for weeks and perhaps never been resolved. But Chapman was not philosophically inclined—he was a problem-solver who willingly put himself at risk financially, and now physically. He co-owned a Main Street lumber yard, owned a frame home and another under construction, all of which were vulnerable to the anti-Chinese antagonists who were "loose cannons." He must have realized drawing attention to himself as the principal leader against the anti-Chinese would exponentially expose him to danger, but the immediate launch of a swift and decisive investigation that produced arrests and prosecutions was required. While Gus Chapman's call to stand up to the anti-Chinese was self-serving, it was also courageous.[4]

The Chapman Committee

The March 1877 meeting drew 150 men. No list survives, but press coverage mentioned the presence of significant town leaders, including John Bidwell, physician William Fitch Cheney, as well as Ed Hoole and George Crosette, publishers of the two Chico newspapers. They immediately elected "Augustus Chapman, Esquire" chairman of the only vigilante committee in Chico history. Chapman's central role in this episode disappeared from Chico history until 2009 when research led to the first and only full account of the anti-Chinese violence.[5]

Gus was ready. He immediately appointed close associates—two Republicans and two Democrats—to his executive subcommittee. He was, of course, one of the Republicans; for the second, he appointed Dr. William Fitch Cheney, president of the California Medical Society and a former Union Army surgeon (who horrified townspeople when they learned he had performed surgery on himself). While Cheney enjoyed wide respect, any Republican other than Chapman would have selected John Bidwell for one of that party's two slots. However, their past strains explain why Chapman invited Bidwell to attend as a "regular" committee member.

Gus chose George Dorn, who had purchased the Chapman, Titcomb & Bush store, and jeweler Charles Ball to represent the Democrats. Ball, like the two Republicans, had been anti-Chinese, but after the Lemm Ranch killings he dropped his membership in the ardent but largely nonviolent Order of Caucasians. His wife Rebecca and Sarah Chapman held both elder seats allotted to North Methodist Church women. Like Ball, Dorn had just dropped his Order membership. (Dorn and Chapman were partners in other local speculations, including the gas and water company.)

At the initial meeting all the volunteers arrived ready to find suspects, make citizens' arrests and deliver prisoners to Chico's jail. They left the lawyers among them to sort out how to charge, indict and prosecute them. Chapman appointed George Crosette and lawyer J. F. Hutton to compose the bipartisan resolution.

The seventy-five men who returned for the second meeting in March approved their draft with some changes. They also approved the Chapman Committee's ex post facto hiring of ex-sheriff Sam Daniels who was already calling on suspects. When members Ball and Bidwell picked up their mail at the post office (formerly Bidwell's post office), they found letters from the perpetrators threatening arson and worse unless they fired their Chinese workers and stopped the Chapman Committee's investigation. Targets included three hotel keepers, two or three merchants and Sydnia Ann Jones, a well-off widow who owned a store and farm. Tipped off by a clerk, Sam Daniels followed the man who mailed the letters, then arrested him at his residence. Despite the risk, the committee members ignored the threats. Although the Chapman Committee had made a strong start, the local anti-Chinese outnumbered the vigilante group.

R. B. Hunt, a San Francisco private detective, and James Hamilton of that city's police department, both hired by the Chinese Six Companies, checked in to the Chico Hotel. By this time, the Chapman Committee was already reviewing Daniels's preliminary findings and a subcommittee was building a reward fund from donations by the state, the Six Companies, Chinese in Oroville, other Chinese and Chico residents.[6] A. H. Chapman donated a well-publicized $20 (about $550 today).

Sam Daniels worked in parallel with the San Francisco detectives. With some help from the now-shamed Chico police, they identified suspects linked not only to the Lemm Ranch crimes but also arsons, killings and assaults that had been ignored until then. Rumors had been rife about likely suspects for months.

Town police or constables started receiving suspects the detectives and Daniels delivered to the Chico jail, which quickly "filled to overflowing." This sweep extended well beyond the attacks on the Lemm Ranch workers. A majority of these arrests, which took place the same month as the killings, were made on charges linked to crimes committed, but ignored, in 1876.

The Chapman Committee also handled public relations. Chico was receiving hard hits in national newspaper coverage. Apparently Gus's job was to repair the town's reputation. He delivered

Chico's "line" to editors in New Orleans, Chicago, Boston and elsewhere. In order to throw them off the scent, he declared the murderers and arsonists were probably Chinese warring among themselves. Chapman's public relations approach succeeded. It diverted the out-of-town newspapers from reporting on the extent of anti-Chinese influence on Chico's town government.

That version also fitted with Republican Chapman's still characteristic loyalty to working white men, recently renewed on his trip east. Although now well-off, his empathy was anchored in his Michigan days when he, too, was poor and struggled to rise. Now a businessman, he recognized that men of all classes were valuable clients at his lumber yard.

Even though Chapman had excluded John Bidwell from the group's executive committee, the rancher was a key part of the vigilante campaign. He had alerted the post office staff in his office building to stay alert for threatening letters. His established reputation as Chico's best known leader meant he was the committee member the state press sought first for information and opinions about developing events. When press outsiders asked him about Chinese labor in Chico, Bidwell wrongly told them "no one anywhere" in Chico had replaced white men with Chinese workers. He also declared anti-Chinese activists had attracted idlers to Chico and that "cases of real want are rare, but when known they receive immediate attention from the Chico Relief Society."[7] In the latter comment, he crossed a line with Relief Society women, probably including Sarah Chapman and Annie Bidwell, who were indignant at his understatement about the needs they struggled to address. So Gus donated $50.

With District Attorney Leon Freer's approval, the Chapman Committee hired attorney Park Henshaw to interrogate arrestees. Henshaw and Chapman worked together on the board of directors at the Bank of Butte County. There were so many suspects other lawyers helped Henshaw with depositions. Outside, around City Hall, the Chico Guard and the local militia kept the jail under around-the-clock surveillance. This was not to protect the anti-Chinese prisoners from escaping or being lynched, but to prevent their "rescue ... from outside" by a growing coterie of their friends and families.[8]

Known as a skilled writer, Chapman had long been called on

to draft resolutions, prepare application essays and later, submit extensive reports to the state. In his telegraphs to eastern newspapers and journalists about the perpetrators' arrests, he omitted mention of the defendants' broad local support and assured that prompt justice was underway. After that, the national press's interest began to wane and soon died out altogether.

In April 1877 wagons packed with almost two dozen men were escorted from the Chico jail to Oroville for trial. The Chapman Committee, helped by the Oroville Chinese and the Chinese Six Companies, retained Chico lawyers Albert J. Gifford and J. F. Hutton to assist county attorney Freer in prosecuting the suspects. The Grand Jury swiftly dismissed charges—or, as the *Record* reported, "ignored charges"—of arson against eight of the men. Trials for the remaining defendants began in late April. For almost two months, Chico attorneys for both sides, law enforcement officials and citizen witnesses were in Oroville at the Superior Court.[9]

Among those convicted was carpenter Hayden Jones, 51, the rabble rouser Chapman knew as a customer who lived near his lumber company. Jones had been one of the most zealous speakers during the December night anti-Chinese rally in Bidwell's forest east of downtown (probably the area now known as Annie's Glen by Big Chico Creek). He implored spectators to join a "secret" group ready to use violence to oust the Chinese from Chico. Later, during Jones's trial, Chapman happened to be in Oroville serving as a juror on a different case. Even though Jones had entered a full written confession, character witnesses on his behalf from men like Chapman, whose praise of him as a working man, albeit modest, gave him hope. He was visibly shaken, therefore, when the jury convicted him of arson and sentenced him to twenty years in San Quentin State Prison.[10] There is no way to know why Chapman helped Jones, apart from Gus's years of familiarity with him as a neighbor and regular customer.

When the trials of the Lemm Ranch suspects ended in late May 1877, the court released every arson suspect except five who participated in the murders; all five pled guilty. Judge Warren Sexton, on the Butte County bench since the early Gold Rush days, assigned all but one to twenty-five years at San Quentin.

The Chapman Committee distributed the reward fund. Although local men pressed the members to deny any share to the San Francisco detectives, the committee assigned them a portion. With the committee's work now completed, it dissolved and Chico's town trustees turned to other divisive issues until the next round of anti-Chinese crimes.

Gus Chapman had built his reputation over almost twenty years in Chico, only to endanger it in the school site issue. His formation of the 1877 vigilante committee investigating hate crimes against the Chinese undermined his popularity, but not his reputation as a man of principle, courage and leadership. That, and his contributions to Chico's development, positioned him to address more of the town's problems at the same time his longtime associate, California's next governor George Perkins, invited him to address issues at the state level.

11

Republican and Workingmen's Party Candidate

By early summer 1878 Augustus Chapman was ready to draw on his political capital. He was financially successful, had demonstrated courage in launching vigilante justice against the anti-Chinese criminals and his efforts to split the county had garnered him public respect. Of particular value, he maintained good relations with Democrats despite his switch to the Republican Party. In addition, Gus was well-regarded by the editors of both Chico newspapers and had managed a civil relationship with Republican John Bidwell, despite their lingering strains. He was ready to try again for election.

His opportunity arrived via a circuitous route. In 1878 the depression in San Francisco led thousands of men to rally against Chinese workers and their employers and jointly accused them of stealing jobs from whites. Rousing speeches by Denis Kearney and William Wellock called for violent attacks to drive them out of the country. Their message reached Chico where it energized local anti-Chinese and worried farmers dependent on their labor. As the popularity of Kearney and Wellock's new Workingmen's Party spread, Democrats and Republicans were both thrown on the defensive. Across the state they suspended their rivalry and allied with one another to stop this rogue third party. Unlike the established parties, which had ignored issues of unemployment, poverty and immigration, the Workingmen vowed that, in their hands, state government would resolve all those issues by driving Chinese labor out of the work force. To that end, the Workingmen's Party demanded a new State Constitution.[1]

The Chico Relief Society

In fall 1876 Ruth Hobart Gilkyson, founder and stalwart leader of the Chico Relief Society, gave San Francisco economist Henry George a tour of Chico prior to his speech that evening on the depression's effects on California. She offered firsthand examples of local "mechanics and laborers" whose unemployment or low pay left their families impoverished and reliant on church women for food, medical help and rent money. In his classic work, *Progress and Poverty*, Henry George found similarities between the situations of rural workers in California and industrial workers on the East Coast.

Prior to the Civil War, factory workers in the east had found seasonal unemployment relatively painless, and even productive, because layoffs gave them a "break from routine" and a welcome chance to go home and help on family farms. Similarly, in the 1850s when young Gus Chapman worked in a pre-war farm town, he was able to return home to help his mother with harvests. By the late 1870s Chico laborers, whose families were across the continent, had nowhere to go when they could find no work.[2]

In March 1878 forty-nine men converged at Town Hall and launched Chico's branch of the Workingmen's Party.[3] A Chapmantown resident, Pennsylvania native Joseph Campbell, 56, became the local party's first president. Members included bootmaker Bob Bill Baker, a Mexican War veteran and California gold miner in the 1850s who nicknamed his daughter "Money." Also joining was James Chamberlain, carpenter, property owner and taxpayer since the 1860s. His role was to sell subscriptions to the group's newspaper.[4] Six of Chico's boot- and shoemakers followed the lead of their fellow artisan William Wellock and joined the new party.[5] Elias Stuckey, Chico public school teacher and beekeeper, urged fellow members of the new party to "crowd out the old [Democrat and Republican] party men and supply their places with honest laboring men."[6]

In addition to Joseph Campbell, some Workingmen members lived and worked within two or three blocks of Gus's home and his lumber company. Some were his employees and customers. He was their customer and their children knew his children.

Chapman & McKay's lumber outlet was the Junction precinct's polling place where the Workingmen's Party was favored.

Joseph Campbell scored a coup when he scheduled William Wellock to give a Chico speech. Wellock was launching his first promotional party tour, which featured a Sacramento rally. However, after a hostile crowd there frightened him, he canceled his Chico stop and returned to San Francisco. Although disappointed, Chico members kept up hope because of their party's impact in San Francisco, where support for the Workingmen's Party leaders Kearney and Wellock was at a peak.

The Chico branch's members, while loyal to the Workingmen, stood on the moderate side of its spectrum. For one thing, they were uncomfortable about Kearney's reputation as a rabble-rouser because they did not consider themselves "rabble." The term "Kearneyism" captured a fleeting place in Chico's lexicon as a code word for anything extreme or radical. It described, for example, the disheveled condition of Dr. Carnot C. Mason after he experienced buggy problems near Chapman's mill. By the time he reached Chico, Mason looked "more like a broken Kearneyite than a professional gentleman."[7]

Dr. Mason and his good friend Gus Chapman were likely uneasy about the new party's direction, which went beyond their own perennial concerns about slow growth, unemployment and education. Like them, Chico Workingmen accepted core values of the existing political and economic systems. While they endorsed economic individualism and private property, it never occurred to them that government should be a problem-solver in their personal lives. Whatever the Workingmen stood for, and they were divided among themselves, socialism was not their goal. They did not want to control government so they could seize property; after all, private property was a core tenet. The moderate Workingmen's Party model represented the general longing for ownership of small farms and businesses.

Chapman never forgot the privations of his youth so he understood the Workingmen's issues, but also the necessity of private investors to drive the economy. Republican Augustus Chapman, therefore, dealt with the contradiction by becoming, in effect, an intermediary between his party and the local Workingmen. There is no way to know when he realized his good relations with the new party during the depression could benefit his own political ambitions.

Earlier attempts to rewrite the 1849 State Constitution had been unsuccessful. However, in late 1877 a majority of voters defied their traditional parties and supported the Workingmen's referendum to convene a state convention to replace the original State Constitution with a new, more egalitarian one. The next question, therefore, was which party would dominate in crafting a new plan for the state of California.

State residents were to vote in mid-June 1878 to elect the party delegates they wanted to represent them at the constitutional convention in Sacramento. Faced with the remarkable growth of the Workingmen, Democrats and Republicans quickly adopted a novel strategy. As Neil Larry Shumsky put it, "The election was to be a contest between the Workingmen on one side and every-one else on the other."[8] Following the agreement their leaders negotiated, Butte County's Republican and Democratic parties merged into a single "Nonpartisan Party" with the common pur-pose to stop the Workingmen from rewriting the Constitution in their favor.

Workingmen's Party members had only to choose their constitutional convention delegates from among their county members. In contrast, the Democrats and Republicans, in their unfamiliar and unwelcome roles as Nonpartisans, had to get together in advance of the convention and pick which Repub-licans and Democrats would run against the Workingmen's candidates for convention delegate seats as Nonpartisans.

In 1878 Gus engaged in the series of elections: the selec-tion of convention candidates, the writing of the Constitution and the looming election of the next governor. Each is treated separately.

The Nonpartisan County Convention: Testing the Waters

In June, elections in each county would designate delegates to the constitutional convention. The Republicans and Democrats, as Nonpartisan Party members, had to field candidates from the northern and southern parts of Butte County to run for the Nonpartisan slots on the ballot. They had to choose candidates with a chance to draw votes for the delegate position away from the Workingmen. For Democrats and Republicans to share the preliminary county convention and vote together on candidates to represent them was unprecedented. In order to do so, they had to be civil and willing to compromise.

However, first they had to confront a familiar problem: the Chico men refused to meet in Oroville and the Oroville men refused to meet in Chico. They finally agreed to meet and work through their differences in the village of Biggs, a reasonable distance from each city. This convention provided Gus Chapman a political opportunity at a time in his life when private business had lost its appeal.

The Republicans and Democrats from Chico who went to the Biggs county convention were town leaders, but they reflected only part of the town's political diversity. Central Chico was substantially Republican; in south Chico the combined Oakdale and Chapman's Addition's precinct was divided among the two major parties and Workingmen. The Junction and Dumpville districts had previously been Democratic but were now precincts where the appeal of Workingmen particularly threatened to pull voters away from the Democrats.

Despite their nonpartisan nomenclature, the delegates who gathered at the depot to await the southbound train's arrival that morning were still Democrats and Republicans at heart. However, they knew they had to stand with their rivals against this upstart party of outsiders that excited their common disdain, resentment and fear. This meant they had to pick candidates from among themselves who could best attract voters tempted to back the Workingmen. At the depot that morning the major Republican names considered to represent northern Butte County were Frank Lusk (a Democrat in his Ohio years), John Bidwell, Augustus Chapman and Josiah Boucher. However, Bidwell had declined the nomination and declined to attend the convention.

Frank Lusk would later become a principal player in Chapman's life, but, at this point, they were only part of the general town leadership with little else in common. Lusk was still new in Chico, having made his start there in the mid-1870s when he entered general legal practice with A. J. Gifford, a genial and respected litigator. Before long, Lusk's advice to the town trustees led them to appoint him town attorney and town clerk.

Disapproval never fazed Lusk; he focused on building his legal practice to represent the powerful. While Chapman was an occasional client and John Bidwell became increasingly important to him, his retainer from San Francisco's Chinese Six Companies infuriated local anti-Chinese who casually accused him of "double dipping" from the town's treasury. Lusk's defense of the Chinese made no claim for their civil rights as understood today. With backing from the Chinese consul, Six Companies contracted its immigrant labor force to interior Valley farms and ranches. For over a decade its distant directors relied on Lusk to defend their Sacramento Valley countrymen in trouble, be they perpetrators or victims. In late 1877, for example, he defended two Chinese defendants who ran lotteries Marshal York Rundel wanted to close. Lusk also assisted in prosecutions of Whites who wronged Chinese. In 1879 he backed up Butte County's prosecution of a man and his sons who murdered two Chinese miners on Butte Creek. In 1878, therefore, because Lusk was a Nonpartisan candidate whose record could never attract Workingmen's votes, both parties declined to back him as a delegate.

Among the Republicans, John Bidwell was the obvious choice to run for delegate to the state convention. He was not only the town's founding citizen, he had been a delegate to the 1849 state constitutional convention. (He acknowledged later that business commitments had kept him from its proceedings.) Even George Crosette was ready to endorse him.[9] However, Bidwell was emphatic—he did not want to be a delegate. Only three years previous he had lost a bruising campaign for governor. In addition, the ongoing potential for anti-Chinese violence against his property kept him at home to personally patrol it. Although Bidwell was not among the men headed for the Nonpartisan county convention in Biggs, some men present discounted his protestations as false modesty and kept his name on the ballet.

Republicans Josiah Boucher, 59, and his brother David had arrived in California from Pennsylvania in 1855 to seek gold but soon became cattle ranchers. Old timers in Chico remembered that, even though the Boucher brothers had lost 5,000 head of cattle in the floods of 1861-1862, they had prevailed after a mighty struggle. David Boucher won election to the State Senate but died before completing a single term. He left his bachelor brother to look after his family. David's daughter was a classmate of Mary Chapman. Josiah Boucher's solid reputation and community sympathy for his personal circumstances made him an attractive candidate.

While Augustus Chapman had long been drawn to political office, financial demands had allowed him little time for anything but his business enterprises. As president of Humboldt Road Co. and Chico Water & Gas Works, he was constantly dealing with maintenance and improvement issues. However, as an active Republican Gus made time for the Nonpartisan convention. He went to Biggs with no organized support and was unprepared to fight for anything complicated. He carried only his own vote and two proxies from his Oakdale precinct.

The political passengers jockeyed with one another for support as their train rolled south to Biggs. Like the northern Butte County Republicans, the Democrats would also pick a candidate for their half of the Nonpartisan delegates. However, the Democrats on board considered this journey a relaxed get-away because they had already decided to nominate James Reavis, 31, for the north county slot. While apprenticing to become a lawyer, he was the bookkeeper for his family's major ranch between Chico and the Sacramento River. Reavis championed farmers' rights in general but condemned the Workingmen as communists for challenging land monopolies.[10] The Reavis family's origins in the Deep South were reflected in their lingering loyalty to the Democrats, even though Republicans were more simpatico to their economic interests in California.

The ongoing depression was driving an exodus of Democrats to the Workingmen's Party. This exasperated *Record* publisher George Crosette, who, even through the Civil War years, never waned in his loyalty to the Democrats as the only friends of the poor. However, men at a Workingmen's meeting in Chico had heard Crosette vow to oppose the Democrats joining with Republicans as Nonpartisans to defeat the Workingmen. Then, when information filtered north about Denis Kearney's inflammatory rhetoric at packed San Francisco rallies, Crosette decided he could best stand up for Democrats by running for that party's spot on the Nonpartisan ballot. When told at the depot that party members had already picked Reavis to represent them, Crosette relaxed and, fortified by the whiskey in his flask, traded jokes with a farmer while enjoying the train ride.[11]

When the Northern Butte County delegates from the downtown, Junction, Dump, Oakdale and Dayton precincts exited the train in Biggs, they suspended their horse trading to acknowledge the Biggs Brass Band's welcome and greetings from their host Marion Biggs, 55. While some split off to stop at the Plantation Hotel bar, the rest strolled on to the Baptist Church with Biggs, a "sturdy prairie schooner" of a man. In California since 1850, he established his large southern Butte County farm in 1864. The *Enterprise* described Biggs as "tall and slender. He combs his hair like Andrew Jackson, he has a nose like Roscoe Conkling and a voice like George Tickner Curtis."[12] A Democrat, Biggs had completed two terms in the State Assembly and, at the time of this 1878 county convention, was president of the State Agricultural Society.

When Biggs, a family man with a roving eye, convened the Nonpartisan convention, he opened with his characteristic appreciation of "the ladies," commending them to the visiting men as sweet, intelligent—and fecund. Even in a speech to school commissioners, "the subject of ladies predominated." The *Record* publisher, in an indulgent mood, euphemized Biggs' line as "gallantry."[13] Biggs's additional remarks were evidently less notable.

At their close, the uncomfortable churchwomen escaped and the politicos moved pews, positioned spittoons and lit their cigars—they were ready to negotiate. Crosette was in his element. While he had "kind of wanted" to be a Democratic candidate, he settled back and took notes. He had rarely or never witnessed the inside workings of his favorite quarry, Chico Republicans. As they squabbled, he worked on his column for the *Record*.[14] Watson Chalmers, editor of the Republican *Enterprise* and delegate from the Junction, also took a keen interest in the "log rolling, button holing and wire pulling" of his party leaders.[15]

Democratic nominee Jim Reavis chaired the meeting and

called for the county's Nonpartisan local party leaders to create a joint statement of objectives they could adopt to lend credibility to their appeal against Workingmen in the coming election of delegates to the convention. Reminded the joint "platform" must attract Workingmen's Party voters, they agreed to ban Chinese immigration and declared vague support for the division of "large" but otherwise unspecified landholdings. They endorsed four-year terms for county office holders. With longer terms, Republicans and Democrats could keep their usual hold on county-elected offices long enough to shut out upstarts like the Workingmen's Party which they expected to die out over time. Their platform distinguished between "men of property," industrious, worthy citizens like themselves, and "men of money," the monopolists and land speculators who, they argued, were the real culprits the Workingmen should oppose.

With a platform in place, next on the agenda was for Democrats and Republicans to pick who would run as Nonpartisans against Workingmen in the June 19 election for county delegates to the constitutional convention. When the Oroville Democrats arrived in Biggs they were already unified behind their south county man M. R. C. Pulliam and their north county man Reavis from near Chico. While the Democrats arrived prepared to relax, Republicans in northern Butte County were, as usual, at odds.

The open Republican slot centered on Chico where competition was intense. When the remarks of A. J. Gifford failed to raise a groundswell for his law partner Frank Lusk (until recently an inactive Democrat), he seconded Oroville Republican Charles St. Sure's nomination of John Bidwell.

As Gifford pressed the case for Bidwell, however, he encountered the reservations of men who had urged Bidwell to run but had heard him adamantly refuse. Gifford also heard from men who cautioned that, like Lusk, Bidwell was unelectable because he was unpopular with both Democrats and Workingmen. Nevertheless, his backers kept him in the running.

Josiah Boucher's candidacy was an easier sell for the Republicans' north county Nonpartisan slot. He was an uncontroversial, well-liked, solid citizen who wanted the job. When Reavis called for the caucus's first straw ballot, the north county delegates cast fourteen votes for Boucher, twenty-nine for Bidwell and nine for surprise candidate Gus Chapman. Without a majority, they had to vote again. In this round there was again no majority, but the vote totals had been close enough that control of a third vote would fall to Gus Chapman's handful of votes. While Chapman had initially declared himself out of the running, his name continued to surface. His civic and Republican leadership, as well as his history of friendly relations with Democrats and Workingmen, kept his name in play.

Why would Chapman allow himself to become a "spoiler"? The politics of the situation invite speculation. He may have felt tempted to keep the contest open until Boucher could pick off some Bidwell votes and, with Chapman's votes, overtake Bidwell's lead. He also may have believed that, based on Bidwell's wishes, the rancher's name would be removed. In that case, the contest would come down to Boucher versus himself. That might give Chapman a real chance. As the Chico area delegates returned to the church after a break for drinks at the Plantation's saloon, they remained in a deadlock. They knew their failure to assemble a majority behind a candidate looked bad, but that was an old story in Chico politics. As they walked, they shared a laugh: Oroville had brought two undertakers and a coroner expressly to "lay out" [prepare the corpses of] the Chico men who regularly lost to Oroville candidates.

Chapman had a slight advantage because of his good reputation in Oroville, which he had frequently visited on lumber mill business. Chapman's nominator, for example, was Dr. Lewis Burwell, a "Virginia gentleman" whose affability and courtesy won him friends across social classes and political parties. A lumberman from Dogtown (now Magalia) near Chapman & McKay's mill, Burwell was a veteran Southern Democrat who had developed ties to the Workingmen's Party.[16] The Republican Chapman's seconder was County Sheriff William Schneider, Oroville's anti-Chinese Democratic delegate, who was also affiliated with the Workingmen's Party. Chapman's strong support from Chico anti-Chinese and Oroville Democrats with links to the Workingmen represented a small but politically potent coalition in the present political climate. That support suggested Chapman could draw votes from the significant population of anti-Chinese in the county's two major towns.

However, just when Republican backing for Chapman's candidacy was attracting notice, he rose, thanked his supporters and withdrew his name, swinging his supporters to Josiah Boucher's column and, thus, the winning margin. George Crosette later recalled that "if he [Chapman] had only consented to run no one could have beat him."[17] Chapman explained, with politically appealing "modesty," that he had withdrawn because he carried two proxies' votes who told him whom to support. For him to win, he might have needed to cast those ballots for himself and, had he done so, those individuals might have felt "betrayed." As Chapman had done in the 1860s store issue when he left Bidwell's store and in the 1874 school issue, when he won the school location for his subdivision, he once again prevailed over John Bidwell in a public arena.

The Biggs convention rewarded Chapman's "generosity" by nominating him as the Nonpartisans' candidate for an unusual delegate position—he was to run against Workingmen to represent a third district—Butte, Plumas and Lassen counties—at the constitutional convention. This position was newly created in accord with tactics of Deep South legislators who used it to limit the power of elected Blacks. In the California version, legislators gerrymandered or configured a few urban districts to concentrate Workingmen voters. Then, to build a majority favorable to their own candidates, they combined many lightly populated, rural districts dominated by Democrats and Republicans. The Nonpartisans picked Chapman to run in one of those districts.

When word reached Bidwell that he had lost the delegate nomination, albeit in a contest he had expressly declined to enter and, all the worst, one in which Chapman played a role, he was livid. Bidwell charged into the *Record* office where he exploded at Crosette: he felt "deeply humiliated by the disgraceful proceedings inaugurated by the idiots who introduced his name as a candidate after telling everyone who asked that he would not be a candidate because business duties would keep him at home."[18] Bidwell apparently added this to his list of Gus Chapman's offenses.

After his rant appeared in print, Bidwell returned to the *Record* office where, contrite, he asked Crosette to publish a more conciliatory statement. In light of the profuse, probably abject, apologies of his supporters, he offered absolution. He granted that his friends had acted with "partiality in an emergency and under great provocation."[19] To this assessment, Crosette appended his comment that Bidwell had no idea what had gone on at the Biggs convention.

The Workingmen Prepare to Run

In early June 1878 the Workingmen's convention to select their northern candidate met at Antonio Pazle's store in Chico. Fifteen of them were to pick men to run against the Nonpartisan candidates in the north and south sections of the county that the Biggs convention had just chosen. Another would run against Chapman for the third district slot. Teamster David Campbell opened the nominee selection to anyone who subscribed to the Workingmen's ideas or platform: equal taxes for rich and poor, opposition to Chinese labor, salaries of public officials graded to the wages paid to skilled mechanics and restrictions on both water and land monopolies.

The Butte County men took hope from news that not only had Sacramento just elected a Workingman as mayor, Santa Cruz elected Workingmen as mayor, city clerk and a councilman. On the other hand, these northern Butte County men also knew that the radical reputation of "Kearneyism" had cost their party seats in Santa Rosa and San Rafael.

Among moderate Chico Workingmen were Elias Finley, Chico town trustee and hotel owner, and Thomas Broadwater, builder and arch-antagonist of publisher George Crosette. Broadwater sustained extensive injuries when Crosette, for some political reason, beat him with his cane on West Second Street, near the entry to the newspaper's upstairs office. Another Workingman, farmer Samuel Crose, worried about the futures of his four sons. The youngest was 14 and none had work prospects in Chico beyond their jobs as day laborers. Crose was a recent state leader of the Order of Caucasians.

The Workingmen nominated as their candidates lawyer John T. Daly for the north county and Dr. J. T. France of Gridley for the south county. Each would run against their Nonpartisan counterparts recently selected in Biggs. The victors of that summer election would go to Sacramento in the fall to work on a new Constitution.

The Workingmen could not settle on a candidate to run against Augustus Chapman, the Nonpartisans' candidate for the multi-county Senatorial district slot. With few members and less organization in Lassen and Plumas counties, their prospects of competing with Chapman were dim. At first, they decided to forego a nomination to that seat. Then they made a bold, even stunning, move: they would not run against Chapman, they would nominate him. They declared he was "one of the same stamp as the men nominated in [the Workingmen's Party convention in Marysville] and ... not an old party hack like the majority of Nonpartisan nominees."[20] With this, the Republican Chapman became a candidate of the Workingmen *and* the Nonpartisans for delegate to the constitutional convention.

The Oroville *Mercury* agreed, declaring Chapman was "heart and soul with the people as against the monopolists."[21] In support, the *Mercury* cited his support for equitable property tax rates—the well-off must pay their full share. Chapman's endorsement by Democrats, Republicans and Workingmen indicates he had won the esteem of dedicated partisans who ordinarily opposed one another's views. That cohesion was short-lived. Lassen and Plumas Workingmen took exception and demanded their party choose one of their own, ending Chapman's brief moment as the Workingmen's choice. The Workingmen withdrew their pick of Chapman and chose William Wagner, who ran Buck's Ranch, a mountain hotel.

In the June 19 election Chapman won the third district slot by 841 votes, suggesting he carried some Workingmen's votes. Even though Wagner did not campaign, perhaps because his business tied him to his remote location, he grumbled that "the press and the pulpits" refused to back him. In addition to the *Mercury*, the Biggs *Register* noted Chapman's unique political strength and endorsed him as "peculiarly fitted, through an evenly-balanced mind" and possessed of other virtues.[22] With Chapman representing the third multi-county district, rural Chico's Josiah Boucher would hold the northern Butte County slot and Biggs's M. R. C. Pulliam would represent the southern position. Marian Biggs would win a competition for a statewide seat.

Although the Workingmen lost in the delegate elections, in Chico their party attracted numerous Democrats who resented their party's partnership with Nonpartisan Republicans. For example, in the central Chico precinct, the Workingmen's ticket won 32 percent of the votes. South across Little Chico Creek in Oakdale's and Chapman's subdivisions, they polled 40 percent. In the Dumpville district where many flume workers resided, they won 90 percent. The populous Junction precinct between Chapman's Addition and the downtown was another Workingmen's stronghold. There, they most likely won a majority of delegates but both newspapers omitted that outcome.[23] Both Chico newspaper publishers feared the Workingmen's Kearney associations and regularly challenged that party's legitimacy.

Despite its strong showing in Chico's 1878 delegate election, the Workingmen's Party activities subsided while the new Constitution was under construction in Sacramento over the winter of 1878-1879. The Nonpartisan Party evaporated immediately and the traditional parties again parried with one another and the Workingmen in the intense ratification campaign that followed in the late summer. Gus Chapman had to dance around issues at a furious pace the whole time. But he found firm footing in the subsequent governor's campaign when his good friend George Perkins ran for governor. His renewed commitment to the Republicans would result in the greatest—and most ruinous—opportunity of his life.

12

Delegate to the State Constitution Convention

The lumber business was at its season's peak in September 1878 when Gus Chapman headed for the state constitutional convention in Sacramento. With no qualified buyers for the lumber company in sight, he left George Turner, veteran of the Mexican and Civil wars, to cover for him at the Chico lumber yard while Bill McKay continued milling lumber at Powellton.[1]

By the late 1870s Gus had won respect for his business comebacks and appreciation for his civic work. The convention represented a different kind of opportunity, a chance to make a stellar contribution, one that might qualify him for a significant public position.

However, circumstances worked against him. He arrived in Sacramento late because his chronic malaria had flared up in August. At home in bed, he slipped in and out of fever and chills. Sarah kept the children busy with chores, while she administered his quinine and alternately sent for ice or piled on blankets.

By the end of the month, he felt well enough to go camping with "Uncle Dan" Bidwell, half-brother of John Bidwell (who found him something of a trial), and Charles Faulkner, their mutual friend at the bank. If Chapman, no outdoorsman, expected this mountain escape from Chico's blistering heat to top off his recuperation, he miscalculated. Soon after they made camp, he slipped into a full-blown relapse. Although his companions realized he should return home, he was too frail to ride for hours on the rutted roads to Chico. Bidwell and Faulkner stood watch, tending Gus as best they could while they waited out his bouts of fever and chills.[2]

Because Chapman didn't reach the convention for its formal opening in mid-September, he missed all the preliminary jockeying for positions. Had he been there early and become a "player," he would not have had to fit himself into the margins of the "game." Early arrivals had already written the rules and appointed the committees.

When Gus checked in, fellow Nonpartisan delegates—Republicans and Democrats—briefed their new delegate representing the third district—Butte, Lassen and Plumas counties.[3] Gus found himself in the same position as the Workingmen's Party delegates, who also arrived too late to count for much. Even though they had forced Democrats and Republicans to draft a new State Constitution, the Workingmen had only elected about a third of the delegates from the few districts the Legislature had gerrymandered to concentrate their voters. When those neophyte delegates arrived in Sacramento, they encountered politically savvy Nonpartisan delegates already in the key positions. Nonpartisans stood ready to outvote Workingmen on one parliamentary technicality after the next. Their tight organization not only kept the Workingmen on the defensive, but the Nonpartisans' long mastery of knotty parliamentary propriety secured them opportunities to weave into the new Constitution the same core policies and practices by which they and their predecessors had been governing California from its start.

Making it all the worse for the Workingmen, they were not unified. The urban and rural delegates regularly defied their party's positions, voting with Nonpartisans. Therefore, they were never able to challenge Nonpartisans' control over most committees. While clashes between Democratic and Republican delegates occasionally compromised their "nonpartisan" facade, in the main, their alliance held.

Despite having been finessed out of plum assignments Chapman could have used to showcase his skills, he tackled the work assigned him in his usual quiet way. For example, he was one of the Engrossment Committee's lawyer members. As the adjunct to the powerful Rules Committee, its members drafted the legal language of the resolutions that would go to a final vote.[4] An experienced lawyer, he found no challenge, let alone glory, on that committee because it kept him off the floor and out of debates. On the State and Municipal Indebtedness Committee, his only proposal became the constitutional mandate that voters pay their taxes in the district where they elected their assessor.

However, Chapman did have one meaningful appointment: chairman of the Education Committee. He had never forgotten how, as a poor child, public education readied him to better his life. Since then, he had learned school management as a Chico public school trustee during the 1860s and 1870s. There is no direct way to assess Chapman's accomplishments in the Education Committee's meetings because "the business of the State Constitution for the most part took place in [unrecorded] Committees."[5] However, Gus reported its actions to the Chico press. He was among those arguing for the new Constitution to require popular election for the state superintendent of schools. In addition, he drew on his Chico experience when he authored the mandate that every school district must keep a free public school open at least six months each year.[6] At that time, schools stayed open only until funding ran out. According to Chapman, he proposed four-year terms for county superintendents of schools and supported other measures that advanced local control of public schools. When he backed the obligation of school districts to fund foreign language instruction, he helped the Workingmen who had many immigrant members.[7]

As a leading supporter of the Chico Academy, Gus was aware of Reverend Woodman's use of corporal punishment. No committee record reveals his position on beating as a school discipline, but the proposal to outlaw it did not prevail. His long experience with schools that educated women and men together and his plans to send Mary to college suggest he was in the majority that guaranteed continuance of women's admission to all the University of California's academic programs.[8] Some Chicoans had reservations about his support for a proposal to transfer control over schools from local district residents to county superintendents; he evidently considered the county local enough. He favored no public funds for any "religious sect or denominational school whatever" or any private school. This particularly targeted Catholics' demand for Bible readings in public schools.[9] In addition, Chapman voted to make the University of California a constitutional corporation, a status that guaranteed its independence from political incursions. He also vindicated the Workingmen's earlier trust in him when he supported, on the floor, their proposal to reduce the workday on public works projects to eight hours.

The Education Committee's productivity was possible because most educational issues lay outside the current political line-of-fire which focused on Chinese labor and railroad issues. Complaints about the 1879 State Constitution over the years have overlooked its positive contribution to public education. According to historian Andrew Rolle, the committee Chapman chaired treated issues "with dignity and foresight."[10]

The Butte County Delegates in Action

Until mid-winter 1879, when the Education Committee finished its work, Chapman's responsibilities shrank to drafting motions off the convention floor with other lawyers on the Engrossment Committee. Because its members spelled one another, Gus was able to make returns to Chico to oversee Chico's gas and water services. His presence at home acquainted him with the growing controversy there, like elsewhere, over the Constitution's draft. For example, in Chico the Republican *Enterprise* fretted about delegates who "gave away the store" to the radicals, while the *Record* fulminated that property "rode herd."

Unlike Chapman, Josiah Boucher and Marion Biggs, the other northern Butte County delegates had hunkered down in Sacramento for the duration. While the contrast between the city of Sacramento and Chico, a farm town, must have fascinated Boucher, maneuvers by the convention's shrewd politicians left him on the sidelines. More comfortable in the churning political mix was Marion Biggs, Butte County's Democrat under Nonpartisan cover. A veteran of the State Legislature, the Missouri-reared farmer was a glib orator whose call, "Mistah Chahman [chairman]," resonated through the chamber.[11] While always ready with an opinion on any issue, thrift was Bigg's favorite cause. He prodded delegates with persistent and passionate, albeit unpersuasive, pleas to eliminate expensive convention minutes. Biggs also worked hard to reduce the seeming prerogatives of public employees with their regular pay and long-term jobs.

He championed the popular cause of railroad regulation and opposed Chinese immigration.

Chico Water & Gas Works

While Chapman had been an investor in the Chico Water & Gas Works since 1874, his January 1879 acquisition of the majority interest came at a time when his confidence was at a peak.[12] He believed, as principal owner, he could make a difference. He knew he had built a reputation as a "turn around" man: while other lumber companies were failing, he and McKay were keeping their lumber company afloat and Chapman had narrowly rescued Chapmantown from its early sales crises. Now, with a compatible board of directors, he could make improvements to each service. He evidently had faith that effective utilities could make a profit and also pay off in political support from a grateful community.

As the new president and general superintendent of the utilities, he intended to expand public interest in gas lighting. However, there was an immediate crisis: "[T]he fluid of questionable compound now being drawn from the water pipes around town contains too much water to burn and rather too much gas for a beverage."[13] Resolution to such company crises would soon test him.

The Next Challenge: Ratification

While business demands were compelling, politics continued to lay claims on Gus, who had to be in Sacramento when the constitutional convention closed on March 3, 1880. Butte County's representatives voted with the convention majority to approve the new Constitution. A statewide referendum would decide whether to ratify it. Although Nonpartisans, heavily influenced by lobbyists, were disappointed that state regulation of railroads had passed, they had successfully protected other major interests and thus voted for the new Constitution.

The moment the convention disbanded Democrats and Republicans resumed their traditional rivalry, relishing the recovery of their genuine political identities. Democrats still opposed the new Constitution, but, if ratified, the party was determined to control its interpretation. Beyond that, their priority was to destroy any future role for the Workingmen's Party.

After the constitutional convention closed, Chapman remained in Sacramento for the Republican caucus's March 8 meeting. He heard party leaders instruct him and the other delegates about to leave for home that, even though they had just voted to pass the new Constitution, they were to organize local campaigns to defeat its ratification in their districts. They had created the document under pressure from the Workingmen and now they were determined to destroy it so California would revert to its original Constitution.

Gus had plenty of time to mull this over with Josiah Boucher on their way back to Chico.[14] Back home, he ignored the party mandate. He rarely criticized the proposed Constitution and, in general, avoided his party's campaign for its defeat. Chapman apparently did not fear the terms of the new Constitution.

For once, work at the lumber company appealed to him. He spent an unusual amount of time in Powellton, where he made up to Bill McKay for his extended absences by purchasing over 2,000 acres of timber near the mill.[15] This was another example of Chapman's willingness to buy against the market. This time it was timber. A few months earlier it was the troubled water and gas utilities. Whatever his private thoughts, Gus Chapman was still a risk-taker, something of a gambler and certainly a speculator.

The Public Debates and Votes

With the gubernatorial election looming, the ratification campaign would either be a useful warm-up for Republicans or it could undermine support.[16] With this in view, Chapman's restraint in the ratification campaign allowed him to avoid becoming controversial. That was important to his new political direction: unify Chico behind the candidacy of his Oroville friend and backer George Perkins.

But voters were not ready to think about the gubernatorial election. They worried about how the new Constitution would affect their businesses, farms, schools, Chinese labor and taxes. Townspeople regularly conveyed their concerns to Biggs, Chapman and Boucher. When challenged, Chapman had no choice but to acknowledge he and Republicans had voted for ratification in the convention, then switched to oppose it. There was no way to reconcile the conflict. Therefore, when he had to take a position, he limited himself to ambiguous statements about his support for his party's platform. However, the other representatives' responses were direct and vigorous: Democrats Marion Biggs and Josiah Boucher supported the new Constitution's passage and ratification, even though they disagreed over some of its implications.

Other Republicans were adamantly opposed. In brief, they claimed the few Workingmen's provisions in the new Constitution made it too radical for California. In the debate that followed, Chapman was fortunate because his cautious restraint provoked no criticism from the Democratic *Record* or the Republican *Enterprise*. Perhaps their editors gave him a pass because Chapman had cultivated support from both of them with copies of documents and regular observations to fill out their convention coverage. In the end, both newspapers opposed the "New Constitution," which George Crosette branded "Kearney's Kommunistical Konstitution." The Chico press's skepticism was common across California, except for its only significant champion, the *San Francisco Chronicle*.[17]

Chico was typical in its spirited debate, pitting "new Constitution" and "old Constitution" supporters against one another. Residents' keen interest satisfied Thomas Jefferson's vision of a free people who pursue the truth "according to their own lights." The all-male voters from every section of the township packed meetings to debate the draft from every conceivable angle, as often as three or four evenings a week for more than two months. All the while, Chapman fended off considerable pressure from fellow Republicans to assume a more active role in rejecting the new Constitution.

Workingmen brick mason Evan Knapp and Baptist preacher Elias Finley created the New Constitution Club to lead the adoption campaign. Desperate for every vote statewide to protect their modest gains in the new Constitution, Workingmen had managed to insert a slightly reduced property tax, which succeeded in attracting votes for the Constitution by farmers like John Bidwell. Chico Workingman Joseph Campbell praised

Chapman's Education Committee, which had been generally supportive of the new party's egalitarian values. Charles Ball, president of the town trustees and a member of the Order of Caucasians, also campaigned for the new Constitution.

However, new Constitution backers were at a disadvantage, particularly in Chico, because one provision required a two-thirds popular vote to secure a county split. Chico residents, still keen to break away from Oroville and Butte County, could never garner such a large majority. In addition, the provision stipulated that if Chico, for instance, were to lose again in the next election to form a separate county, its supporters could only try again at four-year intervals. Chapman's credentials as a county-split leader suggest he was unhappy with the new Constitution on that account. In their votes at the convention, his opposition had neutralized Boucher's vote for it. Boucher's vote certainly defied his and his northern Butte County constituents' determination to split away from Oroville.[18] In a lengthy poem about the convention, Crosette attributed this "treachery" to Boucher:

A Colloquy on Kearney's Bilk:
Between the Writer and an Ex-delegate

Concerning the county seat, of course
I must confess
That the power to reorganize the same is taken
from the mass.
If my constituents were swindled, I'm sorry
and all that
But I had to ring that in, my boy, to accommodate
Judge Pratt.[19]

Boucher denied he was under the sway of Orrin C. Pratt, a land mogul who liked the new Constitution's tax relief. Dismissing Crosette's attack as sour grapes, Boucher explained that he had refused to loan the *Record*'s publisher some cash he needed to get home from Sacramento. Crosette, always stubborn, countered that Boucher had "worked against his own [north] end of the County." He chided Boucher that if he "never finds any owner for the earrings which the chambermaid at the Capitol

Hotel found in his bed, he can send them to us with history of the same...."[20] This might have packed a wallop had Boucher not been an elderly bachelor accountable to no one.

The New Constitution Club's campaign coup in Chico was a Town Hall speech by Charles J. Beerstecher, who led the Workingmen's Party at the convention. A German-born lawyer from San Francisco, he was campaigning for one of three seats on the new State Railroad Commission. Crosette, leery that a Workingmen's Party revival would threaten Democrats, repeatedly reminded readers that Beerstecher was "one of Kearney's lieutenants, a regular sand-lotter [Kearney supporter]."[21] Such warnings drew a large, enthusiastic crowd to Town Hall at Third and Main. They were excited to hear one of California's most infamous orators.

Cheer after cheer greeted Beerstecher's appeals. For two hours he championed the proposed Constitution, discounting charges that the Workingmen's support meant it was a radical measure. George Crosette had to admit that Beerstecher impressed him: "His appearance is prepossessing, and he has a good voice and a stock of funny stories." At the meeting's close, he conceded the speaker was roundly cheered. "We confess that we rather like Beerstecher. He is a communist and 'sand lotter' of the first water and has pluck enough to defend his faith."[22]

While John Bidwell criticized the new Constitution, he pointed out that the tax breaks would benefit him and, therefore, would vote to ratify it. Bidwell allowed the Workingmen and farmers of the New Constitution Club to use his forest grove for their dance and concert after Beerstecher spoke. In return, the Club's officers urged their guests to drive carefully through his grounds and to respect his shrubbery.

On hand were Democrats Marion Biggs and Josiah Boucher who were friendly with "Doc" Burwell, the Magalia Democrat. He nominated Republican Chapman for a delegate seat at the Biggs convention. "Beerstecher is evidently one of the boys and circulated ... until a late, or rather an early hour in the morning...."[23] No record tells where Gus Chapman was that night, but his pleasure at the progressive Tilden speech he and his son Fred had heard in New York suggests he would have made a point to hear Beerstetcher's California version.

Chico men also organized an Old Constitution Club in opposition to ratification. Its odd mix of members could just as easily have supported the new Constitution, based on their previous political positions. For example, the club's supporters included both *Record* publisher George Crosette and the *Enterprise*'s new editor Bill "Dad" Atwell. Joining them against the proposed new Constitution were men from the Order of Caucasians who opposed Chinese labor. They included shoemaker Bob Bill Baker, '49er carpenter William Bradley who, along with carpenter Schuyler Walker, had remodeled Chapman's farm house, and merchant G. W. Dorn. Republican town trustee A. F. Blood had signed on, as had Democrats brewer Charles Croissant and Constable Ridgely Tilden, son of Chico's late Democratic leader Dr. William Tilden. The popular new owner of the Pony Saloon, Henry McLennan, also opposed it. Dr. Carnot C. Mason circulated a resolution against the new Constitution which was endorsed by "over 100" old Constitution supporters.

On May 7, 1879, Californians voted by a margin of 10,825 to adopt the so-called "child of the Workingmen's Party."[24] Interior valley farmers, rather than laborers, provided its margin of victory. In the Sacramento Valley, such supporters included three of California's largest landowners: Hugh Glenn, John Bidwell and Orrin C. Pratt. In Butte County the new Constitution squeaked to victory by only 55 votes, 1,508 to 1,453.[25] The Chico precincts again divided by narrow margins. In fact, central Chico was evenly split with 150 votes for and against ratification. The Junction precinct, which included Gus Chapman's business sites, supported the Workingmen's campaign for the new Constitution: 136 votes in favor and 97 against. The Workingmen's efforts also carried the Dump precinct. The editors of the *Record* and the *Enterprise*, which had each opposed the new Constitution for different reasons, mulled over how little influence they had wielded. Passion about the issues lingered into December when a Chico waiter punched a Kearney man.

Republicans' claim that its passage hurt California's reputation in the East mirrored *The Nation*, which claimed it was "not the constitution of a civilized State" but rather "the first incorporation into American constitutional law of *pure* communism."[26]

By contrast, Henry George, the populist economist declared, "It [the new State Constitution] is anything but agrarian or communistic for it entrenches vested rights—especially in land—more thoroughly than before, and interposes barriers to future radicalism by a provision in regard to amendments which would require almost a revolution to break through."[27] The farmers celebrated its delivery of tax relief and took hope from its promised check on the power of the railroads. The new Constitution aroused both anticipation and dread.[28]

The Gubernatorial Election: Chapman's Takeoff

In the upcoming contest for the governorship, Republican and Democratic parties were again rivals for state offices and both vied with Workingmen candidates. Pending this election, Chapman continued to be discrete but his abiding affinity for long-held Democratic Party causes such as labor and public education for the poor lingered on. The renewal of his friendship with George Perkins at the constitutional convention had given him a focus and avenue for his own driving political ambition. As one effect, this made him a disciplined Republican.

Gus Chapman's attention now was the campaign for governor. He would devote every hour he could spare from his other business ventures to advance the election of his old friend, benefactor, and mentor George Perkins of Oroville.

Little Chico Creek bridge, looking south, on the Oroville-Shasta Road.

William "Willie" Winthrop Chapman (left) and Augustus "Gussie" Chapman Jr., sons of Gus and Sarah Chapman.

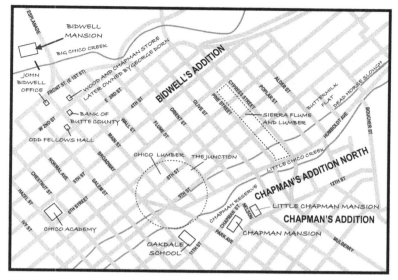

Chico in the 1870s, showing Chapman's subdivision, Chapmantown (Chapman's Addition), and other sites.

In his competition with Bidwell for the location of a second public school, Chapman became a school board trustee to ensure the Oakdale school was built across from Chapmantown. He later made up for his conflict of interest.

The original ranch house on Doc Smith's Sunflower Farm, purchased by Chapman for his family. Connie Ballou, illustrator.

Architect Henry Cleaveland designed and expanded the Chapmans' ranch house as a showplace for his new Chapmantown subdivision. The house, in a present-day view that still closely matches Cleaveland's design, was placed on the National Register of Historic Places as the Little Chico Mansion in the 1980s.

Flume carrying lumber to Chico. The flume also carried goods, the injured and thrill seekers to town. Chapman & McKay preferred their less expensive and more reliable oxen-drawn freight wagons.

WATER AND GAS WORKS, CHICO, CAL.

When Chapman was president and owner of the water and gas utilities, he had the water tower built.

The water and gas utilities' downtown office. (Note the spittoon.)

A check to A. H. Chapman for $134 from his friend Daniel Bidwell.

Chinese workers in John Bidwell's fields.

Although Ben True was the town marshal, the anti-Chinese ran him out of town after the Lemm Ranch murders and trials. Here he is a Sacramento railroad officer. Courtesy of James A. Dimmit.

RESIDENCE OF AUG. H. CHAPMAN,
CHAPMAN'S ADDITION, CHICO, CAL.

Chapman's mansion on Chapman St. (now E. 11th St.). He bought and kept open land all around it as a private park. It was converted into the Sisters of Charity Hospital which burned down in 1909. Oroville-Shasta Rd. is in the foreground.

William Earll was an important source of funding for Chapman. His mansion, built in the 1870s, compares with that of Chapman's. Both men understood the importance of owning beautiful homes as visible financial assets used to secure business credit.

Fred Chapman (not pictured) was an agent for the Wells Fargo & Co. Express, located in the Bank of Butte County.

13

Avoiding Chico's Fight Over the New State Constitution

While in Sacramento as a delegate to the constitutional convention in 1879, Gus Chapman revived his friendship with George Perkins. The former Oroville merchant had been a leading Republican in Butte County during the 1860s, then served as a state senator and was now a state party leader ready to run for governor. On the basis of unfolding events, it is clear that Perkins was influential in Gus Chapman's new role as president of the Chico Republican Club.

Bidwell had established links with Perkins when both were principal leaders in Butte County during the 1860s. Bidwell's store was a significant client of Perkins's wholesale business. As buyers for Bidwell & Co., first George Wood and then Gus Chapman stayed in Oroville, sometimes for days, to work on orders and organize deliveries to Chico. Perkins's confidence in both Bidwell's partner Wood and their employee Chapman led him to back the two men's break with Bidwell to open their own store. Perkins may have turned against Bidwell over the Chico man's leadership in the initial county-split campaign that erupted in the early mid-1860s.

In the early 1870s, after Wood & Chapman was underway, Perkins, the first president of the Bank of Butte County newly opened in Chico, appointed Augustus Chapman to its first board of directors. Therefore, while both were in Sacramento for the 1879 convention, they reignited their friendship. During this period, Chapman signed on to support Perkins's run for governor.[1] This may have influenced Republican Club decisions in a meeting in Bidwell Hall on Broadway, reopened for a few years after George Dorn turned Wood's Hall into offices. The party's planning was underway for the upcoming Republican Party's county nomination convention in Oroville. In previous county conventions, the Chico men had low expectations about their candidates winning the party nominations. The Oroville majority had rarely allotted Chico more than the school superintendent position. This time Gus, Carnot Mason and their committee had reason to hope the Oroville-run Republican Party would nominate north county candidates for county positions, including sheriff and assessor. Their optimism rested on the apparent private understanding that Chapman and Mason's agreement to run Perkins's campaign for governor in northern Butte County precincts would be rewarded by Oroville support for Chico candidates on the pending ballot.

The Chico Republicans were not disappointed. When they reached the convention in Oroville, their counterparts surprised them with hearty greetings and warm admiration for their choices. They savored the respectful treatment, which culminated in confirmation of their hopes. The first signal of their new influence was that Oroville business leader Max Brooks nominated Gus Chapman to chair the convention.

Gus led the meeting through nominations, then called for votes.[2] By the meeting's end in 1879 the Oroville leaders not only re-nominated Chico's Jesse Wood as county school superintendent, they allotted the county treasurer slot to Richard De Lancie, an Order of Caucasians member and Oakdale school teacher. Then they backed A. H. Chapman to run for county assessor. At the convention's end, the Democratic *Record*'s George Crosette evinced a hint of sarcasm when he complimented county Republicans on their "well-oiled machine."[3]

Chapman could now be confident of Chico Republicans' support in Perkins's election and, in exchange, Chico Republican names would be on the ballot for county jobs. Butte County Republicans caught the train to Sacramento where the state Republican Party convention was to nominate its candidate for governor. Mason and Chapman brought drafts of their speeches conveying Perkins's home county's support for his nomination. Although he had been living away from the county for almost a decade, their affirmation at the statewide event would represent party support from his home base—"the people who knew him when." At the end of the convention, the party nominated George Perkins, who now counted on party unity to develop a formidable election campaign.

George Perkins

Republicans statewide unified behind Perkins for governor because they respected and trusted him. All the same, they harbored other considerations. Because Republicans anticipated the Democratic and Workingmen's parties would unite against them, they hoped Perkins's early life story would convince some Democrats and Workingmen to cross over and vote Republican.

At the age of twelve, Perkins ran away from his Maine home to work on various ships; when one docked in San Francisco in his early teens, he debarked for good. From there he followed miners to the Sierra Nevadas where he briefly panned for gold and was counted in the 1850 census. Then, after a stint as a teamster, he went to work in an Oroville grocery store where he rose from carry-out boy to manager. He eventually bought the store and renamed it Perkins & Co., which he developed into a major retail and wholesale business.[4]He was elected to the State Senate in 1869 and then again for another term. In 1873, when State Senator David Boucher, a Chico area farmer and brother of later constitutional convention delegate Josiah Boucher, suddenly died, Perkins sold his Oroville store to his brother and partner James Logan and filled out Boucher's term.

From there, Perkins gravitated to state and national politics as the natural complement to his increasingly far-ranging enterprises.[5] During the 1870s, Perkins was a co-owner of the Pacific Steamship Co., operated passenger and freight carriers and was a principal officer in the Arctic Oil Works, the Pacific Steam Whaling Co. and the West Coast Land Co.

Perkins had earned considerable respect because his steamship line's freight rates undercut railroad rates. However, after he made a deal with Southern Pacific Railroad that led him to raise shipping rates, critics accused him of collusion with the railroad. Similar rumors continued to spread while Perkins's campaign for governor was underway.

Like Chapman, but for different reasons, Perkins was not antagonistic toward Chinese immigrants. In his years as a general merchant in Oroville, he traded with white and Chinese customers alike. The Chinese population there was so large that the two races were more financially interdependent than in Chico, influencing Oroville residents to coexist. Although Perkins was president of the San Francisco Chamber of Commerce, when he ran for governor he remained sympathetic to agriculture's need for Chinese labor. Perkins also intended to monitor the new Constitution's Board of [tax] Equalization and the new Railroad Commission's regulatory powers, both of which Republicans considered a threat to property rights.

Even though Republicans hoped Perkins's appeal could cross classes, they recognized that most voters were divided between the Workingmen's and Democratic parties. That left Perkins with little support outside his own party. On the other hand, it was to Perkins's advantage that Workingmen and Democrats remained rivals after the convention, competing with one another for the same voter base. In that light, Perkins could be elected if Republicans could undermine unity between Democrats and Workingmen.

In order for Democrats to win without an alliance with Workingmen, the party of Andrew Jackson allied with a new fourth contender, the New Constitution Party (originally called the New Constitution Club). Together, the Democrats and the New Constitution Party nominated Dr. Hugh Glenn, a rancher who owned land in Glenn County that adjoined Butte. Glenn was well-respected in Chico where he sometimes did business. On good terms with John Bidwell, Glenn was also acquainted with Charlie Stilson. In 1860 Glenn and Stilson crossed the country from Missouri in the same wagon train party.[6] The 1879 ballot for governor pitted Republican candidate George Perkins against William F. White, the Workingmen's candidate, and Hugh Glenn, the Democratic/New Constitution Party's man.

The Campaign Gets Underway

Perkins was impressive on the trail. Almost six feet tall, his erect posture and large frame projected assurance without arrogance. Despite the time's loose ethical standards in politics and business, his overall reputation was a reasonably honorable one on both counts. His gubernatorial campaign's theme capitalized on him as self-made. According to Chico's Republican *Enterprise*: "Geo. Perkins is emphatically a man of the people.... Mr. Perkins is emphatically a workingman ... who has risen from the ranks by sheer industry...."[7]

Campaign promotions presented Perkins as "the sailor boy," emphasizing his youth as a sailor rather than his present role as a shipping magnate. The campaign linked Perkins's naval imagery to the theatrical phenomenon, Gilbert and Sullivan's "H.M.S. Pinafore." In Chico, both the *Record* and the *Enterprise* emphasized this link. For instance, they referred to Chapman as a "Buccaneer for Buchanan" because, in the 1850s, he volunteered for Buchanan's campaign in Michigan. They also referred to him, Carnot Mason, John Gilkyson and other middle-aged stalwarts as Perkins's "sailor boys."[8]

The *Record* predicted the campaign "will require all [of Perkins's] knowledge of seamanship to steer his craft into the State Capitol." When Perkins campaigned in Chico, he "spliced the mainbrace" for the volunteers who were working hard to elect him.[9] This rhetoric pitched to high excitement when the Amy Sherwin Pinafore Troupe arrived in town. Curious townspeople packed their performance of the operetta "Pinafore" at the reopened Bidwell Hall. The audience included many who "don't understand opera, not even burlesque opera."[10] However, they responded noisily to each appearance on stage of the "Lord High Admiral" whom they identified with "their old neighbor" George Perkins.[11]

The candidate's sailor boys also organized a parade in which torchbearers (only forty-one of them, the Democratic *Record* sneered) led Perkins's carriage up Main Street and down West Second by the light of bonfires. Men and boys carried transparent signs illuminated by flames in lanterns before and aft. They read, "Perkins, Friend of the Workingman," "No More Land Monopoly" and "Perkins, the anti-Railroad Man."[12] From the enormous balcony of the only local "first class" hotel—the Chico Hotel on West Second near Broadway—Perkins exhorted his supporters to keep their faith in party and candidate.

Afterward, Perkins and the Republican Club repaired to a hotel event room to celebrate the evening's success. In the code of the day, critics of Perkins disparaged the size of the crowds by pointing out the sizeable turnout of women who didn't count because they could not vote.[13] Despite the enthusiasm and visibility of the men's support for Perkins, co-chairmen Chapman and Mason were on edge: they knew Perkins had locked up his southern Butte County base, but they were not confident they could secure him a majority in politically divided northern Butte County.

The campaign was more than intense: it reached gridlock when all the candidates seemed to have similar levels of support. With that came calls for unorthodox measures. In Chico, according to the San Francisco *Chronicle*, Republicans were competing with "active and intelligent" leaders of the local Workingmen's Party.[14] However, hoping to improve their chances to defeat Perkins, Workingmen statewide had dropped their party's candidate, William White, and united behind the Democratic/New Constitution parties' candidate Hugh Glenn. That became a crisis for Chapman, Mason and their cohorts. For Perkins to win northern Butte County, the Workingmen had to break away from the Democratic/New Constitution parties.

At the same time, Chico Republicans were uncomfortable discrediting Hugh Glenn. He was the premier rancher in Northern California: his 65,000-acre Rancho Jacinto stretched southwest of Butte County along fifteen miles of the Sacramento River. They understood that, like many Chicoans, he remained a Democrat because he carried deep Southern roots. And under ordinary circumstances, those Democrats reliably voted with Republicans—local and statewide—on property issues.

The Republicans, considered the party of property, next devised a tactic to confuse the Workingmen's marginal voters. Ironically, the party began to denounce Hugh Glenn as a "land monopolist," which had been the Workingmen's standard charge against the political power of big ranchers. The Workingmen were confounded. The Republicans, of course, had stolen such rhetoric about rich ranchers like Glenn to make themselves appear less elite and more compatible to Democratic/New Constitution parties' voters.

While Republicans sought to undermine the alliance of Workingmen with the Democratic and New Constitution parties, they only succeeded in sowing confusion. And no one was more confused than Glenn, known as the state's "Wheat King." He found himself inveighing against "land monopolists" even though he owned California's largest ranch. According to the Perkins's campaign, Glenn's ranch provided no schools, nothing better than bunkhouses for workers and employed a large Chinese labor force. Perkins's Republicans took hope when they heard voters referring to "Ah Glenn" or "High Boss Glenn."[15] The situation was to become even more bizarre.

In August Republicans tried a new tactic to split the alliance between local Workingmen and Democrats backing Glenn. A Workingmen's Party secretary, James Leonard, 78, of Chico, received a letter from a Republican backer of Perkins:

> August 12, 1879
>
> Dear Sir:
> Will you go to the stable, procure a double-seated carriage, come to Oroville Saturday, and preside at the Kearney meeting and take him to Chico on Sunday? The money is in waiting to defray all expense and compensate you for your troubles.
>
> A. P. Waugh[16]

"If a thunderbolt had fallen at Leonard's feet he would not have been more astonished."[17] Why would Waugh, a well-off Oroville Republican, arrange for Denis Kearney to appear in Chico? After all, he was the San Francisco Workingmen's leader whom Republicans most despised and feared. Nevertheless, Leonard took the request to Chico's Republican campaign co-chairman Carnot C. Mason, who conferred with other party leaders.

The Chico Republicans, following state party orders, expected Kearney to give a speech so compelling that Chico Workingmen would return their loyalty to their party, breaking up its alliance with the Democratic/New Constitution parties. He was to convince them to vote, not for Glenn, but for the Workingmen's own original candidate William White. Workingmen had withdrawn support from White but, since the time to remove his name from the ballot fell short, it remained there.

Chico's Workingmen were incredulous when they figured out the Republicans' ruse. Their own Denis Kearney had allowed

Republicans to use him to undermine his own party's campaign strategy to win back the alliance with Democrats. In the end, clinging to faith in their party, they agreed Kearney must have had some valid explanation to justify his agreement to speak in Chico. They brought him from Oroville to Chico for his speech in front of City Hall at Third and Main.

However, when Workingmen's Party leaders James Leonard, Joseph Campbell, David Campbell and John Daly met with "prominent Republicans" to receive payment for Kearney's transportation expenses, they had second thoughts and backed off. They felt they were being bribed to sell out their party for the Republicans' benefit and refused to introduce Kearney to the expected crowd. With no local Workingmen willing to cooperate with them on this part, they enlisted a San Joaquin Valley Workingman. The *Record* immediately revealed he was an advocate for Chinese labor, but they went ahead with him anyway.

Kearney's controversial two-hour speech in Chico disconcerted everyone. The Republican *Enterprise* did the best it could to justify its party's strange tactic. It eked out an uncomfortable but surprisingly generous review of Kearney's performance:

> The people met a small man with a pronounced Irish accent, who kept them interested from the beginning to the close of his speech, and that is saying very much for him. All that terrible array of cuss words, all that horrible profanity and vulgarity ... which we all gathered to hear (and were disappointed because we did not hear it) was denied us, and Kearney spoke just about like other men.

> ... Certain prominent and pronounced ... Republicans have been guilty of treating Dennis [sic] Kearney with the common courtesy we all expect to receive. (That is the only thing one can treat him with, for he is a temperance man.) We did not think these men would do so, did not suppose them capable of committing such an unheard-of crime. But we have learned that the charge can be supported by ample evidence.... Yes, Dennis [sic] Kearney has been to Chico, spoke his piece, and if we are rightly informed he has left our town for some oth-

er more congenial clime. Still, he may be here yet. Things are mixed, and facts are only fancies since Dennis [sic] came and upset the moral aspect of Chico.[18]

But, the *Record's* Democratic editor wasn't having it. Crosette could not decide which was worse: Kearney's "perfidy" or the Republicans' cynicism.

Republican leaders in Chico ... were his constant companions during his visit here. Suffice to say that he stayed in Chico and spoke, and that an elegant barouche took him and his reporters to Red Bluff. The Democracy didn't pay for it; we have the assertion of one of the reporters that neither Kearney nor themselves paid for it; the N.C.P. [New Constitution Party] hardly like him well enough to go to any expense in his behalf; and we guess his Republican allies will have to stand it.... We thank thee, Oh, Denis, for allowing the light of your illustrious countenance to shine upon us! We are grateful to thee for showing us to what depths the once proud Republican party can descend to gain political advantage.[19]

Chapman's name does not appear in any of this coverage. He may have deferred to his party co-chairman Carnot Mason or suddenly had pressing business in Powellton or simply stood back. He had been known for his compatible relationship with the Workingmen and had been their nominee only months before. The Lemm Ranch murders excepted, he had long avoided central speaking roles in controversies.[20]

The Workingmen's disillusionment with Kearney for his collaboration with Republicans led them to publish a letter in the *Record*, declaring they would not break up their alliance: "We are now for Dr. Glenn for Governor and so are forty other voters who intended, until Kearney's visit, to vote for White."[21]

Chapman, Mason and their cohorts found no immediate way to recoup a lead after Kearney's speech. Of course, the Democrats were relieved when the Workingmen renewed their commitment to vote for Hugh Glenn. Had they not done so, the additional forty to sixty Workingmen who threatened to vote for White could have swung the Chico tally to Perkins.

Political leaders knew how evenly split Chico was between Democrats and Republicans because they always kept track of the votes on county ballots for the coroner. Voters never crossed over to vote for a candidate other than their own party's man. In a 1877 town election, for example, Chico Republicans won 273 votes and Democrats 256—a difference of 17 votes.

To produce a winning margin in the 1879 race, the Democrats reached deep into their own bag of tricks. Because anti-Chinese sentiment was still entrenched in Chico, they sponsored P. S. Dorney's appearance on behalf of Hugh Glenn. Dorney had founded the statewide anti-Chinese Order of Caucasians to which Chico's chapter had provided not only a large membership but also statewide officers. Dorney's Chico audience for the election brought out about 150 men who heard him announce a promise from Hugh Glenn to oppose both Chinese labor and land monopolies. Glenn's position was getting stranger by the day.

A joke circulating in Chico pointed to land owner Glenn's discomfort as the candidate for the anti-monopolist Workingmen: "On Tuesday evening after Dr. Glenn left a saloon where he had treated the boys, an Irishman exclaimed, 'Be gorra, I've worked for him two years an' it's the first time he treated me. An' be dad if he is elected Governor, it's the last time he'll treat a workingman.'"[22] The election provoked an onrush of cynicism:

The Candidate

Husband who is that man at the gate?
Hush my love, 'tis the candidate.
Husband, why doesn't he work like you?
Has he nothing at home to do?
My dear, whenever a man is down,
No cash at home, no money in town,
Too stupid to preach, too proud to beg,
Too timid to rob and too lazy to dig,
Then over his horse his leg he flings,
And to the dear people this song he sings:
Howdy, Howdy, Howdy do?
How is your wife and how are you?

Ah! It fits my fist like no other can
The horny hand of the workingman.[23]

On election day George Perkins carried the state. In Butte County he won 1,715 votes, Glenn drew 1,477 votes and 253 votes went to the Workingmen's candidate White, whose voters just could not bring themselves to vote for Glenn despite their leaders' pleas to support him. Had those votes gone to Hugh Glenn, he would have defeated Perkins in the county by 15 votes.[24]

Perkins's exhilarated supporters lit bonfires along downtown streets where most celebrated with liquor, their lubricant of choice. Celebratory gunshots competed with cheers, while band music "oompahed" throughout the night. Supporters fired so many salutes to Perkins from Chico's plaza cannon, the Civil War relic, that residents began begging for them to stop. According to the preliminary count (the only one still available), Perkins won Chico by only two votes. His team had eked out that narrow victory even though he had opposed Chico's county-split attempt as late as the previous year. Perkins credited Chapman and Mason for his thin victory in northern Butte County.

At the same time, Chapman's campaign for county assessor, an appropriate position for him in light of his business and civic experience, was a casualty of his exertions in the governor's campaign. Working night and day, Chapman was too invested in campaigning for Perkins to work on his own campaign, which would have required him to travel across several counties. The election result, which left him a distant third, was an embarrassment. This loss is ironic since his committee work for the new Constitution created the position of elective county assessors.[25]

Chapman surely had not pleased Chico Workingmen when he stood back from endorsing the new Constitution. After all, they had tried to nominate him to represent them in the convention. He no less tested his relationship with his own Republican party when he stood back from opposing it. Unlike Chapman, the other Butte County delegates to the constitutional convention had entered the ratification fray straight on: they stepped up, stood their ground and accepted the consequences. Chapman, who had wanted elective office since 1859 and who had built up political respect from local Democrats and Workingman, had given no quarter in his aggressive campaign for Perkins.

The 1879 state election was California's "laborers and mechanics" final effort in the nineteenth century to form their own party. While the state Workingmen's Party officially disbanded in 1881, Chico's party lingered on as late as 1886, when, at best, it amounted to a fraternal order or, at the least, a network of friends. In 1888, a small newspaper article noted Denis Kearney's social visit to the White House. Already a political has-been, he struck a patronizing reporter as just a used-up labor agitator.

The Perkins campaign shifted Gus Chapman's focus from local to state politics. Although Chicoans expected him to serve a new term as a school trustee, he bowed out, supporting Henry Camper who won the election. Perkins promoted him from a Bank of Butte County board member to bank vice president. As a bank founder, Perkins could bestow such a reward on his local campaign leader.[26] Then, the governor-to-be offered Chapman one of the then most significant positions in state government.

Republican businessmen like Gus Chapman were relieved by Perkins's election, which engendered renewed confidence about recovery from the depression. They counted on Perkins and future Republican governors to ensure that "responsible" men like themselves could moderate or neutralize elements in the new Constitution they considered "worrisome."

Although Chapman's anchor remained Chico, he was looking toward state service, which meant he had to leave his business in order. To mollify William McKay, he bought more timber land near their mill, "[t]he finest belt of sugar pine timber now accessible to this market. In connection with their mills and equipment for lumbering, this is one of the finest properties in Northern California."[27] Publicizing this purchase underlined his image of success, an asset that attested to his political and social weight going forward. By every overt measure he had "made it"—his family was secure, McKay had the timber he needed for the mill and Chapman had staff to cover the lumber sales. Whether he could rely on all this was an issue because he had to service the successive bank loans that made it all possible. Nevertheless, Gus took a long-term perspective: he finally had his chance to enter a high level of public service—with no need for an election.

As governor, Perkins was in a position to promote some elements of the 1879 State Constitution and downplay others. While his opponents focused on his ties to the railroads and his steamship line, he vowed his personal priority was not self-serving. He intended to make reform of the state's prisons his top priority. Fraud and abuses at San Quentin had long been a public scandal and the new prison under construction at Folsom presented an opportunity for proper management from the onset. Who could Governor Perkins rely on to transform the prisons? Augustus H. Chapman of Chico.

The drama of state politics, the satisfaction of engagement in key problems of the day, the opportunity to work with powerful leaders—all this diverted Augustus Chapman's attention, for days or weeks at a time, from the issues that encumbered him in Chico. A nationally powerful man, Perkins had bet on him to handle challenges beyond any he had tackled to date. In an earlier autobiographical essay prepared for the constitutional convention, Gus Chapman offered a revealing admission: although he identified Michigan men who helped him rise up in his youth, he omitted mention of his only Chico mentor, George Wood.[28] Since Wood's departure, Chapman had advanced as his own man. Now he was George Perkins's man.

14

The Hon. A. H. Chapman, State Prison Director

In 1880 Governor-elect George Perkins acknowledged Dr. Carnot Mason's work on his campaign by appointing him to the State Medical Board and offered Augustus Chapman the chairmanship of the State Prison Commission.[1] Fellow Butte County Republicans approved both of Perkins's choices. The Chico *Enterprise* said of Chapman, "few men ... selected for this position ... could command more respect than he."[2]

In that period of California history, when government had a narrow range of responsibilities, the State Prison Commission was not only powerful but prestigious. While other state departments operated in the background, the public closely followed news about San Quentin State Prison, opened in 1852. When Chapman entered the scene, Folsom State Prison was due to open and speculation flew about how it would compete with or complement San Quentin. Also, because former warden William Irwin had become governor in 1875, politicians considered prison positions a steppingstone to advancement.[3]

The offer from Perkins was the best public service opportunity in his life. Chapman's response to his appointment effected appropriate modesty. However, before accepting it, he would have been well-served to weigh the issues such a position presented. First, appointments to public office and elected representation are political. While both rest on determination and luck, each requires distinctive political and bureaucratic skills he had acquired, but not yet mastered. Second, the stakes at play in Chico and Butte County politics did not compare with the reach and complexity of those in state politics. Third, the prison position would require extended absences from his family and lumber business, the financial base he took for granted, although he already knew the lumber business was not necessarily a stable earner because it was subject to changing economic conditions.

In addition, Chapman might have weighed the implications for him of San Quentin's reputation. It was infamous for incompetent, cruel and corrupt management. Newspapers focused on abuses there as a reliable source for copy and Folsom Prison was already scandal prone. In the recent constitutional convention in Sacramento, Democrats and Republicans had mainly focused on other issues so their leaders let changes in prison policies slip through to appease the Workingmen's Party.[4] For example, needing to keep prisoners occupied, the San Quentin warden contracted prison labor with private manufacturers who were unwilling to pay the higher wages outside white labor demanded. They paid low wages to Chinese workers hired to work with less skilled prison labor. The new Constitution prohibited the hire of Chinese at both prisons. A further challenge Governor Perkins accepted was to make San Quentin and Folsom self-supporting without income from private business contracts. However, San Quentin depended on such income to supplement inadequate state appropriations.

It seems curious that the new governor would call on an obscure lumber mill owner experienced in farm-town retail to take the leading role in California prison reform. However, when Perkins and Chapman reconnected as friends at the constitutional convention in 1878, it apparently emerged that Chapman had admired reformatory prison policy since his experience back home in Michigan. In the early 1830s he was a child in Jackson County when the town of Jackson became the site of Michigan's first state prison. In the 1850s, when Gus had been educated, practiced law and became a co-owner of Smith & Chapman thirty-five miles from there, the state erected substantial buildings on a sixty-acre campus, making Michigan Central State Prison the leading institution in the region. As a local leader, Gus Chapman was aware of Warden F. H. Hatch's emphasis on reformatory rather than punitive policies. The prisoners received a basic education and training for work on prison farms. They also learned how to manufacture products for state and private contractors. Michigan Central State had become a reformatory nationally known as a center of industry.[5]

Neither Michigan Central nor any other American prison has ever resolved many of the prison labor issues Chapman encountered. One hundred years later, U.S. Supreme Court Justice Warren Burger urged legislators to assign prisoners "meaningful productive work to help pay the costs of prisons."[6] In 1984 Justice Burger called for contracted prison labor capable of producing marketable products. This is what Governor Perkins challenged Chapman, as chairman of the Prison Commission, to accomplish in 1880. (This issue is ongoing.)

Governor Perkins assigned Chapman to make San Quentin a grain-sack mill and to organize a granite-production business based on the quarries near Folsom. At a minimum, each prison would require total reorganization, construction work, equipment purchases, sales contract systems, skilled supervisors and retrained prisoners. That Perkins also entrusted his reformatory mission to Chapman underlines the depth of his respect for the Chico businessman.

Why such respect? From firsthand acquaintance over twenty years, Perkins was aware of Chapman's contributions to building Chico from a small scrappy village to a dynamic incorporated town. He had observed Chapman successfully navigate political conflicts in northern and southern Butte County. For example, despite Chapman's staunch leadership on Chico's behalf in the county-split challenges, he maintained respectful relationships with Oroville businessmen. George Crosette, still publisher of the Democratic *Record,* and, in 1880, a member of the Board of Supervisors and president of Chico's Democratic Club, praised Perkins's choice: "The numerous political and personal friends of Hon. A. H. Chapman of the county ... believe that Mr. Chapman would be one of the best men in the State to carry out the views of Governor Perkins."[7]

The Republican *Enterprise* was no less emphatic: "A.H. Chapman [is] a representative man for one of the State Prison Commissioners.... His long life spent here in this community and his constant efforts in every direction towards building up and sustaining the best interests of the State and county speaks louder than words.... Few men could be selected for this important office from the northern portion of the State who could command more respect than he."[8] And, of course, Gus Chapman and Carnot Mason's Butte County campaign had produced a "miracle" in Perkins's victory there. The Chico Republican Club they chaired had spared the governor the embarrassment of having lost his home county.

Perkins explained his choice of A. H. Chapman:

> After the 1st of Jan., under the organic law, no contract for convict labor in the State Prisons can be let. In view of that I felt the necessity of making the selection of such men as I believed to be thoroughly honest, competent and progressive in ideas. I received over sixty applications for the position of Prison Director, but I did not appoint one of them. I was determined to appoint only those from experience I believed were fully competent to discharge the duties of the position ... I selected Mr. Chapman because I had known him for several years as a thoroughly good businessman, of an excellent reputation, and thoroughly reliable. I deemed him eminently fitted for such a position and I told him I was going to appoint him. He did not ask for it, it was I who asked him to accept it, and after some time for consideration he did accept.... I appointed Mr. Chapman purely from personal feelings and a knowledge of his capabilities.[9]

Having, as Chapman explained, "consumed the greater part of [my] life in getting [my] living," Perkins's offer was his entrée into work more satisfying than he found in the marketplace.[10] On January 1, 1880, Gus, Sarah and Mary, 15, set off for Perkins's inauguration. To the teenager's delight, also on board their train to Sacramento were forty members of the Chico Guard. They, not the Oroville militiamen, would march in front of Perkins's carriage in the parade to the Capitol.[11]

Perkins's inaugural speech endorsed the 1879 State Constitution's abolition of contract prison labor. He underlined prison reorganization as his top priority. While prisoners at Folsom would support themselves through work in the granite quarries, San Quentin had no natural resources to exploit. Perkins laid out his plan. On the prison that sits in San Francisco Bay, prisoners would manufacture grain sacks. Coming from Butte County, the new governor grasped the value of this for wheat growers. Every year wheat farmers were forced to buy millions of Calcutta-made hemp bags because international shipping companies required containment to prevent shifts of loose grain in vessels' holds. Since the 1860s, western grain depended entirely on international sales because midwestern growers monopolized the country's domestic wheat market.[12]

That evening, as the Chapmans socialized at the Inaugural Ball, Gus introduced their guest John Gilkyson, failed farmer and insurance agent, to the other prison director appointees. Gus brought Gilkyson to make introductions that could lead to the Chico man's employment. Gilkyson was a hardworking, respected fellow Methodist who struggled repeatedly to find a livelihood. And now, again, he needed work to support his large family. Not only had a sheriff's sale taken his farm, but the conflagration that consumed a major part of downtown Chico had destroyed his insurance business.[13] Gilkyson and his wife Ruth were responsible for their seven children, both sets of grandparents, as well as boarding two farm children who stayed in town to attend the Chico Academy.

As the Chapmans and Gilkyson circulated around the ball they exchanged greetings with John Bidwell. Out of deference to Sarah's Methodist scruples, she and Gus did not dance. But, because Sarah loved music, the orchestra playing in the Senate and Assembly chambers thrilled her. The elegance of the occasion furnished the Chico contingent with colorful accounts for their friends at home. John Bidwell was unusually profusive in pronouncing the event "a grand and brilliant affair."[14] He did not mention Chapman's presence there.

Gilkyson accompanied Gus and Sarah to Sacramento again for Perkins's reception where Gus received his official appointment to a six-year, full-time position. That Gus Chapman had an official place in such grand festivities meant a great deal to him. Always an ambitious man, his official role in the inaugural events declared him "arrived."

Chapman's Introduction to State Politics

While politicians cherished few prerogatives more than the right to reward supporters with public jobs, the 1879 State Constitution changed that when it came to the Prison Commission. It required governors to appoint men from both parties to its board of directors. In addition, the commission was distinctive because the length of appointees' terms extended beyond the terms of the governors who selected them as a means to reduce partisanship on the board and protect appointees from politics. (While this provision seemed sensible, later manipulation of it would become a critical issue for Chapman and his colleagues.) Perkins offered positions to two Democrats: William Irwin, a former governor and San Quentin warden, and Martin Miller, a serving State Senator.

However, Irwin declined the offer and the State Democratic caucus, ignoring the new Constitution mandate, forbade Miller to accept an appointment from the new Republican governor. Even the Democrats' ally, the *Record*, objected when Perkins honored the terms of the new law: "If George Perkins has any ambitions beyond being Governor, he had better take the back track on his proposition to make appointments from the Democratic Party. Gov. Haight drove one-third of his party from him by such action, and his political fate should be a warning to Perkins. To the victor belong the spoils, and the victors should have them."[15]

Governor Perkins had tried to make appointments according to the new Constitution's bipartisan rule but gave up on Democrats and appointed two more Republicans in their places. The four men he appointed to work with Chapman were Perkins's State Senate colleague J. H. Neff, whom the governor considered "an honest, upright man"; Wallace Everson, a businessman who brought Oakland backing; Dr. W. F. McNutt, because he wanted a capable, certified physician in the mix; and former judge F. W. Schell.[16] While Perkins's decision to appoint two more Republicans quieted the political uproar for the present, repercussions would follow.

Following Perkins's lead, the Prison Commission members, informally called the board of directors, appointed fellow

Republicans to staff positions. To bring Folsom online, they chose John McComb, a successful printer and National Guard brigadier general who had mustered 5,000 men to control San Francisco's anti-Chinese rioters in 1877. The appointment Chapman's board members made next, the warden, should have alerted him about what lay ahead.

For the San Quentin warden's appointment, Chapman would later remember that he and the other directors reviewed "no scarcity of applicants."[17] Chairman Gus and the other commissioners sat through lengthy meetings which eventually culminated in the appointment of Joseph P. Ames, despite Gus's opposition. Ames was a San Mateo County businessman, Republican State Assembly representative and a "friendly acquaintance" of George Perkins. For reasons no longer available, Ames carried a checkered reputation. Chapman's resistance to Ames's appointment was later deemed prescient.[18]

Chapman may have made a deal for giving in and voting for Ames because this was also when the board approved John Gilkyson as assistant commissary at San Quentin. Since 1862, when bad food led to a riot, prison officials had been careful about commissary appointments. On the downside, Gilkyson's appointment meant moving his family to the prison, depriving his lively teenaged daughters of their Chico companions. The girls' Teardrop Victory Club sent one of them off with a jaunty salute: "We are sorry to find that the new Constitution has not only sentenced criminals to San Quentin, but also one of our club."[19]

With the Prison Commission and its key staff in place, Chapman launched a grueling travel schedule. The Constitution, notorious for its detail, required a monthly meeting at each prison. The directors' agendas were so far reaching, however, that any single meeting might require stays of a week or more. One Folsom meeting required a full month to complete the agenda. As chairman, Chapman worked additional days out of the commission's San Francisco office at 410 Kearney Street. He also briefed Governor Perkins and legislators.

Because the *Record* regularly printed lists of arrivals and departures at the depot, townspeople followed his travels. In only six months, January to June 1880, the commission held thirty-four meetings, including twenty-one in San Francisco, nine at San Quentin and four at Folsom. In addition to that, Gus handled the administrative work. Some Chicoans considered Gus Chapman's frequent, extended absences abandonment of their town. How did Sarah respond? When Mary, Gussie and Willie started their summer vacations, she took them to Michigan where Fred joined them for a family visit. Gus was on his own.[20]

When he made business stops in Chico that summer, it was not unusual for the head of a family like himself to be living in an empty house. Intense heat temporarily drove better-off wives and children to the new vogue: foothill and mountain cabins or a new option—the Santa Cruz beach. George Crosette captured this for the *Record*: On "the approach of hot weather, almost every train and stage-coach bears away from one to a dozen of the gentler sex whose radiant presence has thrown effulgent rays of light and joy around the family circle.… However, there is one consolation left to the fond husbands, these poor demented creatures, and that is, the hotter the locality, the cooler tastes a nice julep or iced punch, and there's no one at home to chide."[21] His wife Sarah summered in their Powellton cabin.

Gus found relief from the valley heat in the summer chill of San Francisco. While there, after meetings in his office or across the Bay at San Quentin, he returned to a hotel room where he wrote letters, read reports and drafted memoranda by gaslight. He brought that work home to Chico, where he also tended to his own affairs and made time for the Republican Club, renamed the Garfield and Arthur Club in honor of its presidential ticket. Chico events supplied at least a paragraph when he wrote Sarah. What could he talk about? A defective stovepipe burned down their former home on West Sixth Street where Mary was born in 1865. That house had passed to Fred's high school teacher Hiram Batchelder, whose family escaped without injury.[22] Whatever its shortcomings, Sarah remembered how conveniently close it was to her Methodist church, stores, friends and the Chico Academy.

Gus could also tell her about arrangements for President and Mrs. Rutherford B. Hayes's Chico visit in company with Civil War General William T. Sherman. The men in the party were curious about Sierra Nevada gold mining. Town leaders were eager for positive national press coverage to compensate for the damage Chico suffered by eastern editors' fascination with the 1877 Lemm Ranch murders. Gus's reception committee planned the welcoming parade, a job he and the rest had done for many politicians. This time they enhanced the production value, adding flower-laden carriages to carry the president's party from the depot. A band welcomed the visitors and led them up Fifth Street where the Canfields, Crews, Campers, Joneses and other residents of Chico's most fashionable street had decked out their homes with banners, bunting and flags. After the parade traveled up Main and down Second streets, John and Annie Bidwell hosted the president's party. The Chapmans' neighbor Addison Blaire Collins later drove the president's carriage on their gold country excursion.

Chapman also likely told his family about the mammoth sugar pine their company's loggers had cut down. It produced 22,080 board feet, an amount slightly more than a single day's usual production from several large trees. Half of its yield was top-rated clear wood and six boards were sixteen feet in length.[23]

In return, Sarah briefed Gus on their Michigan families and Fred's return to New York for a new semester. She arrived home at the end of the summer with the boys and Mary, ready to start her senior year at the Chico Academy.

Chairman Chapman

As head of the Prison Commission, A. H. Chapman became a man of interest to the Republican Party. When the party's State Central Committee summoned him to discuss prison reform, Gus had his first chance to display his growing expertise on prison management.

James A. Garfield's presidential run added luster to the already high respect for Dr. Carnot Mason, a relation of the candidate. Because his State Medical Board meetings required less travel and time than the Prison Commission required from Chapman, the physician assumed his friend's leadership role among Chico Republicans. While John Bidwell was ever the local party's respected elder, he had retired from its management. That summer, the party's finance committee—Chapman, young rancher W. W. Durham and Llano Seco Ranch manager Addison Blaire Collins—won bragging rights for the $79 they raised in a single meeting. A tiny sum today, at the time it approximated many Chicoans' monthly wage.[24]

Work on the Prison Commission invigorated Gus Chapman. By the time he reached home for Christmas in 1881, ending his first year as chairman, the commission had transferred 200 prisoners from San Quentin to Folsom to finish the buildings and grounds. These prisoners, some with skills in crafts and trades, saved the state the cost of hiring workers. Chapman was proud that improved conditions bolstered prisoner and staff morale. The commission had separated adults and boys pending a new institution for the younger inmates, ended the beating of prisoners and introduced full funeral services. The directors paid San Quentin Prison inmates 50¢ a day (about $14 today) to paint cells and make other improvements. Assistant Commissary John Gilkyson and his cohorts met the Prison Commission's diet objective: food that was equivalent to boarding house fare. The Chapman board also had plans to expand the San Quentin yard and followed Perkin's directive to review sentencing and recommend pardons.[25]

During Gus's first year as commission chairman, the board received cutting and sewing machinery he ordered from Scotland to make jute grain sacks. Chapman hired the men who arrived with the equipment to stay on as production supervisors. Meanwhile, in order to someday manufacture the bags from California grain, Chapman and other directors distributed bags of twine and jute seed to farmers. In Chico on a visit home, Chapman met with both newspaper editors who publicized his call for jute crops. (A Colusa man abandoned his attempt—they needed a Mediterranean climate.) The editors did their part: "The farmers of Chico township are, as a general thing, pretty wide awake on the sack question."[26]

The *Enterprise's* editor marveled at the changes townspeople saw in Gus Chapman. While they still groused about his absences, he was less reserved. He had become outgoing, even voluble, about every aspect of the grain-sack plan and prison improvements in general. His enthusiasm had overcome "the general reticence which characterizes his business transactions, either public or private."[27] Such reticence was no longer appropriate as the governor's man responsible for the public's business. It is notable that Augustus Chapman immediately understood that distinction.

Perkins and Chapman found support in the enthusiasm of California's powerful wheat farmers. For years they had griped about the high cost of imported bags that shippers required them to buy. They specifically resented merchant Isaac Friedlander who had long monopolized the supply. The former Wood & Chapman, now Bullard & Dorn, was Friedlander's Chico outlet. When Chapman owned the store, in 1869 alone he bought grain bags in several lots of 60,000 each, then 100,000 more, and then another 100,000. California farmers annually purchased 43 million bags. Governor Perkins's grain-sack factory resolved a statewide problem and ended the perennial Chico refrain: "Could not more be made by a sack factory in Chico?"[28] Because the sacks were an ongoing issue in Chico but irrelevant in Oroville, where mining hung on and Perkins had been away from for a decade, there are grounds to speculate that Chapman recommended grain-sack production to Perkins in their conversations at the constitutional convention in 1879.

Chicoans took new interest in California prisons not only because of their townsman Augustus Chapman's leadership, but also because he helped find a good position for John Gilkyson. He and his wife Ruth Hobart Gilkyson had moved their large family to a commodious staff house on San Quentin's grounds. Despite the daughters' reluctance to leave their childhood friends, they enjoyed the roomy new house—one they did not have to share with boarders.

In November the Gilkysons invited their Chico friends to a party in the prison schoolhouse, which inmates set up for the event. Since Sarah had so recently arrived home, she excused herself from the Gilkysons' San Quentin get-together. The large party of Chico people who made the train trip ranged from boisterous teenagers to John Bidwell. In his diary he noted his presence but, as usual, added no comment. Gus Chapman led them all on a tour of the grounds, while the young people played games and gossiped over supper prepared by prisoners. The guests jocularly declined Gilkyson's invitation to stay overnight in another new building, the as yet unoccupied officers' quarters.[29] They caught the train to Chico later that night.

Disaster Calls Chapman Home

At the close of 1881 Gus Chapman could find satisfaction in his accomplishments. However, in January 1882 he was called home from a prison meeting because a large fire had destroyed the newer Chapman & McKay mill in Somerset, two miles from Powellton. The previous November, when snowstorms threatened, William McKay shut down both mills for the winter. Somerset workers had closed a profitable season with 1.5 million board feet of stacked pine to fulfill a major contract once the roads reopened in the spring. The guards McKay posted to protect this inventory were there in mid-December when a growing blizzard threatened to cut them off from protective quarters. Snow conditions were so severe that horse teams could only move with 14-inch squares of wood attached to their feet by iron clasps. The men left for refuge in Powellton.

Because they were aware of recent fires in the area, every few days the guards made their way back to check on the outlying mill. During the second week in January, however, heavy blowing snow stopped all travel. It was January 18 before the guards could return to the Somerset mill. When they reached a crest above the mill, they paused in confusion. There was nothing. The mill's building, its machinery, and towering stacks of lumber had vanished. Had they had made a wrong turn? When they approached for a closer look, however, the men discovered the stable was intact beneath the snow. From there, they figured out where the mill was and dug down through the snowdrifts to find only ashes.

William McKay received the news at his Bidwell Avenue home in Chapmantown. He telegraphed his partner and immediately headed for Powellton, reaching there with difficulty because floods had taken out bridges along the way. After a stop at his cottage in the village, he headed for Somerset where he examined the site and identified six places where arsonists had lighted fires.[30] Chapman's Prison Commission schedule was so tight that he could only return to meet with Bill McKay in Chico for a single evening's briefing. The evidence produced no arrests. Estimates of Chapman & McKay's uninsured losses ranged up to $30,000 (over $800,000 today). Chapman left McKay to handle all the after-effects, again taxing the men's already strained relationship.

Back to Prisons—and Politics

Gus Chapman moved from one problem to the next, whether in San Francisco, Folsom or Chico. His lumber mills became his lowest priority. Despite the substantial advances the Prison Commission made in its first year, political attacks began breaking out in mid-1881. This added a new dimension to Chapman's responsibilities as chairman of the board. He and his colleagues could never again focus solely on prison reform.

For example, the *San Jose Mercury* accused the board directors of misusing funds. Until then, the State had reimbursed the directors for their mileage, room and board. In 1881 an Assembly committee noted the Prison Commissioners' far-flung responsibilities kept them away from their homes and businesses for much of the year. The Assembly committee made such a strong case for fairness that they secured *unanimous* passage of a new law. It authorized the directors to recover their monthly expenses and be paid another $100 monthly as a token "salary." (Chapman's monthly $100 was one-third less than he and George Wood paid their store clerk Charlie Stilson in 1865.) When Gus and his colleagues filed for compensation under the more generous formula, which all agreed they had not proposed, the *San Jose Mercury*, first, then other newspapers, accused them of exploiting public service for private gain.[31]

Coverage of state affairs in Chico newspapers was always sketchy. In this case, brief mentions fed local gossip with inferences that Chapman was a "rich" man linked to shady games with state funds. For example, the *Record* mentioned Chapman's $2,723 invoice for a year and eight months to cover transportation and room and board while traveling extensively on commission work. The article omitted that the Legislature recently had given unanimous support for the raise because the members had reached bicameral agreement that the former pay formula was unfair to the directors. The *Record* noted Chapman's reimbursements as the highest of all the members and noted his original request for $3,678.07 to reimburse his expenses. The newspaper noted that in one month (in which he had traveled 1,432 miles on prison business) he had only documented expense claims for $296.40. That was for cash Chapman had spent out-of-pocket that exceeded the $100 allowance expenses plus the $100 salary which the new law granted.

Governor Perkins appointed a Board of Inquiry to examine the new law's compensation allotments and make recommendations. There was too much information for Chico papers to print, but the inferences about Chapman scandalized his hometown readers. For them, the accusation must have seemed all the more compelling because Chapman offered the *Record* no explanation either for his expenses or the history of the Legislature's pay formula.

With this talk circulating in Chico, the return of Chapman's reticence at home did not work to his advantage. Only a few friends who asked him about the issue, if he even responded, had the opportunity to hear about his constant travel, its purpose, the cost of trains, ferries, buggies and the like, as well as his full-time stays in hotels where restaurant kitchens prepared his daily fare. Other directors who lived in the San Francisco-Sacramento corridor didn't accrue the amount of mileage Chapman did during his travels between his distant home and back and to other meeting sites. Only Chico's readers of the *Sacramento Bee* had a fuller grasp of Chapman's situation.

When the Board of Inquiry asked for Attorney General A. L. Hart's opinion, he concluded that, contrary to the law's wording, contrary to the record of the committee that proposed it and contrary to the unanimous vote of the legislators who understood its meaning when they voted, the law intended only to cover actual expenses and the legislators lacked the right to add the extra $100 to their pay because that would be, in effect, a salary. He declared the law did not permit board members to be paid a salary.

This confounded the prison directors. Their demanding work for the state required so much time and attention that they neglected their businesses and professions, seriously impinging on their private incomes. Therefore, while, in the first place, none had even asked the Legislature to grant reimbursement for their time, inconveniences and financial losses away from their businesses, now they decided that the "symbolic" $100 added to their expenses was only fair and due them. Gus Chapman, more than any other board member, carried on the commission's work between scheduled meetings. This meant he was constantly away from his family and businesses in order to work virtually full-time on prison responsibilities.

Therefore, the prison directors sued the State in A. H. Chapman's name as their chairman. Pending legal resolution, the State responded by suspending the directors' entire compensation through the winter of 1881-1882. This made the directors' financial strains even worse. All the board members now had to continue their prison work away from their homes without any state compensation, forcing each to spend his private funds to cover expenses. Relief came when the Superior Court upheld the commissioners' higher compensation, citing the formula set by the State Legislature's original, unanimous vote.

However, Attorney General Hart immediately appealed that decision to the State Supreme Court, which overturned the Superior Court. With that, the State reverted to the original formula which limited their compensation to mileage and minimal expenses. Any amount above that had to come from their personal funds. Gus Chapman and his colleagues bowed to the court's restoration of the old pay formula and returned their income from the State since 1881.

The State Assembly's Democratic Party-controlled Board of Inquiry next issued three other judgments hostile to the Republican Prison Commission. First, its August 1881 report concluded the commission had violated the 1879 State Constitution's provision mandating bipartisan appointments. Perkins had appointed only Republican commissioners, who appointed only Republican wardens, who appointed only Republican staff. The Board did not take into consideration that Perkins and the commission initially offered appointments to Democrats, but, at that party's demand, each declined to serve. It had been the Democrats, not Perkins, who insisted on continuing the customary "winners should take all."[32]

Second, the Board's investigators identified no significant problems with the jute mill policy and operation. However, they declared the Prison Commission had set up the jute grain-sack factory with inadequate authority because Perkins had exclusively relied on his executive powers. This was correct. However, the Legislature had issued no objections until after the San Quentin operation was in place and underway. The Board also criticized Chapman's board of directors as excessively generous to prisoners:

> The are humanely treated, are well clothed and well fed, while the entire prison within is cleanly and well kept. The books and accounts are plainly kept, and the system of purchase such as to merit approval. Our Inspection brought under … observation the table fare, and we found it to be fully equal to that of the average boarding-house fare, and in many respects superior to the daily food of the honest and industrious laboring population. With regard to food, clothing, shelter or toil, prison life in [San Quentin and Folsom] is not a hardship. In all these respects, the condition of the convict is better than that of the free laboring citizen, and much superior in point of plenty and comfort to any of the almshouses or hospitals maintained at the cost of either public or private benevolence. *The State treats her criminals with a generosity that is not accorded the indigent or the worthy poor* [emphasis added].[33]

Third, the Board of Inquiry frowned on the board's policy that ended beatings because members agreed it was wrong to ease prisoner discipline.

Chapman must have felt satisfaction with the board's "compliment" to John Gilkyson's work on the improved quality of prisoners' food. He certainly agreed with its observation that constitutionally prescribed travel on prison business was excessive, causing "heavy expenses necessarily paid out by the Directors [personally] in the discharge of their official duties, or the serious personal losses resulting to each member of the Board on account of his necessary absence from his home and neglect of his own private business."[34]

A judge who chaired the Legislature's review concluded that, despite any concerns he had mentioned, "The Board of Prison Directors are gentlemen of intelligence, integrity, and well-established business character."[35] He added that "many marked improvements have been made by the present management, both in the matter of treating prisoners and in the construction of buildings for those in charge."[36]

With this, the newspapers moved on from the prison issues. However, reporters remained alert for more Democratic attacks. Commissioner Wallace Everson, a businessman like Chapman, resigned in disgust at what he considered unwarranted accusations. Chapman, on the other hand, decided he would continue to pursue the reforms his friend and patron Governor Perkins had set in motion.

15

Divided Concerns: Wooden Pipes and Prison Politics

The issue of prison directors' reimbursement for state service continued through 1883, when Gus Chapman was embroiled in creating the jute grain-sack factory at San Quentin. Disgusted at the politics in play, confident of the prison board's record and eager to move on, the directors, as the commissioners were now called, negotiated an agreement with Attorney General A. L. Hart. The members returned the monthly $100 the existing law had allotted to them as a supplementary stipend above the reimbursement of their expenses. For its part, the state agreed to revert to the former rules and pay only their expenses.

However, the state controller refused even to process their expense claims. He explained he could not pay the directors under the expired rules because the Legislature had to pass a new compensation law to guide him. Governor Perkins stepped in and urged the Legislature to pass such a bill "and thus end the trouble and annoyance which these Directors have been compelled to undergo."[1] However, the Democratic Party-controlled Legislature declined to pass any new bill to pay the Republican prison directors. For Chapman, this meant not only had he already been personally subsidizing the state for all his expenses as essentially a full-time chairman during the first year of his term, now he had to continue this into the indefinite future, all the while financially responsible for his business and family.

For example, he was paying Fred's college costs in New York and Chico Academy tuitions for Mary and Gussie; he also had to make loan payments on his 1878 purchase of controlling shares in the floundering water and gas utilities, on his share of the uninsured loss in the Somerset mill fire and on his purchase of another 549 acres from the Central Pacific Railroad. The latter had relieved William McKay's worry that the Sierra Flume & Lumber's acquisition of large tracts of land across Butte Creek could cut off their access to Chapman & McKay's other timber stands. Now McKay wanted the old Empire mill's equipment so he could upgrade their product from rough boards to finished wood. Chapman, otherwise of no help to McKay in any other aspect of their joint business, made the purchase.[2]

The timing of these purchases suggests Chapman was, in effect, compensating McKay for all the time he spent away from their lumber business. A mill machine exploded in fall 1881, injuring Bill McKay and others. The big man took no time off to recover; instead, he worked on repairs for the four days the mill was down. When Gus again excused himself in favor of Prison Commission business, McKay was not surprised. Throughout the two men's entire partnership, Gus had always preferred town life and only went to the mill when necessary. In November 1881 an *Enterprise* item from a Powellton source captured this: "Mr. Chapman saw the storm coming this week and made haste to get to the Valley, where he can run around with more freedom."[3]

A Happy Moment at Home

With crises simmering at every point in his life, when Chapman woke up some mornings he must have needed a moment to orient himself. A typical month saw him travel 1,500 miles, for which all his reimbursements remained frozen by the Legislature's refusal to act. When he stopped at Chico, he arrived home to two little boys to whom he was almost a stranger, a daughter who had turned into a teenager, an exhausted wife, an edgy lumber partner and pressing responsibilities at the Chico public utilities.

But March 27, 1883, differed. Gus and Sarah hosted a celebration for their shared birthday and their twenty-fifth wedding anniversary. Because townspeople still considered Chapmantown a country destination, Gus engaged the Union and Chico hotels' omnibuses to drive many of the one hundred or so guests to their Chapman Street home. Cigar smoke hovered in the air as men debated the day's hot topics. After supper and receipt of their guests' joint gift of a sterling silver serving set, Fred

Chapman and his pals in the Chico Cornet Band provided the entertainment.

Water, Water, Water

Since becoming head of the Prison Commission in early 1880, Gus's responsibilities for Chico's water and gas services regularly distracted him from commission work. Neither were in good shape. However, if, as their new principal owner, he could resolve their problems, income from them might provide him a financially feasible exit from Chapman & McKay. On the positive side, the improved economy had raised lumber prices. In the meantime, utilities issues and the demands of transforming San Quentin Prison's financial base meant he had insufficient time for any one task.

Meanwhile, Chico's gas and water services demanded his attention. Neither utility would become profitable, let alone attract investors, until their management could restore public confidence.

As in every opportunity Chapman had embraced, he was confident of his management talent and approached the utilities problems with a positive spirit. Well-managed gas and water systems were imperative for Chico to attract new residents and make up for the population loss during the depression. Town leaders were under pressure to expand Chico's development because of an unexpected challenge from Southern California. A flood of immigration there from the East had created a boom. "Northern California was dumbfounded. For decades its residents had mocked the [southern California] cow counties, now it tried to imitate them."[4] Chico's leaders had to re-imagine their farm town as a resort.

The Chapmans were proud of the blood orange tree in their front yard a decade earlier; now, citrus groves were replacing wheat fields. Promoters held "fruit fairs where meretricious displays of imported oranges were heaped under waving palm and banana fronds.... Palermo dubbed itself the Riverside of the Sacramento Valley. Thermalito called itself the Pasadena of the north."[5]

Then an announcement brought an immediate and more practical focus on Chico's prospects. When the California &

Oregon Railroad declared it would extend its tracks north from Redding to the Oregon border, town leaders, for some reason, envisioned Chico as a potential site for the "terminal station of [the] freight division."[6] Determined to impress railroad officials, they expanded their cleanup campaign in an effort reminiscent of Chico's 1860s effort to attract settlers. Like their forerunners, storekeepers cleared away the cartons, barrels and refuse cluttering boardwalks. Pedestrians discovered they could resume the pleasure of strolling side by side rather than single file. Town officials hired a man to rake trash from the gutters. They tasked constables to corral family cows, pigs and off-duty buggy horses who had been grazing along the streets for the past twenty years. To avert fines, owners began cooperating.[7]

When town trustees graded the broad downtown thoroughfares, the result made such a striking difference that a few residents graded the streets in front of their homes. They planted palm trees and "picked up" their front yards, repaired and painted fences. But still a considerable number of outliers, resentful of any change, fumed about taxes or made fun of all the commotion and made no effort to participate in the clean up.

Diversion arrived with residents' introduction to progress of a different kind. John Bidwell named a colt "Telephone" after the invention that puzzled everyone when a traveling salesman at a downtown store stretched "talking attachments" between two points and invited onlookers to give it a try. "Usually," the *Record* snickered, "the boys operating it talk loud enough to be heard two blocks away. The principal word sent into the tin can and over the cotton twine is 'Louder!'"[8] Because practical uses for telephones eluded the imaginations of most, such promotions only provided a good laugh.[9] However, before long the value of telephones became obvious in the countryside, where they connected large ranches and lumber camps to town businesses and residences. Still, two more years passed before telephones replaced telegraphs between Chico and Oroville.

What mattered most was water. Of course, Chico had always been alert to water issues, not only for safe drinking, but also to realize its ever elusive vision of "flouring mills, woolen mills, paper mills, and printing plants and ... agricultural irrigation."[10] Now, in 1881, the most prominent water issue was fire protection. This problem came to Chapman's attention when the town's steam-driven noon whistle, for which his company's water supplied the pressure, began to call townspeople to dinner at different times every mid-day. As soon as Gus returned to Chico, he ordered his engineer to raise the water pumps' pressure. While that solved the whistle problem, Gus knew it was only a temporary fix because the underlying reason for the pumps' irregularities was the poor condition of the water pipes that fed them steam. Therefore, seeking to raise public pressure on town trustees for a subsidy to replace them, Chapman announced on March 11 that the water company could not afford the $6,000 (over $170,000 today) required to buy and install the pipes.[11] The trustees ignored him.

Chapman, exhausted and distracted, raised the ante. He published a notice: the water utility would "cease operating the water works on Saturday, April 21, 1881."[12] The company, he said, was open to negotiations with the town trustees and, of course, he regretted "the inconvenience to the health and beauty of the city, and the want of ample protection in case of sudden conflagration and destruction by fire."[13] His stark references unleashed community fears. Only months previous his own mill had burned, a couple of years earlier downtown blocks had burned, and three years previous a Sierra Flume & Lumber mill had burned.[14] Every building in town was at risk from wood stoves in winter and dry grasses in summer.

Chapman's tactic worked. When the town trustees relented and appointed a citizens' committee to report on options, he probably felt encouraged about the outcome because he had been a volunteer member of various town committees for almost two decades. Some would remember that the water company was first ready to deliver to customers in 1874 when Chapman headed the company. When he learned there was a shortage of iron pipes, the only option was to install six miles of temporary wooden ones. High water pressure levels started cracking some of those pipes as early as 1875 while surviving ones were deteriorating.

The new trustees' committee met at the water company where Chapman opened the ledgers to the members so they could verify his statements about the extent of the firm's financial problems. He presented cost estimates to dig up the old pipes and buy and install iron replacements. Initially Chapman and the committee flirted with the cheapest solution: ignore the old pipe problem and add new pipes to bring clear mountain water to town. However, the committee knew John Bidwell owned all the rights to Big Chico Creek water out of Iron Canyon, seven to eight miles northeast of town.[15] When the committee approached Bidwell about sharing those rights with Chico, he explained that his flour mill and farm operations required all of it.[16]

The trustees' committee backed Chapman's request for a temporary tax increase to buy iron pipes. Hearing that, he made ready to order and install them immediately; to offset the costs, a new water rate would have to be negotiated later. On May 6, 1881, however, when the town trustees heard about the committee's endorsement of Chapman's proposal for a tax increase, they not only refused, they informed him that, as long as his company held the town's water franchise, it was his responsibility to replace the wooden pipes. Furthermore, they informed Gus that, if his company could not meet the expense, it must forfeit the franchise.

The public was furious at the impasse. Any lapse in water service terrified them. Since drought had lowered the water level in the cisterns under downtown streets, high water pressure for the fire hoses was more necessary than ever. Supporters of a tax to pay for iron pipes included rancher John Bidwell and druggist Jerry Noonan, both of whom owned arson-plagued buildings. Furniture and casket builder Martin Loy, who had lost his planing mill to fire, also signed on. Even carpenter Zion Moore, a former Workingman who was often out of work and called himself one of the "poor ones," offered to pay something. (Another speaker recommended residents like Moore be exempt from a hike.[17])

At the meeting's end, the trustees finally voted for the tax. Chapman immediately left for San Francisco to order iron pipes and catch up on prison business. By the time the new pipes arrived in Chico a couple of weeks later, water company workers had already dug many of the trenches. While that work proceeded, property owners cooperated with town trustees on another advance: assigned street addresses, including numbers they painted by their front doors.[18]

Even when the new pipes were in the ground, there was no rest for Chapman. The gas utility mounted twenty street lamps. More fully lighted streets were part of the town improvement agenda but the trustees were leery. Outside vendors had been approaching them to install the latest invention, electric street-lights, which were more appealing than the exasperating gas ones. However, the trustees hesitated to sign a contract because stories circulated about places like Nevada City where fly-by-night electric companies defrauded the town.[19]

The gas light problem touched on political sensitivities. Along the six blocks of Salem Street's elegant newer houses there were four gas lamps, whereas along the eight blocks of 1860s cottages on Sycamore (now Normal Avenue) there was only one lamp. Chapman managed to ignore the lighting problem until November 1881 when the trustees suspended payments to the company for poor service. Gus, occupied by prison problems, responded by terminating street lighting altogether.[20]

A few citizens, accustomed to the little blobs of flickering gaslight on their street, attached boxes containing their own kerosene lamps to the street posts nearest their houses. Volunteers lighted them for awhile. Then, when their diligence dropped off, the ink-dark nights became regular reminders of Augustus Chapman's seeming disregard for Chico's problems. At the same time, Chico's claims on Gus diverted him from his state responsibilities. While the new water pipes had offered him some redemption, the streetlamp problem raised new doubts about his commitment to Chico.

Then the water pumps failed. In August 1881, the hottest month of the year—only months after Chapman replaced the water pipes—the pumps, only two years old, shut down. After emergency fixes, Chapman ordered the pressure reduced to extend their use. The company also published an irrigation timetable.[21] Residents could only water their yards, gardens and orchards between 5 and 8 o'clock in the mornings and evenings. Water users were not permitted to run water at night lest they drain the tanks by midnight and leave the town without water for fire service. Chapman appended a vague threat to make examples of water users who did not comply.

Gus's Thoughts about Prisons and the State

Trusting his customers would observe this schedule and the pumps would hold to forestall another expensive crisis, Gus turned from Chico demands and caught up on writing the annual prison report. On reviewing the Legislature's criticisms of his prison board of directors he emphasized in the report that it was less critical of his board's management than of San Quentin's chronic failure to reform inmates. He insisted legislators were unreasonably holding this board responsible for problems that predated their service of only one year. Nevertheless, this criticism spoke to his charge from Governor Perkins to turn the prisons into reformatory institutions once they became self-supporting.

Chapman's extended report provides a window on how he, as a California farm town resident and businessman, understood the state's social problems. He centered considerable blame for crime on economic conditions. He argued that California's pervasive poverty and inadequate schooling were producing parents whose neglect criminalized their children. Beginning in life as thieves of "wood, coal, vegetables," some turned into young hooligans who frightened town and country people alike.[22] Chapman did not name any towns, but he knew from his state travels such patterns existed in Chico and elsewhere. He pointed to California's influx of newcomers who hoped for riches but instead found destitution and, in response, resorted to crime.

Apparently influenced by the analysis of San Francisco economist Henry George, Chapman traced the source of California's economic problems to the structure of its agriculture. Vast ranches in the hands of a few were characteristic of the state's holdings. Virtually no new arrivals could find a foothold in agriculture—that is, own a small farm. His own experience was anchored in the northern Sacramento Valley where Chico's farm town businesses, like others elsewhere, were stymied without a growing population base centered on agriculture. Local people concluded their futures were in jeopardy unless principal land monopolists—he did not mention John Bidwell, O. C. Pratt or Hugh Glenn by name—broke up their vast landholdings and sold parcels to small farmers.

This concentrated ownership, Chapman's report argued, had deprived California of the stable foundation that moderately sized family farms established in the Midwest and the East: "[T]he mode of farming here does not provide homes for farm laboring, but promotes roving and unsettled habits [as well as] financial uncertainty."[23] He observed how the depressed economy was "tossing men about, throwing them out of employment and leaving them adrift in straightened circumstances."[24] Their evident awareness of Chapman's views had led earlier Chico Democrats and Workingmen to their joint endorsement of Republican Chapman in 1879.

Chapman's report preserves this glimpse of his values and intellect. The complex issues he confronted on the Prison Commission elicited all he had to offer. His report presents a steady, thoughtful approach not only to the operation and development of the prisons, but also to the broader social and economic contexts in which they operated. The content and even tenor of his prison reports supported Perkins's confidence in Chapman as a man suited to the broader scope of state affairs.

Although public life had attracted Chapman, he brought to the work no previous experience in the labyrinth of state elective politics. That was the world now closing in on Gus, who would increasingly find it narrowing and imperiling his prospects. His sense of vulnerability—even bewilderment—in that milieu surfaced in his report: "The Board asks only that fair treatment be accorded them ... rather than that they should be the subject of constant and unjust criticism and unmerited abuse."[25]

Governor Perkins, ever under fire from Democrats, relied on Chapman and his board to implement prison reforms he hoped would fuel his own political rise. Determined to realize Perkins's vision, the prison board of directors laid the foundation for the next phase of their work. They assigned Chapman to tour eastern prisons and identify prison products which, in addition to grain sacks and granite, could keep the state prisons self-supporting and avoid competition with non-prison labor. The recently added chair factory and the jute mill at San Quentin employed only half its inmates; most of the other men were idle. Folsom prisoners who did not work in the granite quarries also needed productive activity. Chapman left for the tour just as the Chapman & McKay lumber mills started up for the new season—just when he should have been dealing with seasonal sales. Once again, he left Bill McKay on his own to "take care of business."

16

Prison Successes Collide with Chico Water Issues and Family Rebellion

On March 4, 1882, Chapman did not consider his Chico problems resolved but under control when he set off from the depot to begin his national prison tour. Iron water pipes were in place and the pumps struggled on. In January the Bank of Butte County's board of directors had re-elected him vice president.[1] However, it was clear that, without income from Chapman & McKay, he could not afford unpaid work in public service. Unlike the Chico utilities draining his time, reputation and finances, retail sales of lumber were overall reliable. There were still strains between Bill McKay and himself and he was mulling over how to change that.

While the personal expenses incurred by his Prison Commission work were inescapable, he was resigned to them because, with George Perkins's support, he qualified for yet another high public position. He had also become aware that, in the highest public circles, personal fortunes insulated men like George Perkins against the machinations of political opponents. Gus Chapman was very well-off, but he was not rich like his mentor or John Bidwell. Since he was playing "out of his league," he had to calculate his every move.

However, even though Chapman & McKay generated Gus's major source of income for twenty years, he did not want to resume an operational role in the partnership. His journey east to examine other states' prison manufacturing production provided the only unbroken rest that Chapman had enjoyed since he arrived in California. His hours on trains gave him time to strategize how to keep his income flow from Chapman & McKay without dealing with the production end in the mountains.

Once in Michigan he was refreshed and ready to launch his survey. His destination was Addison, where he had owned the general store. His purpose was to consult with the warden of the Michigan Central State Prison in nearby Jackson, whose reformatory approach had interested him and George Perkins when they considered the problems overwhelming California prisons. While in Addison, he had a chance to see Sarah's Sickley family and meet the family of his half-brother George Babcock. At Jackson, after meetings and a look at prison-made products like wool hats, he concluded present California prison products were more suited to the West Coast. In Detroit he visited a prison chair factory that confirmed his board's recent decision to expand San Quentin's furniture production. In a letter to publisher George Crosette, Gus mentioned his recent arrangements with John Bidwell to send a freight load of second-growth oak to San Quentin for table and chair manufacturing. With proper conservation, Gus predicted purchases of Butte County wood could supply the prison's factory for another fifty years.[2]

In Trenton, New Jersey, where he watched prisoners make team whips, he concluded that California prison tanneries could weave them from leftover belting and shoe scraps. Recalling steam-driven laundry machinery from the Philadelphia Centennial he and Fred visited in 1876, he was impressed by a prison machine "which would puzzle a Chinaman to imitate." He considered it superior to the skilled handiwork in Chico Chinese laundries "that now seem necessary."[3]

At Elmira and Auburn state prisons in New York, he concluded the wheel-axle production had potential once materials were available from the steel mills being considered for Oakland. To his enthusiasm about carpet manufacture, he appended a plaintive non sequitur about the amount of energy Californians wasted on "political discussion."[4] He expressed exasperation at the social and political content in the Board of Inquiry's report. It had criticized the Prison Commission for providing more decent food for prisoners and halting guards' use of corporal punishment.

Chapman returned to California with renewed confidence.

Throughout his tour he had compared ideas with wardens and prison directors who were like him and his colleagues. They too had entered public service as civic leaders with backgrounds in business or professions and drew on their pragmatic common-sense approach to management. He learned that other, long-established prisons constantly wrestled with problems like those of San Quentin and Folsom. Chapman had gained expertise, proclaiming "the subject of scientific penology that seems to addle the brains of some would-be reformers, [has not] been awarded that place in penal economy and reformation that fancy or honest desire might wish."[5]

Smarting at the inquiry's claims that prison board members were accountable when freed inmates misbehaved, Chapman allowed himself another barb at critics: "Penology, as an inexact science, is at a discount, except in California."[6] His polished report, full of fresh observations and analysis, suggests that, despite its challenges, he found in public work the satisfaction that had long evaded him in business.

In May 1882 Chapman returned to Chico, according to the *Enterprise*, "full of penology, prison discipline and the working of criminals for their own good, and the benefit of the State which has to support them.... We know Mr. Chapman intimately, as a shrewd, thorough-going business man, and ... something beneficial to the taxpayers ... will be developed and the best interests of criminals subserved."[7]

Fred Returns to the New Water Problems

Fred Chapman's arrival from New York in June 1882 as a college graduate raised Gus's spirits. Friends and family admired how he had slimmed down, yet filled out and matured. He returned a better-than-ever musician with a warm personality, credited to his mother's influence, that contributed to his developing skills as a salesman. In that and his preference for town life, Fred resembled his father. Now that Fred was educated and well-traveled, Gus considered him "finished"—ready to carry out his father's plan for his future.

Gus envisioned he would be to Fred what George Wood (and George Perkins) were to him. With Fred at work in the lumber company, its income would continue to support the family and

Gus would be free to concentrate on developing his career in government or politics. While Gus was pressing William McKay to teach Fred the mill end of the business, Fred made his start at the gas and water utilities where his former schoolmate and Sunday School pal John Kempf Jr. was on the staff. (Employees of young Kempf's father, without his knowledge, had killed the Chinese at the Lemm Ranch.) There were few Chicoans Fred Chapman and John Kempf Jr. did not know. With the public upset over the water and gas utilities' shortcomings, they found public relations part of their jobs. Fred had missed the pipe challenge, but he was on hand for the pump crisis.

Acting on the flicker of public approval Gus's pipes deal had brought him, Gus asked the town trustees to extend the temporary monthly tax they had allotted him to replace the water pipes. Chapman explained it was essential because now the company had to buy new water pumps. However, a recent election had replaced town trustees Henry Camper and grocer Newman Johnson, both fellow Republicans and supporters of the water service in the previous pipes crisis. Taking their places were Democrats jeweler Charles Ball and brewer Charles Croissant, whose votes made a new majority against Chapman's tax extension proposal.

The tax extension debacle was complicated behind the scenes by the close friendship between Bertha Croissant, Rebecca Ball and Sarah Chapman in the North Methodist Church, where Sara and Rebecca held the "elder seats" allotted to women. The *Enterprise* echoed Chapman's frustration: "[Republican] businessmen, capable to fill the position [of town trustees], are not willing to sacrifice their time to such a thankless position, they are not willing to accept a position to be abused by the element who have no other than a selfish interest in the city, and who pay little or nothing for its support."[8]

When his proposal to replace the pumps with help from the existing tax failed to sway the new town trustees, Gus ran out of alternatives. By refusing to transfer the water pipe tax revenue to a pump subsidy, as the trustees had threatened, the company could only relieve the old pumps' life by reducing water use. That meant the company could only keep enough water in the tanks for fire responses, kitchen gardens and hygiene.

As townspeople saw it, Chapman was threatening their safety to protect the company. According to Gus's business perspective, the financial economies from the pumps' reduced operation would help keep the water service afloat. While the irrigation schedule the company imposed in the 1881 pipes crisis had irritated customers, in this round the siren's silence aroused fear of fire.[9]

As the town trustees' differences with Gus Chapman over water service hardened in this round, a significant side effect informally reshaped town government. This body of trustees abandoned their traditional deference to the policy preferences of the business-based citizen committees. Now they began to rely on their own experience and political sense of representing an amorphous "public" against private interest; in this case, Chapman's utility services. In the face of their intransigence, Chapman could not stand down. If he did not secure the tax, the fragile company could collapse. His strenuous defense of it cost him, at least temporarily, respect and influence he had built over years within the citizens' committees.

The trustees were discovering they could fan new popularity "on the street" and, primed by the steam whistle's silence, they excoriated the Chico Water Co. The trustees and townspeople's antagonism re-sensitized Chapman to the urgency of their needs and to his own need for their approval. Not only was he proud of the high regard he had built in Chico by public service, any future he had in politics depended on not alienating potential voters. He quietly withdrew his threat to shut down the pumps. The pumps struggled on, the steam whistle resumed and the water company continued to flounder.

By 1883, while all that was unfolding, Chapman's investors became nervous about the level of his debt. He reassured them that they should have no reason to doubt him and began to reorganize his assets. First, he sold most of the thirty-acre creek-side parcel, the Chapman Reserve, that extended from the Boucher Ranch east of Chapman's Addition to an area behind the Bidwell Avenue farm house he and Sarah remodeled in 1871. Perhaps to protect the garden view across to the creek from the front of his present house, Gus retained approximately a block of the creek bank acreage.

There is no document setting out the reasons behind Chapman's need for the Bank of Butte County mortgage he took out in 1881. However, the sale of his creek-side parcel fell short of his need to cover the loan. In addition, he continued buying timberlands, paying for tuitions and college travel, subsidizing the water and gas utilities and facing the rebuilding of Chapman & McKay's Somerset mill that arsonists destroyed. A later comment by Gus suggests the expense of rebuilding that mill was at the core of his financial problems. And, on top of all that, two years of ongoing heavy expenses for his Prison Commission service had not been reimbursed. It did not help that he, Chapman & McKay's most successful salesman, had neglected that responsibility in the partnership for years.

To see himself through, he turned to a private lender, a standard method to raise money before banks were in place. Since the mid-1870s, as a member of the Bank of Butte County's board of directors, Gus had taken out a loan there about the time he bought the gas and water utilities. Now that he faced paying down mortgages, he needed to find another source of funds.

A loan from a private source to pay off the bank loan became feasible thanks to an economic rally after the 1870s depression. Gus was well-known as the owner of significant business and prime domestic property. He also had a sterling reputation in business and with the community. All this emboldened William Earll, a new arrival in Chico, to loan him the extraordinary sum of $20,000 (over $540,000 today).[10]

Because William Earll's loan would have reverberating effects on Chapman's future, he merits fuller discussion. He had moved his family to Chico from the village of Dunnigan, 59 miles south of there, in 1879. As an experienced businessman, and consistent with financial practice, he recognized Chapman's properties as ample security for the loan. Adding to Chapman's history of credit worthiness, he also had the confidence of George Perkins and Republican leaders on the state level. Earll was further reassured because he and Chapman had much in common. Like Chapman had done with George Wood, Earll had started his Chico hardware store with help from a silent San Francisco partner.[11] (According to the Earll family, a very wealthy investor, Cyril Hubbard, was William's backer; therefore, it seems likely

Hubbard was the actual source of Earll's loan to Chapman.)

Chapman and Earll were approximately the same age and both were natives of New York who had grown up in Michigan. In the early to mid-1860s each had closed retail businesses there to head for the Sacramento Valley. Although they arrived in Chico nearly twenty years apart, each quickly became a civic and business leader. While, according to Charles Stilson's diaries, Chapman was fair to his employees, Earll was both fair *and* generous. For example, after a grueling store audit he paid for all his clerks' dinners at Tom Dooley's Oyster Bar & Saloon on West Second Street.[12] In addition, at the time of the loan both Chapman and Earll had enrolled or soon would enroll daughters in elite New England women's colleges. The younger Earll's daughter Flora and Mary Chapman became close friends at the Chico Academy.[13]

As businessmen, Chapman and Earll understood the importance of tangible assets. Like today, businesses required good credit, but today's sophisticated measures of credit worthiness had yet to be developed. The usual measure available to lenders at the time relied on reputation and image such as publicly visible property of value.[14] Chapman and Earll ensured that their families were among the most beautifully housed in Chico. Therefore, a loan to lumberman A. H. Chapman, the governor's friend and a high public official, whose pressing state responsibilities temporarily left him little time to address home concerns, appeared secure. And Chapman had a history of assuming risks and turning them into profit.

The Earll loan freed Gus Chapman to concentrate on prison issues. Meanwhile, as the water pump controversy continued, he realized he had to burnish his relationship with the local press. But his timing was off. In 1882 his reliable supporter George Crosette won a Board of Supervisors seat, sold the *Record* and bought his wife a "perfect bijou [jewel] of a cottage" on Ivy Street. The couple had recently moved there after their longtime residence, the Chico Hotel, burned down. Chapman likely provided their curbstone or mounting block (a high step used to mount or dismount a horse or buggy) which still sits in front of the house. The curbstone's dark granite resembles products mined and finished at the prison's Folsom Curbstone Works.

This left Chapman no "in" with the new editor of the *Record*. For the first time, its coverage of Chapman turned harsh. For example, with respect to the still faulty gas streetlamps, which Chapman had relighted after the 1881 cut-off, the paper's editorial urged the trustees to withhold the town's payment.[15] Chapman found one brief break in all the negativity after he paid a water witch to search for fresh, gas-free water in town. Wielding an apple branch, he located a new source just east and in sight of the downtown, well away from outhouse pollution (the water tower stands today). This positive moment receded with his return to Sacramento and defense of the Prison Commission against legislators' partisan attacks.

Fred: Flying High

Fred Chapman had returned to Chico from college with high expectations from his parents. However, he had different priories. Fred was ready to take his place in the town's social life. His activities focused on card parties and dinners at private homes, church events, buggy drives along country roads and picnics. In October, when he and his friends organized a hayride, they acquired use of a large, flat header wagon used to transport harvested wheat. They cleaned it, spread clean straw, then scattered bales for seating, reserving space for hampers of refreshments. Before heading for the beach on the Sacramento River, they and their guests drove to the Chapmans' house and then along West Fifth Street to serenade their families. While Fred immersed himself in pleasures, his father had other plans for him.

Of all Gus's concerns about Fred's social inclinations, alcohol was not one of them. His parents did not disapprove of moderate social drinking. Therefore, they must have been astonished when Fred announced he had adopted temperance. It was a cause they had personally avoided. For example, Sarah and Eliza Camper remained best friends even after Eliza became so committed that she traveled to participate in temperance gatherings. Fred's decision came from a revival of the Band of Hope meetings at Miss White's School on Broadway. This national youth organization had its first meeting in Chico in 1868. In Chapman's days, it had drawn crowds upstairs to Wood's Hall for lectures and entertainment that discouraged alcohol, swearing and tobacco.[16]

When Eliza Camper became its sponsor, it moved its meetings to the North Methodist church.

Fred had fallen under the "righteous" influence of former classmate and now girlfriend Magnolia Wood, the daughter of Alice and Jesse Wood, who had remained the county super-intendent of schools since before he defeated Gus Chapman's candidate Selena Woodman. Magnolia had moved with her fam-ily to the outskirts of Oroville to accommodate her father's work at the county seat.

Eventually Fred, financially dependent on his father, submit-ted to his pressure. He left his girlfriend, his friends and his job at the gas and water utilities to work in Powellton during the lum-ber season. Once Fred could independently run the production end, it seems Gus planned to buy McKay's share of the company and replace him with Fred. This may seem a "leap" in conjecture, but, in light of the present context and later events, it fits.

It took almost no time for Fred to confirm one unfortunate resemblance to his father: he loathed rural life in the foothills. Fred's opportunity to learn the family business was not compen-sated by Powellton's natural beauty or its colorful characters. What weighed on Fred was its location: to attend parties and concerts in Chico, he had to ride up to ten hours by stagecoach each way. Even so, whenever he could get away, he headed for Chico. For a couple of days, he could try out the latest sheet music with his close friend Charlie Camper, play in the Neubarth Band and court Magnolia.

She was under pressure to remain with her family on their new farm. But, like Fred, she longed for life in town and left for Chico to teach at the Oakdale School, in sight of Fred's home across the Oroville-Shasta Road. Magnolia's impact on Fred became unmistakable, first with his embrace of temperance and then his switch to the Presbyterian Church. While neither choice reflected his parents' preferences, Fred's adoption of the young woman's upright values gave his parents' hope he was at least growing more responsible.

Magnolia began spending family time with the Chapmans. This included stays at their Powellton cottage, where she kept company with Sarah and Mary while Fred worked for William McKay. While initially Sarah's stays in Powellton were dutiful, she discovered the moderate mountain temperatures offered relief from the valley's heat. Keeping up the cottage was easier than supervising and tending to the maintenance of her big house and grounds on Chapman Street.

Mary Ann McKay's prominence in Powellton might have presented a social conundrum to Sarah, but she was not competitive. Although the two women were winter neighbors in Chapmantown, their husbands' strains had created a social distance. Since several of Sarah's Chico friends summered in Paradise, she joined them for birthday parties, to make rag rugs or to pass time with them on their porches. While Sarah valiantly attempted to keep her family's life on course, by the mid-1880s her husband's and her children's problems evolved in directions no one expected and she could not avert.

1880s

17

Governor Stoneman *v.* A. H. Chapman: Justice Is Best Served Cold

When Gus Chapman returned from his 1882 prison tour, the Prison Commission's board of directors met to hear his findings about other states' prison-made products. Members were still weighing their options when the fall election replaced Governor Perkins with Civil War Union veteran Major General George Stoneman, a Democrat. The positions of Chapman and most of his colleagues appeared secure because most of them had half of their terms ahead of them. But, with no Republican governor to protect them, the Democratic legislators' lingering hostility was now cause for unease. The board members were concerned that the state still had not reimbursed their expenses for more than a year. And Chapman, still under financial pressures at home, was owed more than the rest for his extra expenses from extensive travels as board chairman.

The prison directors were aware of Stoneman because in 1879 he was elected as a Workingmen's Party advocate to California's new regulatory agency, the Railroad Commission. He was already a kind of "Forest Gump," whose life unrolled ongoing connections to important persons and events.

For example, Stoneman's West Point classmates included Civil War officers George McClennan and Stonewall Jackson. George Pickett of Pickett's Charge had been his roommate. As a Mexican War veteran, Stoneman had switched to the Democratic Party after the Civil War because he believed Reconstruction policies that protected former slaves infringed on the property rights of white Southerners. In California during the Perkins administration, Bidwell and Stoneman exchanged memories of their meeting as young men in 1851 when Army Lieutenant Stoneman's unit escorted the federal Indian treaty commissioner to Rancho Chico for negotiations with the Maidu.[1] In 1881 John Bidwell lobbied Stoneman and the other Railroad Commission members at a Bidwell mansion dinner out of concern that they had almost immediately turned into "de facto" allies of the railroad. With Stoneman at Bidwell's dinner was fellow commission member Charles Beerstecher. In 1879 Bidwell had lent "Annie's Glen" on Rancho Chico grounds to the Workingmen's Party for its campaign party after Beerstetcher's new Constitution rally at Third and Main streets.

Democrats, like Workingmen, opposed workforce competition between free labor and prisoners. Both were suspicious of a prison factory churning out wheat sacks for the profit of "rich farmers." In contrast, Chapman and his board members under Perkins found initial support from the *San Jose Mercury* and a scattering of Democrats in the Legislature. Perkins was proud when his prison board brought the jute grain-sack factory on line so quickly that, in its second year, San Quentin forwarded a $25,000 profit to the State Treasury.[2] Thirty years later—well after Chapman's death—U.S. Senator George Perkins would continue to remind voters that he had launched "one of the most important industries carried on in any penal institution in the nation, namely the great jute-bag manufacturing industry which continued at San Quentin."[3] Of course, his authority had launched it, but A. H. Chapman's management made it happen.

When Perkins finished his only term as governor in 1883, grain-sack production had reached 6,000 to 7,000 bags a day. California farmers bought them as fast as prisoners could make them and at cheaper prices than they had paid for sacks shipped from Calcutta. When Chapman brought San Quentin sacks home to show the *Enterprise* editor in June 1882, he pointed to an improved seam stitch. He explained that each sack cost the state 6¢, sold for 8½¢ and was produced in a factory at San Quentin where all but four workers were prisoners.[4] In only two years Chapman and his colleagues had shipped and installed the equipment from Scotland and fully implemented Perkins's grain-sack goal. This alone had satisfied the new

Constitution's mandate to establish prisoner self-support.

In December 1882, as Governor Perkins prepared for his departure, every able prisoner worked in shops, made bricks or grain sacks, or laundered. At Folsom, they built furniture or worked on granite projects. Perkins responded to Democrats' harsh criticism of Chapman and the other directors by reminding Californians that he did not believe they intended "that their public servants shall ... render their services without compensation or reward." Emphasizing the point, he said he did not believe that public servants "shall [have to] pay the costs and expenses necessarily incident to the performance of their official duties out of their own private funds."[5]

But, of course, the Prison Commission's board of directors carried on under those terms. Among themselves, they found no comfort in the new governor's inaugural speech in January 1883. Like Perkins, Stoneman announced his primary focus would be the prisons. By contrast to Perkins's emphasis on reformatory policies, Stoneman stressed a return to harshly punitive ones. He prescribed hard time for criminals, whom he said the Chapman board had coddled.

Stoneman's problem was political. Governors prized the Prison Commission because it was one of the few agencies that had positions they could dole out to supporters. In this, Stoneman was stymied. Perkins's board of Republicans was in place serving terms that, in some cases, extended beyond Stoneman's own term. As previously mentioned, Perkins had invited Democrats to serve, as the new Constitution required, but that party had refused to let them serve, insisting on the tradition of partisan control. That edict from Stoneman's own Democratic Party in 1880 now thwarted his ambition to replace the Prison Commission's members with Democrats. Until he could appoint enough Democrats to make a commission majority, the Perkins holdovers could ignore his preferences at will.

He was right. Chapman and the other Republicans ignored him and continued to forge ahead on their reform agenda. They kept their humane changes in place, continued to refine the grain-sack operation and were getting ready to add new products for prisoners to manufacture. On the latter point, their discussion centered on the report of Augustus Chapman, who had become California's principal expert on prison management.

Still, Those Pumps

In 1883, as in 1881 and 1882, Chapman had to divide his attention. That March a new round of water problems met him when he detrained at the Chico depot. The town trustees had refused to extend the monthly pipe tax to purchase new pumps. However, he persuaded them to approve a small, municipal tax that enabled the water utility to repair the existing pumps so that the water pressure level could be raised. To the relief of everyone, once done, a test of the fire plug at Second and Main produced a water stream that reached over half a block, the best force the company had ever produced—"So far, so good."[6] The pumps' fix had to hold because the company still could not afford new ones. Neither Chico, Sacramento nor San Francisco provided him escape or respite. Chapman and his partners confronted one crisis after the next.

Stoneman's Challenge

In May, Chapman's prison headache turned into a raging migraine. Now that the Democrats' man was governor, their majority in the State Legislature amped up their partisan war on both the prison and railroad commissions. Although complaints about the latter were bitter and rife, Governor Stoneman, who had given up his seat on it, ignored the attacks.

Instead, he focused on the Prison Commission. He decided to drive out its entire Republican membership.[7] After they refused to resign and no standard procedure permitted him to fire them, he charged every member with civil misconduct. This second push for them to resign also did not work. The governor immediately geared up to remove them himself.

Stoneman's lofty position presented ironic testimony to the height of Chapman's rise. Local newspapers broadcasted the charges Stoneman borrowed from the Democratic Party-controlled State Senate.[8] Legislators alleged the directors were lax in their oversight and that their appointee, San Quentin warden J. P. Ames, had committed financial abuses. Stoneman also followed the Democratic senators' lead in reviving the previous year's pay issue. However, when the comptroller moved to reimburse the directors for their personal outlays, the State Legislature refused to pass the proposed reimbursement revision. Therefore, with no new law to replace what the court had struck down, Chapman and his colleagues continued to personally pay for their state service. Stoneman also charged the Prison Commission directors had implemented the jute grain-sack mill solely on the basis of Perkins's executive action, when it should have had legislative approval.

The Chico newspapers provided no context when they reported the new governor's charges against Chapman and his colleagues. In this round, the *Record* editor who replaced Crosette planted a dig. In the regular column listing arrivals at the Chico depot, the previously noted "A. H. Chapman" became "Hon. A.H. Chapman State Prison Director."[9] In other words, Gus's title, one he considered the great honor of his life, was now seen in his hometown as associated with scandal. While Gus was moving at the usual fast pace among Chico, Sacramento, San Francisco, San Quentin, Folsom and Roseville for meetings with packed agendas on prison business, he now had to fit in time and expenses for conferences with lawyers.

Chapman and the other directors took what reassurance they could find in the *Sacramento Bee*'s assertion that Stoneman had no grounds for his charges, that the charges were only a tactic to drive out Republicans so that he could appoint Democrats. Less reassuring, the *Bee* also concluded that, nevertheless, the Commission directors had no choice but to slow their prison work and other ventures to work on proving their innocence.

Three Republican Party state leaders stepped forward to defend Chapman and his Prison Commission colleagues in the pending hearing. Second chair W. H. Sears of Marin County was a member of the early State Senate committee that had investigated prison management and cleared the directors. Judge C. B. Darwin, a former San Francisco district attorney, assisted the defense. First chair was Augustus Hart, who had been Governor Perkins's attorney general. A populist, Hart believed California would be great only if it would champion "the poor as well as the rich ... [the State must] ever look to the laboring classes, the men whose property, though small in degree ... are equal to those of the richer classes."[10] Hart's part in the defense was significant because he was the principal state official who had issued an opinion unfavorable to the Prison Commission when the Legislature granted them a salary in 1881. A celebrated speaker, Hart's voice resembled "the thunder of drumsticks on the bottom of a milkpan" while "his gestures were like the swaying of cornstalks in a gale."[11]

When Governor Stoneman announced he himself would be the hearing officer who would render the verdict, the defense attorneys were irate: the directors' accuser was to be their judge! Chapman and his co-defendants backed their lawyers' call for a criminal trial where an independent jury could deliver a binding verdict.[12] They were confident they could prevail under the discipline of legal procedures. However, when the governor refused to stand aside and they appealed to the State Supreme Court for relief, it rejected their arguments.

Chapman had to confront the reality that Stoneman's "witch-hunt" was unstoppable. The ongoing attack on Gus Chapman's work and his good name provided juicy yet often distorted scuttlebutt in Chico, except for his friends and associates who followed the *Sacramento Bee*. However, he could find no way to penetrate the unverified rumors spread at home in the *Enterprise* and the *Record*.

Despair

Augustus Chapman was so humiliated he must have considered suicide. He penned his will within days of the first hearing. It does not look or read like an abstract document vaguely directed at the future. His hand was shaky, his script spidery and his provisions suggested imminent death. It is possible that one of his bouts with malaria had left his hand unsteady, but wounded pride, anxiety and a sense of defeat are palpable in the legal document. Chapman was not reticent about his pride in the place he had made for himself in society. He requested funeral arrangements "with proper regard to my station and condition in life and the circumstances of my estate."[13] The Chapman & McKay mill and the timberland properties made that significant. Despite the setbacks at the Chico Water & Gas Works, he had negotiated a favorable contract with the town and the company was turning around. But none of that mattered now with the prospect of public disgrace at Stoneman's hands. Gus specified a family monument of "California Granite free from sop or corroding substances," a suitable memorial to his work on behalf of Folsom Prison's great granite quarries.[14]

In his will, Chapman expressed concern about a fair distribution between his older and younger children. Although in the previous four years of public service he had spent little time with Sarah or any of their children, Chapman now contemplated how his family would manage without him. His feelings for Sarah were clear with references to her as "my beloved wife." Making her his executor out of respect for her "ability to manage my estate and devotion to our children," he directed that she employ his assets to her support and that of "Gussie" and "Willie Winthrop."

In particular, he told her to set aside money for those boys equal to the amount in travel and education he had provided Mary and Fred. Once the two boys, then still in grade school, were secure and her own "ample support" provided for, he instructed Sarah to divide the remainder among the four children as she judged best. That said, he scrawled a frail version of his usual, vigorous signature. On June 2 at the Bank of Butte County, where his position as vice president still proclaimed his high station, his friends and bank board allies Charles Faulkner and John Robinson were witnesses.[15]

However, Chapman stepped back from suicide, if that had been his intent, and now appeared determined to face, endure and fight back—but how? When Stoneman launched the hearings, Gus and the other board members agreed to stay away from all except those to which they were called to appear. The inquiry was held in San Francisco, San Quentin and Folsom, with breaks between June and October 1883.

There was irony in the anguish churning below the subdued, almost mechanical exercise. In the main, onlookers were *Sacramento Bee* reporters who observed the defendants' lawyers deal with their combined accuser, judge and jury—the governor himself. Meanwhile, administration of the prisons was practically nil.[16] The *Sacramento Bee* reported on additional meetings in June and July.

Despite his intent to stay away, Gus and Fred stopped in at a San Francisco session during the second week. After they heard the governor refuse to amend his hearing procedures in the interest of fairness, they headed home. There, water service issues now seemed like a welcome diversion. Gus wandered around upper Iron Canyon with other businessmen looking for new municipal water sources. Bidwell carried the rights to Butte Creek's water and had declared he needed all of it. Meanwhile, in San Francisco, Augustus L. Hart and former Judge Sears launched the directors' defense.

Hart conceded Governor Stoneman's charge that former Governor Perkins had not met the constitutional requirement to make the Prison Commission bipartisan. He responded that, if there was an offender on this charge, it was Perkins who had appointed the directors—they had not appointed themselves. As mentioned earlier, the Democrats Perkins had invited to serve on the board had turned him down at their party's insistence. Chapman and the Prison Commission had followed his lead, however, and appointed only Republicans to the staff positions. Even so, Hart argued they had acted for Governor Perkins, who was ultimately responsible.[17]

The defense also argued that, when the directors had cut through one constitutional and several technical requirements to rush the grain-sack mill into production, their actions were only temporary ones necessary to keep the institutions running until the improvements underway were in place. For example, for a time the Prison Commission had ignored the new Constitution's ban against the public employment of Chinese. The penalty for employment of the eighteen prison Chinese workers skilled in weaving burlap was removal from office. Hart explained to Stoneman that, once "reminded" that the Constitution's bar against Chinese employees in the prisons was absolute, the directors fired them. The directors dismissed the Chinese workers even though compliance meant they then had to temporarily shut down production. Without the skilled Chinese workers, the prisoners had no productive work.[18] That meant San Quentin was generating no income for its support.

With hearings underway, the directors could not launch production of promising products that Gus recommended after his eastern tour. Instead, the directors left the warden to supervise prisoners' work under existing contracts in the furniture and new harness departments at San Quentin State Prison. Profits from the "jute mill" (grain-sack factory) and new products had been projected to free the prisons from state politics. As the Chapman board envisioned, self-supporting prisons could generate income to facilitate development of a juvenile facility, a women's facility and additional reformatory programs. The directors believed California had a lot to lose if they were to leave their posts.

Stoneman found no grounds to charge the directors with corruption. However, he made that charge against Warden J. P. Ames, who, with his clerk R. V. Ellis, had permitted questionable expenditures.[19] In this, Chapman found bitter vindication for his earlier lone objection to Ames's appointment. Trust in the former judge proved the board's biggest vulnerability.

During June 1883, the first month of the trial, Governor Stoneman heard the bookkeeper Ellis explain irregularities in the books he kept for Warden Ames. Ellis acknowledged that Ames had made a contract with a private individual who employed prison labor to build a private boat on San Quentin grounds. In their defense, Ames and Ellis testified no harm was done because nearly all the expenses were borne by the builder and the prison was to have free use of the boat to transport prison supplies across the San Francisco Bay to San Quentin.[20] In addition, when questioned, Ames and Ellis verified that Chapman and other prison directors had "acquired" some prison-made goods. However, Stoneman had to accept documented evidence that they each had paid for their acquisitions.

The single dramatic moment in the entire trial occurred when the court's clerk handed Ellis a telegram as he testified. He paled and left the hearing room for Governor Stoneman's chambers where reporters and observers could overhear him sobbing. The death of his aged mother caused a week's hiatus in the proceedings.[21]

When Gus Chapman testified, the governor asked him about a former Folsom warden who requested work. Chapman replied he had reservations, so referred this application to the board as a whole and after that to Governor Perkins, who consulted with the board on several appointments. When Governor Stoneman later asked that former warden why an earlier board majority—prior to Chapman's board—had asked him to resign, he responded, "Incompetence, I believe."[22] The Chapman board did not hire him so Stoneman had to relent.

While Stoneman's hearing was underway, Chapman and his colleagues ignored calls to appear before the State Senate Democrats who had established the hostile State Prison Commission Board of Inquiry. In shaping his offensive, Stoneman had employed early Board of Inquiry claims. Meanwhile, Chapman and his board directors, who, for two years, had regularly been fending off the Senate subcommittee's partisan attacks on their work, caught up on their businesses at home where they scanned the *Sacramento Bee* for information about the hearings.

According to Chapman and the other board members' defense, most of the relatively minor "misdeeds" were like grains of sand in the ethical desert that was California business and politics of the 1880s. Their attorney W. H. Sears reminded Governor Stoneman that Ames's violations had taken place without the board members' knowledge. In addition, he reminded the governor that some actions were temporary technical violations necessary to achieve important state objectives. He called for consideration of the larger result: two high functioning prisons with factories that gave prisoners work and, as a result, now relieved the state of all prison expenses. After the hearings concluded in San Francisco, they moved to Sacramento for July and, from there, to San Quentin so Governor Stoneman could observe the jute mill operations.

At Home: "Trouble in River City"

While no press on the scene reported on Chapman's testimony, influential Chico readers of the *Sacramento Bee* and the *San Francisco Examiner* drew their own conclusions. Although most had respected Chapman, they also were skeptical of "politicians." Aware of this, Chapman launched a spirited campaign at home where he counted on positive newspaper coverage to neutralize the negative effects of prison hearings coverage. Now he needed his friends. It was fortuitous that a Masonic convention was pending in San Francisco. Gus traveled there with bankers

A. H. Crew (Bank of Chico) and John R. Robinson (Bank of Butte County), as well as Dr. Carnot Mason. He had plenty of time to give these significant leaders a full picture of his situation in state government.

Once Gus was back in Chico for weeks at a time during the hearing, he evidently welcomed travel to Powellton. Fred was there at work for Bill McKay, but had won a transfer to Chico for training in lumber sales. Later developments would demonstrate sales were not Chapman's principal goal for Fred. McKay must have been skeptical about his partner's sudden enthusiasm for any part of the business.[23]

Chapman's Next Project—The Odd Fellows Lodge

Any recovery from the Stoneman affair and any future in politics would require renewed support from Gus's Butte County "base." His "campaign" quickly found an opportunity to recover his reputation as a Chico leader by helping the Odd Fellows unscramble a troublesome problem. Although an Odd Fellows member for at least twenty years, he had only been active the first ten. After that his commitments shifted to the crises he faced by his Chapmantown development, businesses and state politics.

The Odd Fellows's problem concerned real estate. In 1879 the group paid $3,000 for a deep lot at the northwest corner of Third and Broadway. The majority of members envisioned a lodge upstairs with first floor rentals to pay for the building construction. The members who objected to taking on debt had managed to block further progress and, in 1883, found a way out to the whole club's advantage when Frank Lusk approached their board of directors.

In spring 1883 Lusk, on his way to becoming Chico's most powerful lawyer and a colleague of Chapman on the board of the Bank of Butte County, had lost his suite at the Chico Hotel when it burned down. Determined to build a combined home and office downtown, Lusk offered to buy the Odd Fellows' lot for $5,000, a handsome sum. The members were in a turmoil as they debated how to proceed. Would they construct a building or would they sell the lot?

Frank Lusk was known to be aggressive, driven and cold.

No one crossed him lightly. For Chapman to refuse him could be a costly decision. Nevertheless, rather than selling the lot to Lusk, Chapman agreed to spearhead the Odd Fellows project by raising the funds and overseeing the construction on his own. Trusting Chapman, who had built two Chico schools and a subdivision, the board appointed him president of the Odd Fellows Building Association and, while the Stoneman hearings continued, Gus led a summer fund drive that raised $30,000, an extraordinary amount at that time (over $900,000 today). In September the building committee he formed called for bids to build a three-story, ornamented brick building with commercial space below, professional offices in suites and well-appointed lodge rooms on the second floor and a ballroom on the third floor.

Then, during winter 1883-1884, Chapman worked with the contractor as the building went up. By now hypersensitive to issues of ethics, he bought lumber from Oregon rather than Chapman & McKay.[24] When the handsome structure was complete, the celebration brought Odd Fellows members to Chico from across the region.[25] As Oakdale School had done, the Odd Fellows building won him community appreciation.

Of course, none of Chapman's new efforts at home—not his and McKay's rebuild of their Somerset mill, not the Odd Fellows Hall's ongoing progress, not his installation of fifteen new gas lights on town streets—could overcome Stoneman's blows.

The Verdict

On September 13, 1883, one day before Governor Stoneman delivered his verdict that removed the Republican prison board and opened their seats to his choices of Democrats, the governor met with John Bidwell at the State Fair.[26] Nothing about their conversation survives. However, Bidwell was the most important client of Frank Lusk, who, for years, had quietly been a Democrat who avoided party politics. But he "came out" to secure a post office job to help the children of the late physician Samuel Sproul. In 1879 he had briefly tried to become a Republican candidate for the Nonpartisan Party. Now, in 1883, he found it useful to be a Democrat when Bidwell was reestablishing his own old links to the state Democratic Party through the election of his distant acquaintance to the new state governor George Stoneman. At this point, Republican Bidwell and Democrats Stoneman and Lusk all had issues with Augustus Chapman. While this set a tone of menace associated with Chapman's "fall," no evidence other than Stoneman's meeting with Bidwell the day before the verdict, confirms that Bidwell influenced or tried to influence Stoneman on the Prison Commission issues.

Governor Stoneman, unsurprisingly, rendered a guilty verdict. He pronounced all the Prison Commission board of directors guilty and removed them from office "for cause." He also castigated Governor Perkins for making all partisan appointments, in violation of the new Constitution. He then filled the entire board with Democrats—violating that same mandate himself. In October, when the new Prison Commission chairman resigned, Stoneman appointed William C. Hendricks, an Oroville Democrat, to fill the position Chapman had held. His brother Thomas lived in Chico where he met with Bidwell several times during this time.[27]

Based on deep reporting on events through the prison hearings, the *Sacramento Bee's* editorial concluded the Prison Commission hearing had sustained none of Governor Stoneman's serious charges. Chapman and the other directors excoriated Stoneman in the *Sacramento Bee*: "You have become so eager for the feast of spoils that you are ready and willing to trample truth and facts under your feet in order that place hunters in your party may lead their voracious appetites to the public crib."

Without George Crosette at the helm, Gus no longer had the *Record* at his back. The new editor welcomed the Prison Commission's return to Democratic Party control: "The Ex-Directors should have the stamina and pluck to stand punishment when their party is put out. The people had repudiated their party and it's eminently proper and right that the control of the State Prisons, as well as the State Government, should be in the hands of friends of the people."[28]

The *Sacramento Bee* introduced its readers to Governor Stoneman's Prison Commission appointee William Hendricks, who had narrowly defeated Chapman for the State Senate seat in 1873. Manager of the Hendricks Hydraulic Mine in the Morris

Ravine, twelve miles from Oroville where it produced several hundred diamonds, he was "intensely Democratic in politics."[29] (His brother Thomas was likely named for their uncle, Thomas Hendricks of Indiana, who was briefly the vice president to sitting Democratic President Grover Cleveland.)

In the mid- to late-1880s, when Stoneman hearings had receded from general interest, Bidwell's diaries and occasional press items documented regular exchanges of visits between the Bidwells and the Hendrickses in Sacramento and at Rancho Chico. Hendricks evidently considered Bidwell his patron.

John Bidwell and his lawyer Frank Lusk paid close attention to Governor Stoneman's attack on George Perkins and, by extension, Chapman. Gus's life had long been influenced by the old strains between Bidwell and Perkins, whose financial interests clashed when Bidwell moved the Chico hamlet off his ranch to the south across Big Chico Creek and named it Chico Village. Its potential threatened Perkins's leadership of the county, based in Oroville. Bidwell's ambitious plan developed into a viable town, culminating in Chico's serial attempts to break up Butte County. Perkins's backing for the Wood & Chapman store in 1865 led to the failure of Bidwell's Chico store, alluded to in earlier chapters. In sum, Bidwell evidently considered Chapman disloyal but, in subsequent clashes presented earlier, when Chapman was a town leader, Bidwell's attempts to undermine him failed.

As for Lusk, Chapman's influence in the Odd Fellows had deprived Lusk, not a man to cross, of property he coveted. He also had an eye on Chapman's position as vice president at the Bank of Butte County. And, of course, he was determined to become invaluable to his client John Bidwell. Therefore, both men, each for his own reasons, relished this long-deferred opportunity to see Perkins and Chapman "pay." And, all the better, their interface with Stoneman stayed "off-stage." For that reason, Bidwell likely believed that Stoneman had rendered justice, or at least vengeance, at no cost to Lusk or him.

Despite all this, Chapman and Bidwell continued to publicly cooperate on civic projects. In small towns, personal breaches can simmer for decades, but sophisticated leaders with shared civic and business interests often mean to keep them private. This was so with Chapman and Bidwell, who were proud and inner-directed by nature; five years later, in 1888, the two remained at odds. Chapman's reputation had again become vulnerable because there were rumors about his debt problems in the small business community. That year, when traveling in the Sierra Nevadas, Bidwell learned he was only two miles from the Chapman Lumber Co. in Powellton. Although curious and tempted to see it, he drove on.

The Aftermath

In the months, then years, to come, Gus Chapman followed news about the Prison Commission's board of directors on which W. C. Hendricks and his successors served. Like Chapman's board, the Stoneman appointees grappled with political charges and countercharges, but this time they were on the receiving end by Republicans primed for vengeance. In learning about their problems, Chapman never would find more than psychological vindication—and there was little of that. In 1885, when Stoneman's directors declared they would dismantle the San Quentin grain-sack factory, outraged California farmers demanded that the State Legislature not only continue but expand it. In the coming year, the Democratic prison directors relented. They shifted prison labor and funds from curbstone and furniture production to grain-sack manufacturing.[30] Later, with the fuller development of electricity in the 1890s, the Prison Commission would shift the factories to 24-hour production.

As the years passed, Chapman could look back on the jute grain-sack's creation as the major achievement of his life.[31] He had other reasons to take satisfaction in prison improvements he and his colleagues had accomplished. During Chapman's tenure, the directors ended the flogging of prisoners. They mandated evaluations of inmates to record such things as age, type of crime and medical conditions. They assured a funeral service for all prisoners. They provided prison food equivalent to boarding house fare. Finally, they provided a "moral instructor" whose assignment was to "encourage and develop" in prisoners even "a single [remaining] spark of manhood or honor." While the Chapman board found vindication as their replacements expanded on work they had launched, later boards dropped many of their most humane advancements.[32]

Chapman could not miss press coverage and local recognition for Hendricks who went on from the Prison Commission to serve two terms as California's secretary of state.

He had no sympathy for George Stoneman when the Democrats—his own party—turned on him, refusing to consider him for a second term. Until his 1894 death, George Stoneman struggled in every aspect of his life. His eastern gravestone mentioned his several Civil War campaigns but omitted his governorship of California. However, he resurfaced in 1970 when songwriter J. R. Robertson remembered him in "The Night They Drove Old Dixie Down": "Virgil Caine is the name, and I served on the Danville train, 'Till Stoneman's cavalry came and tore up the tracks again...."[33]

San Quentin's role as a grain-sack factory continued. However, Perkins and Chapman's hopes to fund a youth facility and create reformatory programs with its proceeds vanished.[34] By 1910, grain-sack production grossed $2.63 million (over $70 million today). San Quentin operated as a state-owned factory which, for the next two decades, pressed most of its inmates to manufacture sacks for California's wheat farms. Despite brutal conditions that taxed their health and led to prisoner revolts, the production of jute products continued until 1956.[35]

18

Money Trouble: Chapman's Slippery Slope

By 1884 Gus Chapman was finally in Chico full-time, but he had not recovered from Governor Stoneman's expulsion of his Prison Commission from state service. While his work to bring about the Odd Fellows building must have neutralized the harm of Stoneman's insults to a degree, his successive Chico projects represented efforts to fully reclaim his public standing at home. Resolution of a new outbreak of problems in the water and gas utilities might win back the admiration of his townsmen.

Moving On—Honey Run Road

However, a more appealing opportunity for restoring his standing was already underway. Gus signed on with John Bidwell, William Earll and other downtown businessmen negotiating with the county to build a direct road between Chico and the Magalia Ridge—the Carr Hill Road (soon renamed Honey Run Road).[1] When problems arose, however, Bidwell and the rest left Chapman to take the blame.

This idea had sparked talk as early as 1864 and as recently as 1878 when John Bidwell agreed it would make lumber deliveries to Chico more reliable than the flumes which were regularly in disrepair, out-of-order and costly to maintain or rebuild.[2]

A new road was of keen importance to Chapman & McKay whose freight wagons regularly traveled south on the rough mountain roads to Oroville where the drivers and oxen stopped to rest. The next day they continued northwest for twenty-five miles to the Chico landing. With a direct road from the Magalia Ridge to the landing via Chico, freight wagons and buggies could avoid ten or so hours of tedious and sometimes dangerous passage by way of Oroville. Such a road could also trim by half the cost of hauling lumber to the valley.[3] This was a Chapman project even William McKay endorsed, at least at the start.[4]

Even more important to Gus Chapman in late 1883 as he, in effect, started over in Chico, was his long-standing determination to buy his way out of the partnership with William McKay. In preparation, he had insisted Fred work at the Powellton mill on arriving home with his diploma. The partners' attempts to split up their lumber company in the late 1870s had been stymied for years, but, since the constitutional convention in 1879, McKay had carried on their business on his own with little more than sporadic lumber contracts Chapman fitted in while on the Prison Commission. Gus's periodic timberland purchases only temporarily appeased his partner's ire.

It was McKay who rebuilt their Somerset mill and upgraded it with finishing machinery from the Empire mill.[5] In summer 1883 he had it in peak condition. Thirty employees at both the company's mills delivered 2.5 million board feet of lumber to the Chico train depot. Much of that fulfilled a contract with a San Francisco door and window firm. Always an exceptional salesman, Gus had long brought in lucrative contracts from the Bay Area to Salt Lake City. However, during Chapman's immersion in state politics his work for his business was negligible. In addition, by late 1883, when Gus returned from Sacramento to Chico for the last time, McKay was no longer the simple woodsman in the mountains whispering to oxen; during Chapman's extended absences, McKay alone represented the company. In this role he built up enough confidence to hire Frank Lusk, Chico's most aggressive lawyer, to represent him in dissolving Chapman & McKay. This suited Lusk, still angry at Chapman's role in thwarting his attempt to buy the lot on Broadway. By this time as well, Lusk had designs on Chapman's position at the Bank of Butte County.

Lusk drove a hard bargain on McKay's behalf. According to an item the lawyer planted in the *Enterprise*, the agreement enabled McKay "to take things easy and live upon the earnings of twenty years labor."[6] When their split became public on April 18, 1884, news of the breakup caused a sensation in Chico where old timers respected Chapman & McKay as a leading pioneer firm. Chapman was left with the Chico Lumber retail store at Eighth and Main and the older Powellton mill, which he renamed Chapman & Co. McKay retained considerable timberland and the upgraded Somerset mill, which Chapman was entitled to use in certain circumstances.[7]

The *Enterprise* cited Chapman & McKay and then Chapman & Co. as among the three or four lumber firms with the most to gain from a road between Chico and the Magalia Ridge.[8] But in Chico, now calling itself "Butte's Metropolis," retailers and professionals also savored the prospect of trade from hundreds of rural residents. They envisioned clients and customers streaming down to Main Street from mining claims, small farms and hamlets scattered along the proposed road's path. Therefore, in addition to Bidwell and Chapman, Chico's Ridge road promoters included Jo Wertsbaugher of the Union Hotel, merchant Z. W. Burnham, hardware dealer W. R. Faunce (Charles Stilson's partner) and Dr. Carnot Mason, Faunce's father-in-law and Chapman's old friend, a veteran of difficult journeys to treat mountain patients.

In spring 1883 John Bidwell and William Earll had represented Chico's Carr Hill Road committee in urging the supervisors to form a county exploratory committee. The board was reluctant to build the road but agreed to call for bids. Surveyor James McGann submitted a plan which would cut five to seven miles and six hours of travel between Chico and the Magalia Ridge. If the road proved popular, tolls would eventually repay investors. However, Oroville's influential businessmen erupted at the prospect of losses they would suffer by the route change. In response to their alarm, the supervisors reduced the county's contribution. Chico's businessmen, moving quickly to make up the difference, formed an ad hoc road construction committee and elected A. H. Chapman chairman.[9]

He was a likely pick because he was a longtime member of Humboldt Road Co.'s board of directors and for years had been its president. The Humboldt Road board had dissuaded the supervisors from making the proposed Ridge road a free public highway. The Carr Road committee preferred a toll road because that would guarantee funds for road maintenance. On the basis of almost forty years of experience, the Chico men did not trust the Oroville-dominated Board of Supervisors to maintain a road that would funnel trade away from Oroville. In addition, Bidwell and Chapman agreed with fellow Chico members that, since the supervisors only approved a new road under pressure, they would likely shortchange or even ignore county maintenance of a free public one. In that case, the Chico businessmen believed the public would eventually stop using the costly new road as it deteriorated and revert to the present, longer route through Oroville to reach mountain locations.

When considering the options for Magalia Ridge access, the Chico businessmen also considered an extension to the old Neal Road, the existing circuitous route from the Sacramento Valley south of Chico to Dogtown. As an investor in Neal Road, which his lumber wagons used, this route was tempting, but instead Chapman joined the Chico businessmen who opted for a new road instead. It would follow the trail at the valley entrance to Butte Creek Canyon, less than three miles southeast of Chico, and run along the creek for about 4½ miles. Then, the new road, cut out of precipitous cliffs, would rise to the Ridge, about 5½ miles, all the while following the creek.[10]

That fall, when Gus's embarrassment and anger at Governor Stoneman's takeover of the prison board was fresh, he called on the Carr Hill Road committee members to consider the road proposal by McGann and another submitted by surveyor William O'Donnell. McGann recommended a gradual grade which required a longer and, therefore, more expensive road than the one O'Donnell proposed. The O'Donnell route was shorter because it used an existing old road through the Carr Hill Ranch. Although this followed a steeper grade in the higher sections, the surveyor assured it could be built to meet safety standards. John Bidwell had considered the O'Donnell proposal the past April, just before he and William Earll met with the supervisors. However, in October Bidwell told the committee that he thought it looked like "a very steep and rocky way."[11]

As the decision drew near in early December, Gus Chapman rode from Powellton with Magalia businessmen to "a considerable elevation on the mountain side opposite the celebrated Carr Hill and above the babbling mountain brook known as Cherry Run."[12] There, they met the Chico road committee members—Bidwell, Mason, Burnham and Faunce, who had ridden out to Butte Creek Canyon early that morning to make the rendezvous. The Ridge men accompanying Chapman that day included farmer E. R. Powers and storekeeper D. C. Proctor. Later, in a lengthy joint letter to the *Enterprise,* they opposed the O'Donnell route because of its steep grade.[13]

The Chico men were conflicted. While a minority could not overlook the dangers of the O'Donnell route's grade, Gus Chapman, John Bidwell and others in the majority concluded that, although the O'Donnell route "is a heavier grade than [McGann's], it is compensated to some extent by the fact that distance [between Chico and the Ridge] is considerably less."[14] And, the O'Donnell route would cost less.

Determined to review their own inclination to favor the O'Donnell plan, Gus and his old friend Carnot Mason drove out again to look it over. Back in Chico, the salesman and physician reported that "a splendid road can be built for a small sum of money, and without much trouble."[15] However, when the bids for each plan exceeded the amount the backers had pledged, the committee members told Chapman to call for new bids while they set out to raise more money.[16]

When the second round of bids again exceeded the backers' funds and the road project was about to collapse, Gus stepped forward and offered to "save the day." As in the past, if something was difficult, Chapman would tackle it— securing the school for his suburb, fixing the water and gas utilities and his current work on the rising Odd Fellows Hall. Now, Chapman would build the road. As a man who considered himself politically savvy, despite the Prison Commission debacle, he apparently projected that his success with the road would unify Ridge and Valley residents in a political base he could call on for his return to public life.

In October 1883 Chapman announced the committee's choice of the steeper O'Donnell route. He signed on with John Bidwell, William Earll, Charles Faulkner and others in creating the Carr Hill Road Corporation. While Bidwell handled fundraising, Chapman hired experienced road overseer Henry Buschman to supervise a crew of thirty laborers. Although Chapman had built two schools and a store with considerable setbacks due to rain, once again he did not wait for the coming summer to launch its construction. As heavy winter downpours moved in, Buschman and his crew headed to Butte Creek Canyon and commenced work on the road.

The men labored along Butte Creek in the cold, driving rain. The ten inches that fell in February alone turned Chico's board-walks to mush, forcing pedestrians onto the streets where they waded ankle-high in mud and puddles while dodging the spray from buggies and wagons. Heavy clouds forced migrating geese to fly low, making those "miserable pests" easy targets in a full-scale hunters' campaign to wipe them out.[17] Men cleared away the resulting multitude of dead geese that filled a two-acre field almost a foot deep. Meanwhile, downpours washed away sec-tions of the new roadbed along Butte Creek, particularly at the higher grades, as fast as the men could build, then rebuild them.

While a shorter distance between Chico and Magalia would financially benefit Chapman and McKay in their now separate lumber properties, as Bill McKay observed work on the steep road underway he kept in mind the men who would have to drive down it at the reins of freight wagons stacked high with lumber. Theirs was treacherous work even on decent roads.

McKay had had enough of Chapman. In October 1883, as the new road was underway, McKay announced that he and Mary Ann would move from their Chapmantown house to another across the Oroville-Shasta Road. For years townspeople had nav-igated their way around the tensions between the two men. For example, after Charles Stilson married, he and his wife Emma socialized separately with each couple. Until the McKays' actual move a year later, the situation had become even more fraught for George and Millie Miller, whose Oroville-Shasta Road home was between the Chapmans' place and the McKays'. Like the Stil-sons, the Millers divided their attention between both couples.

While the transformation from Chapman & McKay to Chap-man & Co. in Powellton was a satisfying accomplishment for Gus, sole ownership meant he was responsible for the mountain mill distant from the valley lumber outlet. However, he had a plan. Once his father took over the company, Fred relented and headed back to the mountains to work in late April 1884.[18] With Fred there to take on McKay's role, Gus could now renew his focus on sales at home and out of town. However, the father and son had hardly started their collaboration when, after only a few weeks at the mill, Fred quit and headed back to Chico. He had never liked the production work and each time he tried it during college vacations, he had taken every possible opportunity to return to Chico. Without Fred in Powellton, his father had to be both places. McKay, still operating the Somerset mill, and Chapman both had cottages in Powellton, so they must have crossed paths on the street or in its only general store.

Meanwhile Gus remained responsible for seeing the new road to completion. Its name, Carr Hill Road, had already been dropped in favor of Honey Run Road. On July 1, 1884, after Gus's first trip down it, he announced to the press that he found the road ready for general travel.[19]

For buggy drivers like Chapman, daily stagecoaches, horseback riders and drivers of light wagons, the road was a challenge but manageable. However, confirming early concerns, teamsters who tested it with freight wagons found the O'Donnell grade too steep, the curves too tight and the surface too loose.[20] Urgent calls appealed for reconstruction of the dangerous, steep sections. When some referred to Honey Run Road as the Chapman Route, they were not paying Gus a compliment. As chairman of the committee behind the road's construction, the public considered him the most accountable for the road's shortcomings. This was so despite the fact that the whole committee, including John Bidwell, had opted with him for the cheaper O'Donnell option.[21] Gus Chapman's determination to push the road into reality through the rainstorms, probably in his search for redemption, led to a fully publicized reversal in his drive for public acclaim.

Despite initial concerns, once in place, the road erased any doubts about the advantages of a direct connection between Chico and the Magalia Ridge. In April 1886 the supervisors bowed to constituent demands and reworked hazardous sections of the new road according to the McGann plan.[22] A contractor drew on eager volunteers who tackled the roadwork themselves. Although the new final grade meant this revised route was several hours longer than the original one, the road was safer. "The poorest plug team in the hills can haul a full load up such a grade as that...."[23] Even so, an elderly woman later recalled her childhood fear on family trips: terrified that her father's wagon might crash over the steep cliff alongside Honey Run Road, she would lie flat, clinging to the wagon bed and, closing her eyes, never look over the side.

Family Struggles

While Sarah Chapman understood that Governor Stoneman had railroaded her husband, a hint of suspicion about Gus lingered with Chico residents who had little interest in the granular details of Sacramento politics.

Initially, all of this only amounted to background noise in Sarah's life. Her driving purpose was service to her husband, their children and her circle of friends in the North Methodist Church. However, Gus Chapman's embarrassment in 1884 evidently drove her to impress on Chico her family's positive role. To accomplish this, she marshaled support from her own constituency in the church. There, as an elder, her established leadership complemented Gus's efforts to call on his old strength in the business community.

Sarah launched a variety of church events at their home. In March John Bidwell joined the Methodist "missal exercises" in Sarah Chapman's parlors. A North Methodist before he married and an occasional contributor thereafter, by now he was frustrated by the demands on him by Annie Bidwell's Presbyterians. In addition, Annie spent months away from Chico for many years making visits to help care for her ageing parents in Washington, D.C.[24] In April, Sarah invited the church women for lunch, followed by singing and Fred's instrumental music. Then, she held another social in May. All her events had newspaper coverage. Gus and Sarah—each in their way—were reminding their friends, neighbors and business associates that the Chapmans, although weathering a bad time, were still the good people and solid citizens Chico knew.

During the miserable winter in 1884 Gus was about to start up the season's lumber production. It did not take long to discover how much he had underestimated the skills Bill McKay brought to the cutting, processing and transporting of their company's lumber. Fred's quick withdrawal from the business destroyed his father's plan for the company's management. While, in retrospect, Fred's departure seems inevitable, his decision was not only because he missed social life in Chico.

Like his father, Fred Chapman lacked the mechanical bent the mill required. He was terrific with a trumpet, in a quartet or at a piano, but he had no interest in steam engines. Nor did he find the felling of raw timber an attractive challenge. In addition, while Fred was smart, his internships with McKay had not taught him how to manage the rough-and-ready teamsters twice his age. The purchase, training, maintenance and driving of oxen presented no skillset he cared to master.

The abundant talents of Gus and his son were evident, but the similarity of their strengths precluded a workable division of labor. Like his father, Fred's nature and outgoing disposition were perfect for retail, so he might have thrived in the lumber sales end of the business, but both father and son had a horror of being stranded in the mountains for lengths of time, over-seeing steam-driven lumber mills. The irony is that Bill McKay had no interest or experience in sales. Despite their tensions, the clear division of responsibilities between Gus Chapman and Bill McKay had made Chapman & McKay an imperfect but lucrative and well-oiled enterprise.

Fred resumed his former job at the water and gas company. He also plunged back into Chico's social rounds and became more active in the Chico Guard, a posh "club" for young men. His father approved and contributed to construction of an armory hall at East Fifth and Main streets. In the meantime, because Gus had to stay at the mill to oversee production, it was hard for him to make the lengthy trips needed to negotiate sales. When he managed to get away from Butte County in October, his compet-itors had already fully mined his sales targets. He could not sell enough lumber to meet his expenses, let alone the payment due on at least one of his loans at the Bank of Butte County. Thus, on October 20, 1884, when his payment came due, he deeded to the bank eighty acres of timber, along with its "buildings and appurtenances" in a nearby township.[25]

No End to Conflict

Despite his travails, Gus presented a positive attitude as he made time for Republican Party politics. No longer head of the party in Chico, in 1884 he was one of thirty-five so-called vice presidents campaigning to elect James Blaine president of the party. In planning for the visit of a speaker in a scheduled rally, he and his cohorts, as was usual for big events, arranged for West Fifth Street homeowners to light up their houses along the torch-lighted parade route east from the train depot to Main Street, then north onto Broadway and then west onto West Second Street, still the leading business street.

In early 1885 Frank Lusk was ready to take over Gus's vice presidency of the Bank of Butte County. As Bill McKay's lawyer in the division of Chapman & McKay's property, Lusk knew how financially strapped Gus had become.

In 1885 the onset of the struggle between Chapman and Lusk caught the attention of businessmen who read the *Enterprise*. For example, after the bank's annual meeting that January, its weekly notice in the newspaper listed Frank Lusk, not A. H. Chapman, as vice president. The board had apparently elected Lusk in his place. Then, in February, the bank report dropped Lusk's name and returned Chapman's. Board members were gridlocked.

Lusk's advantage over Gus improved in April when William Earll called in the $20,000 balance on the loan Chapman had borrowed from him in 1882. Evidently Gus had managed to pay only the interest and almost no principle. Hubbard and Earll could no longer ignore Chapman's steady financial and career reverses. While such experienced men had discounted the Prison Commission outcome as partisan politics, they could not overlook the breakup of Chapman & McKay and knew Gus had to sell land to pay on a loan from the Bank of Butte County.[26]

When Earll called in the loan, it "took many of our citizens by surprise, and many expressions of regret were made as Mr. Chapman has been an active and enterprising businessman for years."[27] John Bidwell was referring to Gus's transfer of land to the bank when he noted in his diary, "A. H. Chapman has made an assignment."[28] As he wrote it, Bidwell may have been indulging in a tinge of satisfaction, although he must also have reflected on his own vulnerability. Four months previous, after army worms destroyed his crops, he borrowed $230,000 in San Francisco, a staggering amount then (almost $7 million today). The following year, Bidwell borrowed the equivalent of $60,000 from the Bank of Chico, then crossed Broadway to pay off a Bank of Butte County debt.

Chapman's financial plight was also of interest in Oroville where Chapman & McKay trade had thrived. According to the *Mercury*, "It has been a hard blow to him and he has been confined to his bed with a fever since Saturday."[29] Weak economic conditions had frustrated lumber sales and devalued his assets just when he needed money to recoup his losses.

Chapman's compulsion to rise in the world had always pushed him to take risks. However, he considered his debt a test of character and launched no legal actions to fend off his obligations, unlike other prominent debtors, including George Gridley and D. M. Reavis, who had launched court cases to exempt themselves from debt. Instead, Gus Chapman negotiated with Earll which assets he would accept as payment. Apparently Earll wanted nothing to do with the lumber business. However, in May Chapman raised cash when he sold Chico Lumber to Lloyd Coggins for $4,500. A local carpenter, Coggins had become a successful builder of wooden fruit crates for the orchards proliferating around Chico and on the Magalia Ridge. Chapman brought Coggins up to his Powellton mill to solicit his business.[30]

Chapman also sold various Chico lots and turned over to Earll his majority interest in the gas and water utilities, which were in good order by then. Only the previous year he had drilled a second water well. This one, across town from the company's gas storage, was untainted.[31] It had only been in January that the board of directors had elected Fred Chapman company secretary. When the companies reverted to Earll, Fred lost his position. Charles Faulkner, his father's friend, stepped in and appointed Fred to be one of Wells Fargo's two "gentlemanly clerks" in its Bank of Butte County office. With these developments, Fred finally registered the enormity of his father's, his family's and his own financial plight.

Still needing additional funds to satisfy the loans from Earll and the bank, Chapman subdivided the eastern end of his Little Chico Creek property, part of the Chapman Reserve. He also sold his barn and some land from the open block on which his house sat.[32] This permitted him to take out a new bank loan that satisfied Earll's demands. He retained his house, a few lots across

Chapman Street and his bedrock business capital: 2,717 acres of timber, $1,500 in lumber (100,000 board feet) on hand, $2,000 in mill equipment, and $1,300 in the wagons and oxen he needed to transport his lumber to the valley floor for Chico sale and railroad shipments.[33] With that intact, he planned his comeback.

These dramatic moves only briefly halted Gus Chapman's problems, however. Beginning summer 1885, the lumber business stalled. By year's end, because he could not sell any more of the mountain property he had wanted to keep for timber cutting, he mortgaged his debt-free fourteen-room family home on Chapman Street, the symbol of his cherished position in Chico.[34] Meanwhile, although the contest between Gus Chapman and Frank Lusk over the vice president position at the bank had seemed resolved, neither man relented.

19

Chapman Starts Over

As if all of the debt drama was not enough for Gus Chapman to deal with in 1884 and 1885, the following year was no sooner underway than Frank Lusk arose like a specter. While he first failed in his January 1885 attempt to capture Chapman's vice presidency at the bank, he had not given up.

Lusk had been building his stock holdings in the Bank of Butte County as a basis for a move from board member to company officer. Of all the present members, Chapman's political and debt crises made his position the most vulnerable.[1] However, Chapman had taken heart when his February defense felled Lusk's initial attack. A. H. Chapman's position as vice president of the bank mattered so much to him that, in the 1881 city directory, he listed it ahead of his presidencies of the utility companies and the lumber firm. Because Gus was one of few in Chico willing to challenge Lusk, it is appropriate to take a close look at this adversary.

The Lusk Factor

By 1885 Franklin Crawford Lusk had become a leading member of the Northern California bar. A New York native, he arrived in Chico from his Wisconsin home in 1872. He began to build his reputation by advising Chico's town trustees, then went on to try cases before municipal courts, superior courts and the State Supreme Court. About twenty years Gus Chapman's junior and just as driven, he had the financial advantage of having no dependents and a growing fortune which included Chico property. His services to wealthy clients probably generated his most lucrative source of income. He had begun by partnering with Albert J. Gifford, 32, in offices George Dorn carved out of the former Wood's Hall. Down the hall was the *Enterprise* office where the editor commented that the new young lawyer "has most handsomely adorned his office with every appliance looking to comfort."[2] Lusk's handsome decor treatments would grace three successive offices in his long practice. So fastidious was Frank Lusk about his image that, in 1880, he refused to give the census taker his age. Still in his twenties, it was professionally important that his well-healed clientele think of him as a seasoned professional.

On the other hand, in order to reach higher courts in Oroville, Sacramento and San Francisco, Lusk had to leave his well-appointed office and spend hours in the saddle or bouncing on buggy seats. At least once his horse tossed him into the mud. On another occasion, after a late start for home, he wandered lost in the dark, then gave up and slept in the Sacramento Valley's marshy swales until dawn revealed his location.[3] Although his first case before the State Supreme Court in 1878 established his professional career, Lusk based his practice in Chico, where he didn't give a second thought to his new role as a lightning rod to white Workingmen. They resented his retainer from the Chinese Six Companies in San Francisco which assigned him to defend Chinese laborers in Butte County. However, the Six Companies' purpose meshed with Lusk's representation of big farmers, the principal employers of Chinese. In this, Lusk's work was compatible with the interests of the bank's larger stockholders.

While Lusk's professional and economic success ensured his entrée into Chico's social circle, it never made him popular. In the mid-1870s he figured in parties of the younger set whose ambitious parents would have welcomed the rising lawyer to their families. Yet no lasting commitments evolved. Over decades, some women must have been at least briefly intrigued by the luxuries he displayed, but eventually even those could not compensate for his frigid personality and arrogance. Fifty years or more after his death, wisps of gossip about Lusk's flirtations survived, one with a single working woman, one with a widow and another with a disappointed married woman.[4] Lusk's intellect was more impressive than his social graces. He was "a man not to cross ... a man considered not to have any compassion whatever."[5]

By contrast to the starchy Lusk, his partner Albert Gifford was an unpretentious man whose laconic style and dry wit had wide appeal. Gifford housed his boisterous family on Wall Street where boarding-houses stood next to whorehouses up the street. In 1878, when Lusk wanted to move their firm to the Bank of Butte County's new offices, which featured marble fireplaces, Gifford resisted and the partners went their separate ways. Having put up with Lusk's fixation on décor, Gifford joked that he planned to set up shop over the Pony Saloon.[6]

Lusk's soft spot emerged, however, when a man he immensely admired, Dr. Samuel Sproul, died and left teenaged children. First, Lusk arranged for Bessie, the Sprouls' daughter, to become a clerk at the Chico post office where she could support herself and her mother. Then, he concentrated on Jo Davis Sproul, Fred Chapman's school mate, whom Lusk sent to the University of California. When Jo did not succeed there, Lusk secured him an appointment at West Point. After that military academy expelled the high-spirited Sproul for minor misconduct, Lusk brought the young man home to Chico for his own close supervision. Like others who had not succeeded at West Point—James McNeil Whistler, Edgar Allen Poe and George Custer—Sproul turned himself around.[7]

Jo D. Sproul apprenticed himself to Lusk, whose disciplined study of law he accepted. He not only became a capable practitioner, but his mastery of rhetoric eventually made him Chico's favorite public speaker. "Possessed of a magnificent voice, a keen mind, and an ever-present sense of the deepest humor, he was always listened to with the greatest delight. There were none who could equal his pathetic and wondrous word-pictures, and had they been preserved many of his orations would have become permanent features of American literature."[8] Lusk's success in shaping young Sproul to such a degree brings to mind the senior man's encounter with a bystander who complimented the skill of his sulky driver T. B. Daniels at the Chico track. Lusk acknowledged the compliment to his employee, "I taught him and when I teach anyone anything he knows how."[9]

Jo D. Sproul's reputation for compassion and generosity recalled the characteristics of his Kentucky-born father whose medical practice treated not only well-off patients but also poor

Whites and the desperately ill Mechoopda dispatched to the Round Valley reservation in 1863.

Despite the two men's different characters, which had consequences for Gus Chapman, Lusk and Dr. Sproul were old school Democrats. Both opposed the politics of George Crosette and the "Dickerson Democrats" who advocated the populist positions of laborers and small businessmen.[10] Instead, they embraced the genteel, old Jeffersonian identity still associated with Chico Southerners. As a retailer dependent on sales to people of all stripes in both parties, Chapman had taken a risk of alienating Democrats when he changed to a Republican after the war. Yet somehow he had managed his shift skillfully enough to retain the respect of men in both parties.

Lusk had privately remained a Democrat through his early years in Chico, when Jo Sproul, loyal to his father's party, became, in effect, his ward. This made political party a household issue. When Lusk helped Jo's sister secure the post office position he had to draw on his party affiliation to lobby Democrats in control. After that Lusk discovered his Republican clients didn't care. From then on, when it served some advantage, Lusk identified as a Democrat of the elite Jeffersonian faction. During Gus Chapman's term on the Prison Commission, Lusk again raised his profile, this time to align himself with Democratic Governor George Stoneman to drive his fellow Chico Republican from office.

While Lusk and Stoneman initiated their collaboration, John Bidwell seemed on the sidelines, but he must have remained close to Lusk because entries in his diary show regular meetings with him in their business and private lives. In 1880, when the Perkins administration was just underway, Republican Bidwell hosted a dinner at his home for members of the state's new Railroad Commission. The guests included Civil War general Stoneman, who was the Workingmen's Party and Democratic choice for the commission. While Stoneman had run for his place on the commission as an opponent of the railroads, once elected to regulate them he backed off and protected them. Bidwell's disappointment in the commission was reason for Bidwell and Lusk to lobby him.

Stoneman took on significance to the two men again when, in

October 1882, after the Republicans' candidate for governor Morrice Estee lost to Stoneman, Bidwell and Lusk met with Estee, evidently to commiserate and compare notes on Stoneman. Having stood back from the Republican Perkins, Bidwell would ordinarily have resumed his commitment for Perkins's Republican successor.

With Estee's loss and Stoneman's rise, Lusk needed to bolster his recently renewed connection to the Democratic Party. At the same time, Bidwell had already reminisced with Stoneman, who was a State Militia officer at Rancho Chico during the 1851 Indian Treaty events. His dinner in Chico to lobby the new Railroad Commission had also been cordial. In turn, the new governor, controversial as a recent immigrant from the Deep South, relished these prominent constituents' solicitation.

After Stoneman won, he and Lusk stayed in touch. For the Chico lawyer's campaign support, Stoneman awarded him a notary public license, a valuable gesture then. In Stoneman's inaugural speech, which revealed his priority for governing, the new governor may have been "carrying water" for Lusk and Bidwell.

On September 13, 1885, Bidwell and Stoneman met at a State Fair event in Sacramento and later lunched as they traveled by train. In October, after ousting Gus Chapman, Stoneman appointed Democrat William C. Hendricks as Prison Commission president. In spring 1886 the Bidwells hosted Governor Stoneman and his family at Bidwell Mansion. The Stonemans reciprocated by hosting the Bidwells at lunch in Sacramento as both couples were returning home from San Francisco visits. Bidwell's diaries mention other social contacts with Stoneman family members.[11] It was not usual practice for Chico Republicans to exhibit such personal interest in the well-being of any Democratic governor; particularly in light of Stoneman's treatment of their respected townsman. At the Chapman home twelve blocks south from Bidwell Mansion, it was "message received."

The Bank War

When Lusk decided to go after Chapman's seat on the bank board, he called in a valuable chit his actions suggest he had curried for that purpose. While Chapman had retained Perkins's backing on the bank's board, Lusk found an opening to gain the support of Perkins's full partner in the bank, Norman Rideout of Marysville. In 1883, therefore, when Chapman registered the seriousness of Stoneman's challenge, Lusk positioned himself to be due a chit from Rideout. Lusk filled in for him as the on-site agent for Hugh Glenn's estate. A mentally disturbed and alcoholic bookkeeper, Huram Miller, had murdered the rancher, the 1879 Democratic nominee for governor. Norman Rideout was Glenn's estate executor. He and George Perkins of Oroville had been founding investors in Chico's Bank of Butte County. Although the urbane Rideout had agreed to be Glenn's executor, he was unwilling to take up residence on Glenn's vast, remote and troubled ranch during the long probate. Frank Lusk sprung forward to "rescue" him by agreeing to "take up his headquarters at Jacinto not only as attorney for the estate, but as the Administrator's special agent."[12] This required the elegant Lusk to sequester himself on the dirty, neglected ranch.

In August 1885, while Lusk was staying at Rancho Jacinto, Chapman's name dropped from the bank's weekly newspaper notice and no other name appeared in his place. Until the previous January, when Lusk's name had briefly replaced Chapman's, such elections had been pro forma exercises.[13] The vice president position remained empty in newspaper notices pending the January 1886 meeting when Lusk's advocate, Norman Rideout, and Chapman's ally, George Perkins, were to attend in Chico and resolve the issue.

Entering the Battle

George Perkins was not Chapman's only ally on the board of directors. Bank cashier Charles Faulkner, with whom Chapman took his occasional camping trips, had significant bank shares and he was also a major stockholder in the gas and water utilities for which Chapman had exerted extraordinary efforts to reorganize. Faulkner ran the independent Wells Fargo & Co. Express, located in the Bank of Butte County, and hired Fred Chapman as an agent. He and Gus Chapman were Odd Fellows and Masons from their first days in Chico. As recently as January 1883, Chapman and merchant George Dorn had put up Charles Faulkner's bond when he became town treasurer. In addition, Faulkner and Chapman traveled together to accept the State's Triennial Commission awards for their civic contributions.[14] Finally, Faulkner was considered a compassionate man—for a banker.

Chapman also could count on banker John R. Robinson, a personal friend and brother in the same fraternal organizations. Both men had known Chapman at least since 1871. When Gus was at his lowest point, they were the men he chose to witness his will. These three bank officers—Perkins, Faulkner, and Robinson— believed that Augustus Chapman could surmount his reverses.[15]

However, when the board met in January 1886, Lusk's backer Rideout was present, but George Perkins had been called to Montreal to negotiate a deal between his Pacific Coast Steamship Co. and the Canadian Pacific Railway.[16] Chapman could not win reinstatement without Perkins on hand to lean on Rideout and back up Robinson and Faulkner.

Therefore, Lusk prevailed and in the bank's next weekly newspaper notice his name appeared as vice president. Then, suddenly, Lusk's name vanished again. Again the notice had no name next to the title. It appears probable that only one absent member of the bank's board had enough power to demand Rideout step back: George Perkins. Had a telegram reached Perkins in Montreal?

Whatever intervention suspended the final decision, it prolonged Chapman's hopes. However, six weeks later, in February 1886, Lusk was finally selected to replace A. H. Chapman as bank officer. His continuing place on the Bank of Chico's board of directors afforded some consolation, of course. In order to reduce the demands of business and establish a political life, Chapman had severely diminished his financial assets, jeopardizing his family. He must have found it bittersweet to hear the cheers of Chicoans, whom he had envisioned as his own constituents, when his old friend Marion Biggs, the new member of Congress, paraded with fellow Democrats down Second Street. In December he endured a personal blow from his old friend George Dorn who named his new son Stoneman Cleveland Dorn. (In 1888 the entire image of Chapmantown was obscured in Chico's new "point of pride"—an elegant illustrated map.)

In July 1886 Gus Chapman took yet another punch from

Frank Lusk, who hosted a large party for Governor Stoneman and the Hendrickses at his new home, the full second floor above his office in the two-story "brick" on West Second Street. His entertainment in Governor Stoneman's honor doubled as a housewarming. The guests who gathered to honor Chapman's nemesis included fellow Republicans John and Annie Bidwell and leading local Democrats such as D. M. Reavis, at whose country home and private race track the Chapmans had been guests.[17] The ladies, entertained by Lusk's mother Mary, savored the opportunity to marvel at her bachelor son's luxurious quarters. The men were drawn to his billiard table, which warranted its own room. It is likely the Chapmans were not on the guest list and their absence quietly noted in private conversations.

Chico's New Face

In the second half of the 1880s the growing popularity of Southern California as a tourist venue flummoxed Chico, where the *Record*'s editor grumbled: "The immigrants coming are not all one lunged consumptives! There will be a large sprinkling of the enterprising manufacturing class, and that is the kind we want as population."[18]

While Northern California cities formed an Immigration Aid Association to develop a counter strategy, ideas circulated through town about ways to make Chico more competitive. For its part, town trustees ended the gas lighting in favor of electric-light wires workers strung along tall wooden posts and, from there, to every subscriber. The posts and wires defaced the streetscapes of every neighborhood. However, few found the price too high. Weak light at the flip of a switch freed everyone from dependence on the dim, flickering glow from kerosene lamps. The *Record* urged businessmen to buy bulk newspaper subscriptions for eastern libraries to help readers discover Chico.

In their efforts to approximate the appeal of Southern California, residents planted citrus trees in wheat fields and palm trees in front yards. Everyone rued the 1882 fire that had consumed the first-class Chico Hotel on Second Street, especially when they heard that "tourists" who streamed to the "barren plain"—Los Angeles—appreciated modern hotels with every comfort. Surely, they surmised, if people favored that dismal part of the state because of comfortable accommodations, they were sure to favor Chico if it could again offer a good hotel.[19]

As an inveterate traveler over the years, Gus Chapman understood the appeal of a good hotel. In 1884 he and George Dorn agreed Chico had the means to replace the Chico Hotel with another substantial hostelry. While Chapman was circulating downtown, talking with potential investors, he learned the town trustees' agenda that day included protecting boardwalks by cutting out the overhang of "old and dangerous" trees. He stopped in to listen and realized the trustees were talking about removing downtown trees. He spoke up, emphasizing the mature trees' beauty and precious shade they provided.[20] His appeal saved the trees but he could not convince investors to get behind the plan for a new hotel: there was local money, but it was committed to investors' other projects.

Then, a second large hotel burned. In August 1886 flames destroyed the Junction Hotel in view of Humboldt Road. Gus Chapman, again relying on loans and with one or more partners, bought the plot and, in 1890, built a two-story, frame hostelry, the Chico Hotel, a substantial, practical place. While somewhat attractive when new, it did not feature the amenities of its grander counterpart, the Chico Hotel built in 1861. However, investors considered it's potential: it faced the Junction roundabout that received traffic from the Humboldt and Oroville-Shasta roads.

Chapman's family history may have inspired him to tackle his latest project. His father built the still historically recognized Cataract Hotel overlooking Niagara Falls. Gus and Sarah co-managed the hotel and hired George Sisk, a teenager new to Chico and on his own. George unloaded guests' baggage from buggies, carried messages among businesses and was on call for other errands.[21] While at the hotel, young Sisk got to know his future wife Eunice Curtis, whose parents were married in the parlor of the Chapmans' remodeled farm house, previously owned by Dr. Smith. The Chapmans' hotel ownership, like their other property, was soon sacrificed to satisfy bank debts.

Gus Chapman's last surviving financial hope came down to reviving the lumber mill that had long anchored his fortune. While he still disliked the production end of the lumber business, his family survival from economic peril was tied to the mill's close management and an economy demanding lumber. While young Fred had disliked the lumber business so much that he had quit it soon after he returned from college, by 1886 Fred realized his father had no other options and he no other prospects. He agreed to try again. In April, while John Bidwell was entertaining the Stoneman family at Rancho Chico, Fred headed for the mill to set up the season's operations. However, within a week he returned to Chico to perform with a choir at the Odd Fellows picnic. Then he headed back to Powellton. This pattern continued. Even under these desperate circumstances, Fred and his father were still only at the mill when they had to be.

Despite Sarah's efforts to mediate disputes between her husband and their son, the partnership teetered.[22] By now it must have been clear to his parents that Fred was no more suited than his father to work in a rough, demanding business while isolated from the refinements and social rounds of town life. Fred remained at work through their first season as Chapman & Co., but at its end he gave his father notice. When the mill shut down for the winter, he resumed his job with Wells Fargo and did not return to Powellton the next season.

Lost in all of the family's concentration on Fred's withdrawal was an irony, one clearer in retrospect than at the time. Although only in middle school, Fred's young brother Gussie had begun to exhibit potential for machine work. He thrived at Powellton. The mill machinery sparked his lifelong fascination with engineering and mechanics. Had he been old enough to handle millwork with his father covering sales during the crucial years of the 1880s and after, the two might have saved and restored Chapman & Co.

His Political Test

Chico confronted a revival of anti-Chinese actions in 1886, bringing back ironic recollections of the violent acts and aftermath of 1877. That year, when he organized the vigilante committee that brought the anti-Chinese killers to heel, he had passed the test of leadership. However, the conditions in 1886 differed. The current events centered on a local anti-Chinese boycott of John Bidwell's ranch products. It quickly became so popular to boycott John Bidwell goods that other owners began to fear their businesses might become the next targets. Businessmen, farmers and others who relied on Chinese labor joined Bidwell's Committee of One Hundred. Its mission was to hold anti-Chinese labor activists to account, protect property and thwart the boycott. Bidwell opponents emerged among some of his own employees and among business owners who complained that Bidwell conditioned their Rancho Chico employment or contracts on joining his pro-Chinese labor group. For this and other reasons, the Committee of One Hundred fell short of that number. (An essay on the anti-Chinese period in this author's *Exploring Chico's Past* sets out the clever tactic by Frederick Bee, consul to the Chinese Six Companies, with John Bidwell's knowledge, to crush this round of anti-Chinese aggression.)

Chapman, whose political roles in Chico since 1861 were well-known, attended the committee's March meeting. His successes in the 1880s had helped him overcome his old reticence. He was one of the men who addressed the crowd, denouncing the boycott of Bidwell's products.[23] However, for some reason after that event he stepped back from Bidwell's group. Despite the committee's efforts, the defiant anti-Chinese continued to protest at numerous public events.[24] Even though arsonists burned down Old Chinatown on Flume Street in July, imperiling the surrounding property, it took several months for George Dorn, Chapman's successor as owner/manager of the water company, to persuade town trustees to subsidize new pumps to raise the water pressure levels for fire service.

In 1886 Frank Lusk led a substantial campaign to establish the second branch of the State Normal School (now California State University, Chico) in Chico on six acres of Rancho Chico donated by John Bidwell. When word of Chico's victory arrived, Gus Chapman's name is absent from the long list of local men grateful to the rancher for his land and other contributions to the new campus.[25]

The Odd Fellows did not turn their backs on Chapman, whose help had been instrumental in erecting their new building. They added him to their board of directors in 1888. Nevertheless, while Chapman accepted that board position, he was also beginning to recede from public life for the first time since he arrived in

Chico. His dream of a career in politics had turned his life into a minefield.

Whether Chapman was in Powellton or Chico during the late 1880s, he fixated on Chapman & Co. The Chapmans' only income now trickled in irregularly from mill operations. Although 1887 was a decent year, he worried about the future. Chapman had no reserve to buffer a downturn.[26] He had spent a decade or more juggling business demands, local civic contributions, state service and debts. Taken together, the process exacted a crushing financial and personal cost. His position in the late 1880s recalls a remark John Bidwell made, when he returned from serving in Congress during the 1860s: "I am ashamed to think I got into debt, but I did so by going into politics and going away from home."[27] Gus Chapman had saved himself again and again, so he had to believe it was still possible. This time, however, he was 59 and exhausted. He had no mentor, no rescuer and no luck.

Hotel omnibuses ferried guests to Gus and Sarah's 25th wedding anniversary at their "southern Chico" home in 1883.

Some of Chapmans' wedding anniversary guests bought gifts at Hibbard & Sommer in downtown Chico.

Magnolia Wood Chapman, wife of Gus's son Fred. Sarah and Gus realized the taciturn woman was a good influence on their son, encouraging him to become more responsible and settled.

In response to a Southern California boon in the 1880s, the North Valley competed to attract eastern immigrants by planting orange tree groves in the country and palm trees in town.

Looking north toward the Junction and the Junction Hotel. On the far left is a horse stables. To the left of the hotel, later replaced by the second Chico Hotel, is Broadway; to the right is Main St. Log-bearing freight wagons maneuvered in the wide open space when entering Chico from the Humboldt Road on the far right.

The second Chico Hotel at the Junction was built by investors led by Chapman in the 1880s.

Bank of Butte County (left) and Bank of Chico (right) on 2nd & Broadway. Chapman was an officer at both banks.

Chapman was co-owner of the Chico Steam Laundry, located on his Chapman Street (now E. 11th St.) property.

Chico Steam Laundry wagon.

Chapman raised the funds and oversaw the construction of the Odd Fellows Hall on 3rd & Broadway.

The inauguration of the Odd Fellows Hall. An arrow points to Chapman sitting to the right of the chapter president.

Teenager Will Chapman worked after school at Lee Pharmacy on the ground floor of the Odd Fellows Hall.

George Perkins, speculator, legislator, governor and later U.S. Senator. As governor, he appointed Chapman chairman of the State Prison Commission.

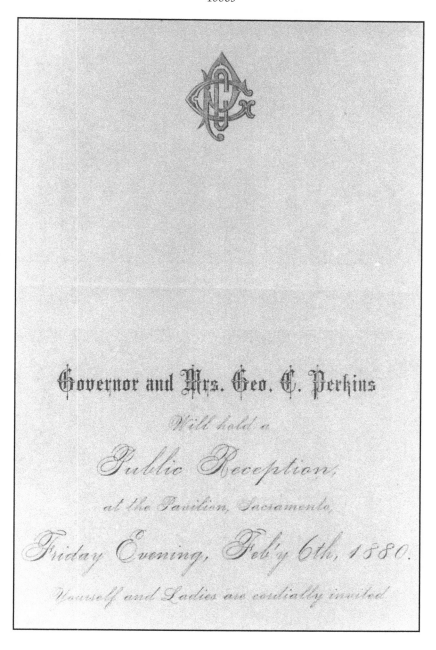

Governor George Perkins's invitation to his 1880 inaugural ball. Gus brought Sarah and the Chico Guards, who escorted Perkins in the parade. Although John Bidwell attended, he opposed Perkins and Chapman, his fellow Republicans.

As George Perkins's chairman of the State Prison Commission (1880-1883), Chapman established the grain-sack mill at San Quentin and granite production at Folsom Prison.

Wheat was a staple crop and farmers had to buy millions of grain sacks from India. By 1869, they were purchasing 43 million sacks annually to ship the grain to foreign markets.

This men's club met on Sundays on the veranda of the Union House. In the 2nd row, from right to left, seated, are Gussie (with fan), Willie (with cane hat), and their host, older brother Fred Chapman.

Sarah Chapman (right) and her good friend Eliza Camper, with whom she and Gus wintered after they lost their home and two of their children.

20

Hopes Implode

Since his days as George Wood's "right-hand man" at John Bidwell & Co. and, finally, as chairman of the State Prison Commission, Gus Chapman traveled extensively on business. Gus's work on the Commission alone kept him away from Chico almost every month for three years. This left Sarah to manage their four children, their home and their town properties.

In 1880 Sarah, who turned 47 that March, had to accompany Gussie, 7, across Oroville-Shasta Road, even though Oakdale School was in sight of their home, due to the dangers of freight wagons, speeding buggies and racing riders. Willie, 5, would join his brother there in another year. Fred, away at college, could not help his mother for another couple of years. The role of mother's helper fell to Mary, 15, although, as a student at Chico Academy, she could not be on call much of the time.

Sarah also made time for her North Methodist Church where she worked with close friends. Church, children and Chico Academy projects were the foundation of her friendship with Eliza Camper. Although Eliza's husband Henry and Gus Chapman never became close companions, they developed an amicable relationship due to the constant presence of one another's children and spouses in their homes and because both men were Republicans and Odd Fellows. It may be recalled that when Chapman declined to run for another term as a school trustee in 1879, he endorsed Henry Camper who won the seat.

Early on, Sarah and Eliza agreed to disagree about temperance. Sarah had not objected to temperance speakers at Wood's Hall in the 1860s. She remained unimpressed by the Women's Christian Temperance Union (W.C.T.U.) in the mid-1880s, when Eliza helped organize genteel gatherings and rallied attendance at lectures by traveling speakers. She was so committed she made a rare trip from home to Santa Cruz for a W.C.T.U. meeting. When Eliza and others made the church a base for that group's activities, Sarah found other tasks.

Both Sarah and Eliza loved music; for years their homes resonated with children's earnest attempts to learn multiple instruments. The mothers' eventual reward was the finished sounds of hymns, popular songs and light classics throughout their homes. Henry Camper's nephew Charles Camper and Fred Chapman, the most accomplished of the elder children, became regular performers for a variety of audiences, including their mothers' guests. When Fred, and later Mary, came home for college vacations, they headed straight for the Camper house— Mary to see Nellie and Fred to catch up with Charlie.

In the early to mid-1880s Sarah became more civically active. While she had always hosted her share and more of her circle's socials, her contributions broadened during Gus's years on the Prison Commission.[1] She and her Ladies' Aide or church or library board members plied benefit attendees with trays of their signature "afternoon dainties." As the *Enterprise* put it, "No one knows better than does Mrs. Chapman how to entertain a party pleasantly."[2]

One 1884 church "social" in Sarah's double parlors was elaborate, featuring a full-blown performance. Nellie Camper and Georgia Dorn sang, while their teacher Selena Woodman collaborated in readings and music. Another of Mary's good friends, pianist Maude Blood, played "one of the finest pieces ever heard here."[3] Had the versatile Fred Chapman not been at the mill that day, he would have recited, played an instrument or sung. When it came to entertainment, Fred was "first chair."

Gussie and Willie were full of fun and mischief that had its charm, but, as an older parent, Sarah must have strained to keep up with them. That and Sarah's socials made her new housekeeper Mrs. Maddox, a widow, all the more valuable. Most Chico families in the Chapmans' circumstances had a Chinese cook, but there is no evidence that the Chapmans employed Chinese. Gus's good relations with the white working men of Chico, who loathed those who hired Chinese, suggests Mrs. Maddox was their only help. During Gus's extended absences, Sarah also began to make her appearance at private parties and public gatherings on her own or with Fred as her escort when he was home.

The Library Campaign

In 1879 the town trustees rejected the appeal by John Bidwell, Gus Chapman and others to approve a small tax to fund the free library. This left their wives to launch the 1880s with another round of private fundraising. Sarah and the other women, who had been library mainstays since the mid-1860s, were aware that their energy was flagging and their health uncertain.

The women who sustained Chico's fragile institutions paralleled the female characters of the same period whom Helen Hooven Santmeyer portrayed in her novel "*... And Ladies of the Club.*" These aging women yearned for freedom from their fundraising tasks but never succeeded and instead passed them on to their daughters and succeeding generations. In addition to the money they managed to pry from the public, they provided all they could through personal gifts and their husbands' labor and contributions. The ancient Rebecca McIntosh exemplified the women's persistence and inventiveness. Once she became too frail to fully participate in fundraising activities for her beloved Methodist Church South, she charged her daughters and granddaughters 25¢ a dozen to finish the buttonholes on their new clothes.

George Crosette reprinted a telling parody of the women's efforts to collect money from the general public: No sooner had a naïve young man paid his entrance fee to a "church fair," than one matron after the other manipulated the fellow's confusion and good will into purchases of a lapel pin, two slices of cake, and a fortune reading—one for himself and one for a cousin. Still another woman guessed his weight and one more sold him two flower bouquets. "'Well, if I ever visit another fair may I be ___d!' he [exclaimed] as he counted over his cash to see if he had car fare to ride home."[4] But all the money the resourceful women collected from such exasperated wage-earners never satisfied churches' needs for long. Pastors had to be paid and leaking roofs repaired.

With no library tax to help in 1880, the women organized a Leap Year dance, similar to the one they had put on as young women in the 1860s. Because Sarah's religious beliefs forbade her dancing, she must have provided other help for the event. Next, borrowing from the W.C.T.U, they created a Blue Ribbon brigade in which a "Soliciting Committee" paired off women to scour the town for donations. Sarah Chapman and Mary Ann McKay, ignoring the strains between their husbands, canvassed Chapmantown together.[5] These library volunteers, in the main, were the same women who had raised money for the Sanitary Fund during the Civil War, the Chico Relief Society since the 1870s and always for their churches. The women's experience had taught them to make calls for donations accompanied by a friend or family member, thereby securing their reputations. Also, as one newspaper remarked, when the volunteers walked away, one might turn to the other and criticize owners who turned them down.

In 1888, overwhelmed again, the library volunteers accepted a proposal by Susan Heath Crew and Annie Kennedy Bidwell to hand over its management to the W.C.T.U. Sarah might have disagreed and stood back on principle, but that year she was too immersed in problems concerning Gus, Fred and Mary to take much interest. From the point of view of Mrs. Crew and Mrs. Bidwell, W.C.T.U. management would solve the library volunteer problem and provide for their organization. Members then could also monitor reading materials in the town's collection. However, the new management was not long in place before dissention among the library board members led to "a parting of the ways."

Now desperate, the board shifted library management to a high school women's group, whose members' elaborate theatrical productions had impressed town elders, some of whom were their mothers. While the teenagers began with good intentions, the library soon exhibited neglect. The "librarians" became more entranced by the young men stopping by to chat than by shelving books or collecting fines for late returns.

College for Mary

When it came to their planning for Mary's education, Sarah and Gus ignored an 1879 *Enterprise* article which cautioned parents that intense mental exertions can cause girls to "break down." Then, in 1882 they ignored a letter from Mills Seminary in Oakland to the *Record* which reassured parents that "out of the 242 graduates, only six are deceased and not one an invalid," addressing the concern that higher education was too stressful for delicate young women.[6] Although not sickly, Mary's name escaped frequent social lists, suggesting she was more retiring than her older brother. The frequency of her name on lists of Chico Academy's best students suggests she was intellectually oriented and perhaps even academically competitive.

The only question for her parents was which college was right for her. The University of California was an option because Gus Chapman's Education Committee in 1879 secured admission there for qualified women. However, Gus's ambition for his children to attend an established eastern campus lingered on as a private imperative. Even in the years they could afford a summer cabin in Forest Ranch, a beach cottage in Santa Cruz or trips to Europe, the couple invested in business, four tuitions and only traveled together to visit family in Michigan. Gus's 1883 will emphasized his desire to provide future education and travel for Gussie and Willie equal to what he provided Fred and Mary.[7]

The Methodist Church in California had recently promoted colleges within their denomination for church members' children. Had Methodism been the Chapmans' consideration, they could have sent Mary to Mills Seminary in Oakland. Had social connections driven their choice, Mills would also have met that criterion. Privileged young women at Mills included all the Chico daughters of premier social leader Sydnia Jones, as well as Nellie Reavis, Mary Barnard and the late Hugh Glenn's daughter Ella, an Oakland resident since her father's murder by his bookkeeper.[8] Even Mills Seminary's founder, herself a Mount Holyoke Female Seminary graduate, made visits to Sydnia Jones' Fifth Street home to recruit young women for her campus.

Instead, the Chapmans enrolled Mary in Mount Holyoke in Massachusetts. Its Methodist affiliation was not incidental to the Chapmans' choice of it for their only daughter. It was also a pioneer campus in women's higher education that served the daughters of leading families on the national level. The Chapmans' choice of a Methodist college in Massachusetts rather than one in California apparently reflected an intellectual standard or some other factor the couple admired about the East. It is hard to overemphasize how remarkable the Chapmans' decision was to send their only daughter so far from home. Out of Mount Holyoke's 289-member student body, Mary Euphrasia Chapman discovered she was the only student from the entire west coast.[9]

Circumstances suggest influences on their thinking. Not only was Mary smart and quiet, she was independent. For example, in 1876, when she was 11, she briefly rebelled and formally withdrew for a time from her mother's church. Another indication of her nature appears in her choices of friends. She admired Maude Blood who, in the late 1870s, attended Wellesley College in Massachusetts until she had to drop out because her weakening eyesight made the intensive reading impossible. Back in Chico, Maude concentrated on her piano skills and private painting lessons for Mrs. Bidwell and other women. While Mount Holyoke's connection with the Methodist Church was reason enough for Sarah, Gus's support for the cross-country plan was probably a sure bet once he learned that banker Norman Rideout sent his daughter to Vassar, a sister school.[10]

Mary's parents must also have concluded that she could live away from her parents because they were confident she was serious and responsible. For example, even though young women (including Sarah) who drove buggies turned heads, they allowed Mary to drive the family's horse-drawn buggy, which spared Sarah the need to chauffeur the little boys and friends.

Fred's friend Magnolia Wood, a public school teacher and something of a bluestocking, won newspaper notice for her solo drives between the Cherokee school where she first taught and her parents' new "Eyrie Villa" in the foothills.[11] Rancher David Reavis's daughter Nellie insisted on going to Chico when no one was available to take her. The press noted she made trips by herself from her family's River Road home to town.

Another compelling consideration that may have influenced the Chapmans to send Mary east was the frequency with which women married at very young ages. Bachelors far outnumbered them. Mary may have had a suitor on the scene whose intentions worried her parents, such as dashing young Henry Jefferson "Harry" McKim, who had moved to Chico and became immediately popular during Mary's high school years, when her parents were considering her options for college.[12] While handsome and well thought of, Harry's prospects did not measure up to her parents' intentions for Mary. Her ambitious parents were wary of financially "inappropriate" unions.[13] They did not, in fact, subscribe to popular admonitions such as "Better life on a crust he earns than a fortune she has brought him."[14] Families like the Bouchers, Moreheads and Chapmans fretted about how sons-in-law might misuse their future legal control over inherited family assets. In the early 1880s, when Mary's college was under consideration, an even more intense wariness gripped them.

In 1880 Elanora "Ella" Boucher, like Mary, one of Chico Academy's top students, left school because she insisted on marrying her prominent family's hired hand fifteen years her senior. The couple lived with Ella's widowed mother and her paternal uncle on the Boucher farm adjoining the eastern border of Chapmantown. In 1881, less than a year after their wedding, when Ella sought a separation from him, her husband shot and killed her and her mother in view of a Chinese servant and her little brother, who came on the scene unobserved and watched while hiding.

To forestall worrisome alliances, Chico parents had long limited their children's entertainments, as best as possible, to "appropriate" social circles. Sarah Chapman's group was religious and preferably Methodist. Chapman children circulated close to their privileged counterparts. Daughters' prospects were troublesome because acceptable female pastimes were limited and they had considerable free time to fill. While sons could work, people generally associated impropriety or tragedy with women's entry into the paid workforce. Therefore, the daughters of better-off parents often were left to pass their days in the kinds of vacuous entertainments that some parents like the Chapmans disdained. The "parlor daughter" was a familiar figure in such families, including that of George Crosette, whose teenager Mattie afforded him firsthand observations. In an essay, he captured the phenomenon.

A great deal of fault is found with the parlor daughter. It is said of her that she stands at the piano and sings

"What is home without a mother?" while the mother in question is toiling over the fire in the kitchen. No doubt this is true for the parlor daughter nearly always has a kitchen mother, a good, plain sensible woman who says "Young people will be young people" and takes every burden from her pretty daughter's shapely shoulders to put them on her own, already bowed down with care.

There are mothers in Chico who work all day to the accompaniment of "Sweet Violets" and "Only a Pan-sy Blossom" … the mother's darling has been all this time trying to learn these tunes and has not accomplished it yet.… [From her mother's point of view, the parlor daughter] is stylish and it pays to dress her well. She has the knack for fancy work, painting and other accomplishments that to the mother indicate genius. Her young friends do not work, why should she? She takes books from the Free Library and when she is not drumming on the piano … she is lying on the couch in the parlor, feasting on an account of how Adolphus rescued his lady love from the dreary Castle.[15]

Off to Mount Holyoke

In 1882, when Gus was consumed with prison responsibilities, Sarah, Mary, Gussie and Willie visited her Sickley family in Michigan. Sarah and Mary left the boys there and visited Fred at his New York campus. From there, they went to Massachusetts where Sarah settled her daughter at the Mount Holyoke Female Seminary. Reassured by the college's culture of rigid propriety and its grueling work ethic, Sarah must have left confident that her seventeen-year-old daughter would gain a fine education while safe from "undesirable" distractions.

However, Mary no sooner arrived on campus than a student rebellion broke out against its new president Elizabeth Blanchard. The young women had ended the previous semester having unsuccessfully demanded relief from obedience to endless rules they considered picayune. Miss Blanchard welcomed the students back that fall with her announcement that, in response to their concerns, she had moderated some of the rules.[16] However, the students were unimpressed by the announced changes and submitted a petition listing their complaints. From among those, the rule that excited their greatest ire was the requirement that they must turn themselves in for even the tiniest lapses in discipline. The students, defiant and ready to raise the pressure on Miss Blanchard, became audacious. Ignoring the rules, they not only donned their jewelry, they knitted and even embroidered in plain sight. Since only nine students out of the entire student body declined to sign the petition, chances are that Mary Chapman endorsed it.

In addition to classes, personal care—hair, clothing, hygiene—and heavy amounts of homework, Mary and her Mount Holyoke sisters had to scrub floors, prepare food, serve at table and, of course, keep their rooms spotless, subject to surprise raids by picky monitors. For the privileged students accustomed to deference from their parents' household staff, it evidently seemed reasonable to demand the school provide employees for building maintenance.

In contrast to the demands on the young women, their male counterparts at Harvard and Yale universities, often from the same privileged families, considered full services and luxuries their entitlement on campus. The women students' labor kept down costs at Mount Holyoke which, of course, was less well-financed than the men's colleges. Housework was also a reminder to the young women—and a reassurance to some parents—that their privileged educations would not exempt them from the domestic duties they would always have to supervise or do themselves.

Mary Chapman tackled it all. She also faced down a prodigious academic load. By the time Mary reached Mount Holyoke, the school had intensified its academic rigor by hiring lecturers from other female and male colleges. In her first two semesters, she completed courses in grammar, rules of arithmetic, analogy, geography, U.S. history, mental arithmetic, written arithmetic, physical geography, algebra, physics, Bible study, botany, modern history, civil government, trigonometry, chemistry, theology, and mineralogy. While most of her schoolmates filled out their schedules with romance languages, Mary signed up for sight-reading and prose composition in Latin and Greek, both courses her father had taken thirty years earlier at Michigan Central College.[17]

Summer at Home

Like Fred, Mary returned home for summer vacations. On her first return, she accompanied Sarah and the boys for stays at the Powellton cottage. Sarah and Gus, who compared Gussie's and Willie's academic performances to those of Mary and Fred, may have found the boys' "B" grades a disappointment. However, they were spared their father's close attention on that issue because Prison Commission problems and financial concerns kept him out of town or preoccupied by business and prison reports at home. As they approached adolescence and beyond, they had the freedom to explore Chico. The boys and their pals watched the big freight wagons roll in and out of the Junction, checked out trains at the depot, swam with the trout in Little Chico Creek and played in marbles tournaments.[18] While the boys' occasional pranks drew admonitions, they were still welcome in homes and stores around the town.

In summer 1883, while the boys explored and Mary caught up with her girlfriends, Sarah was among the church women who had not left town to escape the heat in higher elevations or at the beaches in Santa Cruz. With no church camp meeting to plan that year, the children's absorption in their adventures and her own light schedule suited the late summer languor. However, an unexpected wedding was suddenly scheduled and became the principal project for Methodist women still in town that August. When the event turned overnight into a town scandal, to Sarah's relief it escaped the young boys' grasp; however, it fascinated Fred and Mary.

The bride-to-be "Mollie" White was a well-known reformed Chico prostitute whom Sarah Chapman, Eliza Camper and friends had undertaken to "save" at her request a year earlier. After intense deliberation, they agreed to train White to be a seamstress. When she grew adept, they hired and promoted her and she quickly became a popular dressmaker. Along the way, when she became engaged to a former client, they promised her a marriage ceremony. The women's plan foundered when Mary's fiancé reneged on his proposal. He came by to talk with her about it on the front porch of her Wall Street boarding house. Instead, he quickly died from the strychnine she had bought that day at the Graves Drugstore at Second and Main and added to his port.

After Mollie's arrest, Sarah and her friends took her side, which aroused astonishment and hilarity among Chico men. Townswomen backed Mollie because they considered her victimhood greater than his—her fiancé had betrayed his promise to wed her. However, her extreme revelry, after the judge in her trial dismissed the charges and freed her, soon exhausted the loyalty of Mollie's backers. While waiting for the train to Texas, Mollie told a reporter she intended to become a nun.[19]

By the spring of 1884, when a loan principal came due, Sarah and Gus realized they could not afford to keep Mary at Mount Holyoke past her second year. Their funds were so tight that Sarah had to let Mrs. Maddox go. Not only would Sarah now have to rely again on Mary to help her keep up the big house and look after the young boys, she would also have to help her daughter adjust to the premature end of her formal education and college life. Mary's only consolation was the prospect of a Massachusetts friend's visit the following summer.

With two years of college, Mary, now 20, was qualified to be a teacher. As she reintegrated herself into Chico life, she developed more confidence. She joined a circle of young adults centered on the families of Henry and Eliza Camper, James and Ardenia Morehead, Dr. Carnot Mason and his wife Mariah and the Chapmans' neighbors George and Millie Miller. The group was informal and interacted with other social groups.

Fred Chapman had broken the way for his sister. A core member of the North Methodist group, he also kept up with his Chico Academy friends, some from the Methodist Church South, and increasingly appeared with Presbyterians. These groups became "addicted" to printers ink, supplying each week's newspaper edition with elegant details that distinguished their fêtes. The printed guest lists for private parties created a sense of exclusivity closely monitored by some. Fred's family status guaranteed his access to social events where his outgoing personality was a plus and his musicianship made him an asset at events across the community.

Mary joined in the ongoing parties that moved from one family home to the next. Young people—grown, but living at home—also looked for gathering spots away from their inquisitive parents' oversight. They borrowed their parents' horses and buggies or rented them from a stable and rode out on the dirt roads that webbed the township's farmland and hamlets. After work, it was fairly easy to picnic in secluded spots along Mud Creek, a Sacramento River tributary, and then to reach home before parents became apoplectic.

Group parties were regular events. On an August evening in 1884, for instance, Mary joined Mollie Camper, Nellie Camper Mead, Flora Earll and several young men, mainly the North Methodist group, who packed wagons with food hampers stashed behind mandolin and banjo cases. They drove to the Sacramento River banks where they waded, rowed, flirted, sang and shared a midnight supper until it was time to set off for home along the moonlit roads. Not long after that, even though William Earll had called in Gus Chapman's debt a few months earlier, Mary and Fred were guests at Flora Earll's home for the first dance of the season. Goodwill and polite behavior between the two families remained possible because Gus had reassured Earll that he would promptly repay the funds in full (which he did). The friendship of Flora and Mary became an enduring one.

In summer 1885 Mary's Mount Holyoke friend arrived with news of their friends and teachers, as well as "the latest" regarding the disputes over school rules. After the visit Mary looked forward to her role as a bridesmaid in Nellie Camper's fashionable wedding.

While the Chapmans generally conducted their social life without press coverage, the party Mary gave in January 1885 was an exception. To no one's surprise, Fred's special guest was Magnolia Wood. Harry McKim, by this time the *Record*'s young printer, must have seen to the full newspaper coverage that followed. A baseball player, he had been Mary's schoolmate before she left for Mount Holyoke and now was courting her. If Harry had a bent for publicity, his model may have been the experience of his elder sister Sallie. Chico newspapers had chronicled in minute detail her every move and wardrobe as she set the pace for Chico's younger set during the late 1870s. However, when Sallie suddenly married a traveling sewing machine salesman, her social standing plummeted.

While Sarah tried to keep track of all her daughter's activities, she remained busy with church and library matters. The shock of the day at the North Methodist Church was word that distant church elders had barred female elders from attendance at regional church meetings. The pastors had decided to shift responsibility for local church governance only to men, even though women did everything from housekeeping to fundraising. They were told the new policy would better enable pastors to address men's spiritual needs. The *Enterprise* took the women's side: "three-quarters of the membership ... are women and the active work they perform in maintaining the churches ... entitles them to a voice in its councils. The women have received a rebuff in the house of their friends, and we hope their present discouragement will stimulate them to renewed energy and eventually success in attaining their rights."[20] The irony was that the women were exhausted from their constant work every week of every year. While they might have felt relieved and freed, they lacked confidence in their replacements and their pride was wounded. When no men stepped forward to take their places, district elders withdrew the edict and the women resumed their old roles.

Another Crisis Intrudes

Soon after Mary's party and a few other social events, her name vanished from newspaper coverage. The timing of her new "invisibility" roughly parallels the onset or advance of "consumption," later known as tuberculosis. While her disease progressed slowly and rendered her neither mentally impaired nor helpless, its symptoms included a chronic overwhelming exhaustion that prevented her attendance at social gatherings, particularly late night events such as the house parties or excursions that the young people enjoyed. Determined to be with her friends and sometimes up to driving the horse and buggy, on occasion she participated in events. However, she was no longer of help to her mother on whose attentions she now increasingly relied.

Like Mary's, Sarah's name also vanished from newspaper notices that had lightly traced both their lives beyond home and church in the mid-1880s. Mary benefited from Sarah's experience as Gus's nurse throughout his malaria and other illnesses. Nursing duties on this new scale, however, meant Sarah had joined a kind of "women's club" whose membership spanned Chico's neighborhoods.

These mothers and wives struggled against their own exhaustion as they strove to ease the hardships of their consumptive or malarial spouses and children. Other "club" members included Wilhelmina Pratt Sommers, who had lost children and now looked after her dying husband Carl, Chico's leading jeweler. Just up the street from Sarah, her neighbor Matilda Collins tended to her husband Addison who had managed the Llano Seco Ranch and died in 1887. An example of the toll such women suffered was Mrs. David Craig, wife of a Kimshew Township hotelkeeper, about ten miles northeast of Stirling City, who died from heart failure. Her friends believed she had worn herself out in the care of her consumptive son during his last ten years. John Bidwell severely taxed his own health in order to make numerous trips to visit his consumptive wife at a distant care facility. (Annie Bidwell lived almost twenty years after her husband's death.)

Despite Mary's disease, she sustained the love and loyalty of her athletic suitor Harry McKim. Mary's condition, however, moved the center of their courtship from social gatherings about town to the double parlors and grounds of the Chapmans' now heavily mortgaged home. Even though tuberculosis inspired dread in the late nineteenth century, Americans still considered its symptom, the deepening emaciation that produced frailty and lethargy, "attractive" in women.

Tragedy and Romance

Although Harry McKim was one of Chico's more handsome and engaging young men, his uncertain employment prospects suggest Mary's choice worried her parents. As evidenced by the education they provided her, they had envisioned a more privileged future for her. To Harry's credit, however, he was not a "masher," a male phenomenon that parents dreaded, according to publisher and parent George Crosette:

> What's that, Mother?
> A masher dear;
> You will always find it standing here,
> Posed on the corner of the street
> Proudly displaying its tiny feet,
> Twirling its ten-cent cane
> And stupefying its tender brain
> With the smoke of a paper cigarette.
> Don't touch it, dear; it was raised a pet.
> Will it bite, Mother?
> Well, I should about;
> It will bite a free lunch for all that's out.[21]

Harry was a printer with a passion for baseball, not yet the sport of gentlemen. While that probably did not help him win favor with the senior Chapmans, his ardent pursuit of Mary complicated their response in light of her advancing condition and marriageable age.

After years of financial success and civic distinction, an aura of failure hovered over Gus. Now 60, he experienced the humiliation that accompanies failure, in public and at home. By 1887 Sarah, 54, and he had come to accept Fred's rejection of the family business. The security and satisfaction they had hoped for from their ample talents and work had evaporated. While Gus strove to present himself as upbeat about his future, his disappointed ambitions and growing debt certainly haunted him.

In the meantime, Sarah handled the escapades of their adolescent boys and continued to worry about the breach between Gus and Fred, who had not advanced beyond his job as a Wells Fargo clerk. While her husband was no longer away on state business or on grueling sales trips, now he was mired and miserable in Powellton, trying to resurrect some value from the remains of his lumber company. Together and separately, the Chapmans addressed one knotty problem after the next.

At every stage of her adult life Sarah Chapman adjusted to changes in Gus's finances and objectives and to the life stages of older and younger children. By the late 1880s, Gus was at home with little to do. Sarah continued to run the household and participate in fundraising for the free library and her church. Still active in the Chico Relief Society, she stretched her tightening resources to help the poor such as those in Dumpville, the neighborhood east of the Sierra Flume & Lumber yards. The steady efforts of Sarah Chapman and her friends continued to provide a resource for Chico's poor or damaged. Their work, despite their own personal challenges, refutes stereotypes about the vacuous lives Sinclair Lewis later ascribed to better-off women who lived in small country towns.

21

Money and Marriages

Increased lumber sales in 1888 raised Gus Chapman's hopes again, but the returns did not cover the mortgage payments on his house and the timberland loan.[1] While this was a problem, even more worrisome was Mary's decline in the grip of tuberculosis. In addition, Fred had quit the lumber company, with no future as a Wells Fargo clerk nor any other job prospect at hand.

The future of sons leaving town in their teen years troubled many Chico families. This had been a public issue in the anti-Chinese campaigns which blamed Chinese workers for monopolizing starter jobs suited to white boys. In the 1880s better-off families were also concerned. The son of Gus's friend Dr. Carnot Mason had to move to the San Francisco Bay area for a job. When word had reached Chico about Jo Wood's death in Folsom Prison, townspeople recalled another aspect of the problem: wealthy George Wood's son had been their worst-case example of a failed child of privilege. Gus likely checked on Jo when he was at Folsom on state business. Sarah recalled Jo from the 1860s in the John Bidwell & Co. store, when his unreliability at work exasperated his father. However, Jo made visits to Gus's bedside during malarial episodes and, while there, cut wood for Sarah. After that, he turned into a professional gambler who moved about the region, occasionally visible in Chico while staying with his sister Emily who nursed their mother Caroline, overcome by facial cancer. Each time Jo ran out of local "marks" at the saloons, he took off for more lucrative locations. The *Record*'s George Crosette recalled concern about Jo's "dissolute life and bad company."[2] Some feared their chronically unemployed sons might fall to such temptations.

While Fred's parents knew their son's character bore no resemblance to Jo Wood, Fred's self-indulgence was at odds with their values. He took his advantages for granted and lacked his father's personal drive or ambition. The bitter edge to this was Fred's refusal to work in his father's lumber mill. He was spurning what Gus once considered a golden opportunity and now understood as critical to the family's financial survival. Still, Fred would not step up.

Fred also had another problem. While smart, well-educated and attractive, he could be a prig. For example, the *Record* editor was disdainful when Fred demanded the paper retract its mention of his "tumble into the mud on Wall Street" as he ran to watch a fire.[3] His pride also emerged during his service with the Chico Guard. During their march at Governor Perkins's inaugural procession, members took pride in their "splendid appearance." However, a State Militia colonel visiting Chico, declining to "smear them with taffy," instead sternly advised them how to improve their performance.[4] Although a mediocre marksman in a shooting contest, Fred was devoted to the militia and, while only a private in 1885, threw himself into the drills, weapons maintenance and meetings. His motivation and persistence lent substance to his reputation.

His son's promotion to corporal encouraged Gus, who made a conciliatory gesture. He contributed to the building fund for the armory that went up at Fifth and Main. The militiamen elected Fred drillmaster for his role in their improvement. With "the ladies" present for inspiration, Fred ran rigorous Wednesday evening drills during which the militia men worked their way "through the manual of arms, the maintenance, loadings and firings of weapons and various company movements."[5] The men's new determination turned the Chico unit around.

Therefore, when First Lieutenant W. R. Williams advanced to captain of the general staff, Fred, a corporal (an enlisted rank), decided his own contributions warranted his advancement to Williams's rank. However, Second Lieutenant Charles Coggins, 33, whose father owned the local box-building factory and recently had bought the Chapmans' lumber store on Main Street, had the advantage. He was already an officer whereas Chapman, if elected, would jump from an enlisted rank to that of first lieutenant. In the July 1885 election Fred Chapman received 24 votes to Charles Coggins's 32.

Young Chapman was not a good loser. Instead, he challenged the election's validity on a technicality: the visiting officer who conducted it had done so out of uniform. As a result, Fred became an object of derision not only in Chico, but in Red Bluff, where the *News* issued a sarcastic rebuke: "The mind staggers at the enormity of the [officer's] offense."[6] The paper went on to propose that Coggins and Chapman box "with soft gloves under the Marquis of Queensbury [sic] rules," that is, adhering to a sense of fair play.[7] Fred tried again, this time against three candidates for second lieutenant. He lost. When called on for remarks, the other losers obliged with humor. By contrast, Fred, who had won almost no votes, declined to speak. The company retired to Phil McManus's saloon without Fred.

Despite his loss of support in the militia, Fred rose to officer rank in the "semi-military" Band of Hope.[8] While this earned Magnolia Wood's approval, his temperance isolated Fred from the camaraderie of old friends and militia members who regularly drank together downtown. Saloons were refuges where men relaxed, exchanged news, collected job tips, made transactions and sized up one another. At Phil McManus's that election night in August 1885 the militiamen must have weighed in on Fred's pout over his second election loss. Of greater moment, however, was the approach of a scheduled State Militia drill, a competition on the coast at Camp Stoneman. Fred planned to go, even though the camp was named for the Democratic governor who had smeared his father's reputation.

Because the local militia would vie for judges' approval of their drill techniques against other militias across Northern California, Fred plunged into the practice drills. However, when Chico's men caught the train for Santa Cruz, drill leader Chapman was absent. "Bilious fevers" had sent Fred to bed throughout the first half of August. Determined to participate, he rushed his recovery and "caught the cars" to the coast. No sooner had he arrived in camp, however, than he relapsed. A local minister's wife took care of him until Sarah arrived from Chico.

After Fred and Sarah returned home in mid-September, he resumed his militia duties. Buoyed by praise for their performance at Santa Cruz, the militia members welcomed Fred back into the fold. Then, at a February practice in 1886, as Fred bent over to set targets, his friend Charles Tripp accidentally fired his gun. A single split ball put a hole through Fred's cap, shattered his forefinger and penetrated his foot. While the wounds were "annoying but not … dangerous," they may have contributed to his decision to quit the unit.[9]

Fred was old enough to recognize that, despite Chico's struggling economy, his father continued to provide comforts and advantages, as well as entry into the family lumber business. Now Fred, like his less privileged counterparts, had to make his own way. There was little sustained, desirable work for his generation. Therefore, it became common for members of the first "California generation" to seek work in another town or state. Fred decided to get in on the current boom in San Jose. Because "small properties there had quadrupled in value," people had begun to think of it as the North State's counterpart to Los Angeles.[10] Town leaders, coveting San Jose's success, kept up their morale as they tried to convince themselves that "Chico may be next."[11]

Fred and Magnolia

When Alabama-born Magnolia Wood's family moved to their country place nearer her father's Oroville office as superintendent of schools, she taught in two rural locations. Then, because, like Fred, she preferred town life, she returned to Chico for a position at Oakdale School and boarded in the home of a family friend.

The relationship between Magnolia and Fred became serious not long after he returned from college in June 1882. That November Sarah accepted Magnolia's invitation to a Presbyterian Mite Society social at the Bidwells' home. Sarah invited her close neighbor and fellow Methodist steward Elizabeth Miller to go with her. Although Presbyterian women had joined with Methodist women on the library campaigns and in the Chico Relief Society, by and large each group kept to its own circle. As a native of Maryland and resident of Washington, D.C., Annie Bidwell's diary suggests she was more comfortable with women of the Methodist Church South.[12]

Sarah's presence at the Bidwells' home showed support for Fred even though he adopted Magnolia's favorite cause, temperance, and left his mother's church for hers. While the Bidwell church event may have felt awkward at the start, Sarah found herself surrounded by people she had known for years. Among them was John Bidwell, who still made periodic donations to the North Methodist Church and occasionally attended their services.[13]

In the five years that Fred and Magnolia courted, his family realized there were good reasons to accept his choice. Her exemplary education, serious work ethic and religious devotion represented values they respected. While her personality was rather severe, according to a later inference in Sarah's 1899 diary, his parents must have concluded that this stern and self-disciplined woman would be good for their floundering son.[14]

They all grew closer when Magnolia stayed with the Chapmans at their Powellton cottage during the 1887 lumber season. The presence of Fred's girlfriend lowered the temperature between father and son. She and Sarah were a comfort for Fred, while Gussie and Willie's exploits diverted everyone in the house. The boys romped with other children in the forest and swam and fished in streams near the mill. However, when Magnolia returned to Chico, Fred was not only restless, bored and lonely in the woods, he was exhausted by the dangerous labor and intimidated by the rough, hardy men who knew the college boy, the owner's son, was out of place there.

Magnolia's father Jesse Wood, an 1859 graduate of Emory & Henry College in Virginia, had been headmaster of Tuskegee Female College in Alabama (now Huntingdon College) when he married Alice Tyson, a former student there. Magnolia's birth in 1861 was the start of the couple's large family. At the Civil War's end, the Woods immediately joined the flow of impoverished Southerners heading west.[15] Jesse and Alice took their small children by ship to San Francisco where he ministered to a church. After a disagreement with congregation members, Jesse moved his family to Chico where he became pastor of the Methodist Church South.

Like North Methodist pastors, Jesse Wood drew no regular salary. His family depended on the meager proceeds from the church women's fundraising endeavors. He and his wife Alice were grateful for their wages, sometimes amounting to in-kind offerings of produce, firewood and other goods. However, they were not enough to fill the cash gap so Alice taught drawing lessons and fed her family from her garden, the family cow and the chickens. When Jesse began to supplement their family's income with work as a schoolteacher, his congregation demanded he quit because the church prohibited ministers from taking public jobs. However, out of sympathy for his need to support his large family, the church stewards yielded. With the extra job's boost to the Woods' income, and perhaps with a windfall from back home, the couple acquired an attractive, though cramped, Italianate cottage.

In the mid-1870s, after Jesse lost his first try for election as county superintendent of schools, he "inaugurated" the "Christian Union." For his own interdenominational church, he built a downtown meeting place where he gave his progressive religious ideas another chance. However, like his first congregation in San Francisco, this small congregation soon drifted away. Thereafter, elections to successive terms as Butte County superintendent of schools kept him close to Oroville.

Better times arrived for Jesse Wood in the early 1880s. He briefly published the Chico *Enterprise*. Then, while still superintendent, he bought the Oroville newspaper and moved his family to a farm they called "Eyrie Villa" between Chico and the county seat. Magnolia Wood's decision to move from there to Chico disappointed her favorite brother Tyson, who resembled her in his intellect, although his interests took a mechanical bent. In line with thinking that irrigation's arrival meant the Sacramento Valley would diversify its crops, young Tyson invented a prune and plum pitter and looked forward to enrolling in a technical training college. To stay close to her family, Magnolia made drives between Chico and the Woods' farm, sometimes with Tyson as her companion.

Fred proposed to Magnolia in 1887 when she was 26. Verging on "spinsterhood," she was one of the single women school trustees paid even less than the pittance they paid men. For $30 a month, Magnolia daily faced a classroom packed with as many as sixty children. The *Record* commiserated, clucking that it was "hard work to keep so many little folks quiet."[16] While motivated students took advantage of the opportunity to learn, many impoverished parents considered schools convenient places to stash their children between jobs as wood stackers, babysitters or errand runners. Therefore, Magnolia faced classes everyday with one or another student ready to nap or cause trouble.

Such children tested not only their teachers, but also the general public. Defiant boys defaced Oakdale School property, talked back, swore and brawled between classes in the schoolyard over minor offenses. Like boys of the 1870s, in the 1880s some raced horses through town and others lobbed rocks at the Chinese. Now that a growing web of cement walks were replacing boardwalks, sudden sweeps by packs of roller skaters kept pedestrians on alert to jump out of their way.

Magnolia dealt with schoolboys whose marbles scandal of 1884 confounded Chico's adult populace. Gussie and Willie were probably too young to know the destination of boys who regularly fanned out through their neighborhood that year. They were on their way to faro card games in a deserted barn south of Chapmantown. At first, the young gamblers wagered their bets with red Indian beads they had dug out of a grave that town workers had exposed when they removed a First Street cistern; when those beads ran out, the boys turned to marbles. The boys had switched from poker to faro because, at times, they kept 5,000 marbles in play. Their activities eluded parental attention.

Players began to break ranks, however, after one gathering where a couple of new players showed up pulling wagons stacked with sacks of 1,000 marbles each and declared their intent to "break the bank." They launched the game with a 500-marble limit. When the new guys won all those marbles, they proposed to raise the limit to 7,000—all the marbles in Chico. Around a table that the players had cobbled together from fence boards, each player opened with sacks upon sacks of marbles at his side. When a "leading citizen's" son won all 7,000 marbles, he proceeded to sell them back to the boys at 10¢ for twenty marbles.

While parents were slow to catch on, once they overcame their incredulity, they shut down the "casino." Magnolia's everyday familiarity with such pranksters reinforced the strict propriety she reflected in her advice to a student: "Do what conscience says is right/ do what reason says is best/ Do with all your mind and might/ Do your duty and be blest."

One instance illustrates Magnolia's personal determination to "do her best with all her might." When a student tripped her midway down the school staircase, she plunged a dozen steps, taking the brunt of the fall on her head and neck. In the principal's office, she reassured her rescuers that after a few minutes she would return to her classroom. However, when she did not improve, she allowed friends to take her to her rented room, assuring all that she would return to work "shortly," which she did.[17]

Despite such challenges, Magnolia not only persisted, she worked at improving herself. She became a regular participant in the Annual Teachers' Institute meetings which her father ran to raise Butte County's school standards. The programs she enjoyed most included dramatic performance, which provided teachers with communication skills in classes where they dealt with uneven literacy levels. Entertainment at fundraising events often depended on music and recitations by talented children whom school faculty coached. For one Institute's program, she read an essay, "The Farmers." For another, she sang and played Portia's part in "The Merchant of Venice."

Private schools were not exempt from the behavioral problems encountered at public ones. For example, at the Chico Academy, a few blocks from the Oakdale School, Selena Woodman whipped two boys with peach sprouts after she caught them smoking next to her new schoolhouse that had replaced the one an earlier student burned down. In another incident, when the family of a welt-covered student denounced Mrs. Woodman's stern discipline as "unpardonable" and "an outrage," Reverend Woodman published a defense of his wife. The issue remained alive in 1887 when Justice of the Peace Harmon Bay acquitted the reverend of charges that he had hit a student. While the couple were of age to retire, they had no pensions and few savings. So they kept the Chico Academy going until the mid-1890s when they closed it, sold the valuable Fifth Street land and moved to San Leandro to be near their surviving son, who died within a few years. There, Selena Woodman occupied her last years with work to advance the Women's Christian Temperance Union.[18]

By the late 1880s, Magnolia, still single, could have faced the prospect of a lifetime on her own, with no letup in work or prospect of better pay. By contrast, a late marriage to Fred provided love and some promise of security. In family terms, however, a marital alliance between the Woods and the Chapmans was not a "natural." For decades, the couple's fathers had sat on different sides of local issues. For example, Gus Chapman had supported Selena Woodman against Magnolia's father in the early race for superintendent of schools. As recently as 1886, Wood had signed the anti-Chinese petition which Chapman opposed. Still, the two men managed to get along well enough. Despite Wood's reputation for contentiousness, his native Georgia had shaped him as a man of "grace and elegance peculiar to himself.... [He had a] pleasant smile and encouraging word for all."[19] To the relief of Fred's family, Magnolia had inherited her father's intellect and sober rectitude rather than his occasional compulsion to play the "burr in the saddle."

Like his parents in their day, Fred Chapman and Magnolia Wood were in their mid-to late-twenties when they set their wedding date. Their timing not only meshed with Fred's plan to seek work in San Jose, it made it possible for them to share a double ceremony with Mary Chapman and Harry McKim on January 17, 1888. With all that had to be done for the event, and taking into account the Chapmans' straitened circumstances, Sarah did not return to Michigan where her brothers and sisters gathered around their dying mother.

Magnolia's sense of discretion matched the Chapmans' preference for privacy. For example, when she announced she would resign from her school position on December 24, 1887, a month previous to her wedding, the newspaper surmised that she meant to retire to her parents' home for a needed rest.[20] Instead, Magnolia worked on wedding preparations with Mary and Sarah. The families managed to keep the pending double wedding ceremony quiet until two weeks before it took place. Once the local press learned of its approach, items followed with mentions about plans underway for "the wedding." No further description was necessary in the little town for readers to identify whose wedding.

Mary and Harry

Mary's fiancé Harry McKim arrived in Chico as the teen-aged stepson of Henry McLennan. Although a saloon owner,

McLennan was well-known and well thought of in Chico as a civically active local businessman whose standing gave his new family a boost. While not "refined," he was financially comfortable. Even so, his financial standing and his stepson's social standing were not what Gus and Sarah Chapman envisioned for Mary.

After their wedding in 1877, Henry brought his bride, Harry's widowed mother Sarah McKim, and her two children from Sacramento to Chico. McLennan, an 1850s gold miner, had been a courageous stage driver in mountain country. Then, in the Valley, he acquired the Pony, a popular Chico saloon, and, in the 1880s, bought the Cabinet at 222 Main Street. This was the favored watering hole of "respectable" Chico men, including members of Chico Engine Co.'s Number One who considered it their clubhouse. With Chico's history of devastating fires, volunteer firemen were heroes. They bonded as brothers in companies resembling fraternities. Attachment to either Engine Number One, Number Two or the Deluge Hose Company mattered so much that members are buried in the firefighters' section of the cemetery with their companies' names engraved on their gravestones. Henry McLennan's successive reelections to head Engine Co. Number One led to his seat on Chico's Board of Health. Like Chapman, he was a stalwart Republican.[21]

On shelves flanking the entrance to McLennan's saloon was his display of treasures which featured an exact duplicate of the hatchet George Washington supposedly used on the fabled cherry tree, a scattering of colorful minerals and Indian skulls. In addition, he kept live squirrels in a fancy tin cage and displayed "monstrosities" such as an eight-feet-long snakeskin.

Another collector was John Bidwell, whose cabinet displayed more orthodox treasures such as stuffed small animals. Such exhibits were a vogue of the day and a byproduct of the nineteenth-century enthusiasm for natural science. California residents considered cabinet collections a tribute to the uniqueness of their new western homes.

The Double Wedding

Although the Chapmans' home was one of Chico's larger dwellings, it could not accommodate all the wedding guests.

This may be why they kept the wedding quiet as long as they could. The Chapman, Wood and McLennan families, therefore, began by inviting only a moderate number of guests. However, the guest list grew. As an example of the heightened anticipation about the double wedding, the lengthy account published in the *Record* conveys a sentimentality characteristic of George Crosette. The article recalled the Chapmans' overland crossing to California in 1861 when Fred was a toddler. The Oroville *Mercury* also gave large play to the Chico wedding of Magnolia, its publisher's daughter.

The newspaper reports about this wedding offer the only surviving glimpse of the Chapmans at home. In retrospect, the double wedding was poignant—it was the last celebration the entire Chapman family would share.[22]

Out-of-town guests for the Wednesday ceremony began to appear at the "brilliantly illuminated" Chapman Street house an hour or more in advance of the wedding's 8:30 p.m. start. Workers parked their guests' buggies and watered their horses in the stable area, where, in deference to Magnolia's temperance, discrete guests could find an informal bar behind the hay bales.[23] Greeters at the double front doors alternately collected coats or shawls and passed around the long-handled brushes to whisk mud and dirt from their boots. Guests chatted as they moved through the formal entry into the gas-lighted double parlors. There, Sarah had bedecked two bay windows with winter garlands of smilax, camellias, ivy and pansies. The Chapmans' "little boys participated to the full extent in the family's enjoyment."[24] (By 1887 Gussie and Willie, who inherited their small stature from their parents, were adolescents rather than "little boys.") This night the wedding presented rare pleasures at every turn: lighted lamps and chandeliers, the crush of people, laughter, wrapped presents, the quantity and variety of delicious food on Sarah's silver platters. Mary's friends Maude Blood and Nellie Camper Mead spelled one another at Sarah's piano.

All the guests were obliged to Maude's father Amos Blood who provided the drinks. He had first elevated Chico's palate in 1870 when he hauled ice from Truckee and then introduced machine-made ice at his Chico Soda Works, which produced bottles of mineral waters and flavored sodas that became "must have" treats. Like Gus Chapman, Blood had become successful enough to send his daughter east to college.

Once the guests were seated, Maude launched the wedding music to which maid of honor Mollie Camper descended the entry hall's grand staircase on the arm of best man Tyson Wood. Harry McKim followed, escorting Mary who had piled her hair in a fashionable pompadour. Adding to her sophisticated look, her white satin bustled walking-length dress was accented by a corsage she pinned to its square and tulle-draped neckline.

Fred Chapman, wearing a black suit like Harry, descended the stairs with Magnolia. "Passamenterie" (fancy braid) trimmed her tailored "visiting dress" in brown satin. Mary and Harry first entered the parlor, stopping beneath one of two flower-bedecked arches of the bay windows to face the room. From there, they turned to face the Chapmans' Methodist minister as he read them their vows. Magnolia and Fred then followed suit, standing in front of the adjacent arch and turned toward the Presbyterian minister who read them their vows. According to an observer, each of the four repeated after the pastors with characteristic "sincerity and earnestness." The brides "looked pretty and delighted, while the grooms looked happy and handsome."[25]

At the ceremony's conclusion, the two couples circulated among their families and friends who showered them with good wishes in the midst of "great wit and humor."[26] When Maude resumed playing the piano, the couples led their guests to the dining room where Sarah and her friends presented their elegant buffet. Fred's Neubarth Band colleagues serenaded the couples.

The McKims' deferral of a wedding trip was perhaps due to Mary's fragile health and Harry's rocky finances. Instead, they retired to their new "pleasant home," purchased by Gus Chapman, a few blocks north at Seventh and Orient.[27] They were not going to have their frail daughter live in a boardinghouse. Though Harry may not have been the groom the Chapmans envisioned for Mary, she was happy. By contrast, Magnolia and Fred arrived at the depot close to midnight to catch the only passenger train south each day. John Bidwell and others, waiting at the depot to leave for San Francisco, congratulated them. No less eager to see San Jose was Tyson Wood, who planned to visit once his sister and Fred had found a place to rent.[28]

The family weddings were a matter of pride for Gus who, for decades, had quietly but assiduously fostered, in the words of his will, the Chapmans' "standing and influence in the community." While the public was, to some extent, aware of his financial and political reverses, few others than his bankers grasped the extent and immediacy of his peril. The interest in his children's weddings and the unusually thorough newspaper coverage of the event probably meant more to him than to the new couples. The gathering provided Gus with momentary reassurance that, despite the Prison Commission fiasco, despite his sacrifices to satisfy all his creditors and despite his loss of the bank board seat, Chico still cared about his family. However, the weddings also may have occasioned another insight by Gus. Each of his carefully cultivated elder children had made marriage choices to individuals without financial security. Now Harry and Mary, like Fred and Magnolia, were likely to look to him for financial help.

With his home quiet again, Gus Chapman had to figure out how to handle his debt. He still owed the Bank of Butte County on the most recent mortgages he had taken out to fund that season's lumber business. On the good side, his mill's towering stacks of pine had satisfied concerns about his ability to manage production without William McKay. However, northern California construction was again shaky as the national economy contracted. He had been counting on the prospective lumber sales to meet his expenses and at least cover interest.[29]

While Fred's decision to leave the business was an ongoing disappointment and the economy worrisome, Chapman & Co. confronted an even bigger systemic problem. In the mid-1870s lumber operations had begun to adopt a version of consolidation associated with the industrial model of production. While those changes were suspended by the depression then, by the late 1880s consolidation had became established. Sierra Flume & Lumber owned eleven lumber mills across Butte Creek from Chapman & Co. and north from there. This meant small, independent lumbermen like Gus Chapman had to compete with companies that cut and finished product on a vast scale. By 1888 market prices sunk under the combination of a slow market and a backlog of overstocked lumber.

Tragedy Strikes in San Jose

Meanwhile, in September 1888, as Fred and Magnolia awaited their first child's birth in San Jose, they anticipated a visit from her brother Tyson, 20. Already enrolled in Professor Worcester's Commercial College near their home, he and Chico friend Irving Gilbert had stopped along their way to tour San Francisco's Mechanics Fair. From there, the two young men set off on the narrow-gauge railroad which, in 1876, Gus Chapman had evaluated as a model for northern Butte County. Tyson was particularly excited about this trip because he planned to reveal his design of the peach- and plum-pitting machine to the superintendent of the San Jose Agricultural Works.

In the late afternoon, as the young men's train approached its Julian Street stop, Tyson suddenly recognized Magnolia and Fred's neighborhood. Eager to surprise his sister, he jumped from the platform of the rear car. Equipment caught his foot, however, and drew him under the moving car's wheels.[30] Irving yelled at other passengers to stop the train, then he jumped off to help his friend. However, by the time Gilbert was on his feet and caught his balance, the train had glided on toward the depot. The other passengers, horrified, shocked and confused, never signaled the engineer to stop the train which pulled young Tyson's mangled body for three blocks. Although five doctors worked to save the unconscious patient, their efforts proved futile. He died at seven that evening with Magnolia, Fred and Irving at his side.

When Jesse and Alice Wood received the telegram about their son's death, they were seized with a grief so deep it gripped them for the rest of their lives. An especially attentive son, Tyson had developed their orchard and the lingering sense of his presence permeated their farm, where his projects and plans met their eyes at every turn. His parents buried Tyson in the Chico Cemetery. Over his grave they placed a handsome marker commemorating his life. In 1893, they sold all their Butte County property and moved to Magnolia and Fred's new home in Stockton, where the latest boom was underway.[31]

The Slide Continues

Early in 1889 the Bank of Butte County notified Augustus Chapman that he must satisfy the terms of his now delinquent loan.[32] Foreclosure loomed. Frank Lusk's central position in the bank provided Chapman no comfort under these circumstances. Lusk not only had forced Chapman out as a bank officer and board member, he was leveraging that move to acquire an even more direct role in bank decision-making. (His goal, later realized, was to become president of the bank.) For Chapman, the prospect of dispossession was shameful enough, but to see it coming at Frank Lusk's hands must have been excruciating. Chapman also realized that his enduring allies John R. Robinson and Charles Faulkner could do no more than express their regret at his plight. Lusk was ready to administer his financial "coup de grâce" to Augustus Chapman.[33]

On February 27, 1889, however, Chapman managed to eke out financial survival yet again. Making good on his 1884 debt to the Bank of Butte County on honorable, if humiliating, terms, Chapman signed over the bulk of his 2,700-acre mountain timber properties, four wagons, twenty oxen and 100,000 board feet of lumber. Had it not been for the general economic conditions at the time, the market sale of his mountain of stacked pine might have spared him such disgrace.

Though painful, his losses also represented a psychological victory. Chapman's skills as a deal maker enabled him to prevent Lusk and the bank from seizing his ultimate prize, the Chapman Street house. It was his family's home, it declared his success and was his final evidence of credit worthiness. In addition, because he retained a portion of his Powellton mill property, he could stay in business, albeit it on a much-reduced scale. How did he manage this? Prior to his meeting at the Bank of Butte County, he had a meeting with Alexander H. Crew at the Bank of Chico where he remained a longstanding member of its board of directors.

There, he negotiated a new mortgage with Crew who was about to become the bank's president. On the basis of Chapman's subsequent actions, it appears that he and Crew reached an agreement to this general effect: in return for the Bank of

Chico's assumption of the mortgage, Chapman would subdivide and sell the block of open land surrounding his house.[34] In addition, he agreed to sell more of the Chapman Reserve along Little Chico Creek. He would use the new loan to fund his next year's production at the Powellton mill.

Alexander H. Crew was as popular in Chico as Frank Lusk was disliked.[35] The dignity of his British accent and the eccentricity of his daily routine intrigued townspeople. No matter how inclement the weather, each day he walked east of town to a private spot where he immersed himself in Big Chico Creek. While Crew insisted he was self-made, he was not. He was a trustee and manager of the bank owned by John Conly, his wife Susan Heath Crew's brother-in-law. Not until 1890, after all the Conly men had died, could Alexander Crew become president of the Bank of Chico. To Mrs. Crew, the Heath/Conly connection was so important for its link to the Conly bank that her gravestone reads: "Susan Heath wife of Alexander Crew." He and Augustus Chapman had collaborated on countless civic and fraternal projects over their decades in Chico. Both were Masonic Knights Templar and mainstays of the free library. During A. H. Crew's years in Chico, he had respected Gus Chapman as a substantial businessman, civic leader and friend.

From his vantage point at the bank, Crew recognized that Chapman's financial situation was not unique. However, few others had such considerable property that they could sustain their troubled businesses over as long a period as Gus had managed to do. In the hard times of the 1890s that predominated throughout Crew's depression-time presidency, he repeatedly listened to men of accomplishment and character who set out their plight and plans for recovery. He listened to their pleas for special consideration and heard their heartfelt assurances as they faced the American nightmare—disgrace that followed failure.

Crew had observed Augustus Chapman's perseverance, recognized his talent, respected his record of repayment of every debt in full and even, perhaps, Chapman's ability to surmount serial crises. Gus had satisfied every creditor. He had paid off the loan in full from William Earll and several Bank of Butte County mortgages. He had signed over or sold valuable assets to satisfy every debt, including the latest one. Crew viewed Chapman as an honest man who was willing to sacrifice his last valuable asset, his own house. Crew renewed the mortgage.

Crew's help to vulnerable bank clients like Chapman during the latest depression earned him the townspeople's deep gratitude. As a mainstay of the Chico Relief Society, in which his wife was a leader, Alexander Crew also showed compassion for the poor. When he died, stores closed out of respect and townspeople of all circumstances reacted with sorrow.

With the Bank of Chico money, Chapman announced his plan: "His new mill is now in position and will be ready to start up tomorrow or the next day, when he returns [to Powellton]. With the best little mill in all the hill country and a fine section of virgin timber land to draw upon, he expects to cut lumber for doors, windows and such ... for the San Francisco market at a good profit."[36] Gus remained an optimist—or at least was able to maintain the appearance of confidence without which, he knew well, failure was a certainty.

1890s and After

22

The Chapmans Lose Their Own

Harbingers of better times for the Chapmans came with the Bank of Chico's reprieve and the births of grandchildren. In 1889 Mary and Harry became the parents of Harold Dustin McKim, thereafter called Dustin by the Chapman family and "Harry" or "Mac" by the McKims. In October 1890 Magnolia and Fred named their new baby Willis Tyson Chapman for his young uncles. Having begun their own family, they remembered Chico with new appreciation as a place to rear children. To make possible a return there for his family, Fred became the agent for Brown's Remedies in Butte, Yolo and Colusa counties.[1] When this did not work out, the young Chapmans moved from Stockton to San Diego, where, late that summer, Fred fell seriously ill. Gus could not leave the mill and there was no money for sending Sarah; she and Gus had to make do with Magnolia's reports of his recovery in a series of grim letters.

Gus Chapman Sr.'s bank reprieve became a casualty of slowed construction in San Francisco. To honor his obligation to Alexander Crew, he sold more assets to pay off the Bank of Chico loan. This included the family's barn on the Oroville-Shasta Road, which a carpenter turned into a furniture factory. Gus also sold realtor George Vadney a few undeveloped lots adjacent to his house. Vadney, who had worked for him at Chico Lumber Co., became a major real estate developer who created housing lots south from Sixteenth Street; over time, that also became known as Chapmantown. Chapman also sold timberland near his mill. He kept back a small stand of trees to supply the mill. That and his share in the new Chico Hotel comprised Gus's base for recovery.

The family's continued residence in their distinguished edifice on Chapman Street—the only home Gus and Will remembered—struck a positive note. Their father's "quick saves" with bank loans, their mother's thriftiness and both parents' discretion maintained at least the appearance of normalcy. Gus and Sarah, still determined to provide the younger children with advantages they afforded their older ones, somehow kept current with tuitions for Will at the Chico Academy and Gus at the University of the Pacific. However, their parents' fear of more financial struggles deepened because the house, their last significant asset, was now at risk.

In July 1890 Gus and Sarah ran out of options: they had to sell their house to cover the bank debt. Putting the best face on his situation, Gus assured the *Enterprise* that he had a "contract in the milling business which will last him two years, and a smaller house will now suit him."[2] That "smaller" house was their cottage in Powellton. The large mansion's buyer was farmer Robert Boydston, whose sister Ardenia Morehead was Sarah's old friend. The Boydstons needed a Chico home near a school for their eight children. They paid $3,400 (almost $109,000 today), about $1,000 less than the house's recent assessed value. The Boydstons' new carpets, parlor furniture and other pieces were delivered from Fetters & Williams, who had furnished the house for Gus and Sarah.

Death of Mary Chapman McKim

The comfort Gus found from the sale was that it qualified him for another loan; this one to keep his Powellton mill going. While Gus was on sales trips or in Powellton, Sarah stayed behind to manage the hotel. Instead of keeping an apartment there, the couple likely wintered with Mary and Harry McKim because her mother's attention was welcomed by Mary, whose baby Tommy had arrived as her tuberculosis was advancing. Little Dustin's needs at the age of two were an additional legitimate justification for her parents' residence there. That fall Gus Jr. left Chico for his first year in college, Will started a new semester at the Chico Academy and Gus returned to Chico from the mill for the season. His latest loan from the Bank of Chico enabled him to erect a plain building on one of his few remaining lots in the Chapman Reserve, as the adjacent creek-side land across from their former Chico home was still known. Gus's building housed the Chico Steam Laundry in which Robert Boydston was also an investor. The Chapmans' large shed nearby housed their big house's contents.

Sometimes when Mary rallied, she could still drive her buggy. One trip, when she gave Gus Jr. a lift, nearly ended in disaster. As her horse kept to the right side of a street, two men driving a fast cart came up short behind them. Irritated, the driver suddenly pulled out into the middle of the street and dashed alongside to pass her. His cart's wheels caught those of Mary's buggy so forcefully that young Gus, Mary and the speeders all flew from their seats. The miscreants sprung to their feet, checked their horse, hastily righted their vehicle and fled. Passersby rushed to help Mary and her brother who both escaped with bruises and strains.[3] Such accidents were a common hazard. Drivers, passengers and pedestrians died or sustained injuries, not only from speeding or drunk and reckless drivers, but also from malfunctioning buggies, runaway horses and the hazards of fog or moonless nights on rutted roads.

The Chapmans' lives were already full of financial complications when 1891 delivered a cascade of family crises that dwarfed everything else. On March 16 Mary and Harry's second child, Thomas Augustus McKim, just four months old, died of a severe lung infection which did not respond to Dr. William King's remedies. The family buried Tommy near Mary's infant sister Florence in the Odd Fellows section of the Chico Cemetery. No sooner had they buried Mary's baby than she herself slipped into a rapid decline. Her tubercular body had endured two pregnancies, the illness and death of one baby and the normal demands of little Harry, a healthy toddler. In addition, she tended to her energetic and hard-working husband, while providing a home in town for her parents and teenaged brother who were all in low spirits over a dreary winter.

As Mary declined, the family relied on C. A. Oliver, a homeopathic physician. His approach rested on the belief that bodies are self-healing, but can find some relief from minerals and plants. That and her mother's prayers did not save Mary Euphrasia Chapman McKim, who died at mid-day on May 12, 1891, a month before her twenty-sixth birthday and two months after her baby Tommy died. Friends made futile attempts to comfort her distraught family. At Mary's service in her home, Maude Blood played Sarah Chapman's piano for friends who sang her favorite hymns. Spring blossoms from local gardens blanketed her coffin, covered every surface in her home and spilled onto the porch. Afterward, a long line of mourners' carriages moved slowly along Olive Street (formerly Old Chico Way). They crossed the bridge over Big Chico Creek and entered the graveyard to witness Mary's burial with baby Tommy. Even the *Enterprise* obituary writer's offering was more personal than usual. He captured Mary's resemblance to Sarah in her quiet sweetness and desire to serve. He tried to find meaning in her early death; his remarks reflected the then common view that tuberculosis ennobled and spiritually uplifted its victims.

> Throughout a long sickness and great suffering there came no murmur. Conscious for a long time that the end was near she waited with cheerful resignation, trusting with a fervent Christian faith and hope in an all-wise Providence. Possessed of a retiring and sympathetic nature, home life possessed her greatest pleasure.
>
> Surrounded with her family and kindred and friends and ministering to their comfort and pleasure was greater to her than mere public life. When the needs of charity were known to her it gave her pleasure to alleviate suffering and want in an unassuming and quiet way so far as she could minister to those who needed help.[4]

Even though her parents had known for years that Mary's early death was inevitable, not even the arrival of Fred and Magnolia's second child, Earl Winthrop Chapman, the day after she died could lessen the void that opened with her loss. Nevertheless, Mary's father had no opportunity to grieve; he had to immediately return to Powellton. He faced another lumber season with his grieving wife and young sons dependent on whatever he could eke out of the remains of his mill.

Will Goes Next

In the spring of 1891, Will, almost 16, had been immersed for months in his and his parents' grief over their loss of Mary. With summer approaching, he looked forward to his brother's company during trips with their mother to the mill. Gus Jr. was slated for work at the mill, where his father counted on his help. Will showed a glimmer of his father and Fred's gift for sales. After school, he worked for Lee Pharmacy which had moved from its quarters in the Bank of Butte County to the first floor of the Odd Fellows building on the northwest corner of Third and Broadway. Will's job provided spending money and his presence was a comfort to Sarah who divided her time between the hotel and helping Mary with Dustin.

The pharmacy's small high windows lent an aura of refinement to the store where Will worked. While clerks arranged artful displays of finer goods in deeply carved cases behind molded and paneled counters, he unpacked stock, tagged it and stacked the piles of boxes on shelves. He refilled the horse trough or swept the boardwalk and the store. Wesley Lee also had him monitor the entry to the store's Third Street "porte cochère" where he "ran" purchases out to the ladies waiting in their buggies.

Lee's Pharmacy was a cut above most downtown stores. Its patterned carpet, framed advertisements and a fancy gas chandelier supplemented the dim light. The best part of Will's job was making deliveries to customers' homes all around town where he rarely encountered a stranger. While photographs of Will do not suggest he was robust, his smile was right for retail. Will required two more years of tuition at the Chico Academy, where his parents were anxious for him to graduate before the Woodmans retired.[5] The Chapmans had been paying tuitions to the Woodmans for over twenty years.

That summer Gus Jr. had to leave his mother and brother in Chico while he stayed in Powellton because his skills with mill machinery and general familiarity with lumber production were invaluable to his father. The small mill was not only Gussie's personal laboratory of challenging mechanical puzzles, it was the only business that remained in the family. Both he and Will had long overheard their father anguish over Fred's lack of interest in the mill. By now, Gussie Jr. must have recognized his father's intensity as born from a kind of panic.

After Mary's funeral service, Will realized he had to stay in town for his job and to comfort their mother. Sarah missed her greatest comfort, grandson Dustin, 2, whose father took him to visit the McKim family in Oakland.

Everything changed again in 1891 when Will suddenly contracted a high fever. This time Gus Sr. and Sarah, disappointed in Dr. Oliver, turned to Dr. Amos J. Landis, who informed them he was unsure whether to treat Will for malaria or typhoid. Both diseases were familiar hazards in Chico, though the latter was more associated with children. Because a majority of voters considered a sewer system unworthy of their taxes, contaminated water continued killing residents. Will's condition rapidly worsened, issuing in his death on July 8, two months after the Chapmans buried Mary. Will had been a "bright, active boy" whose promise had sustained his vulnerable parents' enduring hopes.[6] His unexpected death devastated them; it was the loss of yet another innocent and one impossible for the shattered family to absorb, let alone accept.

"[T]hese thrice affected parents" had limited Mary's funeral to family and friends; now they reduced attendance at Will's service to an intimate circle.[7] Nevertheless, as still another Chapman funeral procession in five months again made its way along Olive Street to the cemetery, townspeople who glimpsed it must have shuddered at the sight of the white hearse slowly leading the small train of buggies. Multiple deaths of children were nothing new in Chico and elsewhere, but that made the Chapmans' losses no less difficult to contemplate. Young Will had struck a chord with many because his family was well-known and he was often seen at the drugstore. The financial failure of Will's father attracted sympathy in some circles, but also quiet scorn or pity and ongoing speculation about the reasons behind it. Nonetheless, the sorrow townspeople showed for the Chapmans was genuine when it came to their losses of infant Tommy, Mary and young Will.

At the grave site, friends of Sarah and Gus could not miss that Mary still had no gravestone. Of course, she had died only two months previous. Later visitors would still note the absence of headstones for her and Will. Even in the early twenty-first century, the only stone on the Chapman family plots was the small 1863 stone Gus and Sarah provided their baby Florence, and even that stone had disappeared. Gus Chapman wanted only the best and it was in character for him to believe that he would restore his fortune and then buy his family the handsome headstones of the perfect granite he had envisioned for himself in his 1883 will.[8]

Scrambling to Keep Up

With grandson Dustin away and Gus Sr. and Gus Jr. in Powellton, Sarah organized the house contents she and Gus had hurriedly stored in their large shed.[9] In Oakland with little Dustin, Harry McKim met and courted Celestine Beretta who, like Mary when he met her, was the daughter of a well-off merchant. Following the couple's large wedding in April 1892 in Oakland, Harry brought her and Dustin to his Chico house, where they had planned to live. However, Celestine missed her family so they soon returned to Oakland where the senior Berettas financed a printing plant for Harry. Dustin McKim's contact with his mother's family diminished with time and distance and his father's new responsibilities in the city.[10] With Gus Sr. at work in the mountains, Sarah managed the move from the McKim house to the hotel, which she still managed.

In Powellton Chapman & Co. had everything riding on a two-year lumber contract that was half-completed. That summer Gus Jr. learned his parents could no longer afford to keep him in college. The financial problem was critical, but Gus Sr. also needed his remaining available son for mechanical duties and to represent him at the mill so he could make sales calls. Then a new catastrophe emerged. The expansion that increased San Francisco's housing stock four times between 1880 and 1890 was followed by a national depression that crushed the economy. The result was hardly enough sales to carry Chapman's company. During the 1890s, San Francisco workers' wages plunged by as much as 50 percent and houses found no buyers. Public funds started to feed and shelter the poor who had been the working people Chapman counted on as customers.[11] To forestall unrest, San Francisco doled out landscaping jobs in Golden Gate Park. Other workers paved streets with "Folsom potatoes"—granite cobblestones prisoners fashioned from the state quarry Gus Chapman's Prison Commission had turned into a business.[12]

Chapman dropped the manufacture of doors and windows, which he and William McKay had been proud to introduce to their production. Instead, he reduced his mill to cutting "bolts," crude wood pieces miners used to shore up tunnel walls. While renewed interest in mining throughout the West created a market for bolts, the bulk sales did little to restore the Chapmans' income.

With Gus and Sarah now focused on him alone, young Gus changed. His life after 1891 bore no resemblance to the privileged one he had expected as a confident, even cocky boy. His uninterrupted life in Powellton during the years he lived in the cottage with his father created a bond. In light of the deaths of his siblings and Fred's rare visits, Gus became, in effect, his parents' only child.

Settling

Gus's political ambitions flared up one last time. After William McKay was elected to the Board of Supervisors in 1894, Chapman declared his candidacy for the next supervisor slot, but the voters rejected him.

Also that year, Gus Chapman nearly lost his share in the Chico Steam Laundry.[13] His Bank of Chico loan from A. H. Crew had funded this plain building across Chapman Street from his former home to house the new business. Its employment of poor white women was the basis for its claim that it was "morally" superior to the lingering Chinese laundries.

Mischief at the laundry was afoot. Acting on a tip, Constables W. W. Waite and Charles Woods were secretly surveilling its manager Percy Ryan. On a Saturday evening in late September they observed their quarry climb a ladder to the laundry's roof where he eased himself in through a skylight. The officers approached the building and watched from a window as Ryan reached in a cupboard for a can of coal oil which he opened and poured on the floor as he walked around the building. He then scattered wood shavings on the puddles and left the remainder in a pile onto which he set a lighted candle. Finally, Ryan locked the door on leaving and sauntered down Chapman Street to the Oroville-Shasta Road. While one officer entered and extinguished the candle, the other took off after the startled Ryan.

Once in custody, he offered the officers money if they would look the other way. Chapman's building, on which he still owed $800, survived. Ryan explained to the authorities that before he could launch his own laundry he had to destroy Chico Steam's machinery. If only for the moment, the flurry of press attention on the attempted arson revived Chapman's treasured public identity as an engaged businessman.[14] The constable informed Chapman that Ryan, "representing" the Chico Steam Laundry, had invalidated Chapman's fire insurance policy in advance of his planned crime and the insurer had not alerted the police or Gus.

The years 1895 and 1896 were the first in which Gus's taxes were delinquent, as were his payments to the Bank of Chico. To keep faith with the trust of its president and his friend Alexander Crew, he sold all his parcels (except the storage shed lot) along Little Chico Creek for $1,000. The Chapmans also lost the Chico Hotel. There were no more loans and no more prospects.

Gus and Sarah rented a room for the winter months in the West Fifth Street home of Eliza and Henry Camper, whose children were grown. Sarah's days there were taken up with church work and helping Eliza clean and cook. When in Chico, Gus caught up with newspapers in the downtown free library he and Sarah had long supported. If they tried to make sense of their changed lives, they had plenty of time for reflection.

The cottage at Powellton was now their official residence, although, in practical terms, only from spring through the fall. Sarah welcomed having a place of their own. Then, too, its location on the upper Magalia Ridge was so lovely and cool during summers that the village had turned into a popular resort for valley residents in search of relief from the valley's sweltering summers.[15] In addition, Sarah's cooking, housekeeping and companionship with Gus Sr. and Gus Jr. restored her sense of purpose.

On a minor note, she now lived near Mary Ann McKay, who had long presided over Powellton's female residents. Although as Chapmantown neighbors the two women had maintained a cordial, though distant, relationship, their husbands' quarrels had established a permanent sense of distance. However, Powellton was not too far up the road from another Ridge town,

Paradise, where Sarah visited Chico friends who summered there.[16]

In late fall 1898 Gus sold his interest in the Chico Steam Laundry to F. L. Martinette, a miner-turned-real-estate speculator who had invented an almond huller and the hand-pumped Hydro-Carbon Gas Machine that distributed gas for lighting in the homes of Henry Camper and others. Martinette paid Chapman in gold coin and by letters of patent on Idaho and Arizona mining rights.[17] Because Gus Chapman, now 71, did not plan to take up mining, he put aside the patents to provide an inheritance for Fred and Gus.

Similar to Gus Chapman's failure in the 1890s, prominent rancher James Keefer neared bankruptcy. In Chico, John Bidwell and his wife worried about the possible loss of their home and lands to creditors. They contemplated what it would be like to move from their mansion to live in a cottage, but they stayed afloat due to a $400,000 loan, a staggering sum at the time (over $13 million today).[18] Unlike the Bidwells, of course, the Chapmans had forfeited all their assets over ten years or so. When Gus sold stray remnants of his already shrunken timber stand to satisfy his final loan balance, his remaining lots in Chico and his Powellton mill had little value.[19]

The Chapmans' financial plight was widely shared in the depression of the 1890s. Only Kansas surpassed California in the number of failed banks.[20] The state's population growth dropped to a new low and Chico's population declined.

In August 1898 Chapman informed the *Record* about William McKay's uninsured fire loss at the Somerset mill. In order to make a debt payment, Gus had sold his small remaining share in that mill to his former partner.[21] By this time the McKays were also struggling, although apparently in better shape than the Chapmans. In November Sarah and Gus left their Powellton cabin and "came down from the mountains" for their now usual winter months with the Campers. Gus and Henry maintained cordial relations, but they were not friends. Camper still went to work at his carriage business, which helped weather the economic pendulum that regularly buffeted his lodger. In the depression few clients ordered new buggies but he kept busy repairing old ones.

Gus's status quietly shifted to retired. After completing his daily library visits, he reminisced with acquaintances as he crossed back and forth between downtown and the Campers' place. On occasion, when he exchanged greetings with his former store clerk Charlie Stilson, he probably had a hard time remembering that Charlie was now using his middle name Lewis. In the 1880s Stilson had left retail trade for good after he won election as clerk of Butte County, a position he held for several terms. While at work in Oroville, he apprenticed himself to become a lawyer. In 1894, at the age of 52, he opened a private legal office under his middle name. Over the course of twenty years in practice, Lewis Stilson would earn the sobriquet "Dean of the Butte County Bar."

While Stilson and his wife always remained on good terms with Sarah, Lewis's cool relations with Gus had lingered since the 1860s when he regarded his boss with a mixture of respect, envy and resentment. This may explain why Stilson's lengthy and finely detailed biographical essay in George Mansfield's 1918 *History of Butte County* skipped over the years during which Augustus Chapman supervised him at Bidwell & Co. and employed him at Wood & Chapman.[22] While this may seem curious and even unworthy, it fitted the cold calculation of that time. Economic failure was not just considered unfortunate, it was a mark of personal unworthiness, sentenced by disgrace. Some of Chapman's old acquaintances could no longer "afford" to be linked to him.

However, Gus's relationship with Constable Charles Woods was an exception. The friendship evolved from his gratitude for Woods, who had nabbed Percy Ryan and saved Chapman's laundry company from arson. Woods continued to treat the old man with kindness and respect.

Closure

In mid-January 1899 a new round of his chronic malaria attacks struck Chapman, now 72. Such onsets had usually taken place during the summer. Word-of-mouth spread news of his worsening condition; then, the weekly newspapers recorded his deathwatch at the Camper home. This attention to Chapman's ordeal suggests that his advanced age, the deaths of his children and his impending death had softened townspeople's judgment. Hard-pressed themselves in the depression, they recognized, in his many kinds of losses, aspects of their own disappointments and ongoing vulnerability. On his deathbed, Gus Chapman became a sympathetic, and somewhat pathetic, figure. Alerted by his mother's telegram, Fred arrived from his new residence in Stockton to be with Sarah and Gus Jr. at Augustus Chapman's bedside when he died on January 30, 1899.

While funeral services with the casket in the parlor were customary, since the Chapmans no longer had a home in town, his funeral took place at the North Methodist Church. The pallbearers Sarah chose included bank president A. H. Crew, who had provided Gus so many opportunities to make a new start. Nor did Sarah forget the loyalty of Bank of Butte County officer John R. Robinson who had signed her husband's will and supported him against Frank Lusk. She included Chapman's newer friend Constable Woods and jeweler Julius Behme, who organized the Odd Fellows procession that brought Gus's casket from the Campers' parlor to the church. (Sarah's diary that year suggests she sold back pieces of her jewelry to Behme to raise cash.) She also called on Lewis Stilson, who would soon also serve as a pallbearer for Chapman's former partner William McKay. Longtime neighbor Henry Camper provided other assistance in the ceremony.

According to the *Record*, "An extraordinarily large number of people, especially of the old residents of the town" gathered to remember the pioneer A. H. Chapman. Mrs. Bidwell was present, having returned to town from the countryside where she had brought lunch to share with her husband and his Indian workers who were clearing brush. That Bidwell, who attended others' services, did not attend Chapman's would have surprised no one, but Annie Bidwell made sure to be there. However, John Bidwell took special note of it in his diary, writing in capital letters: "FUNERAL OF A. H. CHAPMAN." He occasionally used such emphases to highlight significant events or individuals without revealing what they meant to him.

In Chapman's case the emphasis may represent John Bidwell's long memory of a man who had crossed him or, as he probably thought of it, had been disloyal. He never forgot that his employee Gus Chapman had accepted George Wood's offer and partnered with him in a new mercantile store that drove John Bidwell & Co. out of business. How could Bidwell forget his embarrassment when his effort to destroy Chapman's questionable but popular capture of the Oakdale School site failed? Was Bidwell still uncomfortable about his poor showing, compared to Chapman's, in the nomination for a seat in the 1879 constitutional convention? Bidwell afterward raged about it to George Crosette, despite the fact that he himself had emphasized to his nominators that he did not want them to put his name forward. Although Chapman and Bidwell had built a civil relationship as they worked together on community or business investments and countless civic projects throughout the decades, there is no evidence they ever shared so much as a meal.

Perhaps Bidwell felt he had achieved justice. In concert with Chapman's "sworn" enemy Frank Lusk, Bidwell had humiliated Chapman by cultivating a publicized friendship with Democrat George Stoneman at the same time the governor was engaged in slandering Gus Chapman.

Friends brought smilax, violets and camellias from their gardens to brighten the North Methodist Church and to cover Gus's casket on that bleak mid-winter day. A quartet included the senior Campers' nephew Henry. He had sung for Mary's and Will's funerals and now he sang for the Camper children's "Uncle Gus." Rev. James M. Woodman eulogized Chapman as his friend since the 1860s when Gus could hear Woodman, an even newer arrival, proselytizing along Broadway near the entry to John Bidwell & Co. One Chapman child or another had been a student at the Woodmans' academy from 1870 until Will's death in 1891. According to the *Record*, "Especially did [Woodman] emphasize the fact that [Chapman] was a man of mild manner, strong intellectuality, honest purpose, and thoroughly worthy of the many important honors he enjoyed."[23]

Methodist minister Seneca Jones stepped forward to recall Augustus Chapman's early years as a poor farm boy in frontier Michigan, his struggle to earn his way through college and become a lawyer. Jones reminded mourners of the "prominence [Chapman] attained in science, economy, and statecraft" during his Chico years. These tributes recalled to listeners Chapman's efforts to establish two public schools, the Odd Fellows building, Honey Run Road, his retail, lumber and real estate enterprises and his accomplishments on California's State Prison Commission.

With respect to the latter, the minister reminded those present of Chapman's report on the eastern prisons and his leadership in the creation of the prison jute mills which had become so important to farmers that grain-sack production was running twenty-four hours a day. As a proud man, Gus Chapman would have savored the luster which the remarks of Woodman and Jones briefly restored to listeners' memory of him. After two decades of losses and hardships, Sarah and her sons must have found such sentiments a momentary salve.

Reverend Jones concluded by noting that Chapman had joined others of Chico's pioneer generation in "going Home." Among those still alive, the minister mentioned Sarah Chapman, John Bidwell and teacher Olive Sproul. The *Record*'s reporter concluded, "The community has lost one of its most substantial enterprising citizens, a man of influence with men in highest places, as well as with those in the ordinary walks of life—a fine old gentleman."

In the Odd Fellows section of the Chico Cemetery Augustus Chapman was interred next to three of his children, Florence, Mary and Will, and Mary's infant Tommy.

There Is No End to It

In early February, Annie Bidwell paid Sarah a condolence visit at Eliza Camper's home. The widow's dire situation was a caution to Chico women. If previous depressions had not impressed on them how vulnerable their own fates were to husbands who failed or died before them, the 1890s depression and the Chapmans' slide over the past twenty years acutely reminded them all—even Mrs. Bidwell.[24]

Two months later the *Record* devoted a full, front-page column to the terms of Gus's 1883 will.[25] The editor who authorized this itemization of Chapman's bequests was, in retrospect, either naïve about the decedent's financial condition when he died or gratuitously cruel—most likely the former. Always hopeful his luck would change, Gus had never altered his 1883 instructions to make Sarah his executor, including guidance for her in dividing and administering his then substantial assets. By 1899, those had dwindled to a few odd land parcels at remote sites of no value, old mining equipment and milling machinery deemed "of nominal value."[26] The proceeds could not support his frugal widow for even a year. The newspaper account must have embarrassed Sarah and Gus Jr. When Fred returned to Chico again two months later, he commiserated with his mother and brother, but rallied sufficiently to head downtown to the Woodmen of the World's "smoker," where he shone as one of the best yarn spinners.

Born poor, Gus Chapman died even poorer than his hardpressed widowed mother, whose circumstances he drove himself from childhood to surmount. In the intervening years, he had always worked, first, to educate himself; then, to gain wealth; then, to obtain a public position; and, finally, to survive. Although his failures became public, only his creditors were aware of one point central to his honor: he had paid off every debt in full. He died owing no man.

On the other hand, he had hardly known his children. He spent years away from them and Sarah as he worked downtown, went on buying or selling trips and handled prison business. Like most Americans, he must have reckoned such sacrifices would spare his children the hardships he had suffered and prepare them to excel. Yet all that he had attempted had not enabled him to save Mary and Willie, keep Fred close or complete Gussie's education. Nor had he spared Sarah the indignities of a long and impoverished old age. Gus Chapman worked hard, met his goals, pursued new ones and finally crashed, pulling down with him the only people he loved or who loved him.

While his life, by necessity, centered around the mill, with his father's encouragement Gus Jr. took up mining. Unable to finish his education, he explored the larger world through reading. For the rest of his life he subscribed to the *National Geographic*, which he shelved with his parents' most precious books. He also acquired a Chico cottage he shared with his mother. Gus became a man of many mechanical talents he used to satisfy his interest, stay employed and represent his honorable family.

23

The Twentieth-Century Chapmans

In the blistering, hot summers of the early 1930s, one of Vern Pullins's errands for his mother included trips to the Polar Ice Co. where "Chappie" put down his tools, wiped the grease from his hands and called out, "What do you want?" He already knew, of course. Sweaty children could count on Augustus Chapman Jr., the balding little mechanic in his 70s, to slip them ice chips to crunch while they pedaled around town.[1] The ice company was on Park Avenue (formerly Oroville-Shasta Road), within distant sight of the remodeled farm house on Bidwell Avenue where Chappie was born. The ice company also overlooked houses on open land that had been his family's park surrounding the big house where he grew up. Everything had changed: his father went broke, his sisters and brother died, they lost their house and he had to leave college. He would always remember what happened in that house, but progressively fewer people around him did.

Gus Jr. was his family's sole survivor in Chico. With the arrival of summer in 1899 after Gus Sr. died, he and brother Fred had set off for Idaho where they mined under the mineral patents their father had acquired in his last business deal a month before he died. Fred's wife Magnolia invited Sarah to stay with her and their two sons in Stockton while he and Gus were away. Sarah declined in favor of the comfort she found in the companionship of her many good friends at home. Now grown old, they braided their rag rugs together or strolled uptown to Hart's for cream sodas on warm evenings. Sarah still lived with Eliza and Henry Camper, but she sometimes stayed overnight at another friend's house when they wanted to keep chatting.

While her "boys" chased their fortunes, Sarah took her familiar position at the cash box for a church fundraiser on the Plaza downtown. Hard as she tried, from her station she could hardly hear anything the preacher shouted. She also attended family funerals every month or so to support her friends in their turns at grief. When she couldn't bring herself to attend services for children, they understood. Sometimes Henry Camper sent a horse and fine buggy from his carriage shop to deliver his Eliza and Sarah to their destinations freshly groomed, without mud on their hems. On days when the weather was mild, Sarah walked south toward Oakdale School and then turned toward the big shed where her former home's contents were stored.

Now in her mid-60s, Sarah was in good health except when her rheumatism flared or a headache pounded. She medicated herself with rest, hot tea and "tomato toast," but her natural inclination was just to keep moving. She still found it disconcerting that her former full and engaged life was now reduced to providing good company and making herself useful in various friends' households.[2] Most days she pitched in and made them a chicken pot pie or a stew. She also tried not to intrude. She spent time picking blackberries for her shortcake, canned their peaches and swept out their "cook rooms." On quiet days at the Campers' place or when rains came she pasted clippings from the *Enterprise* into her scrapbook. Sometimes she just leafed through its pages. But no matter how she felt, she wrote in her diary.

Even though Sarah mended her own clothes, she still counted on her dressmaker for small fixes to her slender wardrobe of widow's black garments. While she alternated between the Chico Steam Laundry and Chinese to launder her outerwear, she continued to wash her undergarments. Lace making was her latest attempt at the crafts her friends favored. However, like other handiwork she had attempted over the years, needlework did not really interest her. Her own best handwork was at a piano. Her other escape was the morality tales and popular religious works she devoured. *Idle Thoughts of an Idle Fellow*, *The Simpletons*, *Dreams of Heaven*, and *The Siberian Exiles* were on her bed table in the summer of 1899.

Once that season's intense heat made life in the valley unbearable, Sarah accepted the Chandler family's invitation to stay with them in Paradise. Although she could have gone to her own cottage in Powellton, she needed the income from her renter. In addition, she and young Gus would have been surrounded there by memories of his father, Mary and Willie. While son Fred had disliked the village for its isolation, Powellton had become a rural summer "resort" where visitors flocked to the hotel or rented cabins and socialized around evening campfires or at candy pulls. Stagecoaches, wagons, surreys and buggies, mostly from Oroville, competed for parking spaces.[3]

On one occasion, after Mrs. Chandler became "wrathy" because her buggy's shaft was damaged while daughter Bessie was at the reins, Sarah mediated between them. The upshot was that she and Bessie drove the damaged buggy down Honey Run Road to Chico where Sarah prevailed on Henry Camper to repair it while Bessie browsed downtown and Sarah ran her own errands. Feeling good about their full day, the two returned to the Chandler home by evening. On other days Sarah drove Bessie to school and made her a birthday cake. Sometimes she and Mrs. Chandler relaxed on the porch and sang old favorites. Alonzo and Olive Curtis, who had married in the Chapmans' remodeled farmhouse in Chapmantown, made stops to trade news and left baskets of bounty from their garden.

All that remained of Sarah's life that mattered was her absent sons who rarely wrote from Idaho, although she never complained in her diary. Sarah welcomed diversions. She tried a Sorosis meeting at Isabelle Tilden Crosette's cottage. New to the area, this female-only group was founded in 1868 after the founder was excluded from an all-male dinner for Charles Dickens. The day's topic interested Sarah: "What are your best reasons in favor of women's clubs?" At a Christian Endeavor meeting, her anxiety at facing life without a purpose appears in her question for the group, "How are we to learn where Christ wants us to work?" Her family had filled that purpose; now she was lost.

From time to time during her extended stay with the Chandlers, she caught Messer's 6 a.m. stage which delivered her to Chico by mid-morning. At her Chapman Street storehouse she worked around her easy chairs, cabinets and tables still stacked in odd clusters. She decided what to sell or gift and what she and Gus Jr. might use when he came back to Chico. If her boys' mining patents proved good, Gus might buy her a little house so she wouldn't have to live in her friend Eliza's spare bedroom.

There were items with which she could not part. She stood there, surrounded by reminders of child rearing, socials, the beauty she created in their home and on its grounds. Did she also think about her lonely years there, exhausted by the children, anxious about Gus's safety when he was on his trips or financial undertakings? How could such a driven, capable, accomplished man, who invested every ounce of himself in work and earned a small fortune, have lost *every* penny they had? Even though it seemed each of Gus's ventures came wrapped in a crisis, his optimism had proved itself time and again. Then, in the 1880s he became convinced he could pass his mill responsibilities to Fred—Fred!—and pursue politics. Did she cringe when she remembered having to pull Mary out of Mount Holyoke and ten years later, young Gus out of the University of the Pacific?

Memories abounded when she gave Gus's Masonic lodge regalia and photos to the club's officers. She sent her boys' little printing press to Dustin, Mary's child. She kept for Gus Jr. the personal volumes that included her father-in-law's 1802 dictionary that she and Gus had brought across the plains. Into her "save" box went the book of household hints Gus gave her at their wedding. She also held back both leather-bound volumes of William Cullen Bryant's *Picturesque America* with "A.H. Chapman" embossed on its cover. Gus Jr. would keep this family library for the rest of his life.

As her financial situation tightened, Sarah forced herself to think of her furniture, china and silver in terms of their cash value. Sarah's situation aroused empathy and also interest in her fine things. They were good buys because she bought carefully and Gus insisted on quality. Rose Oser, the young wife of a downtown merchant, to whom widower Robert Boydston had recently sold the Chapmans' former mansion, moved some of Sarah's bookcases, easy chairs and dishes back across the street. Others left with her flatirons, paintings and most of the family's books.[4]

She took breaks from the storehouse for visits with neighbors who noticed the shed's open door and brought her refreshments. She accepted Mary Nelson's invitation to stop for lunch at the farm house Gus had Henry Cleaveland remodel for her and the children in 1871. Then, after taking care of some errands downtown for Mrs. Chandler, she caught the 4 p.m. stage to Paradise where Bess met her with the buggy. She brought her hostess "clothes bars" (hangers) and other gifts from her stash.

Memories lingered at every turn as her bumpy drives up and down Honey Run Road reminded Sarah of the long, dreary journeys Gus and Fred complained about. She must have also recalled that cold, rainy winter when Gus pushed to complete this new route's construction. The necessity to later ease the grade became an embarrassment after all his proclamations about the safety of the steeper route. Even though the grade was lessened, Sarah still had to look away from the road's edge. As Messer's stage bounced along the dusty road, it swayed in the tight turns and the petite passenger's attention alternated between her own thoughts and other passengers' anecdotes. At houses and camps along Butte Creek they pried themselves from the coach to stretch and walk while the driver rested his horses, collected mail, left messages and passed on "the latest" news. In another decade, what people still called the "stage" would not be a coach, but a big, crowded sedan convertible.

Her "Boys"

At summer's end Fred, 40, and Gus Jr., 26, gave up on the unsuccessful Idaho mining patents. Rediscovering how much he disliked mountain work, Fred returned to sales jobs in Stockton. Decades later, the report of his death emphasized his work in his father's lumber company and made only passing mention of other work.

Despite disappointments, the months away had a positive result for young Gus, who, while in Idaho, met and fell in love with Amelia "Amy" Powers, who happened to be tiny like Sarah. He returned to California without her, however, and went to work near Lovelock, a Butte County mountain village where he tended the lumber mill machinery of Charles Hintz. In the early 1900s he and Amy married. About eighty years later the mill owner's daughter, Vera Hintz Ekwall, would recall overhearing her parents' remark that Amy was twelve years older than Gus.[5] Mrs. Ekwall's only other Chapman memory was that of a tippling Gus falling into a sawdust pile during a

July 4 celebration at her father's Stirling City mill.

Gus Jr.'s work for Hintz, Sierra Flume & Lumber, Diamond Match and other out-of-town firms enabled him to house his wife and mother in an attractive Chico cottage on Salem Street, tucked between West Ninth Street and Little Chico Creek, where he enjoyed the beauty he had known as a child. His skills with steam-driven equipment provided adequate support for the three of them. He also had to deal with an event that embarrassed both women. A Chico constable placed him and two miners in custody because he suspected they had left dynamite sticks in a warehouse window. He came across the three men near the large established transient camp where now Highway 32 crosses Big Chico Creek. Employers headed there to hire hourly workers. Because no evidence connected the three to the dynamite, which was so dusty it appeared to have been in place for some time, Gus and his friends were freed the next day.[6] The officers removed the sticks to their Main Street office where they admonished one another to step softly and considered letting the dynamite sticks drift away in Big Chico Creek.

While Gus's house was close to Sarah's church, age impinged on her ability to volunteer on a regular basis. Although death was regularly taking her friends and co-workers, she remained a loyal member of the congregation forty years after the Civil War, when the two white Methodist branches—North and South—reunited, forming the First Methodist Church. In her reduced role, Sarah became a memorable, if somewhat mysterious, figure to the younger congregations. In the early 1980s a very elderly church woman could only recall Sarah around 1910 as "a dignified old lady" of the church.[7]

The Big House Burns

The church woman may have been aware of Mrs. Chapman because a tragic event had drawn attention to her in 1909. By then, the Chapmans' former grand home on Chapman Street (now Eleventh Street), like the former home of banker Norman Rideout in Marysville, had been converted into a hospital.[8] Until the Sisters of Charity Hospital was opened, originally at another location *within* the town limits, residents had never known anyone who stayed in a hospital.

That January at about 4 a.m., night nurse Alice Warden glanced outside and glimpsed sparks in Sarah's former free-standing summer kitchen at the eastern end of the main house. Wind then ignited flames in the kitchen's wood shingles. Despite a heavy downpour, sparks started on siding along the main house's kitchen and from there reached the house's second-story. Although a hospital employee managed to find a garden hose in the dark, its stream of water fell short of the flames consuming the eaves.

Meanwhile, in response to a call for help, the town telephone operator set off both fire alarm boxes downtown. These had replaced the ring of the water company's bell to which volunteers used to respond.

Hearing the alarm, a fireman mounted his engine and headed toward the Sisters of Charity Hospital's previous location within the city's boundaries. When he reached Broadway, however, the sight of high reaching flames to the south reminded him the hospital had moved outside of town—and, hence, the Chico's fire service jurisdiction. He returned his engine to the station. Another midtown company's volunteers also rallied, but they too quickly figured out that the flames came from the hospital across the Little Chico Creek city boundary. They put away their gear.

In contrast, the Junction fire volunteers ran to their station, pulled out their hose cart and headed for the bridge over Little Chico Creek. However, by the time they were within "200 paces" of the hospital, they were quarreling over whether the hospital, outside the city limits, would pay them for their service. A majority were skeptics and refused to continue. As others in the company pressed them to proceed, onlookers joined in with an offer of one hundred dollars, an arrangement that had sometimes motivated firemen to extinguish fires adjacent to Chico.[9]

In the end, while most of the company headed back to their station, the rest determined to do what they could even though the fire was already at an advanced stage. Taking charge, they joined Chapman Street neighbors who had been passing water-filled fire pails every house was required to keep filled and use only for fires. The firemen organized the bucket brigades. While this, of course, proved inadequate, it was their only option without the new fire equipment the town volunteers denied them.

Meanwhile some neighbors had removed the medical instruments from the upstairs surgery and others had carried patients and mattresses to their homes to await other arrangements.

The fire turned the sky orange; its roar filled the neighborhood. Mary Nelson's grandson Warren, 7, whose parents left their house to fill and pass water buckets, ordered him to stay inside. Almost seventy years later Warren remembered the roar of the fire more than the sight of the flames. When the firemen could do no more, they returned to the Junction where their colleagues were waiting to chastise them for providing town services to a county neighborhood.[10]

The newspaper's fire coverage was extensive, but its content confused histories of the earlier Chapman farm house and the one that burned. For example, it attributed information about that 1859 remodeled house fronting Bidwell Avenue (now Twelfth Street) to the 1877 mansion fronting Chapman Street (now Eleventh Street) and stated that Gus Jr. had been born in the destroyed house/hospital. Perhaps, having moved from their Bidwell Avenue house at age four, he only remembered the Chapman Street house and, so, believed that he had been born there. With the fire even more evidence of Sarah's historical presence slipped away from her— her husband, three children, a grandchild, the old North Church they helped build and now the house they had cherished since Gus's vision of it was a mere pencil line scribbled on a surveyor's map.[11] All was gone.

In 1914, As WWI erupted in Europe, Sarah, 81, moved to Sacramento to live with Magnolia and Fred who had settled there in 1907. Fred claimed his mother's dependence on him as grounds for his exemption from the draft. But both his sons, Willis and Earl, were drafted and served.[12] However, despite good intentions all around, Sarah did not find a haven in Fred's home. She returned to Chico where she resumed life with Gus and Amy.

Still in search of a purpose for her life, Sarah was galvanized when she learned that her sister Lydia Sickley Lamb was overwhelmed by the care of her dying husband. In 1920 Sarah, 87, entrained for Michigan. As she later explained, "I was not well when I left Sacramento to come here, but thought the trip might help me and I would get better, and I could be of some use to my sister who is confined at home with an invalid husband...."[13]

Soon after Sarah arrived, however, she learned that she had cancer. An operation to remove a tumor from her side had to be stopped in mid-course. Nothing could be done. With this, Sarah also became an invalid in her elderly sister's charge.

From Augustus Chapman's death in 1899 until her own demise on March 23, 1923, at the age of eighty-nine, Sarah's only steady income had been ten dollars a month paid from the insurance plan her husband secured during his long membership in the Chico Order of Odd Fellows. When each check arrived, she sent a thank you note. At one point, bedridden, she was in such pain that her sister wrote the acknowledgment for her. Out of the ten dollars, her only indulgence was a subscription to the *Record*.

After Sarah Chapman died, a Michigan banker wrote the Chico Odd Fellows that her bank balance would fall "way short" of the costs her illness and burial entailed.[14] The Michigan Odd Fellows secretary reported to his Chico counterpart that Fred and Gus Jr. had not sent her any money during her time in Michigan. Although Earl Chapman, one of Fred's sons, worked in a nearby Michigan county while Sarah was staying with her sister, he was evidently without the means to assist his grandmother.[15]

Sarah Sickley Chapman is buried in an unmarked grave in Blissfield, Michigan, far from the then unmarked Chico Cemetery graves of her husband and children to whom she had devoted herself. Gus Jr. and Amy chose gravesites near Chico in the Durham Cemetery. Fred Chapman, who died in 1933, ten years after his mother, had several jobs that included a few years as a "well-known" insurance broker in Sacramento where he and Magnolia lived for thirty-four years.[16]

In a boyhood class photo, Gussie Chapman Jr. gazed into the camera lens as a confident little kid accustomed to the best. Instead, circumstance made him an "honest workman" who supported his wife and mother. After his main work as a machinist for Magalia Ridge lumber companies, he became a woodworker for the Chico Normal School campus and helped staff its popular mountain camp for summer students. As a local master of steam engines, he provided equipment repairs and maintenance for the Chico Steam Laundry, the Polar Ice Co. and elsewhere as needed. He died in 1949 at the age of seventy-eight. In the early

1950s, his widow Amy, having no children, could no longer live on her own. Like her mother-in-law before her, Amy Powers Chapman became the beneficiary of her husband's membership in the Odd Fellows.[17]

Unlike Sarah, Amy moved to the Rebecca Home, the fellowship's retirement home for its women's auxiliary. As she prepared to leave for Saratoga, in the foothills of the Santa Cruz Mountains, Amy Chapman telephoned Chico teacher Vera Hintz Ekwall and invited the young woman to stop by her home. Mrs. Ekwall was puzzled. She did not know Amy Chapman and her only memory of Gus Jr. was his name as a former employee at her father's mill. Out of respect and some curiosity for the elderly woman's outreach, she stopped in to see her. There, the now elderly Amy Chapman explained to Vera that she had called because her late husband Gus had admired her. Having had to leave college he, like his parents, venerated education and accomplishment.

Amy Chapman gave Vera Ekwall her husband's collection of *National Geographic* and other family books. Mrs. Ekwall later gave this author the housekeeping manual which Augustus Chapman had given Sarah when they married. Amy Chapman sold other family items to an antique dealer who donated them to the Centerville Museum east of Chico. An oil painting of the Chico Water Co. and other items were loaned sometime after the mid-1980s to local historian Mildred Forester in whose home they burned. The only diary of Sarah Chapman that survived was donated to CSU, Chico's Meriam Library's Special Collections.

The Chapmans' original farm house on Bidwell Avenue, remodeled as a "Downing cottage" when Chapmantown was new, still stands and is registered with the National Trust for Historic Places. Before the big Chapman house on Chapman Street—the real "mansion"—burned down, townspeople referred to the smaller one on Bidwell Avenue as the Little Chapman Mansion. While some consider it pretentious to use that name for the present house because it is clearly not a mansion, the name fits its history and its relative size. That is, it is a smaller but special house. Although contradictory in name, it infers its historic provenance and, to those who know, keeps "alive" a sense of the other, vanished place.

In Sum

Gus Chapman came on his hardest times at an early peak of social Darwinism and was in mid-life when sermons in Chico churches regularly preached the gospel of wealth. Therefore, when those ideas reached their early height, Chapman's failures nullified his successes and marked him as unworthy; a status associated in practice then with social death. In his case, this played out as old associates, in effect, blotted out his part in their lives. The most striking example was Charles Lewis Stilson, whose lengthy and detailed biographical essay never mentioned his start under Gus Chapman's supervision at Bidwell's store, and then his employment at Wood & Chapman. Similarly, John Kempf Jr.'s "Old Timer" series in the local 1930s newspapers ignored Chapman's place in local leadership. Kempf was Fred's schoolmate and in the 1880s was his fellow employee at Chapman's Gas & Water Works. Kempf may not have known his father's employees were key players in the most deadly anti-Chinese violence. He, Stilson and everyone else omitted that, in the anti-Chinese period, it was Gus Chapman who organized the vigilante response that reined in Kempf Sr.'s employees and others who were the perpetrators of murders and arsons.

By contrast, as the present account has set out, records contemporary to Chapman's life demonstrate not only his active influence on early town history, but also suggest the high regard townspeople held for him until the mid-1880s when the Prison Commission "coup" under Governor Stoneman, the Honey Run Road grading issue and news of his financial failures in the 1890s depression made a comeback impossible.

People like the Chapmans arrived in northern Butte County from across the nation. They impressed on California their visions of what a proper town should be. Decade after decade they shaped Chico's institutions, fostered its cultural life and wrestled with wrenching political and economic challenges. They informed their actions with a sense of moral purpose, even when they sometimes fell short of their own aspirations and standards. The Chapmans' experiences in Chico reveal how many dimensions of broader American life influenced townspeople in the Sacramento Valley's little farm towns during the founding decades of settlement.

The disappointments and losses in the lives of Augustus and Sarah Chapman ultimately overwhelmed any memory of their contributions and achievements. Nevertheless, it was the Chapmans, their adversaries, colleagues and neighbors who, together, helped realize John Bidwell's vision: the hamlet enmeshed in Rancho Chico's headquarters on the north bank of Big Chico Creek could be dismantled, restarted from scratch south of Big Chico Creek and, in time, become a real town.

Descendants of Augustus and Sarah Chapman

Since the late 1980s, when I wrote the first version of this book, I periodically searched for Chapman family descendants. I could find none in their line beyond dead-end mentions of Fred's sons in censuses. With the present book approaching publication, I decided to try again, this time using Ancestor.com. That and Google led me through a complex path to the lives of Fred's two sons, who, I discovered, had no descendants living today. However, eventually a path opened to the descendants of young Mary Chapman McKim's sole surviving child Dustin who left Chico as a toddler with his father after her death. The Chapmans live on through the families of Dustin's daughter Janet Goodhow and his son "Dusty."

—Michele Shover

Son Frederick Willis Chapman
and Wife Magnolia Wood Chapman

Willis Tyson Chapman (1890-1971)

Fred and Magnolia's eldest son was a Marine during WWI. While training, he became his unit's boxing coach before being sent to France where he received a battle promotion from sergeant to lieutenant. His great interest in flying led Willis to join the new United States Army Air Service where he made surveillance flights for military intelligence. Upon returning to the West Coast, Willis became a reporter for the *San Francisco Call* and other newspapers. He covered the death in San Francisco of President Harding, the Fatty Arbuckle murder trials, a Mob killing he witnessed and more. He left to join the public relations staff of San Francisco's Palace Hotel, but returned to journalism where he launched a long career as a sportswriter (and boxing expert) and then as an editor of the *San Mateo Times*. He and his wife Madeleine, an advertising company vice president, married in their forties and had no children. He died a year after her in 1971 at the age of 82. The *Times* remembered "Chappie" as a "well-known Bay Area newspaper man." (Both Gus Chapman Jr. in Chico and Willie Chapman in San Mateo were called "Chappie.")

Earl Winthrop Chapman (1891-1956)

Fred and Magnolia's second son received his public education in Sacramento where he passed civil examinations that qualified him for positions as chief clerk in state government departments. Upon his enlistment in the Army for service in WWI, he became a sergeant and ordinance specialist. After being sent for officer's training, he advanced to second lieutenant and served in staff positions at several bases. After the war he worked in a YMCA position in Michigan and married Ruby Sharp, who died in 1919. At the age of 24 he went to Southern California where he married Mary Cole in Pasadena. On returning to Sacramento he became an accountant for state government agencies. Earl and Mary had one son, Norman.

Norman Cole Chapman (1921 – c. 1985)

Norman had completed three years of college in Southern California when he was drafted as an Army private during WWII. In Europe he stepped on a landmine and lost part of one foot. He received a discharge and returned home where he completed college and earned a doctorate, then worked in education. He and his wife Dorothy lived in the rural Calabasas area of Los Angeles, where Earl lived with them in his old age. Norman and Dorothy, who died before him, did not have children. He died at the age of 64.

Daughter Mary Euphrasia Chapman McKim and Husband Harry (Henry) Jefferson McKim

Harold Dustin McKim (1889-1967)

Originally called Dustin by the Chapmans (later "Harry" or "Mac"), he left Chico at age 3 with his father Harry Jefferson McKim after Mary's death in 1891. Within a year Harry married Celestine Berretta and moved to Oakland where her family set him up in a printing business. Now called Mac, he grew up with one stepbrother, Lisle, and had a difficult childhood because, according to his daughter Janet, Mac's father beat him regularly. To escape, he joined the Navy at age 15. According to Janet, Mac transferred into the Army. In WWI "he served as a gunner on pioneer plane sorties for which he earned three medals of honor. At 5' 7" and never above a hundred pounds, he next became a scrappy lumberjack admired as a tree topper. Eventually he settled down with his wife Vera Jones McKim in Tracy and became a salesman in Modesto, where his wife owned a dress shop. His daughter remembers him as a gentle person whose ready wit entertained family and friends at gatherings. Dustin became known for the terrific meals he cooked for those events. He and Vera had two children, "Dusty" and Janet.

William "Dusty" Dustin McKim

Dusty, whose long face resembled that of his great-grandmother Sarah Chapman, became a member of the California Highway Patrol. In 1973, while assigned to provide security for a highway truck stop, he drove in pursuit of a suspect and, for reasons unknown, his patrol car veered across the medium at full speed. It collided with a trailer truck and killed him. His wife Maizie Dunn McKim reared their two children, Scott, a C.P.A., and Mary Ellen, the family genealogist.

Janet McKim Hollis Goodhow (1928–)

Janet resides in her hometown of Tracy. She founded the firm Court Forms Plus, still a respected fixture in Modesto County law and finance. Starting out as a cashier while her young husband Bob Hollis served in WWII, she was hired by an attorney as a bookkeeper. Janet eventually set up her own business, which son Mark and his wife Debra Hall Hollis carry on in association with their son Brian. For longtime customers, Janet still prepares tax forms, which she enjoys working on because she considers them interesting puzzles.

Janet later married Tommie Goodhow, a boxing expert known throughout California's sporting world for his expert broadcasting of matches. (He was descended from the family of famed Civil War Confederate spy Rose O'Neil Greenhow.) Janet grew up knowing then-famed boxer Max Baer who was such a regular part of McKim family events that she thinks there may have been a family connection. (Author's note: The irony here is that Janet's cousin Willis Chapman's favorite anecdote was about his one boxing match with Max Baer. Willis gave it his all, but, despite his love of the sport, fell short.)

Janet's son Mark Hollis and his wife Debra Hall Hollis have a son and two daughters. Son Brian Hollis and his wife Tiffany Nicholson Hollis have three children, Evan, Ethan and Eli. Evan is an outstanding ball player and shows promise for the business world. His brothers are no less promising. Mark and Debra's daughter is Brianna Hollis of Tracy. Their second daughter Brandi and her husband Anthony Silva have two children, Brandon and Gregory.

Through Mary Chapman McKim's only surviving child Dustin the Chapman family lives on.

Note: Janet's biography was adapted from the rendering she provided the author. She was also helpful in the sections about her father and brother. The author also appreciates help from Dusty McKim's daughter Mary Ellen and Janet's daughter-in-law Debra Hollis.

Willis Tyson Chapman, son of Fred and Magnolia Chapman.

Earl Winthrop Chapman, son of Fred and Magnolia Chapman.

Harold Dustin McKim ("Harry" or "Mac"), son of Mary Chapman McKim and Harry Jefferson McKim.

Janet McKim Hollis Greenhow, granddaughter of Mary Chapman McKim and Harry Jefferson McKim.

William Dustin "Dusty" McKim, grandson of Mary Chapman McKim and Harry Jefferson McKim.

Bibliography

Books and Monographs

Adams, Kramer. *Logging Railroads of the West*. Seattle: Superior Publishing Co., 1961.

Ahlstrom, Sidney E. *A Religious History of the American People*. New Haven and London: Yale University, 1972.

Anthony, C. V. *Fifty Years of Methodism: A History of the Methodist Episcopal Church: 1847-1897*. San Francisco: Methodist Book Concern, 1901.

Balmer, Beulah Lynn Lemm. *Heart of the Family Tree*. Kenmore, WA: Homestead Press, n.d.

Bancroft, Hubert Howe. *History of California*. Vol. 25. San Francisco: History Publishing Co., 1890.

Barnhart, Jacqueline Baker. *The Fair But Frail: Prostitution in San Francisco, 1849-1900*. Reno: University of Nevada Press, 1986.

Benjamin, Marcus. *John Bidwell, Pioneer: A Sketch of His Career*. Washington, D.C.: Society of California Pioneers, 1907.

Best, Gerald M. *Iron Horses to Promontory*. San Marino, CA: Golden West Books, 1969.

Bidwell, Annie Kennedy. *Diary*. Northeastern California Collection. California State University, Chico.

Bidwell, John. *Diaries*. 1864-1900. Chico: Bidwell Mansion State Park Historic Park Supporting Association, n.d. [CD-ROM]

Blackford, Mansel G. *The Politics of Business in California, 1890-1920*. Columbus: Ohio State University Press, 1977.

Bonner, Richard I., Editor. *Memories of Lenawee County Michigan*. Vol. 1 of 2. Madison, MI: Western Historical Association, 1909.

Bookspan, Shelly. *A Germ of Goodness: The California State Prison System, 1851-1944*. Lincoln: University of Nevada Press, 1991.

Boyle, Florence Danforth. *Old Days in Butte*. Oroville, CA: Butte County Historical Society, 1941.

Brewer, William. *Up and Down California in 1860-1864*. Francis Farquher, ed. Berkeley: University of California Press, 1974.

Bryant, William Cullen, ed. *Picturesque America or the Land We Live in: A Delineation by Pen and Pencil*. 2 vols. New York: Appleton, 1872.

Buckley, J. M. *A History of Methodists in the United States*. New York: Christian Literature, 1896.

Butte County, California: Illustrations. Oakland, CA: Smith and Eliott, 1877.

Butte Remembers. Chico: The National League of Pen Women, 1973.

Caldwell, Mark. *The Last Crusade: The War on Consumption, 1862-1954*. New York: Atheneum, 1988.

Chan, Sucheng. *This Bittersweet Soil: The Chinese in California Agriculture, 1860-1910*. Berkeley: University of California Press, 1986.

City and County Directory: Yuba, Sutter, Colusa, Butte and Tehama Counties. San Francisco: L.M. McKenney and Co., 1881.

Cleland, Robert Glass, and Osgood Hardy. *March of Industry.* San Francisco: Powell Publishing Company, 1929.

Clough, F. S. *The House at Fifth and Salem.* Chico: Stansbury Home Preservation Association, 1978.

Cole, Arthur C. *One Hundred Years of Mount Holyoke College.* New Haven: Yale University Press, 1940.

Compton, Henria Parker. *Mary Murdock Compton.* Chico: privately published, 1953.

Cox, Thomas R. *Mills and Markets: A History of the Pacific Coast Lumber Industry to 1900.* Seattle: University of Washington Press, 1974.

Cross, Ira B. *Financing an Empire: History of Banking in California.* Vol. 1 of 4. Chicago: S. J. Clarke Company, 1927.

Cross, Ira B. *A History of the Labor Movement in California.* Berkeley: University of California Press, 1935.

Davis, Winfield J. *History of Political Conventions in California, 1849-1892.* Sacramento: California State Library, 1893.

Delmatier, Royce, Clarence McIntosh, and Earl G. Waters. *The Rumble of California Politics: 1848-1970.* New York: John Wiley and Sons, 1970.

De Mille, Anna. *Henry George: Citizen of the World.* Chapel Hill: University of North Carolina Press, 1950.

Dijkstra, Bram. *Idols of Perversity: Fantasies of Female Evil in Fin-de-Siècle Culture.* New York: Oxford University press, 1986.

Dillon, Richard H. *The Hatchet Men: San Francisco's Chinatown in the Days of the Tong Wars, 1880-1906.* New York: Ballantine Books, 1962.

Dimmit, James A. *The Chico Police Department: The First 100 Years.* Sacramento: privately printed, 2020.

1882-1883: Mount Holyoke Female Seminary, South Hadley, Massachusetts. Northampton: Bridgman & Childs, 1883.

1883-1884: Mount Holyoke Female Seminary, South Hadley, Massachusetts. Northampton: Bridgman & Childs, 1884.

Eldridge, Zoeth S. *History of California.* 4 vols. New York: Century History, n.d.

Erskin, Albert Russel. *History of the Studebaker Corp.* Detroit: The Studebaker Corp., 1924.

Faragher, John Mack. *Sugar Creek: Life on the Illinois Prairie.* New Haven: Yale University Press, 1986.

Ferguson, Charles. *Fifty Million Brothers: A Panorama of American Lodges and Clubs.* New York: Farrow and Rinehart, 1937.

Fisher, Walter M. *The Californians.* London: Macmillan and Company, 1876.

Folman, John Kent, ed. *"This State of Wonders": The Letters of an Iowa Frontier Family: 1858-1861.* Iowa City: University of Iowa Press, 1986.

Ford, Tirey J. *California State Prisons: Their History, Development and Management.* San Francisco: Star Press, 1910.

Gates, Paul. *California Ranchos and Farms, 1846-1862.* Madison: State Historical Society of Wisconsin, Madison, 1967.

— — —. *The Farmer's Age: Agriculture 1815-1860.* New York: Holt, Rinehart and Winston, 1960.

Griswald, Robert L. *Family and Divorce in California, 1850-1890.* Albany: State University of New York, 1982.

Josepha Hale, *The Ladies New Book of Cookery,* 5th ed. New York: Sheldon Blakeman and Co., 1852.

Hans, Peter. *Butte County Illustrations:* Smith & Elliott, Oakland, 1877.

Heltzer, Robert F., and Theodora Kroeber. *Ishi the Last Yahi: A Documentary History.* Berkeley: University of California Press.

Here is My Land. Chico: The Butte County Branch of the National League of American Pen Women, 1940.

Him, Mark, Joe Huang, and Don Wong. *The Chinese-American: 1785-1980.* San Francisco: Chinese Cultural Foundation, 1980.

Hittell, Theodore H. *History of California.* San Francisco: N. J. Stone and Co., 1898.

Hollenbeck, Edna. *Family History Manuscript.* Unnamed and unpublished. Joan and John R. Robinson III Collection. Chico, California.

Hoopes, Chad. *What Makes a Man: The Annie E. Kennedy and John Bidwell Letters; 1866-1868.* Fresno, CA: Valley Publishers, 1973.

Horowitz, Helen Lefkowitz. *Alma Mater: Design and Experience in the Women's Colleges from Their Nineteenth Century Beginnings to the 1930s.* New York: Alfred A. Knopf, 1984.

Hubbart, Henry Clyde. *The Older Middle West: 1840-1880.* New York: D. Appleton-Century Company, 1936.

Hunt, Rockwell. *John Bidwell: Prince of California Pioneers.* Coldwell, ID: Caxton Publishing Co., 1946.

Hutchinson, W. H. *California Heritage: A History of Northern California Lumbering.* Santa Cruz: The Forest History Society, Inc., 1974.

— — —. *The California Investment of the Diamond Match Company.* Chico: Diamond Match Corporation, 1957.

— — —. *California: The Golden Shore by the Sundown Sea.* Palo Alto: Star Publications, 1980.

— — —. *When Chico Stole the College.* Chico: Butte Savings and Loan Association, 1982.

Jensen, Joan M., and Gloria Ricci Lothrop. *California Women: A History.* San Francisco: Boyd and Fraser, 1987.

Johnson, Charles A. *The Frontier Camp Meeting: Religion's Harvest Time.* Dallas: Southern Methodist University Press, 1955.

Josephson, Matthew. *The Robber Barons.* New York: Harvest, 1962.

Keysaar, Alexander. *Out of Work: The First Century of Unemployment in Massachusetts.* New York: Cambridge University Press, 1986.

Kinnard, Lawrence. *History of the Greater San Francisco Bay Region.* 2 vol. New York: Lewis Historical Publishing Company, 1966.

Kirkland, Caroline S. *Western Clearings.* New York: Garrett Press, 1969.

— — —. *A New Home: Who'll Follow?* New Haven, CT: College and University Press, 1965.

Knapp, John, and R. I. Bonner. *Illustrated History and Biographical Record of Lenawee County, Michigan.* Adrian, MI: Times Printing Co., 1903.

Lavender, David. *California: Land of New Beginnings.* New York: Harper and Row, 1972.

Lesy, Michael. *Wisconsin Death Trip.* New York: Pantheon Books, 1973.

Lewis, Oscar. *San Francisco: Mission to Metropolis.* Berkeley: HowellNorth Books, 1966.

Lingeman, Richard. *Small Town America.* New York: G. P. Putnam, 1980.

Longstreet, Stephen. *A Century on Wheels: The Story of Studebaker.* New York: Henry Holt, 1952.

Lowrie, Ritchie P. *Who's Running This Town?: Community Leadership and Social Change.* New York: Harper, 1968.

Malcolm, Thomas, and Jennifer Grimmette. *Women in Protest, 1888-1950.* New York: St. Martin's Press, 1982.

Mansfield, George. *A History of Butte County, California.* Los Angeles: Historic Record Co., 1918.

Marcus, Benjamin. *John Bidwell: Pioneer.* Washington: privately printed, 1907.

McDonald, Lois. *Annie Kennedy Bidwell.* Chico: Stansbury Publishing, 2004.

McGie, Joseph. *History of Butte County*. 2 vol. Oroville, CA: Butte County Board of Education, 1982.

McGowan, Joseph A. *History of the Sacramento Valley*. 2 vol. New York: Lewis Historical Publishing Company, 1961.

McGrath, Roger D. *Gunfighters, Highwaymen, and Vigilantes*. Berkeley: University of California Press, 1984.

McIntosh, Clarence. *Bidwell Memorial Presbyterian Church: Its First Century: 1868-1968*. Chico: Bidwell Presbyterian Church, 1968.

Melendy, H. Brett, and Benjamin F. Gilbert. *The Governors of California*. Georgetown, CA: Talisman Press, 1965.

Michigan Central College Catalogue. Springdale: Michigan Central College, 1850.

Moak, Sim. *The Last of the Mill Creeks and Early Life in Northern California*. Chico: privately published, 1923.

Mohr, James C. *Abortion in America: The Origins and Evolution of National Policy, 1800-1900*. Oxford: Oxford University Press, 1978.

Moore, Vivian Lyon Moore. *First Hundred Years of Hillsdale College*. Ann Arbor: Ann Arbor Free Press, 1943.

Morrison, Anna M. *Earlier Poems*. San Francisco: A. L. Bancroft and Co., 1880.

One Hundred-Fifty Years in the Hills and Dales. Hillsdale, MI: Hillsdale County Historical Assn., 1976.

Ostrander, Gilman M. *The Prohibition Movement in California, 1848-1933*. Berkeley: The University of California Press, 1957.

Painter, Nell Irvine. *Standing at Armageddon, the United States, 1877-1919*. New York: W. W. Norton, 1987.

Parrington, Vernon. *The Romantic Revolution in America: 1800-1860*. New York: Harcourt, Brace and Company, 1954.

Pen Pictures from the Garden of the World: Memorial and Biographical History of Northern California. Chicago: The Lewis Publishing Company, 1891.

Phaelzer, Jean. *Driven Out: The Forgotten War Against Chinese Americans*. New York: Random House, 2007.

Pingrey, Marjorie. *1858-1958: Centennial*. Chico: The United Methodist Church, 1958.

— — —. *1858-1976: A Bit of History and Spice*. Chico: Trinity United Methodist Church, 1976.

— — —. *1858-1979: Centennial Plus Twenty*. Chico, Trinity United Methodist Church, 1979.

— — —. *Our Heritage: Trinity Methodist Episcopal Church*. Chico: Trinity United Methodist Church, 1858-1968.

Portrait and Biographical Album of Lenawee County, Michigan. Chicago: Chipman Bros., 1888).

Ramsland, Margaret A. *The Other Bidwells*. Chico: privately published, 1972.

Rogers, Justus H. *Colusa County: Its History*. Orland, CA, 1891.

Rolle, Andrew F. *California: A History*. New York: Thomas Y. Crowell Company, 1969.

Roske, Ralph J. *Everyman's Eden: A History of California*. New York: Macmillan, 1968.

Royce, C. C. *John Bidwell, Pioneer, Statesman, Philanthropist: A Biographical Sketch*. Chico: privately published, 1906.

Saxton, Alexander. *The Indispensable Enemy: Labor and the AntiChinese Movement in California*. Berkeley: University of California Press, 1971.

Santmeyer, Helen Hooven. *"...And Ladies of the Club."* New York: G. P. Putnam, 1982.

Shover, Michele. *California Standoff: Miners, Indians and Farmers at War, 1850-1865*. Chico: Stansbury Publishing, 2017.

— — —. "The Blockhead Factor: Marriage and the Fate of California Daughters." *The Californians* 5 (September 1989): 26-32. Republished as *Mother California Cherishing Her Daughters.*" Chico: Chico Museum, 1989.

— — —. *Chico's Little Chapman Mansion: The House and Its People.* Chico: Association for Northern California Records and Research, 1981.

— — —. *Exploring Chico's Past.* Philadelphia: Xlibris, 2006.

Shirer, William L. *Twentieth Century Journey.* New York: Pocket Books, 1979.

Shumsky, Neil Larry. *The Evolution of Political Protest and the Workingmen's Party of California.* Columbus: Ohio State University Press, 1991.

Slotkin, Richard. *The Fatal Environment: The Myth of the Frontier in the Age of Industrialization, 1800-1890.* New York: Atheneum, 1985.

Smith, Edgar. "Gunny Sacks Galore." *California Territorial Quarterly* 52 (Winter 2002): 18-36.

Smith, Henry Nash. *Virgin Land: The American West as Symbol and Myth.* New York: Vintage, 1950.

Smith, Timothy L. *Revivalism and Social Reform: American Protestantism on the Eve of the Civil War.* Gloucester, MA: Peter Smith, 1976.

Starr, Kevin. *Americans and the California Dream: 1850-1915.* Santa Barbara: Peregreno Smith, 1981.

Stewart, George R. *The California Trail.* New York: McGrawHill, 1962.

Stone, Irving. *Men to Match My Mountains: The Opening of the Far West: 1840-1900.* Garden City, ID: Doubleday, 1956.

Stow, Sarah Locke. *History of Mount Holyoke Seminary, South Hadley, Mass., During its First Half Century, 1837-1887* South Hadley, MA: Mount Holyoke Seminary, 1887.

Sweet, William Warren. *Revivalism in America.* Gloucester, MA: Peter Smith, 1965.

Swisher, Carl Brent. *Motivation and Political Technique in the California State Constitutional Convention: 1878-1879.* Claremont, CA: Pomona College, 1936.

Talbitzer, Bill. *Butte County: An Illustrated History.* Northridge, CA: Windsor Publications, 1987.

Thompson, Warren S. *Growth and Changes in California's Population.* Los Angeles: The Hayes Foundation, 1955.

Thoreau, Henry David. "Life Without Principle." In *The Portable Thoreau,* Carl Bode, ed. New York: Viking Press, 1964.

— — —. *Selected Writings.* Lewis Leary, ed. New York: Appleton Century Crofts, 1958.

— — —. *Walden and Other Writings.* New York: Modern Library, 1950.

Tocqueville, Alexis de. *Democracy in America.* New York: Vintage Books, 1945.

Turner, Frederick Jackson. *The Frontier in American History.* New York: Henry Holt, 1921.

Vivian, T. J., and D. G. Waldron. *Biographical Sketches of the Delegates to the State Constitutional Convention to Frame a New State Constitution for the State of California, 1878.* San Francisco: Francis and Valentine, 1878.

Victor, Frances Fuller. *Atlantis Arisen: Talks as a Tourist about Oregon and Washington.* Philadelphia: J. B. Lippincott, 1891.

Walkley, Christina. *The Ghost in the Looking Glass: The Victorian Seamstress.* London: Peter Owen, 1981.

Wells, Harry, and W. L. Chambers. *History of Butte County, California.* San Francisco: Harry L. Wells, 1882.

— — —. *History of Butte County, California.* Reprint with Introduction by W. H. Hutchinson, Berkeley: HowellNorth Books, 1973.

West, Raymond H. *The Story of St. John: The Ghost City of Glenn County, on the Old Wagon Road to the Gold Mines of Shasta.* Orland, CA: Orland Register, n.d.

Willis, E. B., and P. K. Stockton. *Debates and Proceedings of the State Constitutional Convention of the State of California.* 3 vols. Sacramento: State Office, 1880 and 1881.

Wood, Jesse. *Butte County, California: Its Resources and Advantages for Home Seekers.* Oroville, CA: Butte County, 1886.

Woodman, J. M. *God in Nature and Revelation.* Butte Record Press, 1880.

Woodward, C. Vann. *Thinking Back: The Perils of Writing History.* Baton Rouge: Louisiana State University Press, 1986.

Woolridge, J. W. Major. *History of the Sacramento Valley California.* 3 vols. Chicago: Pioneer Historical Publishing Company, 1931.

The Works of Hubert Howe Bancroft. Vols. 7-24 (1860-1890). San Francisco: The History Company Publishers, 1890.

Worster, Donald. *Rivers of Empire.* New York: Pantheon, 1985.

Terald A. Zall, *The Hospital on the 90ᵗʰ Anniversary of Rideout Memorial Hospital.* Marysville, CA: Glena Hill Press, 1998.

Articles

Annan, Noel. "In Bed with the Victorians." *New York Review of Books* 33 (20 November 1986): 813.

Babcock, Barbara Allen. "Clara Shortridge Foltz: State Constitution-Maker." *Indiana Law Journal* 66 JBCUCD (Fall 1991): 849-940.

"Biography of George Stoneman." http://bufordboys.com/StonemanBiography.html. [website currently unavailable]

Book, Susan. "Ashes to Ashes: Chinese Cemeteries in Butte County, 1880." *Diggins* 17 (Summer 1974): 310.

— — —. "Chinese Settlement in Butte County." *Diggins* 8 (Summer 1974): 1122.

Stanley T. Borden. "Northern California Logging Operations: Diamond Match Company." *Western Railroader* 31 (November 1968): 2-34.

Branson, Grant. "Chico's Chinatown." *Chico News and Review* 29 (January 1983): 25.

Button, Melinda. "Reverend Jesse Wood: Combing the Sacred and Secular Worlds of Late Nineteenth Century Butte County, California." *Diggins* 43 (Spring 2009): 3-16.

Clement, H. N. "Caucasian vs. Mongolian." *Chinese Immigration: Its Social, Moral, and Political Effect.* Report to the California State Senate of the Special Committee on Chinese Immigration, pp. 26684. Sacramento: State Office, 1878.

Conlin, Joseph. "When Chico Was Main Line." *Diggins* 26 (Fall, 1982): 6768.

Cornford, Daniel. "The California Workingmen's Party in Humboldt County." *California History* 66 (June, 1987): 13159.

"The Eventful Yesterdays: The Story of Early Chico." *Enterprise* Series, 29 December 1917-28 January 1918.

Fong, Kum Ngou, "The Chinese Six Companies." *Overland Monthly* 23 (May, 1894): 51826.

Frederickson, George M. "Down on the Farm." *The New York Review of Books* 33 (August 23, 1987): 3739.

— — —. "Redemption Through Violence." *The New York Review of Books* 32 (November 21, 1985): 3842.

George, Henry. "The Kearney Agitation in California." *The Popular Science Monthly* 17 (August 1880): 43453.

Hart, Jerome A. "The Sand Lot and Kearneyism." The Virtual Museum of the City of San Francisco, 7 November 2007.

Hill, Dorothy J. "James John Morehead 1828-1885: A California Pioneer." In *Ripples Along Chico Creek.* Chico: Butte County Branch, National League of American Pen Women, 1992.

Huang, George, "The Chinese Settlement in Chico, California." *Chinese Librarians Association Newsletter.* Northeastern California Collection, Meriam Library, California State University, Chico, n.d.

Johnson, Kenneth. "California's State Constitution of 1879: An Unpaid Debt." *California Historical Society Quarterly* 49 (June 1970): 135-41.

KesslerHarris, Alice. "Laid off in Good Times and Bad." *New York Review of Books* 33 (May 4, 1986): 36.

Laney, Anita. "Marysville's Methodist Episcopal Church: The Early Years." Butte County Historical Society News Bulletin 13, no. 491934, 2-27.

Lenhoff, James. "Butte County's Pioneer Bank Closes Its Doors." *Diggins* 27 (Summer, 1984): 2952.

Lenhoff, James. "From Sailor Boy to Senator." *Diggins* 24 (Summer, 1980): 2750.

Levenson, Rosaline. "Jewish Communities of Butte County: Rise and Development." *Diggins* 29 (Fall and Winter, 1985): 55100.

Lustig, R. Jeffrey. "Private Rights and Public Purposes: California's Second State Constitution Reconsidered." *California History* 873 (2010): 46-64.

MacDonald, Lois. "The Roads and Bridges of Butte Creek Canyon." *Diggins* 38 (Spring and Summer, 1994): 30-38.

— — —. "William Chalmers Hendricks." *Diggins* 37 (Spring and Summer, 1993): 3-59.

— — —. "William Chalmers Hendricks." *Diggins* 38 (Fall and Winter, 1994): 59-112.

McIntosh, Clarence. "A Brief History of California State University, Chico." *Diggins* 31 (Summer, 1987): 2750.

— — —. "The Chico and Red Bluff Route." *Idaho Yesterdays* VI (Fall, 1962): 1219.

"126 Years with the *Chico Enterprise Record.*" Special Section, *Chico Enterprise Record,* 30 November 1979.

"Miramar Meach's Amesport and Judge Josiah P. Ames." Parts 1-4. *Half-Moon Bay Memories and El Grenada Observer,* March 2007.

Orberg, George. "Chinese in Chico."' *Diggins* 4 (Fall, 1960): 1218.

Osborne, Thomas J. "Claus Spreckels and the Oxnard Brothers: Pioneer Developers of California's Beet Sugar Industry." *Southern California Quarterly* 54 (Summer, 1972): 11725.

Parker, Virginia C. "The Chinese Question of the 1870's." *Diggins* 18 (Summer, 1974): 2427.

Shepard, Vida Hills. "The Changing Fortunes of David M. Reavis." In *Butte Remembers,* 72-73. Chico: Butte County Branch, The National League of Pen Women, 1973.

Styles, Florence. "Carr Hill Road: Honey Run Covered Road and the Butte Creek Canyon Area, Butte County, California." In Lois Coleman, and Mildred Forester. *Tailings of Butte Creek Canyon, 1833-1971.* Centerville, CA: Centerville Recreational and Historical Association, 1972.

Trussell, Margaret Edith. "Mexican Land Grants in Butte County." *Diggins* 16 (Spring, 1972): 3-15.

Waterland, John S. "The John Waterland Historical Articles." *Enterprise Record.*

Wood, Reverend Jesse. *Butte County, California: Its Resources and Advantages for Home Seekers, 1886.* Oroville, CA: Butte County, n.d.

Interviews

Brooks, Elsa Boydston by Michele Shover, March 1980.

Ekwall, Vera Hintz by Michele Shover, late 1980s.

Gage, Helen by Michele Shover, April 1880.

Miller, Marja and Claudia Jensen by Michele Shover (regarding the Sisk family), 2006.

Olker, Antonia by Michele Shover, January 1980.

Pingrey, Marjorie by Michele Shover, fall 1980.
Rice, Charles by James Neider, 25 August 1964. SCML.
Stansell, Lois by Michele Shover, 1983.
Stewart, Nancy by Michele Shover, no date recorded.

Newspapers

Chico, California
    Chronicle, 1887-1890. SCML.
    Courant, 1865-1868. SCML.
    Enterprise, 1869-1890. SCML.
    Index, February 21, 1863. JBCBL.
    News and Review.
    Post, 1905-1906.
    Record, 1860-1900.
Oroville, California
    The Oroville Mercury, 1877, 1879, 1888.
Sacramento
    The Daily Bee, 1877, 1883, 1888.
San Francisco
    San Francisco *Alta*, 1877.
    San Francisco Chronicle, 1877, 1878, 1887.

Unpublished Materials

Charles Aldini and Brent Owen, "Chapmantown Master Plan." Unpublished term paper for Prof. Margaret Trussell, Department of Geography, CSUC, n.d.
Balmer, Beula Lemm. *Heart of the Family Tree*. Kenmore, WA: Privately printed, n.d.
Bidwell, John. *Dictation*. JBCBL, ca. 1892.
– – –. *Diaries*. NCCML.
Book, Susan Wiley, "The Chinese in Butte County, 1860-1920." M.A. thesis, SCML, 1974.
Chan, Sucheng. "Anti-Chinese Activities in Rural California in the Late Nineteenth Century." Paper presented at American Historical Association Meeting. December 27-30, 1985.
Chapman, Sarah. *Diary*, 1899. Typescript by Larry V. Richardson. Original was in the possession of Mildred Forester, Paradise, CA, and subsequently burned. Copy available in SCML.
Gabriel, Kathleen Faye. *James Lawrence Keefer, 1850-1901: An Ethno-history Study of a Butte Country Pioneer*. M.A Thesis, SCML, 1981.
Edna Hollenbeck. *Family History*. Provided by Joan and John R. Robinson.
Lee, Wesley. Diary fragment. Property of Mary Hanson, Chico, California.
McIntosh-Jones-Robinson Family Collection. Private collection of Mary Ellen Robinson Amer and Joan and John R. Robinson III, Chico, California.
Orsi, Richard J. "Selling The Golden State: A Study of Boosterism in Nineteenth Century California." PhD diss., University of Wisconsin, Madison, 1973.
East, Owen. *Journal of an Overland Journey from Kanesville, Iowa to Feather Falls in California*, 26 August 1852. Courtesy of Andrew Hammond.
Peery, Eugene R. *The Anti-Chinese Press in Butte County: A Study in Prejudice*. M.A. thesis, SCML, 1968.
Rice, Charles. Oral History Interview by James Neider, 1964. Northeastern California.
Silsby, Mary S. Letter, April 3, 1864. Private collection of John Nopel, Chico, CA. SCML.

Stilson, C. L. *Diaries: 1863-1872*. NCCML.

Trussell, Margaret Edith. *Land Choice by Pioneer Farmers: Western Butte County Through 1877*. Phd. diss., University of Oregon, 1969.

Wood, George. Correspondence with Henry Hallet. Papers of Henry Hallet. Property of Betty Given, Sacramento, CA.

Wynne, Joseph. *The Impact of the Civil War Upon Butte County*. M.A. thesis, SCML, 1967.

Public Documents

Appendix and Journals of State Assembly and Senate, California, 25th sess. Sacramento, 1883.

Bicentennial Message of Gov. George C. Perkins to the Legislature of the State of California, 25th sess., in Appendix and Journals A and S, 25th sess. Sacramento, 1883.

Great Record of Butte County. NCCML.

John Bidwell & Co. Ledger, 1861-1864. JBCSL.

Minutes, Chico School Trustees. NCCML.

Miscellaneous Records, 1860-1900. Butte County, California Records Office, Oroville, CA.

Miscellaneous Records, 1860-1900. NCCML.

Property Deeds, Chico Twp., Butte County, California. Recorder's Office, Oroville, CA.

First Annual Report of the State Board of Prison Directors. Appendix to the Journals of the Senate and Assembly, 24th sess., vol. 2. Sacramento: State printing Office, 1881. California State Archives.

Second Annual Report of the State Prison Board of Directors. Appendix to the Journals of the Senate and Assembly, 25th sess., vol. 6. Sacramento: State Printing Office, 1883. California State Archives.

Third Annual Report of the State Board of Prison Directors. Appendix to the Journals of the Senate and Assembly, 25th sess., vol. 5. Sacramento: State Printing Office, 1883. California State Archives.

Report of the Special Commission of Inquiry into the General Administration of the State Prisons of California. Appendix to the Journals of the Senate and Assembly, 25th sess., vol. 6. Sacramento: State Printing Office, 1883. California State Archives.

Report of the Senate Committee on State Prisons and Prison Buildings. Appendix to the Journals of the Senate and Assembly, 25th sess., vol. 3. Sacramento: State Printing Office, 1883. California State Archives.

Petition of Citizens of Butte and Tehama Counties to Governor Leland, July 1862. Papers of Governor Leland Stanford, 1862. Attachment to 17 July letter from John Bidwell to Governor Leland Stanford. California Indian War Files, California State Archives.

Population Schedules of the Eighth Census of the United States, 1860: California. Washington, D.C.: National Archives and Records Service. United States Census Office.

Population Schedules of the Ninth Census of the United States, 1870: California. Washington, D.C.: National Archives and Records Service. General Services Administration.

Population Schedules of the Tenth Census of the United States, 1880: California. Washington, D.C.: National Archives and Records Service. General Services Administration.

Population Schedules of the Twelfth Census of the United States: 1900. Washington, D.C.: National Archives and Records Service. General Service Administration.

The War of the Rebellion: Official Records of the Union and Confederate Armies. Series 1, part 2. Washington: Government Printing Office, 1887.

Abbreviations

BCCML   Butte County Special Collection, Meriam Library, California State University, Chico

CCCSL   California Collection, California State Library

CCML   California Collection, Meriam Library, California State University, Chico

CSA   California State Archives, Sacramento

CSUC   California State University, Chico

CSUSL   Library, California State University, Sacramento

Diggins   Butte County Historical Society *Diggins*

Enterprise   All name variations, such as *Northern Enterprise, California Caucasian, Chico Enterprise,* and *Enterprise Record.*

JBCSL   John Bidwell Collection, California State Library, Sacramento

JBCBL   John Bidwell Collection, Bancroft Library, University of California, Berkley

JBSCML   John Bidwell Collection, Special Collections, Meriam Library, California State University, Chico

NCCML   Northeastern California Collection, Meriam Library, California State University, Chico

Record   All name variations, such as *Butte Record, Chico Morning Chronicle-Record* and *Chico Record*

SCML   Special Collections, Meriam Library, California State University, Chico

Endnotes

Preface

1   Henry George, "The Kearney Agitation in California," *The Popular Science Monthly*, 17 (August, 1880).

Chapter 1

1   The two houses were those of Dr. Samuel Sproul and the John Barham family, whose house was finished first. Barham file, Chico Heritage Association; David F. Crowder, "The Eventful Yesterdays: The Story of Early Chico," *Chico Enterprise*, 1917-1918.

2   This was reconstructed from newspaper coverage of the burning of the Chapmans' last home on Chapman Street in 1909 and a current county land record designating Olive Street as "Formerly Old Chico Way." Its beginning at the bridge over Big Chico Creek appeared in another document. Sources appear in this author's 2012 *Diggins* article on "Bidwell's Early Mansion." Its start near the Potter gate is visible in an 1859 photo of Bidwell's headquarters from southeast across Big Chico Creek.

3   Mary S. Silsby, Diary, 3 April 1864, SCML; George Mansfield, *A History of Butte County, California* (Los Angeles: Historic Record Co., 1918). He cites Smith H. Hurles who arrived the same year as the Chapmans. Gus Chapman supervised Hurles at John Bidwell & Co. Hurles oversaw another very early business, Duncan Neal's Saloon, which was built on Potter's ranch as soon as Bidwell acquired it in 1860. Record, 15 April 1876. An 1864 photograph of such startup businesses in shacks is found in the photo archive of SCML; Paul Gates, *The Farmer's Age: Agriculture 1875-1860* (New York: Holt, Rhinehart, and Winston, 1960), 277; *Record*, 15 April 1876; *Enterprise,* 24 October 1873, 20 January 1888.

4   Chapman's account in the John Bidwell & Co. ledger showed purchases of porter, popular with street and river porters. According to Wikipedia, "The name porter was first used in 1721 to describe a dark brown beer that had been made with roasted malts. Because of the huge popularity of porters, brewers made them in a variety of strengths."

5   Mansfield, 437. The school was in a two-story frame cottage influenced by the eastern Greek revival vogue. This charming building, restored by Wayne Cook of Chico, still stands as well-maintained student housing on the west side of Normal between West Fourth and West Fifth streets.

6   T. J. Vivian and D. G. Waldron, "A. H. Chapman," in *Biographical Sketches of the Delegates to the State Constitutional Convention to Frame a New State Constitution for the State of California, 1878* (San Francisco: Francis and Valentine, 1878), 19. The author donated a copy of this rare book to SCML.

7   United States Census, 1860, Woodstock Twp., Lenawee County, Michigan.

8   Vivian and Waldron, "A. H. Chapman," 18-19.

9   Ibid. In 1852, for example, 500 men from the county next to Chapman's prepared to leave for California. With the out-migration and labor shortages, local wages rose from $11 to $26 a month. Paul Gates, *California Ranchos and Farms, 1846-1864* (Madison State Historical Society of Wisconsin), 277.

10   Frederick Jackson Turner, *The Frontier in American History* (New York: Henry Holt, 1921), 153, 355; William Warren Sweet, *Revivalism in America* (Gloucester: Peter Smith, 1965), 114; Henry Nash Smith, *Virgin Land: The American West as Symbol and Myth* (New York: Vintage, 1950), 665, chapters 1-2.

11   Turner, 153; Herb Sparrow, "This Train Was Bound for Glory" (not available at this time); Souvenir History of Niagara County New York (New York: The Pioneer Association of Niagara County, 1902). The much expanded and modernized Cataract Hotel hosted landscape architect Frederick Law Olmstead, British novelist Anthony Trollope and the hotel's black help made it a principal stop on the Underground Railroad. Francis R. Kowsky, "In Defense of Niagara: Frederick Law Olmstead and the Niagara Reservation, North America" in adelaide.edu.au/t/trollopeanthonynorth/chapter7.

12   Turner, 153.

13   Federal censuses, 1850, 1860, Woodstock Twp., Lenawee County, Michigan; T. J. Vivian and D. G. Waldron, *Biographical Sketches of the Delegates to the State Constitutional Convention to Frame a New State Constitution for the State of California, 1878* (San Francisco: Francis and Valentine, 1878), 18-19; Gates, 181. Appreciation for the work of certified genealogical researcher Mary Catherine Grobis of Fort Wayne, Indiana, for tracing A. H. Chapman's family in New York, Connecticut and Michigan.

14   Vivian and Waldron, *Biographical Sketches*, 18-19; Caroline Kirkland, *Western Clearings* (New York: Garrett Press, 1969); – – –, *A New Home: Who'll Follow?* (New Haven: College and University Press, 1965); United States Census, 1850, Lenawee County, Michigan; Vivian and Waldron, 19.

15   Turner, 353; Richard I. Bonner, *Memories of Lenawee County Michigan,* vol. I (Madison: Western Historical Association, 1909).

16   Vivian and Waldron, 18-19; *Record,* 31 January 1899. Michigan Central soon moved to Hillsdale where it still operates as Hillsdale College. Bonner, 525.

17   Vivian Lyon Moore, *First Hundred Years of Hillside College* (Ann Arbor: Ann Arbor Press, 1943), introduction and chapter 1; Catalogue of the Officers and Students of the Michigan Central College, 1850. The foregoing information on Michigan Central College was provided by Dr. J. A. Fallon, archivist of Hillsdale College at which the poet Will Carleton was a student and contemporary of A. H. Chapman. According to Fallon, Carleton was "Michigan's beloved Poet Laureate, who was born on a pioneer farm near Hudson, Lenawee County in 1845." Fallon commented in a November 7, 1984, letter to the author, "I was struck by the amazing similarities between Gus Chapman and Will Carleton."

18   A. H. Chapman, *Tally Book, 1854-1855.* Gifted to the author by Larry V. Richardson.

19   Ibid.

20   Henry Clyde Hubbart, *The Older Middle West: 1840-1880* (New York: Appelton-Century Co., 1936), 97-98.

21   Sources on Sarah Sickley Chapman's family have been drawn from *150 Years in the Hills and Dales,* vol. 1 (Hillsdale, MI: Hillside County Historical Association, 1976) and *Portrait and Biographical Album of Lenawee County, Michigan* (Chicago: Chipman Bros., 1888). These were furnished by Charles Lindquist, curator of the Lenawee County Historical Museum.

22   The author was given Sarah's copy of *The Ladies' New Book of Cookery* by the late

Vera Hintz Ekwall who received it from the wife of Sarah's son, Gus Chapman Jr.
23 *150 Years in the Hills,* 26-29, 97-98. General information on Chapman's Michigan home comes from Richard J. Bonner, ed., op. cit., passim. John Knapp and R. J. Bonner, *Illustrated History and Biographical Record of Lenawee County, Michigan* (Adrian: Times Publishing Co., 1903). The Sarah Sickley site on Amazon.com suggested there were some Indian threats to their party, but offered no sources.
24 Vivian and Waldron, 19.
25 The author's great-grandfather John Andrew Shover served in the 7th Regiment, Iowa Cavalry in the Dakotas from 1861-65 under General Alfred Sully, who objected to the necessity that his soldiers protect emigrant trains. Not only was it highly dangerous, but Sully believed they were protecting shirkers and deserters. He queried his superior, "Why will our Government continue to act so foolishly, sending out emigrant trains at a great expense? Do they know that most of the men that go are persons running from the draft?" *The War of the Rebellion: A Compilation of the Official Records of the Union and Confederate Armies* (Washington: Government Printing Office, 1893), part 1, p. 151.

Chapter 2

1 Charles L. Stilson, *Diaries: 1863-1872,* 1 February 1865 (unpublished), NCCML. William Jones, director of the collection, acquired this valuable record. Stilson, 2 July 1863; *Courant,* 6, 7 July, 1866; The United States Census, Butte County, California, Chico Twp., 1860; Letters from George Wood to Henry Hallet, SCML.
2 Stilson, July 2, 1863; *Courant,* 6, 7 July, 1866. Information on George Wood comes from the United States Census, Butte County, California, Chico Twp., 1860.
3 *Courant,* 2 December 1865, 2 April 1867; Mary Silsby letter. The author appreciates the late John Nopel's willingness to share its contents. Prominent Chico residents who immersed themselves in its history believed Bidwell fathered at least one Indian child. Author's interview with Ted Meriam. Cf. Lois Halliday MacDonald, *Annie Kennedy Bidwell* (Stansbury Publishing: Chico, CA, 2005).
4 Stilson, 12 January, 1, 2 February, 1864. The 1863 profits were $3,000 less than in 1862.
5 The sprawling Maidu tribe comprised hundreds of rival clusters (tribelets) who understood each as a tribe unto itself. The Mechoopda, Valley Maidu, were rivals of other Valley tribelets. All shared their fear and distrust of the Mountain Maidu tribelets which anthropologists conjoined with the Valley peoples in an overarching tribal identity they called the Maidu tribe. Indians today recognize the Maidu tribe as comprehensive, but they still identify most strongly with their tribelet identity. Hence, in Chico the tribelet historically in possession of the land and many still in place, think first of themselves as Mechoopda. *Enterprise,* 15 March 1987; Mansfield, 437; *Record, 3,* 17 August 1861, 15 April 1876. For a fuller account of Indian identities, see Michelle Shover, *California Standoff: Miners, Indians and Farmers at War, 1850-1865* (Chico: Stansbury Publishing, 2017).
6 *Enterprise,* 15 March 1987; Mansfield, 437; *Record, 3,* 17 August 1861, 15 April 1876.
7 Census of the United States, 1860, Butte County, Chico Twp., California, and *The Great Record of Butte County, California,* NCCLM; *Record,* 25 January, 2 February 1862.
8 The author's *California Standoff* fully treats the evolution of the problems referred to here.
9 Correspondence, John Bidwell with Dr. J. B. Smith, George Adams Smith, Joseph McCorkle, passim, CSLS. These present the "flavor" of the 1850s culture that remained visible in the 1860s.

9   *Record,* 25 January 1862.

10 Stilson, 12 January 1864, 7 January 1865.

11 Petition of Citizens of Butte and Tehama County to Governor Leland Stanford, 2 July 1862, CSA. For a full treatment of these matters, see this author's *California Standoff.*

12 Vivian and Waldron, 1819; *Chico Weekly Index,* 21 February 1863; *Record,* 7 November 1863; Henry Wells and W. L. Chambers, *History of Butte County, California* (San Francisco: Harry L. Wells, 1882), 159.

13 *Record,* 20 September 1862; *Chico Weekly Index,* 21 February 1863.

14 Butte County California Tax Records, 1862-1863, Chico Twp., Butte County Records Office, Oroville, CA.

15 Mansfield, 607.

16 Clarence McIntosh, "The Chico and Red Bluff Route," *Idaho Yesterdays,* vol. 6 (Fall, 1962), 1219; Joseph Conlin, "When Chico Was Main Line," *Diggins* 26 (Fall, 1982), 6768; Joseph A. McGowan, *History of the Sacramento Valley,* 2 vols. (New York: Lewis Historical Publishing Co., 1961), 17983.

17 The road company was also called the Chico & Humboldt Wagon Road Co. and the Humboldt Wagon Road Co. To avoid confusion, it is called the Humboldt Road Co. herein.

18 Letter, Mary S. Silsby to unnamed, 3 April 1864. Bidwell gave up on many row crops when the Chinese began to set up vegetable farms for local produce sales in large quantities. The older men sold the produce from wagons they drove daily through downtown and the neighborhoods. Mrs. Chapman's surviving diary used the term "cook room."

19 Joseph McGie, *History of Butte County,* vol. 1 (Oroville, CA: Butte County Board of Education, 1982) 93, 107-8; *Record,* 7 November 1863; Stilson, 2 November 1863. The *Oroville Register,* 1 February 1899, states Chapman opened the What Cheer Hotel. He seems to have had some early link to it, according to another newspaper account after it burned, but accounts contemporary with the fire cite no link to Chapman and name a Mr. Cox as the hotel's owner.

20 Butte County Records Office, Oroville, CA. Florence Chapman died on 18 November 1863. She is buried in the Chapman plot in the Chico Cemetery but, according to the late Larry R. Richardson, is erroneously recorded as the infant of Augustus and Sarah Roe. Certificate of Incorporation, Chico Cemetery Association, 18 February 1864, SCML; Stilson, 9, 28 November, 9 December 1863.

21 In February 1864 the Chico Cemetery Association members were John Bidwell, Dr. S. M. Sproul, Dan Bidwell, John Kempf, H. O. Pertan, A. H. Chapman, Andrew Hallet, Richard Breese, Charles Doty, and two others. Articles of Incorporation, vol. 1 (1892-1897), 22-23, SCML.

22 Author's interview with Larry V. Richardson. Florence's gravestone has since disappeared.

23 Stilson, 18, 24 September 1866.

24 Ibid., May 5, 1864. The general observations in this section are inferred from a raft of entries in Stilson's diaries. John Bidwell & Co. ledger, February 1864, SCML. Chapman, *Tally Book,* 1854.

Chapter 3

1   Mary Silsby to unknown, 3 April 1864, SCML.

2   *Enterprise,* 11 January 1918.

3   United States Census, 1860. These percentages are based on 777 white males who were United States born. Not counted were 3 Chinese, 156 Native Americans,

3 African Americans and 76 foreign-born residents of the Chico township. Northerners were 422, border state men were 265 (of these, a heavy concentration were from Missouri and 92 from the Deep South).

4 Edward Pond's employee George Bush was a member of the Union militia. This is an impression drawn from remarks in Charles Stilson's diaries. He and Bush were friends.

5 This impression builds over the course of the Stilson's diaries.

6 Stilson, 12 January 1864; Ira B. Cross, *Financing an Empire: History of Banking in California* (Chicago: S. J. Clark Co., 1927), 237-39; *Sacramento Bee*, 10 December 1865.

7 *Courant*, 26 April 1867; Hubert Howe Bancroft, *History of California*, vol. 7 (San Francisco: History Publishing Co., 1988), 309. While the Methodist Church South made the best financed start of Chico's few denominations, its congregation worked tirelessly to pay off the mortgage and, afterward, to maintain it. *Courant*, 3, 8 March, 1868. The Methodist Episcopal Church erected a church building to serve African-American residents in the later 1860s.

9 The Northern affiliated church became the North Methodist Church. Stilson, 28 March 1864.

10 Wells and Chambers (1881 ed.), 174.

11 *Record*, 15 October 1863. The 1860 United States Census shows a substantial cluster of Missouri natives, as well as those from border states (Delaware, Kentucky, Maryland, Missouri and West Virginia). The Durham areas of Rock Creek and Mud Creek were two areas they particularly favored for settlement. *Record*, 15 August 1865.

12 Ibid.

13 In 1886, according to allegations by Rancho Chico employees and a town tradesman, Bidwell demanded they join the Committee of One Hundred as a condition of employment. See chapter 19. Known Union League members also included Simeon Moak, who wrote *The Last of the Mill Creeks and Early Life in Northern California* (Chico: privately published, 1923).

14 See Shover, *California Standoff*, chapter 6.

15 *Record*, 21 January 1865.

16 Stilson, 20, 22 August 1864.

17 *Courant*, 7 July 1866.

18 Ibid., 10 April 1866; *Enterprise*, 12 January 1918. Chico's cannon was melted down and donated to make weapons for WWI.

19 Andrew F. Rolle, *California: A History* (New York: Macmillan, 1968), 352-53.

20 Vernon Parrington, *The Romantic Revolution: 1880-1860* (New York: Harcourt, Brace and Co., 1954), 139.

21 See Shover, *California Standoff*, chapter 12.

Chapter 4

1 Stilson, 15 June 1865.

2 *Great Record of Butte County*, NCCML; Partnership Agreement, misc. Butte Co. records, Recorder's Office, Butte County, Oroville, CA, 1 January 1866.

3 Rockwell Hunt, *John Bidwell: Prince of California Pioneers* (Coldwell, ID: Caxton Publishing Co., 1946), 367; Stilson, 24 November 1866. In 1865 Wood also opened a wagon shop.

4 *Great Record*; Stilson, 11 October 1867; Author's interview with Larry V. Richardson, n.d.

5 *Courant*, 5, 26 May 1866.

6 Stilson, 12 January, 1 February, 22 April 1864.

7   Ibid., 18 April, 16 May, 3, 20 June, 21, 31 July 1865; *Enterprise,* 2 August 1865.

8   *Enterprise,* 26 May 1866.

9   Ibid., 4 October 1864, 10 October 1867; Stilson, 7 August 1863.

10   Ibid., 4, 11 October 1867; Stilson, 7 August 1863. Hoose is buried in the Chico Cemetery.

11   W. H. Hutchison, *California: The Golden Shore by the Sunset Sea* (Palo Alto: Star Publishing, 1980), 116.

12   *Courant,* 25 November 1865; Clarence McIntosh, "Chico and the Red Bluff Route," *Diggins* 1 (Fall 1962).

13   *Courant,* 7 July, 15 November 1865, 13, 20, 27 January, 7 July 1866.

14   Ibid., 18 November 1865, 7 July 1866.

15   Stilson, 16 March 1866; *Courant,* 10 February 1866.

16   *Enterprise,* 12 July 1867.

17   Stilson, 30 June 1866.

18   Lois McDonald, "The Bidwell Family," *Ripples Along Chico Creek* (Chico: Pen Women Publication, 1992); Stilson, 8 September 1867; *Courant,* 13, 20 January 1866.

19   Stilson, 1 March 1866; *Courant,* 10 February, 24 March 1866; John Bidwell, *Dictation,* JBCBL. Bidwell served in the House of Representatives from 1864 to 1866. Obituary, John Bidwell, undated, unsourced, Bertha Lee scrapbook, property of Mary Lee Hanson of Chico.

20   Stilson, 16 March 1866; *Courant,* 10 February 1866.

21   James Lenhoff, "Butte County's Pioneer Bank Closes Its Door," *Diggins* 27 (Summer 1984).

22   *Record,* 1 March 1868. The mill had been five miles up Butte Creek from the valley. It was started by O. D. Clark who sold it to George Woolle, who sold it to Wood & Chapman.

23   Federal Census, 1860; Lois Halliday McDonald, *Annie Kennedy Bidwell: An Intimate History of Chico* (Chico: Stansbury Publishing, 2004); Stilson, 8 September 1867.

24   Stilson, passim, 1866-1868.

25   *Courant,* 20 September, 20 December 1867.

26   Stilson, 12 December 1866; *Record,* 7 March 1866.

27   Ibid., passim.

28   Ibid., 5 April, 12 December 1866; *Record,* 7 March 1886.

29   Ibid., 16 October 1863, 24, 25 October 1865.

30   Ibid., 23 June, 24 July, 5, 16 August, 5 September 1866; *Courant,* 18 January, 3 October 1868.

31   Ibid., 28 July, 7 August, 5, 8 September 1866; *Courant,* 18 January, 13 October 1868.

32   *Courant,* 10 November 1866.

33   "Wood's Hall Center of Social Life," *Enterprise,* 13 June 1937, Old Timer series, *Historical Articles,* book 1, SCML.

34   Stilson, 28 July, 7 August, 7 September 1866; *Courant,* 15 September, 13 October 1868, passim.

35   *Courant,* 30 November 1866.

36   Stilson, 18 July, 6 October 1866; *Courant,* 22 March, 12 September 1867; *Enterprise,* 10 June 1869, 4 June 1870.

37   Stilson, 15 March 1868.

38   Ibid., 26 January 1864. The railroad's superintendent was Andrew Binney. Its history was not pertinent to the present research except that, for the record, banker Norman Rideout of Marysville purchased it in 1879.

39   *Courant,* 27 December 1867.

40   *Courant,* passim, 1866, 29 June 1868; Cf. Gates, 181.

41   Stilson, 24 December 1864. Eagan was a sign painter in Chico.

42   *Courant,* 14 August 1868.
43   Ibid., 31 March 1866, 14 February 1868; Stilson, 17 July 1865.
44   *Enterprise,* 17 April, 17, 28 August 1868.
45   Wesley Lee scrapbook, property of descendant Mary Hanson of Chico, SCML
46   Ibid., 21 October 1868.
47   Bidwell, *Diaries,* 6 January 1870.
48   *Record,* 2 November 1861.
49   Ibid., 24 January 1868, 22 January 1870.
50   Stilson, 3 July 1869.
51   Wood's investment relationship with tough negotiator Woodman emerges in correspondence on financial matters between Wood in Pennsylvania and Harry Hallet in Chico. This correspondence was saved by a descendant who gave it to this author, who then donated it to SCML.
52   George Wood to Henry Hallet, 25 February 1872, property of Betty Given who allowed its use. Stilson expressed regret about store closings. His sense of personal relief at still surviving while others failed comes through in his entries. Stilson, 3 July 1869, 5 March 1870.
53   Correspondence, Wood and Hallet, 25 February 1872.
54   Ibid., 25 February, 9 June 1872.
55   Ibid., 27 December 1872.
56   *Enterprise,* 17 April 1868, 11 February 1872. Caroline Wood died a terrible death that started with facial cancer. She is buried in a marginal site in the Pioneer Section of the Chico Cemetery; someone provided a dignified headstone.
57   *Courant,* 5 March 1870.
58   Cf. *Butte Record* v. *Enterprise Record* coverage of Humboldt Road's implications for Oroville and Chico, 1883-1885.

Chapter 5

1   *Record,* 2 October 1862.
2   Deed Records, Butte County Recorder's Office, Oroville, CA. The property passed from Dr. J. B. Smith by Sheriff's sale to Tormey and from there to J. R. Woollen, from whom the Chapmans bought it.
3   *Record,* 2, 15 February 1862.
4   Ibid., 1, 8, 19, 22 February 1862.
5   Ibid. Coverage represents the dispute only from Oroville's perspective. In 1862 no Chico newspaper was being published. The sources of Chico's dissatisfaction in 1862 are inferred here from claims published in the *Courant* in 1865.
6   Ibid., 1860-1861, 8 March 1862, 21 January 1865.
7   *Courant,* 11 March 1866.
8   Ibid.
9   Ibid.
10   See chapter 3.
11   *Courant,* 6 January 1866; *Record,* April 1861.
12   Wells and Chambers, 278; Stilson, 3 May 1866.
13   Stilson, 26 January 1864.
14   In 1876 Chico's first Congregationalist church won general support from other denominations because it accepted the poor, that is, those who could not afford the pew rents that Methodists and Presbyterians charged. Cf. George Wood to Henry Hallet, Hallet-Wood file, SCML.
15   Stilson, 12 January 1864.
16   Cross, *Financing an Enterprise,* vol. 1; *Courant,* 26 April 1868, "Three steamers a

week can't take the wheat as fast as it can arrive at the Landing."

17 McGowan, vol. 1, 223; Hunt, 191.

18 *Courant*, 15 November, 13 December 1867. On silk culture and experiments with mulberry trees, see *Courant* 15 March, 6 September 1867. *Enterprise*, 30 July 1941.

19 *Courant*, 22-23 November 1866.

20 Ibid., 21 July 1866.

21 Ibid., 14 June 1867.

22 Ibid, n.d.

23 Susan Wiley Book, "The Chinese in Butte County, 1860-1920" (MA thesis, California State University, 1974), 85.

24 *Courant*, 23 August 1867, 19 June 1868; *Record*, 29 July 1876; *Enterprise*, 26 June 1869, 9 July 1870; *Courant*, 10 July 1870; Cf. *Butte County, California: Illustrations* (Oakland, CA: Smith and Eliott, 1877).

25 See chapter 14 for Chapman's service on the State Prison Commission.

26 The land was between Chestnut and Hazel, from Big Chico Creek south to Fifth Street.

27 *Record*, 29 July 1876; *Enterprise*, 26 June 1869, 9 July 1870; *Courant*, 10 July 1870; Cf. *Butte County, California: Illustrations* (Oakland, CA: Smith and Eliott, 1877).

28 *Stilson Diaries*, April 8, 1868.

29 Ibid., 14 June 1867; Ralph J. Roske, *Everyman's Eden: A History of California* (New York: Macmillan, 1968), 414. Later in the century the Hearsts built a home near Oroville but made little use of it before they sold it.

30 *Enterprise*, 9 July 1870; John S. Waterland, "The John Waterland Historical Articles" *Enterprise; Courant*, 10 July 1870.

31 Originally built in 1870, it was rebuilt in 1892 and is still in use today. In 1987 it was placed on the National Register of Historic Places as the Southern Pacific Depot.

32 The Oroville-Shasta Road was the main north-south highway through the Sacramento Valley (now Interstate 5). The Humboldt Road was a route from the Valley into the Sierra Nevada Mountains.

33 Wells and Chambers, 1881 ed., 183.

34 *Enterprise*, 29 November 1872.

35 *Record*, 25 October 1879.

36 *Courant*, 10 June, 10 July 1868.

37 Jones & Reilly, former Suydam & Jones, was at the southwest corner of Main and Front (now First) streets.

38 *Courant*, 10 May 1868.

39 *Enterprise*, 24 February 1872.

40 Ibid., 27 August, 22 October 1870, 6 January, 24 February 1872, 24 January 1873; Wells and Chambers, 224-25.

41 *Enterprise*, 10 February 1872; Waterland, 21 July 1935.

42 Ibid. The first trustees were John Kempf, Charles Pond, Benjamin Allen, W. K. Springer, city attorney A. J. Gifford, treasurer Charles Faulkner, night watchmen B. F. True and W. A. Taylor.

43 Letter to this author, undated.

44 This subject is more fully explored in chapter 10. In addition, this author and others treat different aspects of the problem in publications cited there.

Chapter 6

1 Sarah Chapman, *Diary*, 1899, unpublished. Typescript by Larry V. Richardson. The original was in the possession of Mildred Forester, Paradise, CA, and subsequently burned. Copy available in SCML.

2   The inscription reads: "Mrs. Sarah A. Chapman/Presented by A. H. Chapman, March 27, 1858." This author is now the owner. Sarah Josepha Hale, *The Ladies New Book of Cookery*, 5th ed. (New York: Sheldon Blakeman and Co., 1852).

3   This impression and others throughout are based on reading Chico newspapers published in post-Civil War Chico four times over four decades.

4   Stilson, September through November 1863.

5   Sara Chapman. Sarah's entries speak of her black clothing several months after her husband's 1899 death. The diary also speaks of a child's funeral. Correspondence, Hetty Hallet to Henry Hallet, February 1869, property of Hallet family member Betty Given, Sacramento, CA.

6   Edith Sommer was born in March 1878 and died in February 1882. Her brother was born in 1883 and died in 1886. C. J. Sommers, 50, died in 1895, leaving his wife Wilhemina Pratt Sommers to raise their daughter Helen Sommers (Gage).

7   *Courant,* 20 October 1866.

8   United States Census, 1870, Butte County, Chico Twp., CA.

9   Sarah Chapman. The poem "The Old Packing Boxes" captures the pastor's problem: "How dear to my heart are the old packing boxes/Piled out of the way in the loft in the shed/Infested with spiders and broidered with cobwebs/Serenely they wait for the verdict of Conference/Undisturbed by the fiat "Go forth" or "Go back"/As the days hasten on for the annual flitting/When the Methodist minister is ordered to pack/The old wooden boxes, the dust covered boxes/The iron bound boxes the preacher must pack./How often when Conference is over we hasten/To pull down the boxes and brush off the dust/And take up the carpets and take down the curtains/And wrap up the dishes, for pack up we must,/Ah, me! Who can tell of the work and the worry/The din and confusion from morning to night/The rush and the whirl, til a well-ordered household/Has lost its headquarters, demoralized quite/The old wooden boxes, the iron bound boxes/The old packing boxes all ready for flight," Mrs. E. M. McKiben, in Anita Laney, "Marysville Methodist Episcopal Church, The Critical Years, 1850-1864," *The* [Methodist] *News Bulletin* 13, no. 4 (1934).

10 Edna Hollenbeck, *Family History* (unpublished), family scrapbooks of Joan and John R. Robinson, Chico.

11 Ibid., The Chico press sometimes covered church controversies, one of which will be discussed later.

12 *Record,* 1 April 1865.

13 *Courant,* 27 March 1868.

14 Ibid., 10 April 1868.

15 Annie E. Kennedy to John Bidwell, 27 August 1867, in Chad Hoopes, *What Makes a Man: The Annie E. Kennedy and John Bidwell Letters: 1866-1868* (Fresno: California Valley Publishers, 1973).

16 *Courant,* 27 March, 27 April 1868; Wells and Chambers, 289. Some of Bidwell's contributions to the Methodists were quite generous.

17 *Enterprise,* 25 July 1873.

18 Hubbart, 43; Sidney E. Ahlstrom, *A Religious History of the American People* (New Haven: Yale University, 1972), 437-39; Marjorie Pingrey, *1858-1979: Centennial Plus Twenty* (Chico: Trinity United Methodist Church, 1979); C. V. Anthony, *Fifty Years of Methodism: A History of the Methodist Episcopal Church: 1847-1897* (San Francisco: Methodist Books Concern, 1901).

19 Records, Archives of Trinity United Methodist Church.

20 *Enterprise,* 21 July 1886.

21 His investor status emerges in correspondence from Pennsylvania with Henry Hallet, his son-in-law in Chico, regarding financial concerns in Chico.

Correspondence was saved by family members, then given to Michele Shover, who gave it to SCML.

22 Mansfield, 624.
23 Henry David Thoreau, *Walden and Other Writings* (New York: Modern Library, 1950), 721.
24 17 October 1873; *Courant*, 28 February, 8 May 1868.
25 *Enterprise*, 3 July 1869.
26 *Courant*, 2, 3 October 1868.
27 Ibid., 8 May 1868; *Enterprise*, 7 April 1868.
28 Tax Rolls, Chico Twp., Butte County, CA, Assessor's Office, Oroville, CA; Sara Chapman.
29 Tax records, Chico Twp., Butte County, 1862-1869.
30 Lydia Steward to *Enterprise*, 3 February 1986.
31 John Bidwell to Annie Bidwell, n.d., SCML.
32 This, of course, is a chancy speculation, but too tempting to resist. It reflects an informal practice noted by George Packer in *Our Man: Richard Holbrooke and the End of the American Century* (New York: Knopf, 2019), 274: "…. Holbrooke had been pursuing her for a long time, if only in his mind. He kept a list of their encounters." The author here also made such entries in her own diaries.
33 *Courant*, 26, 27 December 1865; Stilson, 14 January 1865.
34 Stilson, 29 November 1864.
35 Author's interview with Marjorie Pingrey, Trinity United Methodist Church, April 1981. The baby was Marguerite Pingrey McPhee. References to Sarah Chapman's sociability and menu are based on her own diary and Charles Stilson's 1860s diaries.
36 Ibid., 13 March, 6 November 1868, 12 June 1869; Bidwell, 25 November 1868; Rolle, 344.

Chapter 7

1 *Record*, 23 August 1867, 29 July 1868.
2 *Courant*, 23 August 1867, 19 June 1868. The lots were between Chestnut and Hazel streets, from Front Street south to Fifth Street.
3 Deed, Woollen to Chapman, 20 June 1871, Records Office, Butte County, Oroville, CA; Parcel map, Chapman's Addition, Butte County Recorder's Office, 1871; *Enterprise*, 28 January 1871, 15 November 1881.
4 However, the new house the Chapmans built there in 1877 was long and rectangular and faced Chapman Street. Its landscaped grounds comprised the entire block around it and to the north between that block and Little Chico Creek. On the creekside their grounds extended east approximately from the Oroville-Shasta Road (Park Avenue) to Mulberry Street.
5 Shover, "The Little Chapman Mansion: The House and Its People," *Exploring Chico's Past* (Xlibis, 2005).
6 George Stewart, *The American Trail* (New York: McGraw-Hill, 1962), 303.
7 Andrew Jackson Downing, *Victorian Cottage Residences* (New York: Vintage, 1881).
8 Hannah Borgeson, "A Cottage in the Rhine Style": A Downing and Vaux Residential Design in New Windsor, New York (New York: City College of New York, 2003), 174-75.
9 Tax Records, 1870-1871, Chico Twp., Butte County, CA.
10 Charlotte Hallet Minderman, "Chico's Past Remembered on 100th Birthday" [clipping], *Enterprise*, c. 1977, property of Betty Given who allowed this author to use it.

11 *Enterprise,* 10 December 1870.
12 *Enterprise,* 4 June, 15 August 1870, 15, 18 November 1881; *Enterprise,* February 1936.
13 Ibid., 22, 28 January 1870, 14 October, 28 January 1871.
14 Stilson, 29 March, 1 April, 26-29 June 1871.
15 *Enterprise,* 1, 14 January 1871; Obituary, George Dorn, undated, unsourced, Bertha Lee's scrapbook, property of Mary Hanson, Chico, CA.
16 Ibid., 14 May 1870.
17 Ibid., 6 December 1872; Walter M. Fisher, *The Californians* (London: Macmillan and Co., 1876), 163; Enterprise, 4 December 1876.
18 *Enterprise,* 25 June 1874.
19 Ibid., 14 May, 3, 6, 10 September 1870, 1 August 1873, 4 April 1874; W. H. Hutchinson, *California Heritage: A History of Northern California Lumbering* (Santa Cruz: The Forest History Society, 1974), 10-12; Mansfield, 920-21.
20 Thoreau, *Selected Writings,* 713.
21 *Enterprise,* 5, 14 May, 15 November 1870, 7 August 1873, 21 August 1874; McGowan, 343-44.
22 Ibid., 14 May, 5 November 1870, 2 February 1873.
23 Ibid., 2 February 1873.
24 Ibid., 7 August 1873.
25 Ibid., 10 December 1870.
26 Ibid., 24 February, 28 August, 6, 17, 20 October 1872, 17, 24 January 1873, 10 March, 23 July, 3 September 1875, 2 June 1876.
27 Thomas R. Cox, *Mills and Markets: A History of the Pacific Coast Lumber Company to 1900* (Seattle: University of Washington Press, 1974), 114.
28 *Record,* 5 April 1875; *Enterprise,* 19 March 1886.
29 *Enterprise,* 22 May 1874; W. H. Hutchinson, *California Heritage: A History of Northern California Lumbering* (Santa Cruz: The Forest History Society, Inc., 1974), 7; Cox, 132.
30 *Enterprise,* 1 November, 1872, 2 June 1876; Hutchinson, *California Heritage,* 2-34. The late CSUC professor of history W. H. Hutchinson told the author that he did not include Chapman & McKay in this essay because he was not aware of it as an ongoing independent lumber operation when Sierra Flume & Lumber assembled its timberlands. He said he assumed there were no important lumber holdings across Butte Creek from the lumber company's land.
31 *Enterprise,* 3 March 1871, 15, 22 May 1874; *Record,* 14 August, 10 October 1875, 27 May 1876, 21 November 1879.
32 Ibid., 7 January, 23 March 1871, 30 January 1872. This was the first of several Bidwell avenues. After Chapmantown became part of Chico in 1918, the streets were numbered and it became East Twelfth Street. The current Bidwell Avenue runs along Big Chico Creek.
33 Charles Aldini and Brent Owen, "Chapmantown Master Plan" (unpublished term paper for the late Dr. Margaret Trussell, Department of Geography, CSUC, n.d.). The paper includes a record of the earliest Chapmantown purchases, but the map and information on A. H. Chapman are flawed. The term Chapmantown referred to Chapman's subdivision in the 1870s and continued to do so through the end of the nineteenth century. At that time, an unincorporated area east of Chapman's Addition was hastily developed without planning. Although it was originally called Boucher's Addition, the name Chapmantown replaced it as housing spread over it. The only focus in this book is Chapman's original subdivision, as of November 7, 1873.
34 *Enterprise* 27 September, 1 November 1872.
35 Ibid., 7 January, 23 March 1871; 30 January 1872.

36 Ibid., 13 March 1868.
37 Ibid., 27 December 1872.
38 Ibid., 24 February 1873; Bidwell, *Diaries*, 5 March 1873.
39 *Record,* 29 July 1876.
40 Ibid., September 19, 1873.

Chapter 8

1 *Enterprise*, 6 February 1874.
2 Ibid., 14 August 1874.
3 Ibid., 26 June 1869, 9 July 1870; *Courant*, 10 July 1870.
4 Mansfield, 229.
5 *Enterprise*, 3 April, 10 July, 2, 28 October 1874.
6 Ibid., 27 February, 6 April 1874.
7 Ibid., 20 April 1874; Bidwell, *Diaries*, 19 March 1874.
8 Ibid., 27 February, 6 April 1874; *Record*, 15 April 1875.
9 *Enterprise*, 3 July 1875.
10 Alexis de Tocqueville, *Democracy in America* (New York: Vintage, 1945), 209. On this subject, see Shover, "John Bidwell: A Reconsideration," in *Exploring Chico's Past.*
11 Chico School Trustee Minutes, August 1874. The late John Nopel of Chico led me to these records which the Chico Unified School District allowed me to copy. His gift to me of a copy of Augustus H. Chapman's obituary provoked my initial perception that Chico's nineteenth century was more complex, significant and interesting than existing accounts had represented.
12 Wells and Chambers, 277.
13 A major Bidwell theme in his autobiographical *Dictation* is his cool temperament in the face of provocations, 27 June 1874. Later chapters reveal Bidwell's successful retaliation against Chapman in the 1880s.
14 For an extended account on this, see Shover, *Standoff*, chapters 1-2. The Oroville newspaper reflects such concerns.
15 *Enterprise*, 14 August 1874.
16 Ibid.
17 *Record*, 17 October 1874, 10 July 1875; Wells and Chambers, 278-79.
18 *Enterprise*, 14 August 1874.
19 *Record*, 17 October 1874. In the twentieth century the school was demolished due to earthquake concerns. However, the demolition proved difficult because the iron rods referred to here had made the walls and roof so sturdy.
20 *Enterprise*, 28 January 1871; Bidwell, *Diaries*, 4 January 1871, 2 July 1875; *Record,* 5 February 1876, 5 July 1879.
21 *Record,* 10 July 1875, 3 December 1876.
22 Warren Nelson, interview with the author, late 1970s. The late Warren Nelson was an Oakdale School graduate who told this author about his after-school work cleaning the blackboards and oiling the floors.
23 Mrs. Louis Olker, interview with the author, January 1980; *Enterprise*, 5 April 1872, 5 April 1877.
24 *Courant*, October 2, 1874; *Enterprise*, 18-19 January 1872, 14 August 1874; Bidwell, *Diaries*, January 4, 1869.
25 *Enterprise*, 6 March, 10 April 1874.
26 *Enterprise*, 1 January 1875. The arson information is from the fall 1874 editions of the *Enterprise* and *Record*.
27 It would be years before Chico gained residents' support for a public high school.

28 J. M. Woodman, *God in Nature and Revelation* (Chico: Butte Record Press, 1880). This limited edition book, in the author's collection, was the formal statement of his ideas.

29 *Record*, 20, 24 April, 8 May 1875; *Enterprise*, 23 July 1875.

30 *Enterprise*, 23 July, 27 August 1875.

31 Wells and Chambers, 289-91, 304-5; Melinda Button, "Reverend Jesse Wood: Coming the Sacred and Secular Worlds of Late Nineteenth Century Butte County, California," *Diggins*, vol. 53 (Spring 2009), 13-16.

32 *Enterprise*, 23 July 1875.

33 Ibid., 27 August 1875.

34 No data are known that explain the source of the Winthrop name.

35 Information from Curtis family descendants.

36 *Enterprise*, 23 July, 27 August 1875; *Record*, 30 January 1874, 6 February, 19 March 1875, 7 March, 31 July 1876. Other investors included Dr. C. C. Mason, banker W. S. Heath, John Bidwell and one of his brothers. Bidwell, *Diaries*, 23 February 1876.

37 Gordon Wood, "Revolutionary Shoppers," in *New York Review of Books*, vol. 51 (10 June 2004), 26. Put another way: The market system produced need for credit and credit could only be established by the display of wealth. Without a modern credit and check system, credit was determined by town talk, which depended on people's observations. Bram Dijkstra, *Idols of Perversity* (New York: Oxford University Press, 1986), 7.

38 The author's gravesite is in this section. She checked first for reassurance the Edgar Slough would not reappear. She was told the water had been diverted to Little Chico Creek, over Chapman's objections, because townspeople were afraid that diverting the slough water to Big Chico Creek could cause flooding downtown.

39 *Enterprise*, 14 March 1873, 27 August, 3, 10, 17, 24 September 1875.

40 Ibid., 7 July 1876; *Record*, 29 July 1876.

41 *Record*, 21 February 1874; *Enterprise*, 7 July 1876.

42 Ibid.; Royce Delmatier, Clarence McIntosh and Earl G. Waters, *The Rumble of California Politics, 1848-1970* (New York: John Wiley and Sons, 1970), chapter 2; Hunt, 367-421; JBCBL, chapter 24, 367-69; McGowan, 336-69.

43 Wells and Chambers, 175; McGowan, 337. For instance, according to Chico's Republican *Enterprise*, 6 March 1877, "We … have all the time had full faith that though corruption had insidiously crept into our organization, that although some bad and designing men had prostituted the power and privileges bestowed upon them by a confiding people and had made the Republican principles the stepping stone and means for the accomplishment of base friends and iniquitous wrongs the party has the ability and spirit to correct its problems."

44 *Enterprise*, 17 November 1876.

45 *Record*, 11 November 1876; Mansfield, 395.

46 The vote was 1,665 for Hayes, 1,635 for Tilden. Bidwell *Diaries*, 22 February 1876.

47 *Enterprise*, 10, 17 November 1876, 6 March 1877; McGowan, 337.

48 *Enterprise*, 17 August 1877; *Record*, 31 October 1877.; Author's interview with Elsa Boyston Brooks who lived there with her family as a child, 27 February 1980; Sanford Insurance maps, courtesy of John Gallardo of the Chico Heritage Association. On county records this Chapman house was called "The Chapman Place." Township residents probably it called the Chapman Mansion because their former handsome, but smaller, farm house was still remembered in the 1980s as the "Little Chapman Mansion." Several early twentieth-century Chico homes were known as the "X Mansion." The author learned this about the Chapman house from a very elderly couple referred to her by a descendant of the Chico Ice House owners. The author called on the couple because they once worked there with Gus

Chapman Jr. They told the author, and Larry V. Richardson confirmed, that all three had known the smaller house still at the northeast corner of East Twelfth and Nelson streets as the Little Chapman Mansion. In this case the title has to do with history, not architecture.

49   *Record*, 4 May, June 1878. The slough was filled in later and the water diverted to Little Chico Creek.

50   *Enterprise*, 1 February, 5 November 1875.

Chapter 9

1   *Enterprise*, 1 February, 1878; Mansfield, 287.

2   *Record*, 26-27 May 1876; *Enterprise*, 2 June 1876.

3   *Enterprise*, 27 May, 13 December 1876.

4   Ibid., 21 August 1874; Cf. *Record*, 23 February 1936.

5   *Mansfield*, 283-84.

6   Authors on the development of Ridge lumber companies enthuse about the flumes, but do not identify the problems they presented.

7   Hutchinson, *California Heritage*, 13, 15-16. "The flume property has been looked on as a great source of profit but the expense of building it through the canyons, and keeping it in repair after it was built, has cost them more than the primitive method of teaming lumber from the mills to the Valley," *Record*, 21 February, 24 July, 21 December, 1879.

8   *Enterprise*, 29 October 1875, 12 May 1876.

9   Ibid., 31 January 1876, 14, 26 January 1887.

10   Fisher, *The Californians*.

11   Random items which identify Chapman employees consistently indicated Anglo-Saxon names. In addition, the anti-Chinese never included Chapman among employers of Chinese.

12   *Enterprise*, 3 February 1876.

13   For general coverage of the Order of Caucasians's development see Shover, *Exploring Chico's Past*, although it does not include the complete bibliography and research data files. Those are available in the Michele Shover Collection on Chinese in Chico, SCML. A note of caution, however. Jean Pfaelzer's *Driven Out: The Forgotten War Against Chinese Americans* is a widely publicized and much praised reconstruction published in 2007 which emphasizes the Chico events. Its first edition contained significant errors which this author pointed out to Ms. Pfaelzer for corrections in later additions.

14   *Record*, 13 May, 24 June, 1 July, 16 December 1876, 27 January, 10 February 1877. No Chicoans' participation appeared in their obituaries or historical biographies in county histories or memoirs of the period. The broad generalization is based on those and a close review of Chico newspapers and documents, including the Order of Caucasians's minutes book, SCML. By 1918, when Mansfield's work appeared, anti-Chinese sentiment remained strong but it was no longer a point of honor or pride to have taken any part in the anti-Chinese campaigns. It is possible, in some cases, that an individual attended the anti-Chinese meetings without formally joining the association. The teachers were Hiram Batchelder, Richard De Lancie and Orlando Swain. The lawyers included Hiram Ashbrook, J. A. Clark, John T. Daly and Alexander P. Waugh. Carpenters Hayden Jones and Schuyler Walker (who remodeled Chapman's house) were members. Merchants included B. B. Baker, Martin Loy, Andrew Hallet, John Kempf, Charles Ball, William Waterland and Elias Findley. Additional names include publisher George Crosette, County Recorder Wm. Armstrong, Odd Fellows President W. R. Williams

and Congregational Church pastor Lysander Dickerman. George Dorn attended an anti-Chinese meeting and became an anti-Chinese leader in the 1880s.

15   Ibid., 23 September, 11 November 1876. The following chapter, which treats the events leading up to and surrounding the Lemm Ranch murders, appears in a much fuller account in several essays by this author in *Exploring Chico's Past*.

Chapter 10

1   Ben True was subsequently run out of Chico by the anti-Chinese and became a Sacramento railroad policeman.

2   Blacks who lived across from Old Chinatown worked with the Chinese to dowse the flames. Cf. Shover, "Climbing the Slippery Slope," in *Exploring Chico's Past*.

3   For a fuller examination of these events, see "The Lemm Ranch Murders" in Shover, *Exploring Chico's Past* and other sources mentioned in chapter 9. For additional research, find additional sources in SCML. Local and Sacramento newspapers are the principle sources for this chapter unless otherwise indicated. A recent publication James A. Dimmit, *The Chico Police Department: The First One Hundred Years* (Sacramento: privately published, 2020) is particularly useful because it includes testimony related to arrests and incarceration before those charged were sent to Oroville to trial.

4   *Record*, 17 March 1877.

5   Cf. Shover, *Exploring Chico's Past*.

6   *Enterprise*, 15 September 1960. This is the only source which identifies who paid for the detectives. It gains credibility in light of the careful avoidance in March 1878 coverage about who provided the outside help. The Chinese Six Companies' role explains why the two men encountered such resentment for their work in Chico. The source does say that the Citizens' Committee welcomed them and that Bidwell rewarded the Post Office's Fred Radcliffe who spotted the letters. Cf. *Record*, 3 June 1877.

7   Ibid., 24 March 1877.

8   *Record*, 31 March 1877.

9   Ibid., 16, 21, 27 April 1877.

10   Ibid., 23, 28 April 1877; *Oroville Mercury*, 27 April 1877.

Chapter 11

1   A related treatment of this subject appears in Daniel Cornford, "The California Workingmen's Party in Humboldt County," *California History* (June, 1987), 131-57. The author thanks professor of history Michael Magliari of CSUC for his helpful suggestions on this chapter.

2   Alexander Keysaar, *Out of Work: The First Century of Unemployment in Massachusetts* (New York: Cambridge University Press, 1986), passim. Keysaar was working on this book when he visited Chico for research. Henry George, *Progress and Poverty* (New York: Appleton, 1881).

3   A competing party, "The Janissaries of Light," also tried to get underway in Chico in a meeting at the Third and Ivy home of brick mason Evan Knapp. A Chico resident since the 1860s, he built ten of the downtown's underground water cisterns. Its leader, Mrs. B. H. Chamberlain, called for a "working men and women's Order ... with no distinction between the sexes, considering women as moral and capable, and therefore as worthy as men." There was no response sufficient to warrant additional meetings. *Record*, 23 February 1877.

4   Ibid.; *Record*, 2 February 1878.
5   Ibid.; *Great Register*, Butte County, California, SCML; Cf. Alexander Saxton, *The Indispensable Enemy: Labor and the Anti-Chinese Movement* (Berkeley: University of California Press, 1971), 71. He treats the San Francisco boot- and shoemakers' conflict with the Chinese.
6   *Record*, 23 March 1878.
7   *Enterprise*, 2 April 1883, 14 February 1888.
8   Neil Larry Shumsky, *The Evolution of Political Protest and the Workingmen's Party of California* (Columbus: Ohio State University Press), 208.
9   Ibid., *Record*, 29 March 1878, 26 April 1879.
10   *Record*, 4 October 1879.
11   Ibid., 18 May 1878.
12   Ibid., 2 April 1883, 14 February 1888.
13   Ibid., 17 May 1878.
14   One of George Crosette's young sons died of typhoid within a week of the convention and a second, five days later. Gravestones, Chico Cemetery.
15   Ibid., 17 May 1878.
16   The information about Dr. Burwell is from the Bertha Lee obituary scrapbook.
17   *Record*, 18 May 1878.
18   Ibid.
19   Ibid.
20   *Enterprise*, 8 June 1878.
21   Quoted in the *Enterprise*, 24 May 1878.
22   Ibid., 8 June 1878.
23   *Record*, 29 June 1878.

Chapter 12

1   Mansfield.
2   *Record*, 14 September 1878. Other information not documented in this chapter comes from the *Record* or the *Enterprise* for the time addressed here.
3   E. B. Willis and P. K. Stockton, *Debates and Proceedings of the State Constitutional Convention of the State of California*, 3 vols. (Sacramento State Office, 1880, 1881), chapter 3; Carl Brent Swisher, *Motivation and Political Technique in the California State Constitutional Convention: 1878-1879* (Claremont, CA: Pomona College, 1936), 27-32.
4   Ibid.; Delmatier et al., chapter 3; Vivian and Waldron; Bancroft, vol. 7, 422ff.; Willis, vol. 1, 37.
5   Ibid.; Willis and Stockton, 1298; *Record*, 26 October 1878.
6   Waldron and Vivian, passim; Willis and Stockton, vol. 1, 37, 47, 58; *Record*, 2 November 1876.
7   Willis and Stockton, 1399.
8   Chapman supported Mrs. Woodman for superintendent of schools. He would send his only daughter across the country to attend Mount Holyoke College.
9   Willis and Stockton, 1399; Bancroft, vol. 7, 391-92; *Record*, 2 November 1878.
10   Rolle, 423-24.
11   *Enterprise*, 11 May 1876.
12   The water and gas companies' president and general superintendent was Chapman. Board members were Charles Faulkner, George Dorn, John Gilkyson and E. Rose.
13   *Enterprise*, 21, 29 June 1878.
14   *Record*, 8 March 1879.

15   *Enterprise*, 21 March 1879; Butte County Deed Book 5, 508.
16   Ibid., 20 June 1879.
17   Bancroft, vol. 7, 400.
18   Willis and Stockton, 153, 156-57.
19   *Record*, 26 April 1879.
20   Ibid., 4 April 1879.
21   Ibid., 3 May 1879. Once Beerstecher was elected, John Bidwell entertained him with the other railroad commissioners as they passed through Chico.
22   Ibid.
23   Ibid.
24   Delmatier et al., chapter 3.
25   Wells and Chambers, 1881 ed., 173.
26   Richard J. Orsi, "Selling The Golden State: A Study of Boosterism in Nineteenth Century California" (unpublished PhD diss., University of Wisconsin, Madison, 1973), 28.
27   Quoted in Swisher, 110; Theodore H. Hittel, *History of California* (San Francisco: S. J. Stone & Co., 1898), 647-48.
28   Over time, courts cleared out sections troublesome to the moneyed. The 1880 legislature made similar efforts. Bancroft, vol. 24, 411, 472.

Chapter 13

1   Swisher, 47-48; Bancroft, vol. 5, 410-11; Hittell, 617-18, 649; H. Brett Melendy and Benjamin F. Gilbert, *The Governors of California* (Georgetown, CA: Talisman Press, 1965), 189-96; James Lenhoff, "From Sailor Boy to Senator," *Diggins*, vol. 24 (Summer 1980), 27-50; *Record*, 12, 26 July 1879; Bancroft, vol. 7, 410-11.
2   *Record*, 21 June 1879.
3   Quoted in the *Oroville Mercury*, 20 June 1879.
4   Mansfield, 292-93.
5   Stilson, 1865 passim.
6   *Record*, 13 April 1922; Mansfield, 498.
7   *Enterprise*, September 1879.
8   Rolle, 387-88; *Record*, 28, 29 June 1879.
9   Enterprise, 18 July 1879. According to Wikipedia, the term "splice the mainbrace" originated "as an order for one of the most difficult emergency repair jobs aboard a sailing ship. It became a euphemism for authorized celebratory drinking afterward, and then the name of an order to grant the crew an extra ration of rum...."
10   Ibid., 18 July 1879.
11   Ibid., 29 August, 1879.
12   Ibid.
13   Malcolm Thomas and Jennifer Grimmett, *Women in Protest: 1800-1850* (New York: St. Martin's Press, 1982).
14   *San Francisco Chronicle*, 21 August 1879.
15   *Record*, 23 August 1879; *Oakland Tribune*, 19 February 1883.
16   Ibid.
17   Ibid.
18   *Enterprise*, 22 August 1879.
19   *Record*, 23 August 1879.
20   Ibid.
21   *San Francisco Chronicle*, 21 August 1879.
22   *Enterprise*, 22 August 1879.

23 *Record*, 30 August 1879.
24 *Enterprise*, 12 September 1879. The vote count here and elsewhere cite the Chico vote after the final tally. *Enterprise*, 6 September 1879.
25 Ibid.; *Record*, 6, 13, 20 September 1879.
26 *Record*, 12, 19 July 1879. It was unusual for the bank to make a mid-year assignment; this usually happened at its annual meeting each January.
27 *Enterprise*, 21 March 1879, 10 December 1880; Wells and Chambers, 227.
28 Vivian and Waldron.

Chapter 14

1   *Enterprise*, 26 July 1881.
2   Ibid., 18 December 1881.
3   *Record*, 31, January 1881.
4   Ibid. In May 1879 a Republican set of policy priorities mentioned several others without any mention of prison reform. Winfield Davis, *History of Political Conventions in California: 1842-1892* (Sacramento: California State Library, 1893), 405-6; Hubert Howe Bancroft, *History of California*, vol. 28 (San Francisco: History Publishing Co, 1890), 413-26. At San Quentin in 1875 three contractors employed 421 convicts. The remaining 1,500 prisoners had no work elsewhere. This was still the case when the Chapman board of directors and Warden Ames tackled the situation. Shelly Bookspan, *A Germ of Goodness: The California State Prison System, 1851-1914* (Lincoln: University of Nevada Press, 1991), 34; Theodore H. Hittell, *The History of California* (San Francisco: N. J. Stone Co., 1898), 630.
5   Jackson County, Michigan, Wikipedia.
6   *San Francisco Chronicle*, 3 January 1984.
7   *Record*, 12 December 1879.
8   *Enterprise*, 18 December 1881.
9   Ibid., 26 July 1881.
10 Vivian and Waldron.
11 *Sacramento Bee*, Inauguration, January 1880.
12 Ibid., 1-5 January 1880; Melendy and Gilbert, 191-92; Hittell, 630, 664-74; Davis, 405-8. Grain was shipped on sailing ships because coal was too expensive to send on steam ships around the Horn. Dr. Edgar C. Smith, "Gunny Sacks Galore," *California Territorial Quarterly*, no. 52 (Winter 2002), 18-36. This valuable article erroneously attributes the initiation of prison grain-sack production to Warden Ames. The warden was appointed after Governor Perkins announced his plan and brought in Augustus Chapman to implement it. Chapman's Prison Commission appointed Ames as the plan went underway.
13 *Record*, 15 November 1879, 14 February 1880; *Enterprise*, 23 January 1879.
14 Bidwell, *Diaries*, 7 April 1880.
15 *Record*, 23 August 1880.
16 Ibid., 31 January 1880; Bookspan, 41-3.
17 Ibid.
18 Ibid., 31 January, 7, 14 February 1880.
19 Bancroft, vol. 18, 413-26; *Enterprise*, 3 January, 25 March, 20 May, 1880.
20 *Enterprise*, 29 May 1880.
21 Ibid., 5 July 1880.
22 Ibid., 29 June 1880.
23 Ibid., 22 October 1880; Wells and Chambers, 259-60.
24 *Enterprise*, 29 June 1880.
25 *First Annual Report of the State Board of Prisons Directors*, Appendix to the Journals

of the Senate and Assembly, 24th session, vol. 2 (Sacramento: State printing Office, 1881), 6-11, CSA.

26 *Enterprise*, 15 July 1881.
27 *Enterprise*, 3, 31 March 1881, 12 May 1882.
28 Ibid., 11 March, 9 April, 28 October, 6 December 1881; *Record*, 3 September 1881; *Second Annual Report of the State Board of Prison Directors*, June 30, 1881, Appendix to the Journals of the Senate and Assembly, 25th session, vol. 6 (Sacramento: State printing Office, 1883), CSA.
29 *Record*, 27 August 1881.
30 *Enterprise*, 8, 18, 22, 25 January, 25 February, 30 April, 21 May 1881.
31 *Record*, 9 April, 3 September 1881; *Enterprise*, 6 December, 11 March, 28 October 1881; *Second Annual Report*, 6-17.
32 Ibid., 3 September 1881.
33 *Second Annual Report*.
34 Ibid., 43-4.
35 Ibid., 7.
36 Ibid.

Chapter 15

1 Bicentennial message of Gov. George C. Perkins to the Legislature of the State of California, 25th sess., Sacramento, 1883, in Appendix and Journals A and S, 25th sess.
2 Mansfield, 1075-76.
3 *Enterprise*, 4 November 1881.
4 *Record*, 9 April 1881; David Lavender, *California: Land of New Beginnings* (New York: Harper and Row, 1972), 317-18.
5 Ibid.
6 Ibid., 4 November 1881.
7 Ibid., 2 April 1881.
8 Ibid., 30 March 1878, 3 October 1879.
9 Ibid.
10 Ibid., 2 April 1881.
11 Ibid., 31 March 1881.
12 Ibid., 2 April 1881.
13 Ibid., 7 May 1881.
14 Sierra Flume & Lumber Co. changed its name to Sierra Lumber Co. in 1879 due to a depression that started in 1876.
15 Big Chico Creek runs through then called Iron Canyon, located in Upper Bidwell Park.
16 Ibid., 9 April 1881.
17 Ibid., 7 May 1881.
18 Ibid., 14 May 1881; *Record*, 16 April 1881; Zion Moore, obituary, undated, Wesley Lee family scrapbook, property of Mary Hanson of Chico. Moore would later be elected as a town trustee.
19 Ibid., 21, 25, 28, May 1881.
20 *Enterprise*, 3, 4, May, 15 November 1881; *Record*, 27 August 1881.
21 *Record*, 6 August 1881.
22 *Second Annual Report*, 14-15. The date is December 1881 but the text covers the fiscal year ending January 1881.
23 Ibid.
24 Ibid.; Kevin Starr, *Americans and the California Dream* (Santa Barbara: Peregrine

Smith, 1981), 135-38; Robert Glass Cleland and Hardy Osgood, *March of Industry* (San Francisco: Powell Publishing, 1929), 414-15.

25 *Second Annual Report*, 19.

Chapter 16

1 *Enterprise*, 13 January 1882.
2 *Record*, 1 April 1882; *Enterprise*, 13 January 1882; Bidwell, *Diaries*, 11 April 1882.
3 *Third Annual Report of the State Board of Prison Directors*, Appendix to Journals of the Senate and Assembly, 25th sess., vol. 5 (Sacramento: State printing Office, 1883), 17, CSA; *Record*, 1 April 1882.
4 Ibid., 18. Chapman conducted his research at the following sites: Eastern Penitentiary of Pennsylvania; Illinois State Prison in Joliet; Elmira Reformatory, Sing Sing and Auburn State Prison in New York; New Jersey State Prison in Trenton; Detroit House of Corrections; Michigan State Prison in Jackson; Ohio State Prison in Columbus; Connecticut Prison in Wethersfield.
5 Ibid.
6 Ibid.
7 *Enterprise*, 12 May 1882.
8 Ibid., 13 January 1882.
9 *Record*, 14 October 1882.
10 *Oroville Mercury*, 10 April 1885.
11 Nancy Stewart, granddaughter of William Earll, conversation with this author. Mansfield, 1075-6; *Chico City Directory*, 1880.
12 *Enterprise*, 21 January 1881.
13 *Record*, 27 September 1884.
14 Dijbstra Bram, *Idols of Perversity: Fantasies of Female Evil in Fin-de-Siècle Culture* (New York: Oxford Press, 1986), 7.
15 *Record*, 14 October 1882.
16 *Enterprise*, 21 July 1882.

Chapter 17

1 Melendy and Gilbert; Shover, *California Standoff*, chapter 2; Bidwell, *Diaries*, 12 October 1880, 19 January, 12 October 1882, 19 January 1883, 13 September 1884, 28-29 April 1885.
2 Hittell, 465; "Biennial Message of Governor George C. Perkins to the California State Legislature," *Record*, 17 June 1882; Melendy and Gilbert, 208-9; *Report of the Special Commission of Inquiry into the General Administration of the State Prisons of California* (Sacramento: State Printing Office, 1881), 66.
3 Mansfield, 435.
4 *Enterprise*, 27 July 1880; *Record*, 17 June 1882.
5 *Second Annual Report*, December 1882, 12-13, 17.
6 *Record*, 3 March 1883.
7 Shelly Bookspan, *A Germ of Goodness: The California State Prison System, 1851-1944* (Lincoln: University of Nevada Press, 1991), 40-1. Bookspan assigns ultimate responsibility for these decisions to pressures from anti-Chinese forces. Certainly these were powerful but the prison issue evidence cited here indicates that old-fashioned partisanship was more significant. Cf. Hittell, 674-5.
8 *Sacramento Bee*, 22 May 1883.
9 *Record*, 19 May 1883.

10   Augustus A. Hart, Wikipedia, https://en.wikipedia.org/wiki/Augustus_L._Hart.

11   J. W. Woolridge, *History of the Sacramento Valley*, vol. 2 (Chicago: Pioneer Historical Publishing Co., 1931), 1279; *Record*, 4 November 1882, 13 June 1883; *Sacramento Bee*, 6 June 1883.

12   *Sacramento Bee*, 6-7 June 1883.

13   A. H. Chapman, will, 1883, SCML.

14   Ibid.; *Enterprise*, 2 March 1883.

15   *Record*, 3 June 1883.

16   *Sacramento Bee*, 5, 6, 13, 18 June, 10 July 1883.

17   Ibid., 22 May 1883.

18   Ibid., 27 June 1883; Zoeth Skinner Eldredge, *History of California*, vol. 3, 355.

19   *Record*, 19-20 June, 18 July, 3 August 1883.

20   The defenses Ames and Ellis made to these charges seem more substantive and credible than journalists or the public recognized at the moment. *San Francisco Chronicle*, 18 September 1883; *Sacramento Bee*, 10, 17, 28 June, 10, 28 July 1883; *Record*, 19-20, 28 June 1883.

21   *Sacramento Bee*, 13, 18 June 1883.

22   Ibid., 10 July 1883.

23   *Record*, 3 August 1883.

24   *Enterprise*, 2 March 1883; *Record*, 22 December 1883.

25   *Enterprise*, 27 February, 2 March, 1 September, 24, 1883; *Record*, 6 February, 25 August, 22 September, 1883, 21 November 1884, 8, 23 October 1885, 22 January 1886, 18 June 1887, 31 January 1899. The building still stands, although no longer as "a gift to the street." In the 1950s owners, determined to "modernize" it, stripped away its ornamentation, installed aluminum "slider" windows, and plastered over its brick. Despite such ravaging, the building's quiet dignity stands today.

26   John Bidwell, *Diaries*, 13 September 1883.

27   *Sacramento Bee*, 14 September 1883; Mansfield, 612; Tirey J. Ford, *California State Prisons: Their History, Development and Management* (San Francisco Star Press, 1910), 1-32; *Record*, 24 March , 10 July 1888.

28   *Record*, 22 September 1883.

29   *Sacramento Bee*, 14 September 1883; Mansfield, 612.

30   Ibid., 25 November 1885, 10 July 1886; *Oroville Mercury*, 24 May 1878. In 1886 W. C. Hendricks duplicated Chapman's tour of eastern prisons for the commission, albeit on a reduced scale. *Enterprise*, 22 January 1886; Lois McDonald, "William Chalmers Hendricks," *Diggins* 27-28 (Spring and Summer 1993; Fall and Winter, 1994), part 1, 3-50, part 2, 59-65. These are excellent articles, apart from some errors on the Prison Commission coverage.

31   Ford, 1-32; *Record*, 10 July, 24 March 1888; Edgar Smith, "Gunny Sacks Galore," *Glenn County Territorial Quarterly* 52 (Winter 2002), 33-6; Melendy and Gilbert, 195.

32   *First Annual Report*, 8; *Record*, 19 March 1887, 10 July 1888.

33   "The Night They Drove Old Dixie Down," Wikipedia, https://en.wikipedia.org/wiki/The_Night_They_Drove_Old_Dixie_Down.

34   Melendy and Gilbert, 195.

35   Edgar Smith, 33-6.

Chapter 18

1   *Sacramento Bee*, 14, 21 September, 27 October 1883.

2   *Record*, 18 May 1886.

3   *Enterprise,* 9 March, 21, 23 April, 5, 8 May, 12, 13, 28 July, 27 October 1883. The best comprehensive treatment is by Lois McDonald, "The Roads and Bridges of Butte

Creek Canyon," *Diggins* 38, no. 1-2 (1994), 30-8.

4   *Enterprise,* 21 September, 13 October, 1883, 8 May 1885.

5   Ibid., 2 June 1882, 19 January, 24 August 1883; Wells and Chambers, 1973 ed., 227.

6   Ibid. Chapman would not have let that information slip. They also reported the breakup of Hallet & Loy, an equally long-established firm. M. V. Loy left his furniture business for the lumber business.

7   *Record,* 14 July 1883; Butte County California Tax Records, 1882-1889, BCCML.

8   Ibid., 9 February, 21 September 1883.

9   Ibid., 12 October 1883; *Record,* 28 July 1883.

10 *Enterprise,* 10, 20, 23 April 1883; *Record,* 30 June, 21 July 1883.

11 *Record,* 30 November 1883.

12 Ibid., 24 November, 1 December 1883.

13 *Enterprise,* 30 November 1883.

14 Ibid., 1 December 1883.

15 *Record,* 13 October 1883.

16 *Enterprise,* 30 November 1883.

17 Ibid., 25 January 1884.

18 *Record,* 15 March 1884; *Enterprise,* 30 April 1884.

19 *Enterprise,* 1 July 1884.

20 Ibid., 10, 20, 27 February, 1, 8 May 1885.

21 Ibid., 13 October, 21 September 1883, 8 May 1885.

22 Ibid., 14 February, 23 April 1886.

23 Florence Styles, "*Carr Hill Road: Honey Run Covered Road and the Butte Creek Canyon Area,* in Lois Coleman and Mildred Forester, *Tailings of Butte Creek Canyon: 1833-1971* (Centerville, CA: Centerville Recreation and Historical Association, 1972), 73-6; *Record,* 24 May 1884; *Enterprise,* 3, 24 January 1988.

24 *Record,* 14 March, 21 April 1884; McDonald, *Annie Bidwell,* 83, 157, 161, 191-2.

25 Deed, 20 October 1884, Butte County Records Office, Butte County, CA; *Enterprise,* 24 May, 20 June, 22 August 1884.

26 *Enterprise,* 17 April 1885.

27 Ibid.

28 Bidwell, *Diaries,* 13 April 1885.

29 *Oroville Mercury,* 10 April 1885, courtesy of Mildred Forester; *Record,* 17 February, 10, 24 April 1885.

30 *Enterprise,* 9 July 1886.

31 Ibid., 28 July 1886. Nevertheless, the problem reappeared in 1887; the public response struck a plaintive note: "Gas and water are each good enough by themselves, but we want them separate."

32 Ibid., 17 April, 22 May 1885; Butte County California Tax Records, NCCML.

33 Butte County California Tax Records, 1884, NCCML.

34 Ibid., 1885.

Chapter 19

1   *Mansfield,* 1885 ed., 588.

2   *Enterprise,* 26 January, 13 February, 27 July 1878, 16 February, 26 April 1879, 19 November 1886.

3   Ibid., 18 May 1872, 14 February, 12 December 1873; United States Census, Butte Co., California, Chico Twp., 1880.

4   In this author's interviews with the late Sybil Gage Mathys and the late Mary Ethyl Robinson Amer, independent of one another, each mentioned the widow and the single woman. Margaret Ramsland mentioned the married woman in her book

about the Daniel Bidwell family, *The Other Bidwells* (Chico: privately published, 1972).

5 Larry V. Richardson to author, Richardson files, SCML.

6 A "pony" was a small glass used for alcoholic beverages. In the mining days, a pony in a Butte County saloon cost a pinch of gold. Florence D. Boyle, *Old Days in Butte* (Chico: ANCHR, 2006), 27; The 1880 federal census noted Gifford was "Disabled"; *Enterprise*, 15 December 1886; Bidwell, *Diaries*, 23 December 1878.

7 Cadet Record Card, Official Register of Officers and Cadets of the U.S. Military Academy, West Point, June 1877, supplied by Dorothy Rapp, archives technician, United States Military Academy (West Point); *Enterprise*, 29 June 1877. Jo D. Sproul and Bessie Sproul's sister Alice (1862-1943) would become principals of Chico's State Normal School.

8 Obituary, Jo D. Sproul, undated, unsourced, scrapbook of Bertha Lee, property of the late Mary Hanson.

9 *Enterprise*, Centennial edition, 1960, 9.

10 Dickerson allied with Chico's radical Workingmen who backed the violent wing of the anti-Chinese movement. For fuller information and sources, see Shover, "The Lemm Ranch Murders," in *Exploring Chico's Past*.

11 Bidwell, *Diaries*, 29 September 1885.

12 *Enterprise*, 27 March 1885.

13 *Record*, 29 August 1885.

14 This came from a brief mention in a newspaper item. This author could find no other information on the Triennial Commission. Recipients other years included C. C. Mason, Alexander Crew and Charles Stilson.

15 *Enterprise*, 17 January 1883; Mansfield, 573-4, 712.

16 Ibid., 29 January 1886.

17 Bidwell, *Diaries*, 13 July 1886.

18 *Record*, 26 June 1887.

19 Ibid., 30 April 1886, 26 June, 20 August 1887; *Record* and *Enterprise*, 24 April 1896.

20 Bidwell, *Diaries*, 17 January, 29 February 1884.

21 Kenneth Reid Miller, essay on George Sisk for Professor Lois Christianson, SCML. This essay included the only known photos of the Chapmans.

22 *Record*, 15 July 1887.

23 *Enterprise*, 6, 12 March 1886.

24 Ibid. and 9 October 1886; *Record*, March, April coverage.

25 Rockwell Hunt, 372.

26 *Record*, 5 November 1887.

27 Bidwell, *Dictation*, 62.

Chapter 20

1 Trinity Methodist Church Archive, North Methodist Church, Chico, CA.

2 *Enterprise*, 23 March 1883, 21 March, 16 May 1884.

3 Ibid., 16 May 1884.

4 Ibid., 15 April 1882.

5 *Record*, 13 March 1880.

6 Ibid., and 11 March 1880.

7 Will, A. H. Chapman, Recorder's Office, Butte County Center, Oroville, CA.

8 *Enterprise*, 24 December 1886.

9 Sarah Locke Stow, *History of Mount Holyoke Seminary, South Hadley, Mass., During its First Half Century, 1837-1887* (South Hadley, MA: Mount Holyoke Seminary, 1887).

10   Terald A. Zall, *The Hospital on the 90th Anniversary of Rideout Memorial Hospital* (Marysville, CA: Rideout Memorial Hospital, 1998), 21.

11   *Record*, 6 February 1876.

12   Michele Shover, "The Blockhead Factor: Marriage and the Fate of California Daughters," *The Californians*, vol. 7 (September 1980), 26-32; John Kent Folman, *"The State of Wonders": The Letters of an Iowa Frontier Family: 1858-1861* (Iowa City: University of Iowa Press, 1986), 31.

13   *Record*, 19 April 1881.

14   Ibid., 24 March 1877.

15   *Record*, 24 March 1877.

16   The Mount Holyoke years are derived from Mary Chapman's class records there and supplemented by Arthur C. Cole, *One Hundred Years of Mount Holyoke College* (New Haven: Yale University Press, 1946); Helen Leflowitz Horowitz: *Alma Mater: Design and Experience of the Women's Colleges from Their Nineteenth Century Beginnings to the 1930s* (New York: Alfred A. Knopf, 1984); Stow.

17   Stow, 273; Cole, 186.

18   *Record*, 11 March 1882.

19   Michele Shover, "The Methodist Women and Mollie White: A Morality Tale," in *Exploring Chico's Past* (Philadelphia: Xlibris, 2005), 19.

20   *Enterprise*, 11 May 1886.

21   *Record,* 12 August 1882.

Chapter 21

1   *Chico's Chapmans*, chapters 4, 15.

2   *Record*, 3, 8 July 1886.

3   Ibid., 17 January 1885.

4   Ibid., 4 April 1885.

5   *Enterprise*, 19 June 1885.

6   Quoted in *Record*, 25 July 1885.

7   Ibid.

8   *Enterprise*, 21 July 1882.

9   *Record*, 20 February 1886; *Enterprise*, 14, 21 August, 18 September 1885.

10   Ibid., 6 September 1887.

11   *Enterprise*, 19 August 1887.

12   This is surmised from associations Lois MacDonald referred to in her book on Annie Bidwell.

13   Bidwell, *Diaries*, 21 November 1882.

14   *Enterprise*, 22 July 1887. Sarah Chapman noted Magnolia's pessimism in her 1899 diary.

15   Information on the Jesse Wood family is drawn from Wells and Chambers, Mansfield, and extensive miscellaneous and minor local newspaper items. Alice Wood's family name appears as Tison or Tyson.

16   *Record*, 4 February 1882; *Enterprise*, 9 February 1877. As an aside, married women were not permitted to teach. Cora Wayland Kennedy was an exception to the rule. While General Cosby's wife had made the attempt to continue, her husband's objections eventually prevailed, according to the 1877 *Enterprise*. By contrast, Mrs. Kennedy taught for twenty-eight years. Mansfield, 819.

17   *Enterprise*, 11 April 1884.

18   Ibid., 10 November 1877; *Record*, 14 May 1887, 29 December 1893, 18 December 1914. Both are buried in Chico with their infants.

19   *Record*, 1 November 1879.

20   Ibid., 24 December 1887.
21   Obituary, Henry McLennan, undated scrapbook; *Enterprise* entry; Mansfield biography.
22   *Enterprise*, 19 January 1888; *Record*, 21 January 1888; Oroville *Mercury*, 20 January 1888.
23   The bar in the barn reference is not factual but is inferred from the author's early life in Iowa where some guests at rural weddings subscribed to temperance. The barn/house division offered a way to accommodate both preferences.
24   *Record*, 20 January 1888.
25   *Oroville Mercury*, 20 January 1888.
26   *Record*, 20 January 1888.
27   *Enterprise*, 19 January 1888.
28   *Record*, 21 January 1888; Bidwell, *Diaries*, 19 January, 8 June 1888.
29   Ibid., 10 March 1888; Roske, 420; Orsi, 10; Mansel G. Blackford, *The Politics of Business in California, 1890-1920* (Columbus: Ohio State University Press, 1977), chapter 4, passim.
30   *Chico Chronicle*, 15 August 1888.
31   *Record*, 7 October 1898; Cf. Button, passim.
32   *Tax Records*, Chico, Butte County, CA, 1884-1890, SCML.
33   *Record*, no date, 1910; Mansfield, 712.
34   *Tax Records*, Chico, Butte County, CA, 1891-1899, SCML.
35   *Record*, 19 December 1904; Mansfield, 18-9.
36   Ibid., 23 August 1890.

Chapter 22

1   *Enterprise*, 4 April 1890.
2   Ibid., 25 July, 22 August 1890; *Chico Chronicle*, 26 July 1890.
3   *Record*, no date. Content suggests late 1880s or early 1890s.
4   *Record*, 16 May 1891; Mark Caldwell, *The Last Crusade: The War on Consumption,* (New York: Atheneum, 1988), 23.
5   J. M. Buckley, *A History of Methodists in the United States* (New York: Christian Literature, 1896), 489-90.
6   *Record*, 6 June 1891.
7   Ibid.
8   The information about Florence Chapman's headstone came from former Chico Cemetery clerk and noted local history researcher the late Larry V. Richardson, some of whose voluminous letters on the subject are in SCML. Gravestones were placed in 2022.
9   *Record*, 2 April 1892, 6 April 1893. Interview by this author with Vera Hintz Ekwall regarding her meeting with Amelia Chapman, widow of Augustus H. Chapman Jr.
10   Ibid., 2, 6 April 1892, 4 August 1947.
11   Lawrence Kinnard, *History of the Greater San Francisco Bay Region*, vol. 1 (New York: Lewis Historical Publishing Company, 1966), 107-11; Ralph J. Roske, *Everyman's Eden: A History of California* (New York: Macmillan, 1968), 420.
12   Ibid.
13   *Record*, 13 October 1894.
14   Ibid., 28 August 1898.
15   The Chapmans' legal residence shifted to Powellton. *Record*, 9 March 1898. The 3 December 1897 *Record* edition refers to A. H. Chapman as "a former citizen of Chico."
16   Sarah Chapman, 1899. Larry V. Richardson made his typescript of this document

from the original in Mildred Forester's possession. It had belonged to the Centerville Museum library, a gift from an antique dealer who acquired it from Amelia Chapman, the elderly wife of Gus Jr. When Lois McDonald died it was in a box of her papers donated by her heirs to SCML.

17 *Record*, 14 April 1898. Chico's Michael Lawrence "Larry" Mery, owner of a Chico-based foundry, invented a similar machine a few years later.

18 *Record*, 1 August 1891, 28 August 1898; Mansfield, 322; Blackford, 105.

19 Hunt, 415; W. H. Hutchinson, *The California Investment of the Diamond Match Company* (Chico: Diamond Match Corporation, 1957), 21-2.

20 Blackford, 105.

21 *Record*, 20 April 1898.

22 Ibid., 13 April 1922.

23 Ibid., 31 January 1899. These and the following memorial remarks appeared in the obituary coverage.

24 Annie Bidwell, 4 February 1899; Lois Halliday McDonald, *Annie Kennedy Bidwell: An Intimate History* (Chico: Stansbury Press, 2004).

25 *Record*, 14 March 1899.

26 Ibid., 13 March 1899.

Chapter 23

1 *Enterprise*, 11 August 1947; *Record*, 11 August 1947. In this chapter, references to Sarah's actions come from entries in her 1899 diary, now in SCML. Death certificate, Augustus Chapman Jr., NCCML; Transcript by Larry V. Richardson.

2 Sarah Chapman, Diary, May 28-November 7, 1899. Major parts of this and following paragraphs are sourced from Sarah's diary. Larry V. Richardson made a typescript of this document from the original in Mildred Forester's possession. It had belonged to the Centerville Museum library, a gift from an antique dealer who acquired it from Amelia Chapman, the elderly wife of Gus Jr. When Lois McDonald died it was in a box of her papers donated by her heirs to SCML.

3 Boyle, *Old Days in Butte* (Butte County Historical Society, 1941), 59; *Record*, 29 September 1899.

4 Rose's husband owned M. Oser & Company, located on the northwest corner of Third and Main, a ladies department store from 1878 to 1986.

5 Interview with Vera Hintz Ekwall whose maternal grandfather, D. H. Woods, played a prominent political role in Chico during the 1880s. No date. A collection of his photographs is represented in NCCML. Censuses do not reflect the age difference, but information differs across time.

6 *Record*, no date. Copied by Monica Garcia while reading early twentieth-century papers.

7 Interview with Mrs. A. D. Pingrey, 1981.

8 Boyle, 59; Zall, 28. Before the move to Chapman Street, the Sisters of Charity Hospital was at Fourth and Chestnut. The hospital's operation returned to that location after the former Chapman house burned.

9 In the 1890s firemen responded to a fire in a Bidwell outbuilding but did not put it out. The firemen were willing, but a town official appeared and, after considerable discussion, ordered them away. Bidwell's employees managed to put it out.

10 *Enterprise*, 14 January 1909; Warren Nelson, conversation with this author, late 1970s.

11 Ibid., 11 August 1947, 10 May 1956.

12 WWI draft document.

13 I.O.O.F. Records, Butte County Historical Society, Oroville, CA. Copies courtesy of

Larry V. Richardson.

14   Ibid.; D. H. Johnson to D. W. Cooper, 4 April 1923.
15   Fred Chapman, WWI draft report.
16   *Sacramento Union*, 14 November 1934.
17   Death Index, 1956, Butte County Records, County Center, Oroville, CA.

Index

Note: Common names and places, such as Gus, Sarah and Fred Chapman, Charlie Stilson, John Bidwell, Wood & Chapman, John Bidwell & Co., Big Chico and Little Chico creeks, state prisons, local newspapers and Humboldt Road are not included.

CPSIA information can be obtained
at www.ICGtesting.com
Printed in the USA
BVHW072316130922
646694BV00001B/1